Advance Praise for *Sunny Side Down*

"Lev Yilmaz is a demented and troubled young man. But he's demented and troubled in the same ways as the rest of us, which is what makes this book so funny, captivating, and identifiable. I'm a fan."

—Davy Rothbart, creator of *Found* magazine and author of *The Lone Surfer of Montana, Kansas*

"*Sunny Side Down* is either a really happy book about misery . . . or a miserable book about happiness. Either way, Lev Yilmaz is among my favorite depressed authors who is not dead."

—David Nadelberg, author of *Mortified*

"Hilariously insightful comics for the modern bachelor, and the women who dump him."

—Keith Knight, author of *K Chronicles*

LEVNI YILMAZ

SUNNY SIDE DOWN

A Collection of the comic

TALES OF MERE EXISTENCE

tertainment
n & Schuster, Inc.
e Americas
20

ork of fiction. Names, characters, places, and incidents either are pro
n or are used fictitiously. Any resemblance to actual events or locale
ntirely coincidental.

nt Entertainment trade paperback edition March 2009

IT ENTERTAINMENT and colophon are trademarks of Simon & Schust

out special discounts for bulk purchases, please contact Simon & Schust
00-456-6798 or business@simonandschuster.com.

Paradelo

e United States of America

For the loners, the misanthropes,
and the perpetually alienated.

CONTENTS:

Dear Reader,

Welcome to the first officially published book of "Tales Of Mere Existence", the immensely popular underground comic strip and animation series. Well, at least I think it's immensely popular. That's what some people seem to think. Even if it isn't immensely popular, I suppose I had better say that it is, sounds a lot better than "Moderately Popular".

Well anyway, welcome to my book. This is my story... actually, it isn't really a story. It's more of a memoir... no, it isn't really a memoir either. It's just, you know, tales of mere existence. I bring you just simple little stories of everyday life. I suppose I don't really know if they're all that interesting. When you think about it though, what is interesting is a relative concept: No one person can really say what is interesting... well, that's actually kind of a pretentious thing to say. Forget I said it.

Regardless, here I present to you a collection of cartoons. I hope you enjoy it... it IS just a collection of cartoons. It doesn't really have a plot. To tell you the truth, I don't know if it flows together all that well. Funny, isn't it? I have always wanted to put a book out, and now I'm not even sure if it flows together that well. It actually probably totally sucks, you're going to think it's crappy, everyone is going to hate it, and the whole thing is going to be a total and absolute flop.

So here's the book. I hope you like it, but you're probably going to hate it. Shit. I'm so ashamed of myself.

— LEV

SUNNY SIDE

DOWN

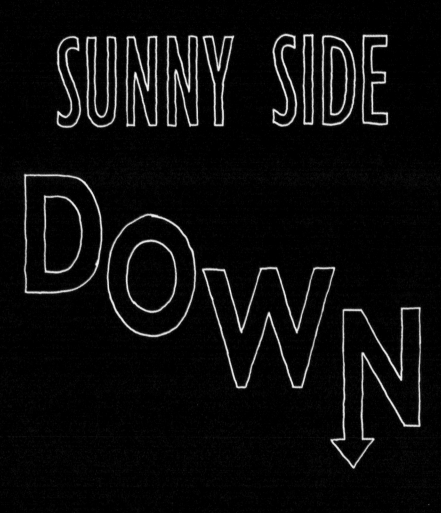

CHAPTER 1:

I was born.

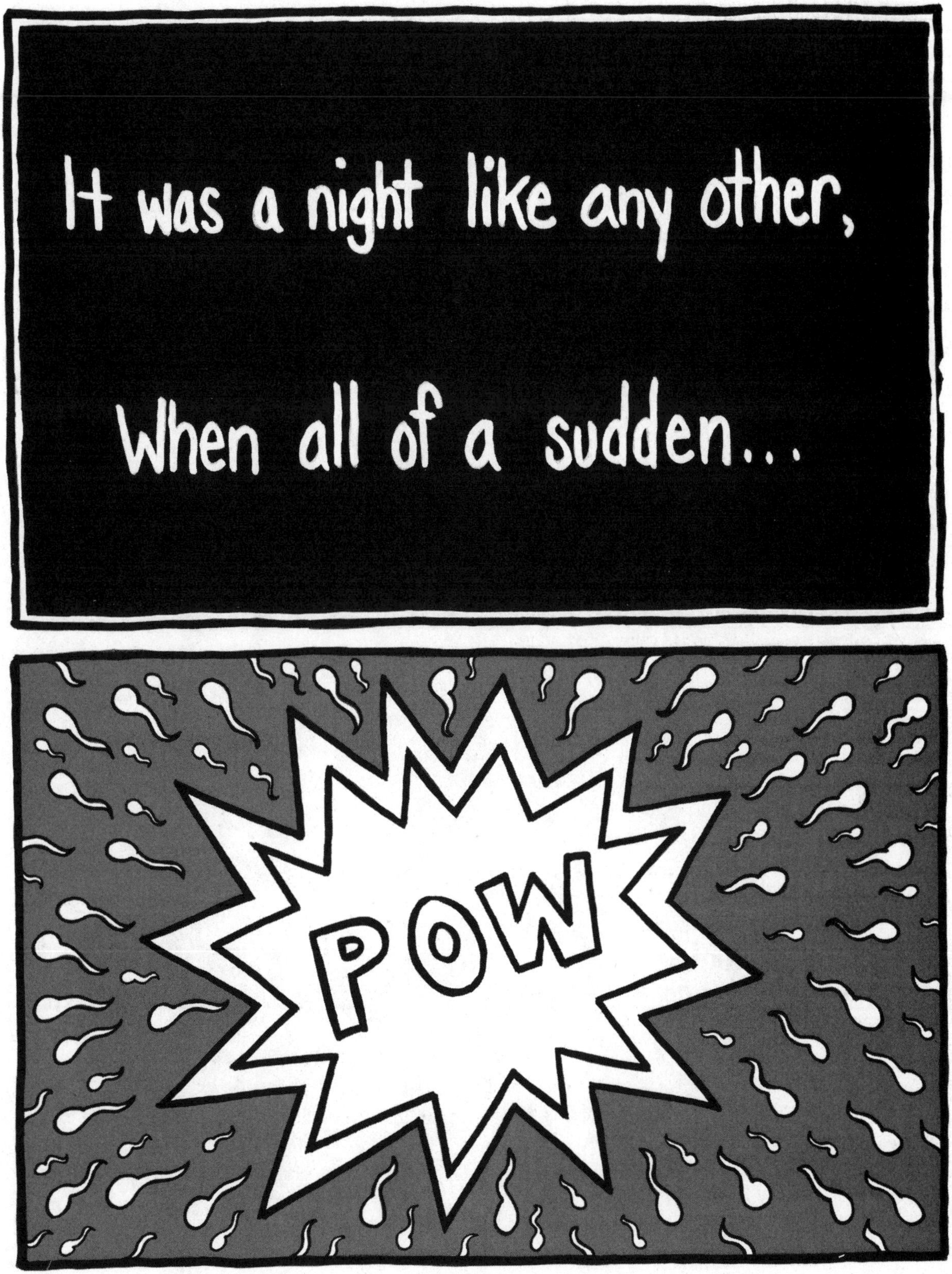
It was a night like any other,
When all of a sudden...
POW

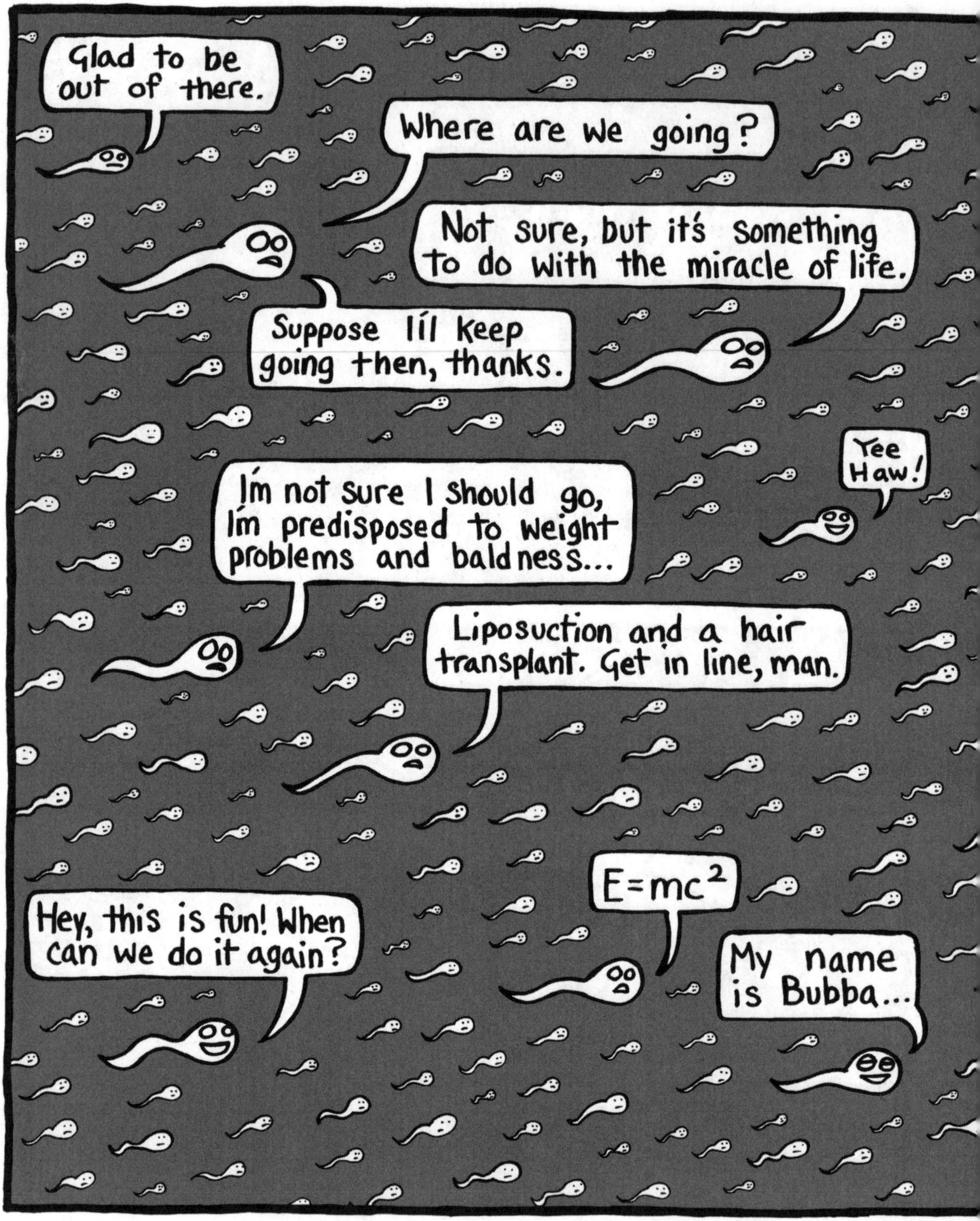
Glad to be out of there.
Where are we going?
Not sure, but it's something to do with the miracle of life.
Suppose I'll keep going then, thanks.
Yee Haw!
I'm not sure I should go, I'm predisposed to weight problems and baldness...
Liposuction and a hair transplant. Get in line, man.
E=mc²
Hey, this is fun! When can we do it again?
My name is Bubba...

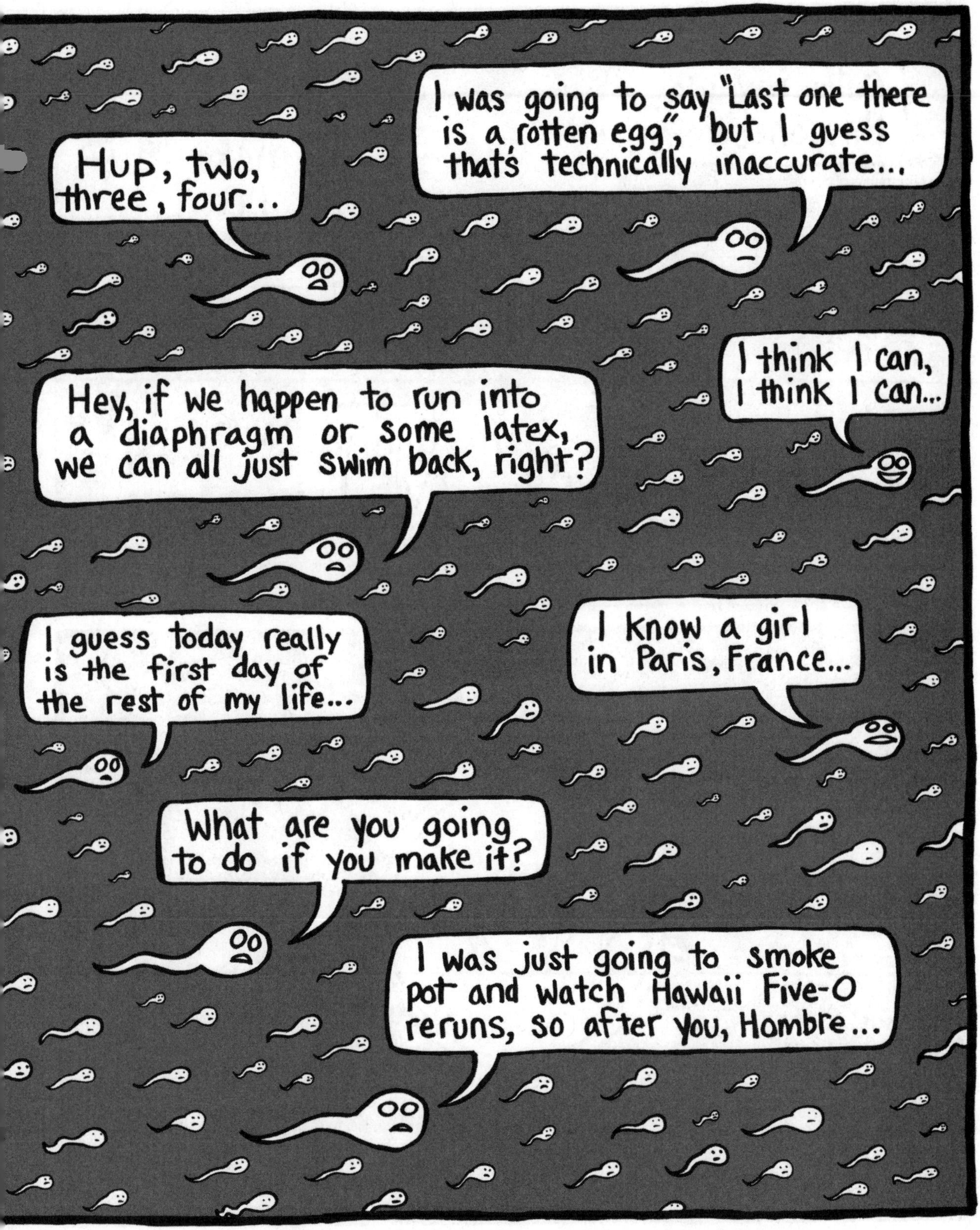
I was going to say "Last one there is a rotten egg", but I guess that's technically inaccurate...
Hup, two, three, four...
I think I can, I think I can...
Hey, if we happen to run into a diaphragm or some latex, we can all just swim back, right?
I guess today really is the first day of the rest of my life...
I know a girl in Paris, France...
What are you going to do if you make it?
I was just going to smoke pot and watch Hawaii Five-O reruns, so after you, Hombre...

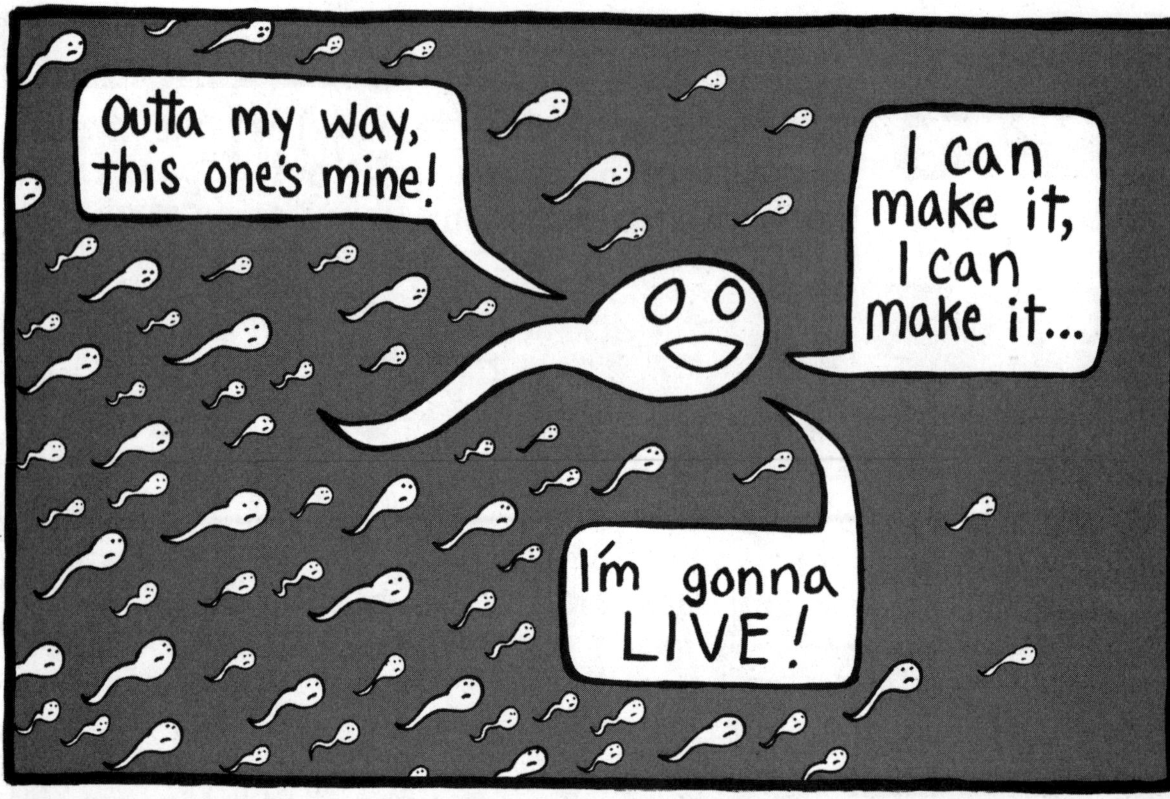
Outta my way, this one's mine!
I can make it, I can make it...
I'm gonna LIVE!

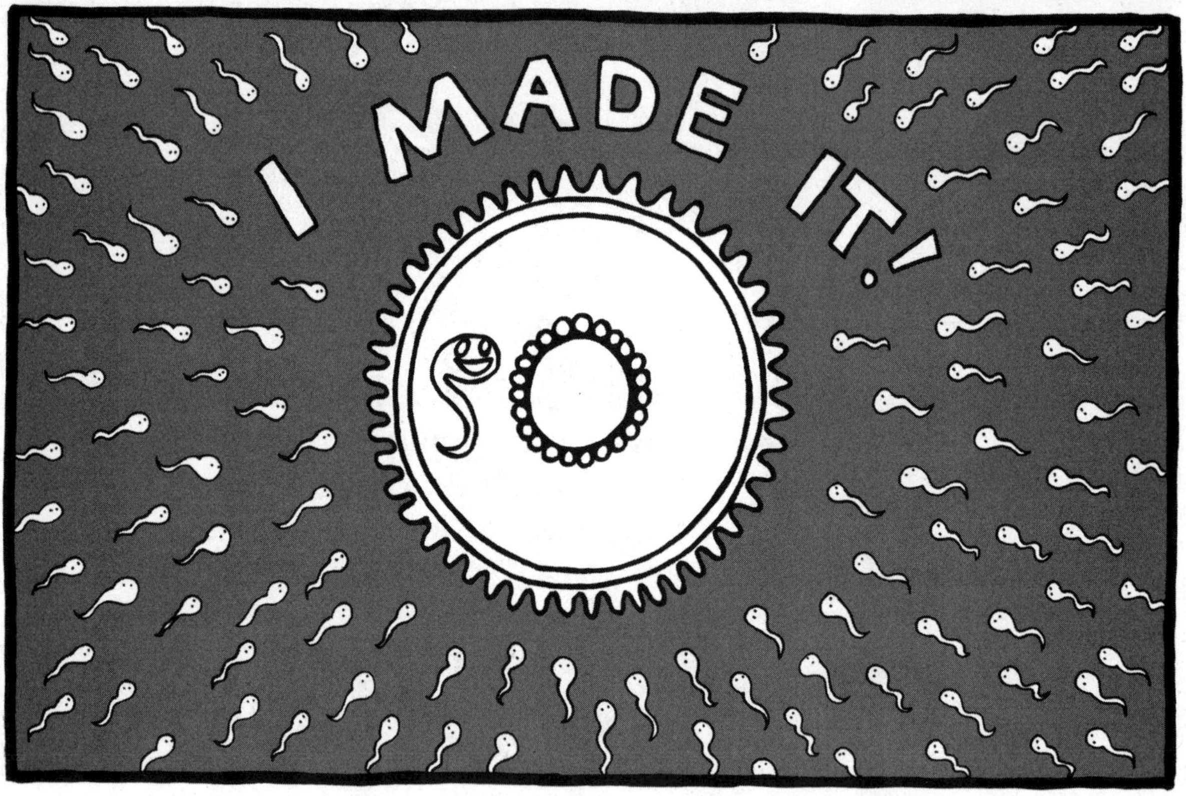
I MADE IT!

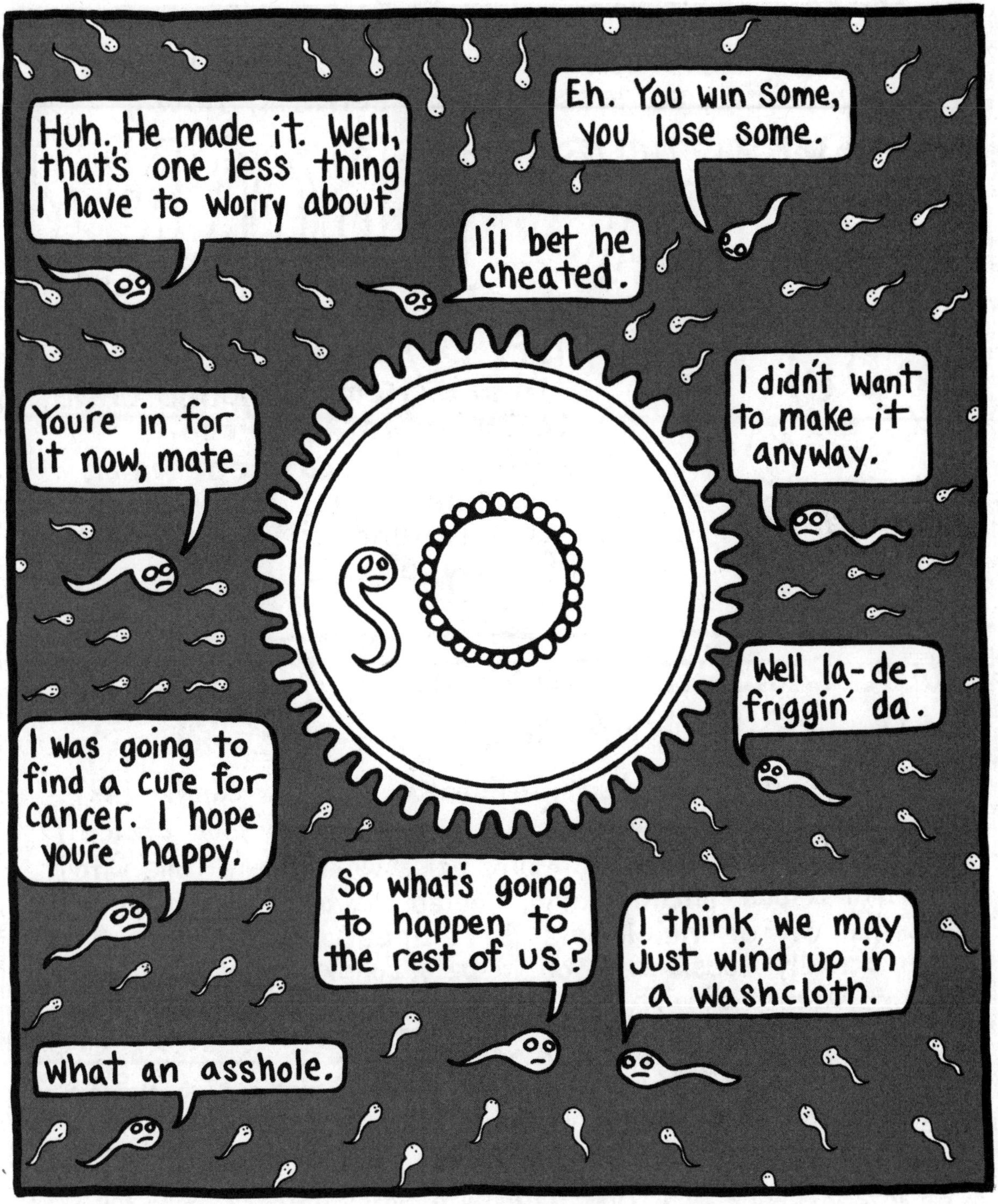
Huh. He made it. Well, that's one less thing I have to worry about.
Eh. You win some, you lose some.
I'll bet he cheated.
You're in for it now, mate.
I didn't want to make it anyway.
Well la-de-friggin' da.
I was going to find a cure for cancer. I hope you're happy.
So what's going to happen to the rest of us?
I think we may just wind up in a washcloth.
What an asshole.

...and so life began.

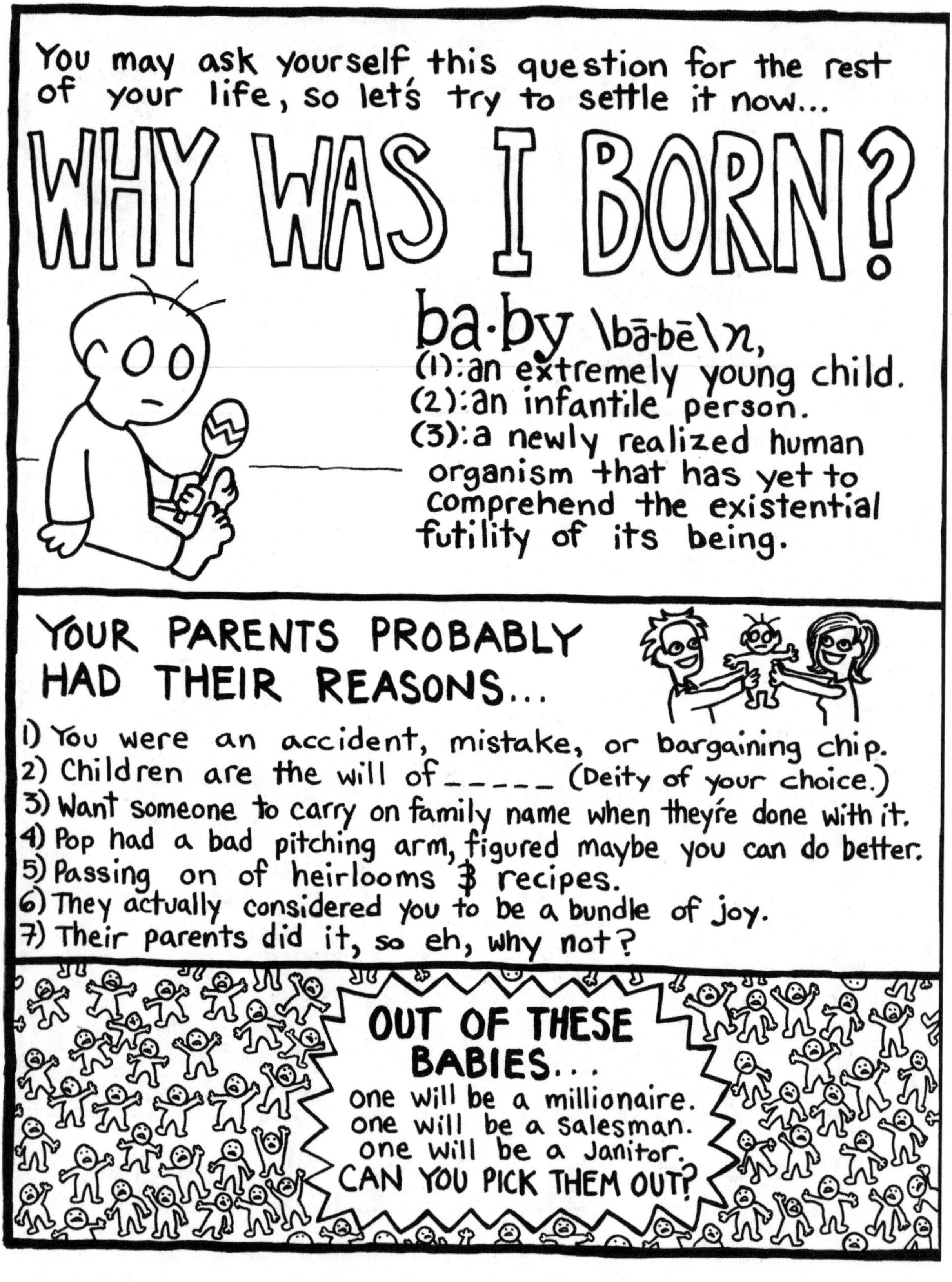

You may ask yourself this question for the rest of your life, so let's try to settle it now...
WHY WAS I BORN?
ba·by \bā-bē\ n,
(1): an extremely young child.
(2): an infantile person.
(3): a newly realized human organism that has yet to comprehend the existential futility of its being.
YOUR PARENTS PROBABLY HAD THEIR REASONS...
1) You were an accident, mistake, or bargaining chip.
2) Children are the will of _____ (Deity of your choice.)
3) Want someone to carry on family name when they're done with it.
4) Pop had a bad pitching arm, figured maybe you can do better.
5) Passing on of heirlooms & recipes.
6) They actually considered you to be a bundle of joy.
7) Their parents did it, so eh, why not?
OUT OF THESE BABIES...
one will be a millionaire.
one will be a salesman.
one will be a Janitor.
CAN YOU PICK THEM OUT?

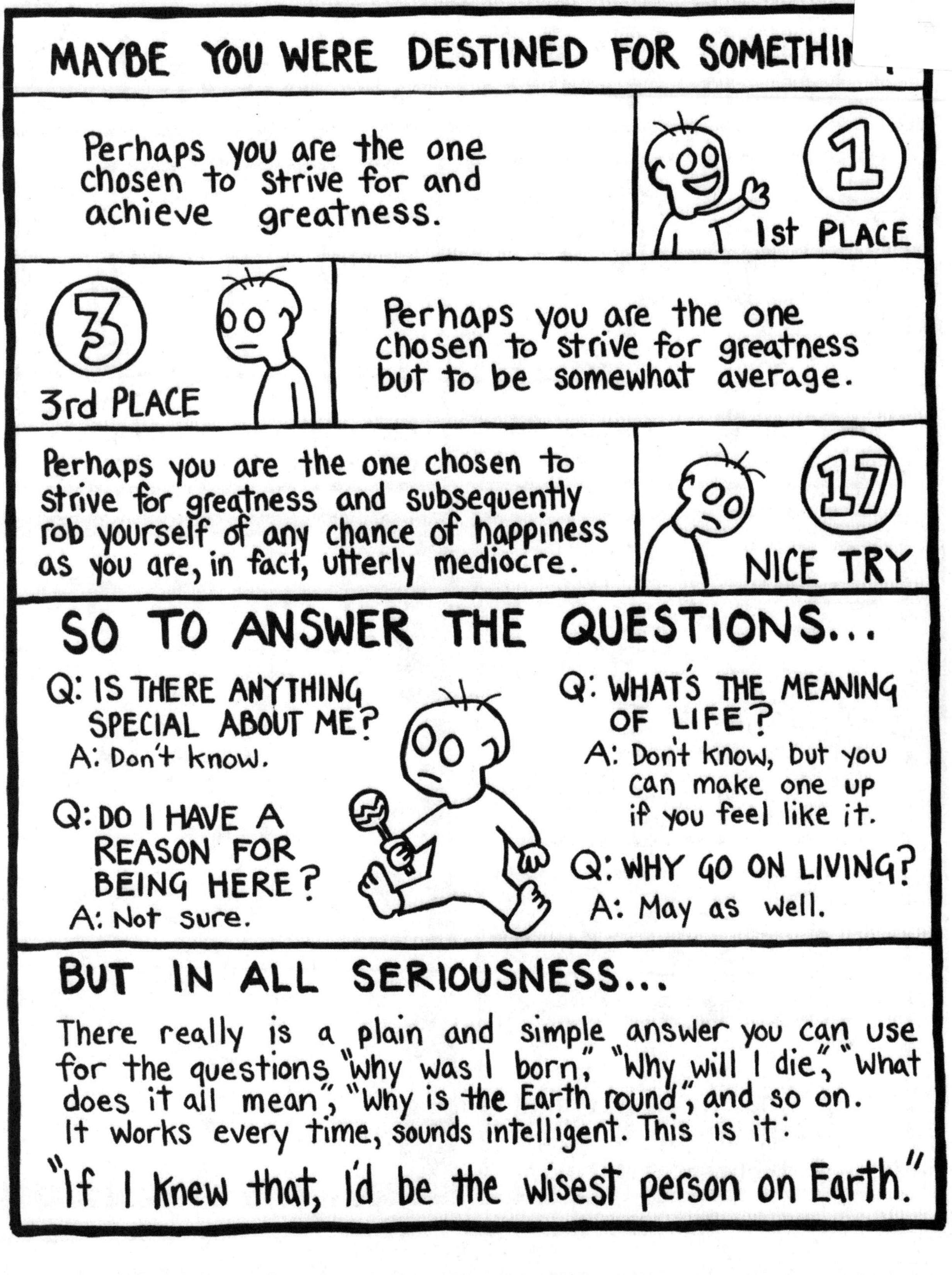
MAYBE YOU WERE DESTINED FOR SOMETHIN
Perhaps you are the one chosen to strive for and achieve greatness.
1
1st PLACE
3
3rd PLACE
Perhaps you are the one chosen to strive for greatness but to be somewhat average.
Perhaps you are the one chosen to strive for greatness and subsequently rob yourself of any chance of happiness as you are, in fact, utterly mediocre.
17
NICE TRY
SO TO ANSWER THE QUESTIONS...
Q: IS THERE ANYTHING SPECIAL ABOUT ME?
A: Don't know.
Q: DO I HAVE A REASON FOR BEING HERE?
A: Not sure.
Q: WHAT'S THE MEANING OF LIFE?
A: Don't know, but you can make one up if you feel like it.
Q: WHY GO ON LIVING?
A: May as well.
BUT IN ALL SERIOUSNESS...
There really is a plain and simple answer you can use for the questions "Why was I born," "Why will I die," "What does it all mean," "Why is the Earth round," and so on. It works every time, sounds intelligent. This is it:
"If I knew that, I'd be the wisest person on Earth."

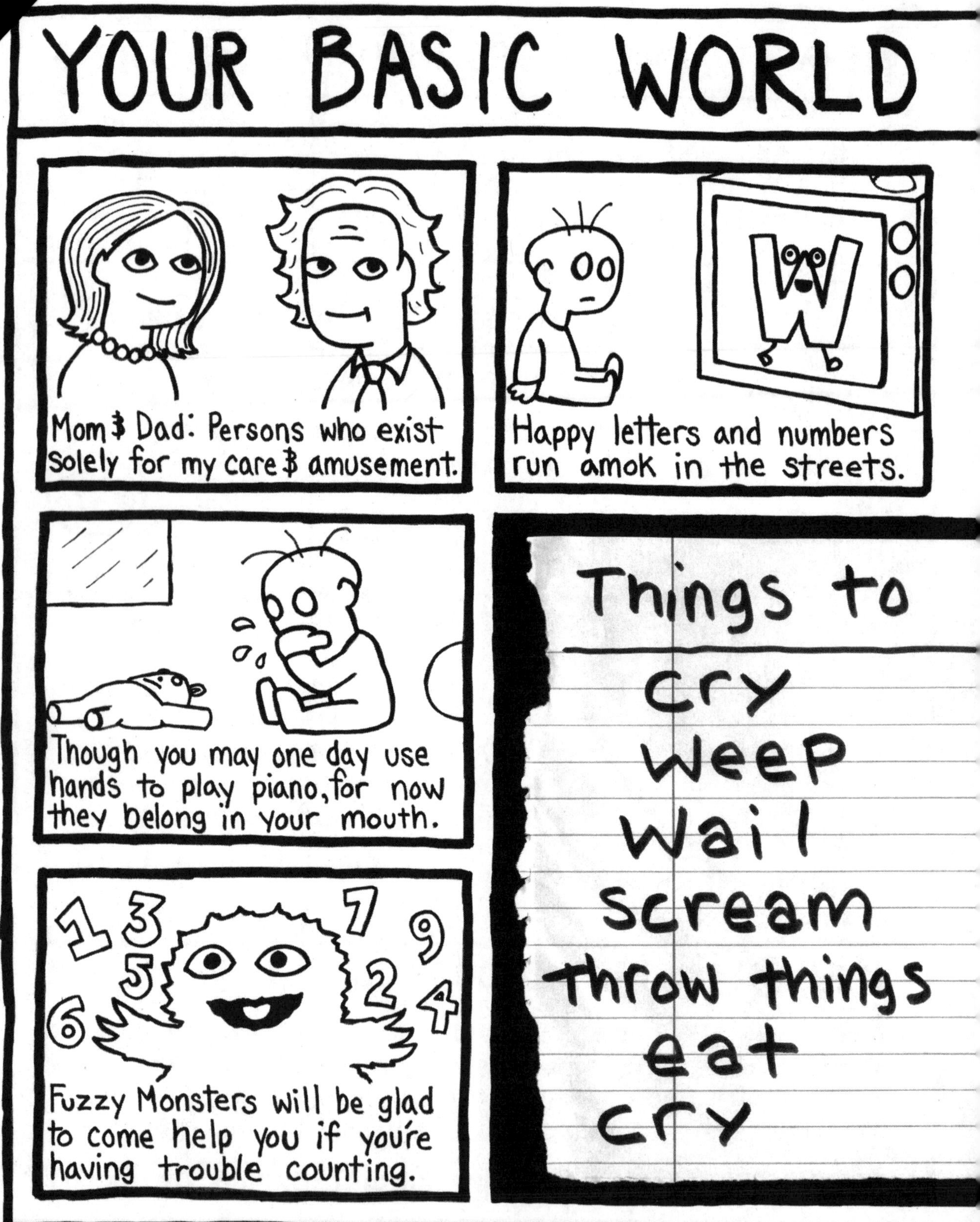
YOUR BASIC WORLD
Mom $ Dad: Persons who exist solely for my care $ amusement.
Happy letters and numbers run amok in the streets.
Though you may one day use hands to play piano, for now they belong in your mouth.
Fuzzy Monsters will be glad to come help you if you're having trouble counting.
1 3 7 9 5 2 6 4
Things to
cry
weep
wail
scream
throw things
eat
cry

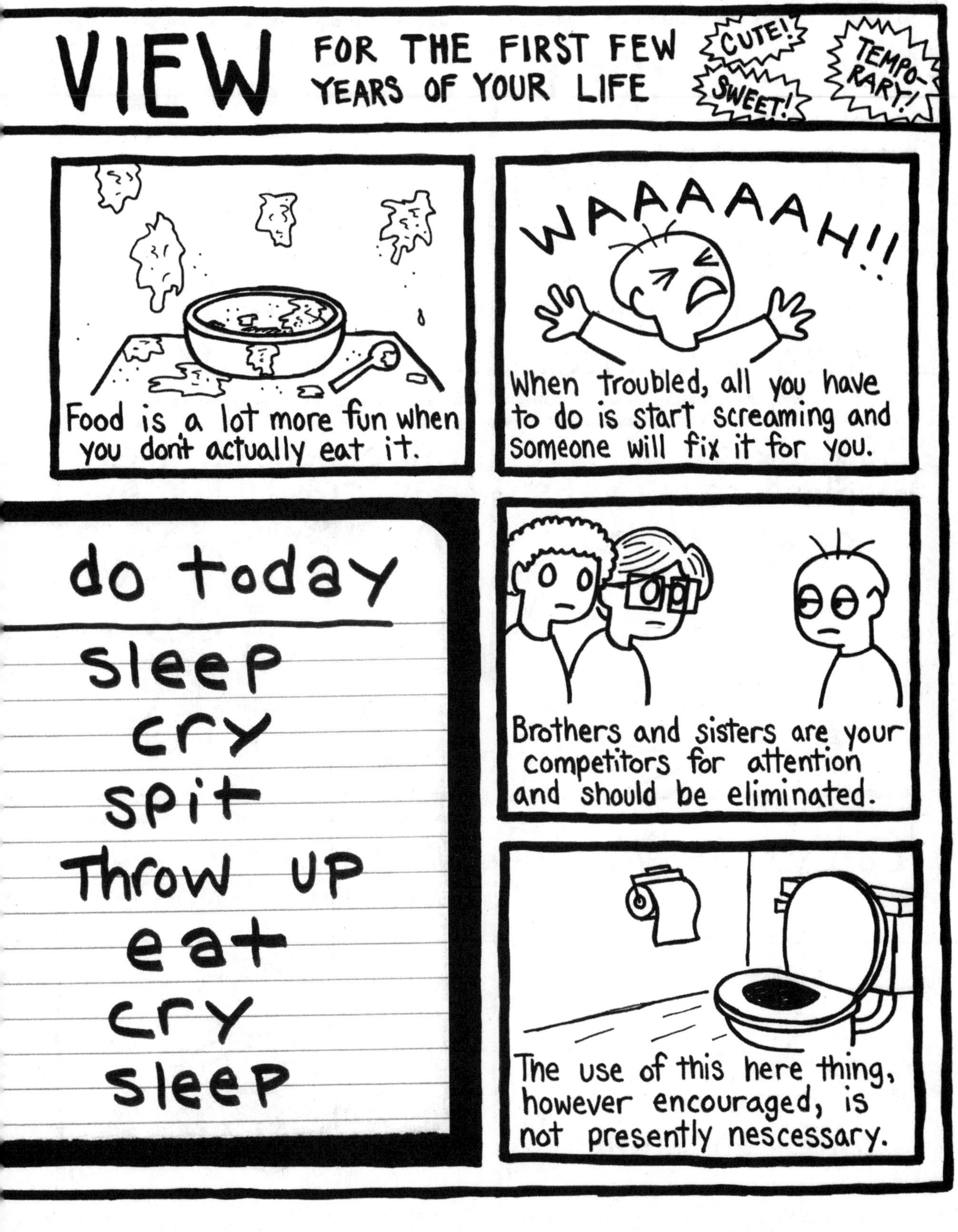
VIEW
FOR THE FIRST FEW YEARS OF YOUR LIFE
CUTE!
SWEET!
TEMPORARY!
Food is a lot more fun when you don't actually eat it.
WAAAAAH!!
When troubled, all you have to do is start screaming and someone will fix it for you.
do today
sleep
cry
spit
Throw up
eat
cry
sleep
Brothers and sisters are your competitors for attention and should be eliminated.
The use of this here thing, however encouraged, is not presently nescessary.

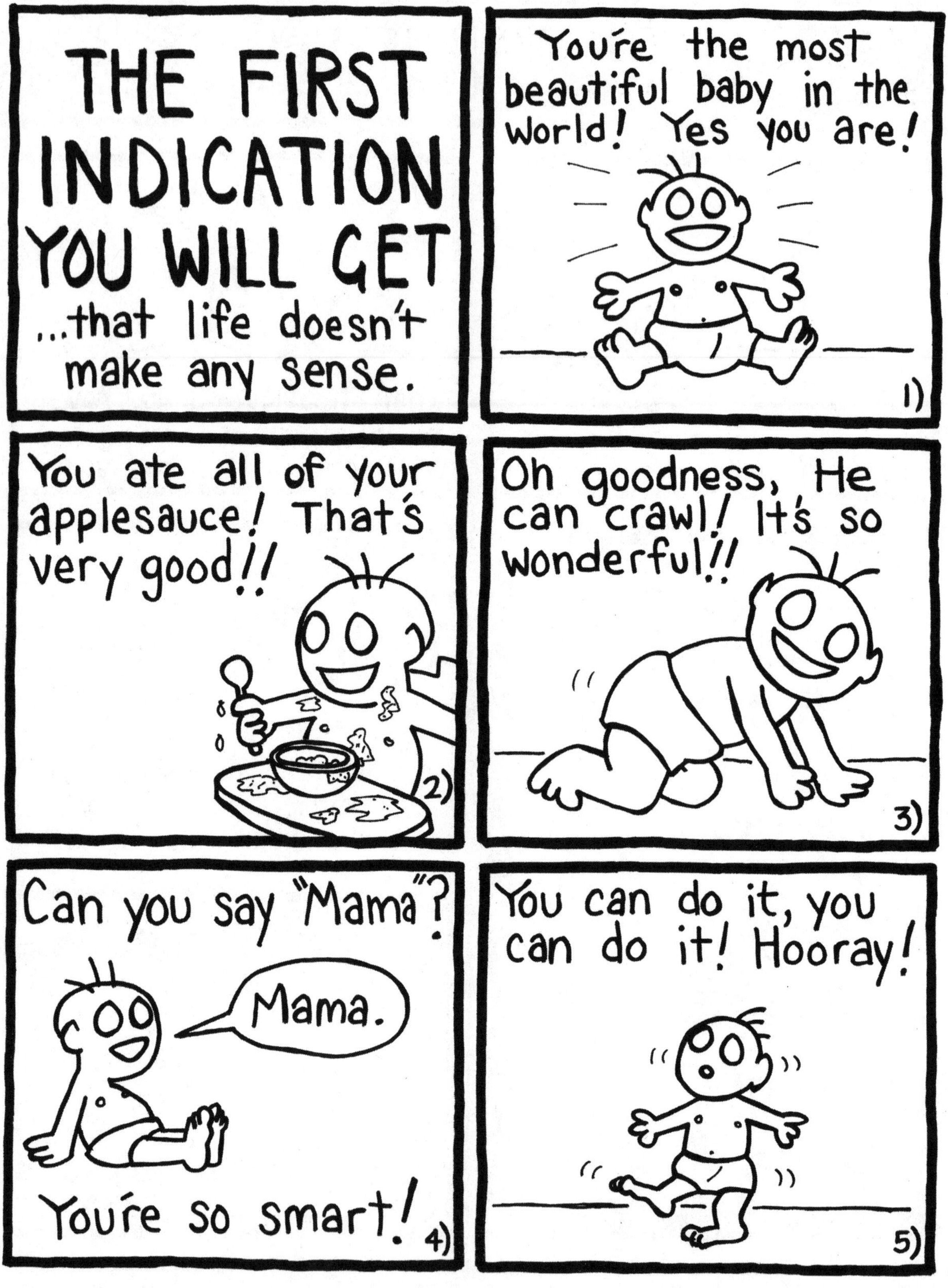
THE FIRST INDICATION YOU WILL GET
...that life doesn't make any sense.
You're the most beautiful baby in the world! Yes you are!
1)
You ate all of your applesauce! That's very good!!
2)
Oh goodness, He can crawl! It's so wonderful!!
3)
Can you say "Mama"?
Mama.
You're so smart!
4)
You can do it, you can do it! Hooray!
5)

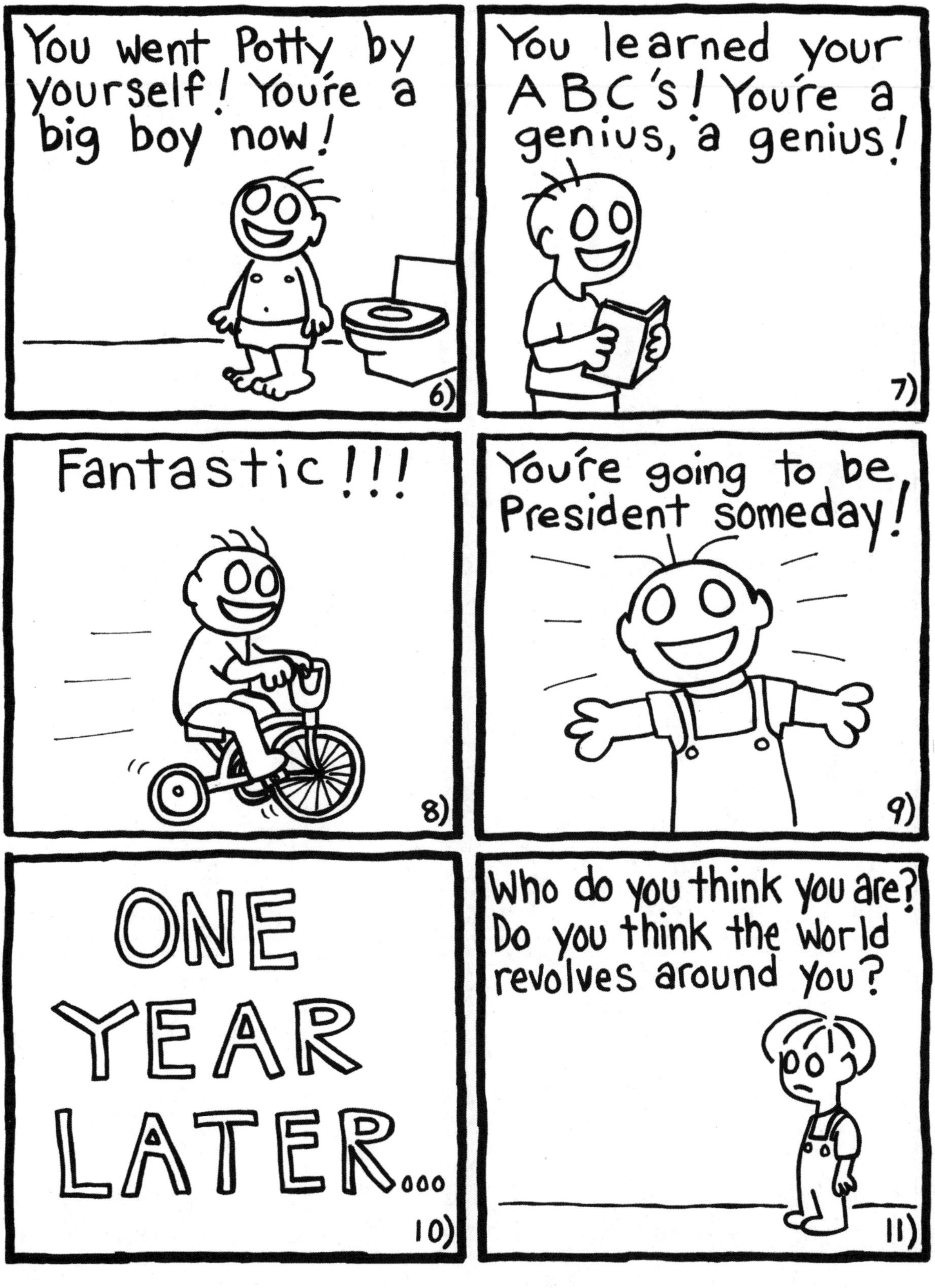
You went Potty by yourself! You're a big boy now!
6)
You learned your ABC's! You're a genius, a genius!
7)
Fantastic!!!
8)
You're going to be President someday!
9)
ONE YEAR LATER...
10)
Who do you think you are? Do you think the world revolves around you?
11)

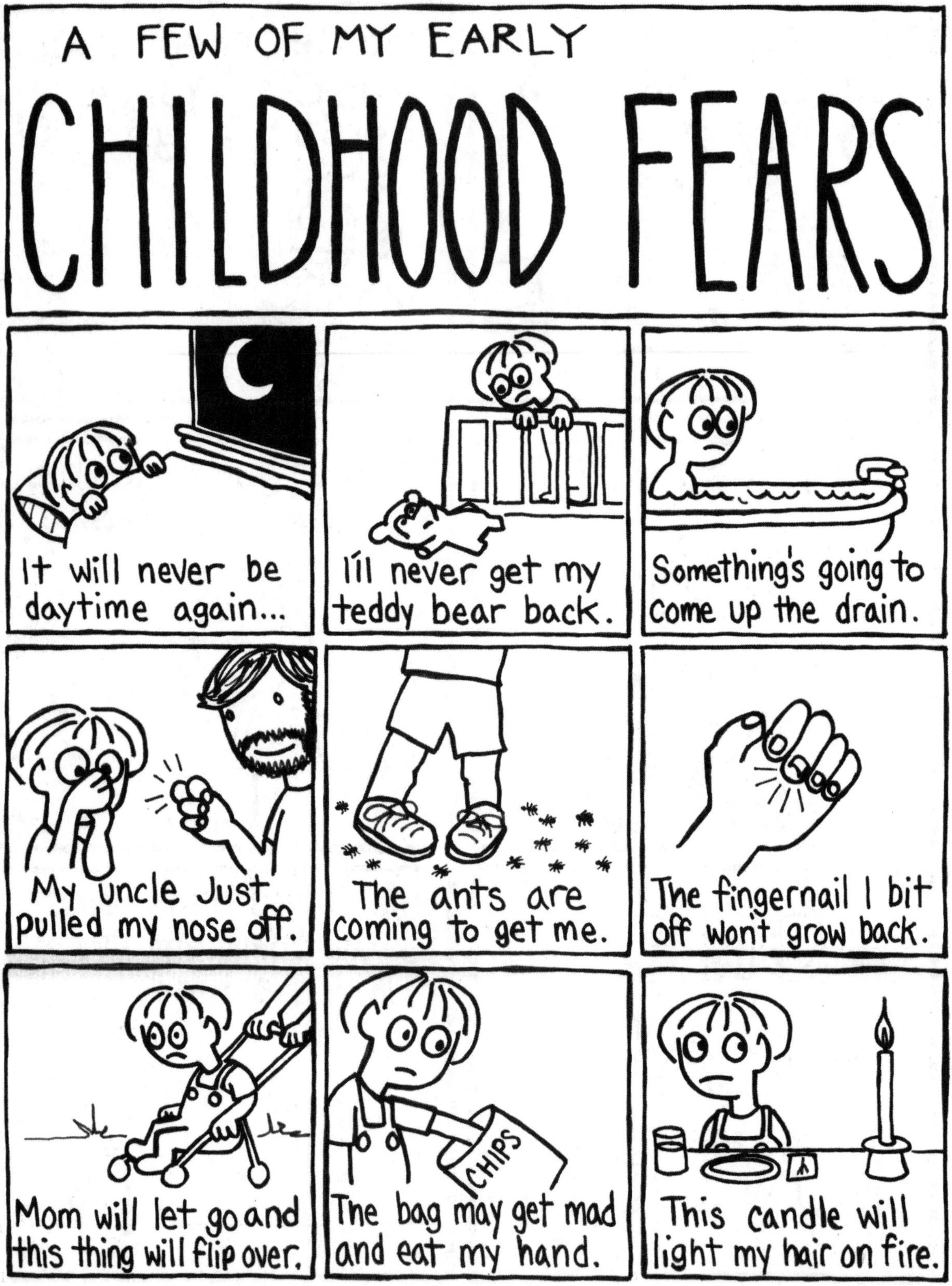
A FEW OF MY EARLY
CHILDHOOD FEARS
It will never be daytime again...
I'll never get my teddy bear back.
Something's going to come up the drain.
My uncle just pulled my nose off.
The ants are coming to get me.
The fingernail I bit off won't grow back.
Mom will let go and this thing will flip over.
CHIPS
The bag may get mad and eat my hand.
This candle will light my hair on fire.

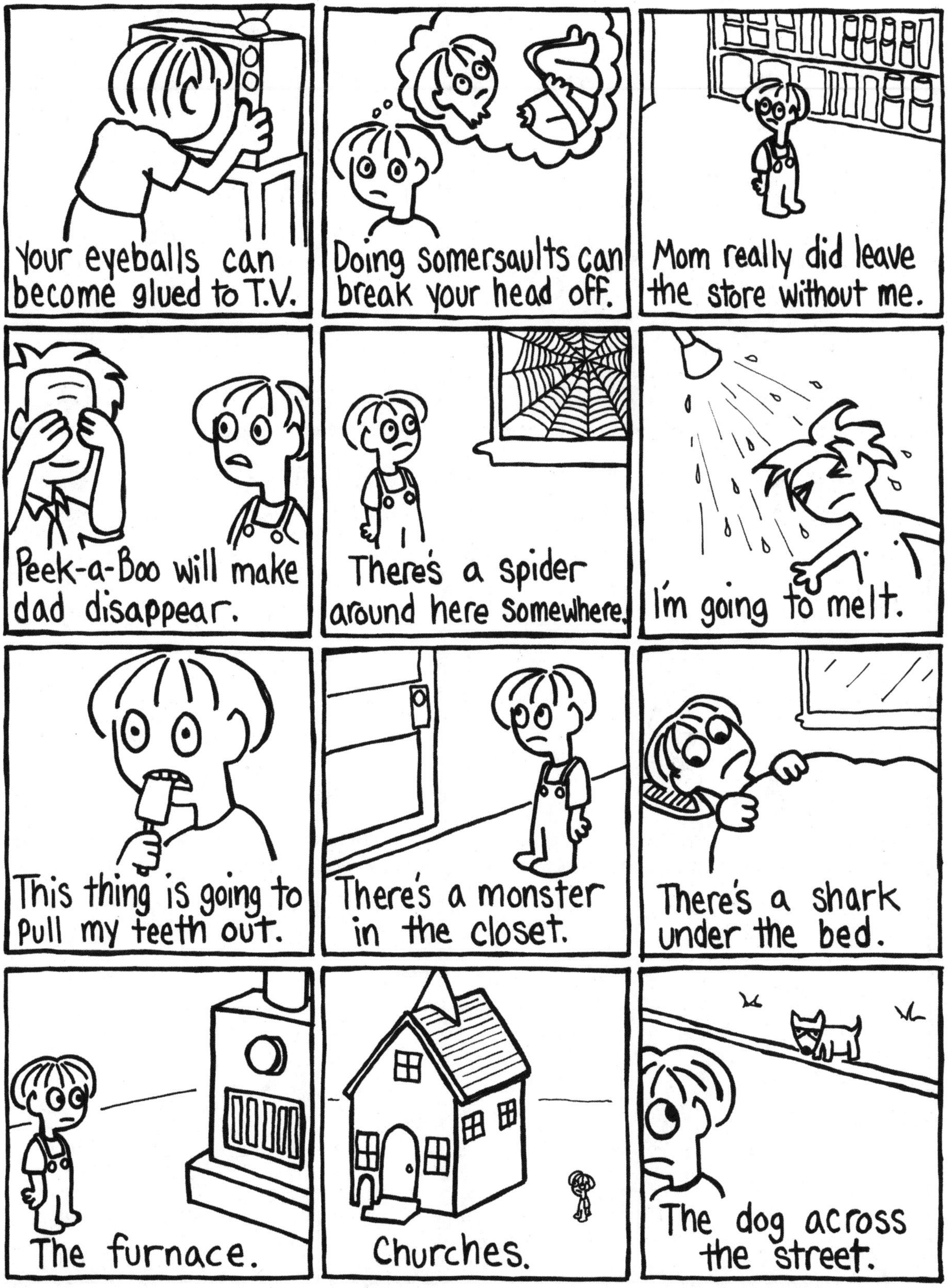
Your eyeballs can become glued to T.V.
Doing somersaults can break your head off.
Mom really did leave the store without me.
Peek-a-Boo will make dad disappear.
There's a spider around here somewhere.
I'm going to melt.
This thing is going to pull my teeth out.
There's a monster in the closet.
There's a shark under the bed.
The furnace.
Churches.
The dog across the street.

STEP ON A CRACK
Step on a crack and break your mother's back.
1)
Step on a line and break your mother's spine.
2)
Step on the grass and break your mother's...
STUMBLE
3)
4)
Oh crap.
5)

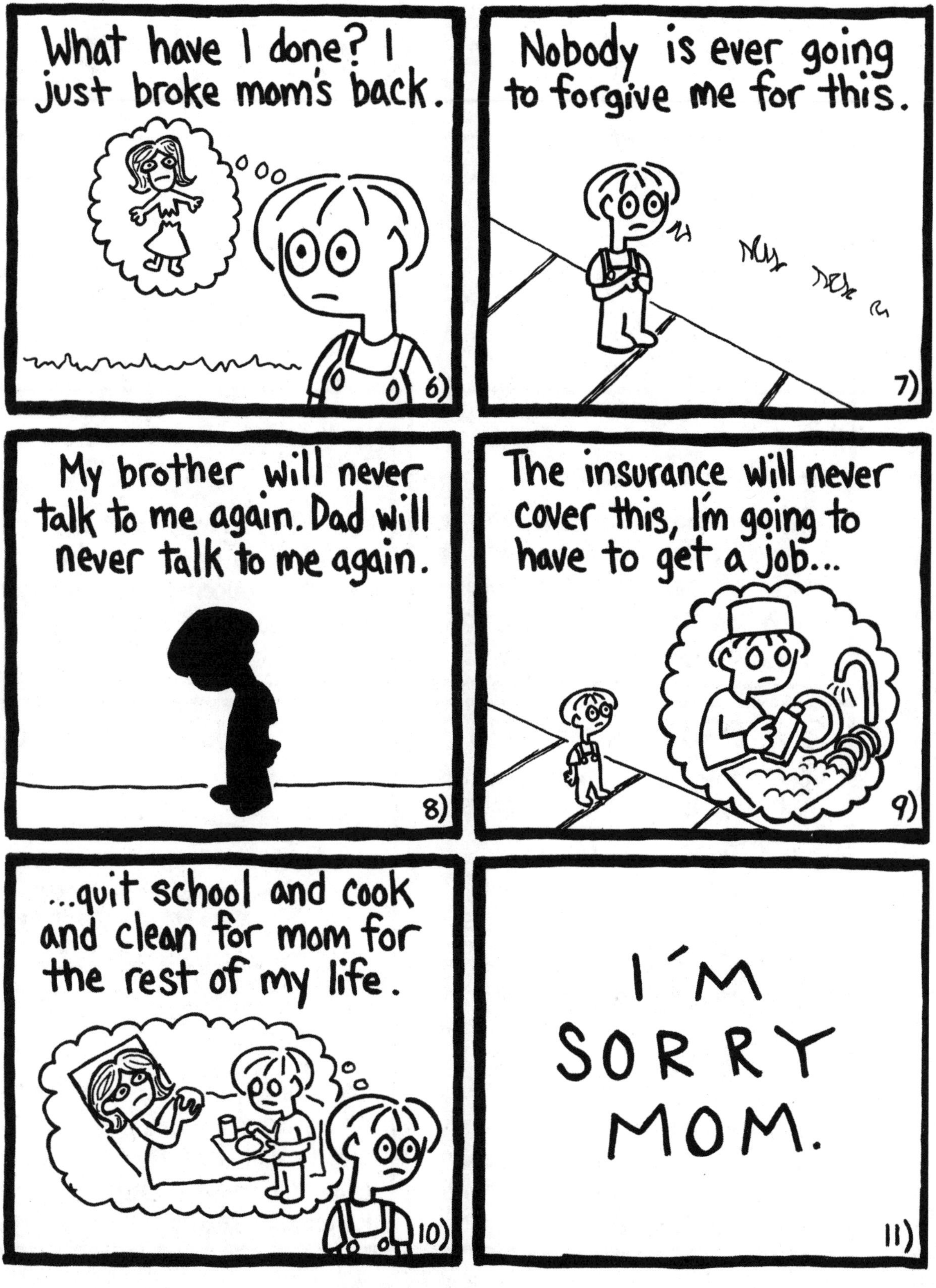
What have I done? I just broke mom's back.
6)
Nobody is ever going to forgive me for this.
7)
My brother will never talk to me again. Dad will never talk to me again.
8)
The insurance will never cover this, I'm going to have to get a job...
9)
...quit school and cook and clean for mom for the rest of my life.
10)
I'M SORRY MOM.
11)

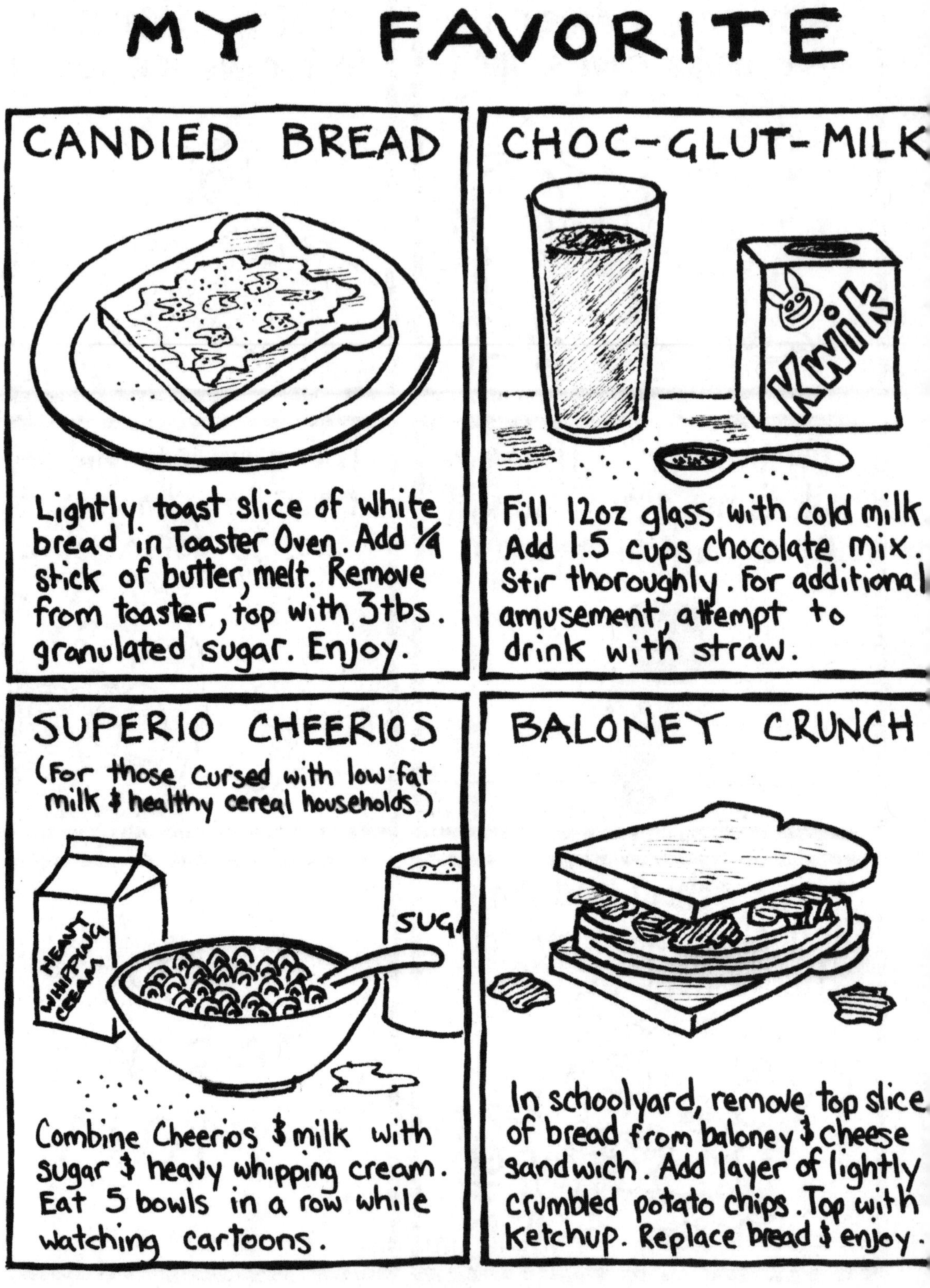
MY FAVORITE
CANDIED BREAD
Lightly toast slice of white bread in Toaster Oven. Add 1/4 stick of butter, melt. Remove from toaster, top with 3tbs. granulated sugar. Enjoy.
CHOC-GLUT-MILK
Kwik
Fill 12oz glass with cold milk Add 1.5 cups Chocolate mix. Stir thoroughly. For additional amusement, attempt to drink with straw.
SUPERIO CHEERIOS
(For those cursed with low-fat milk & healthy cereal households)
HEAVY WHIPPING CREAM
SUG
Combine Cheerios & milk with sugar & heavy whipping cream. Eat 5 bowls in a row while watching cartoons.
BALONEY CRUNCH
In schoolyard, remove top slice of bread from baloney & cheese sandwich. Add layer of lightly crumbled potato chips. Top with Ketchup. Replace bread & enjoy.

CHILDHOOD RECIPES

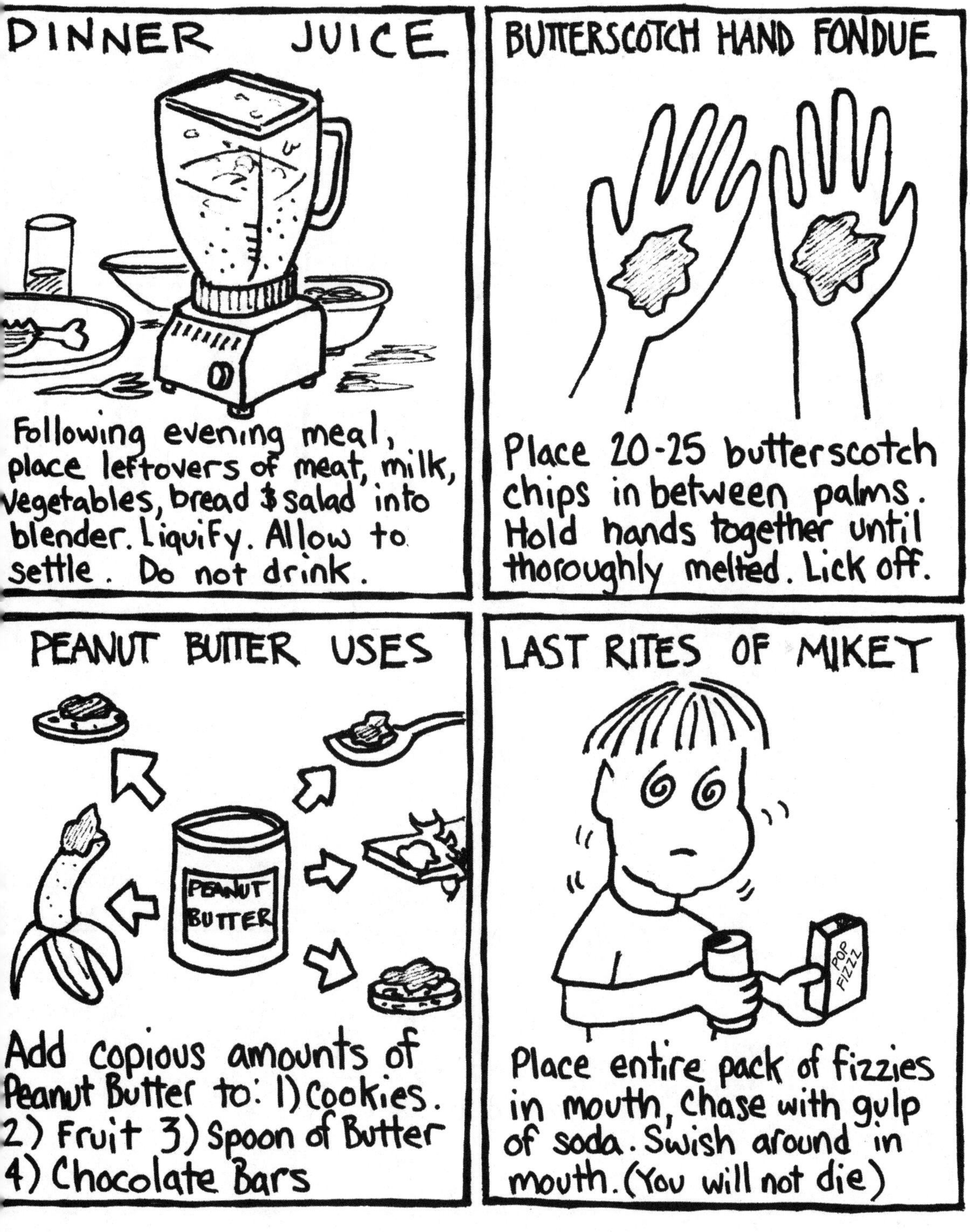

DINNER JUICE
Following evening meal, place leftovers of meat, milk, vegetables, bread $ salad into blender. Liquify. Allow to settle. Do not drink.
BUTTERSCOTCH HAND FONDUE
Place 20-25 butterscotch chips in between palms. Hold hands together until thoroughly melted. Lick off.
PEANUT BUTTER USES
PEANUT BUTTER
Add copious amounts of Peanut Butter to: 1) Cookies. 2) Fruit 3) Spoon of Butter 4) Chocolate Bars
LAST RITES OF MIKEY
POP FIZZZ
Place entire pack of fizzies in mouth, chase with gulp of soda. Swish around in mouth. (You will not die)

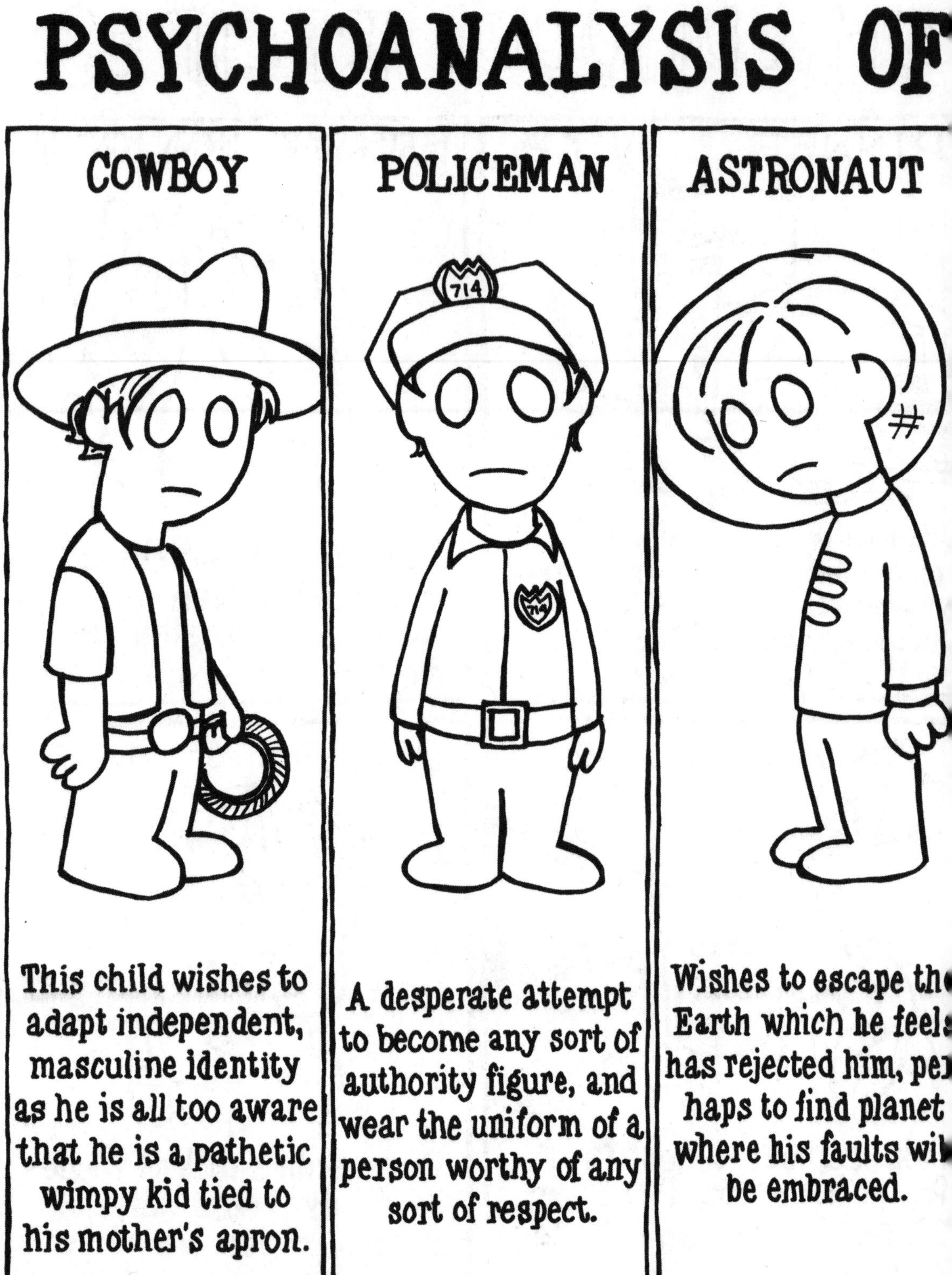
PSYCHOANALYSIS OF
COWBOY
POLICEMAN
ASTRONAUT
714
714
This child wishes to adapt independent, masculine identity as he is all too aware that he is a pathetic wimpy kid tied to his mother's apron.
A desperate attempt to become any sort of authority figure, and wear the uniform of a person worthy of any sort of respect.
Wishes to escape the Earth which he feels has rejected him, perhaps to find planet where his faults will be embraced.

YOUR PLAYTIME

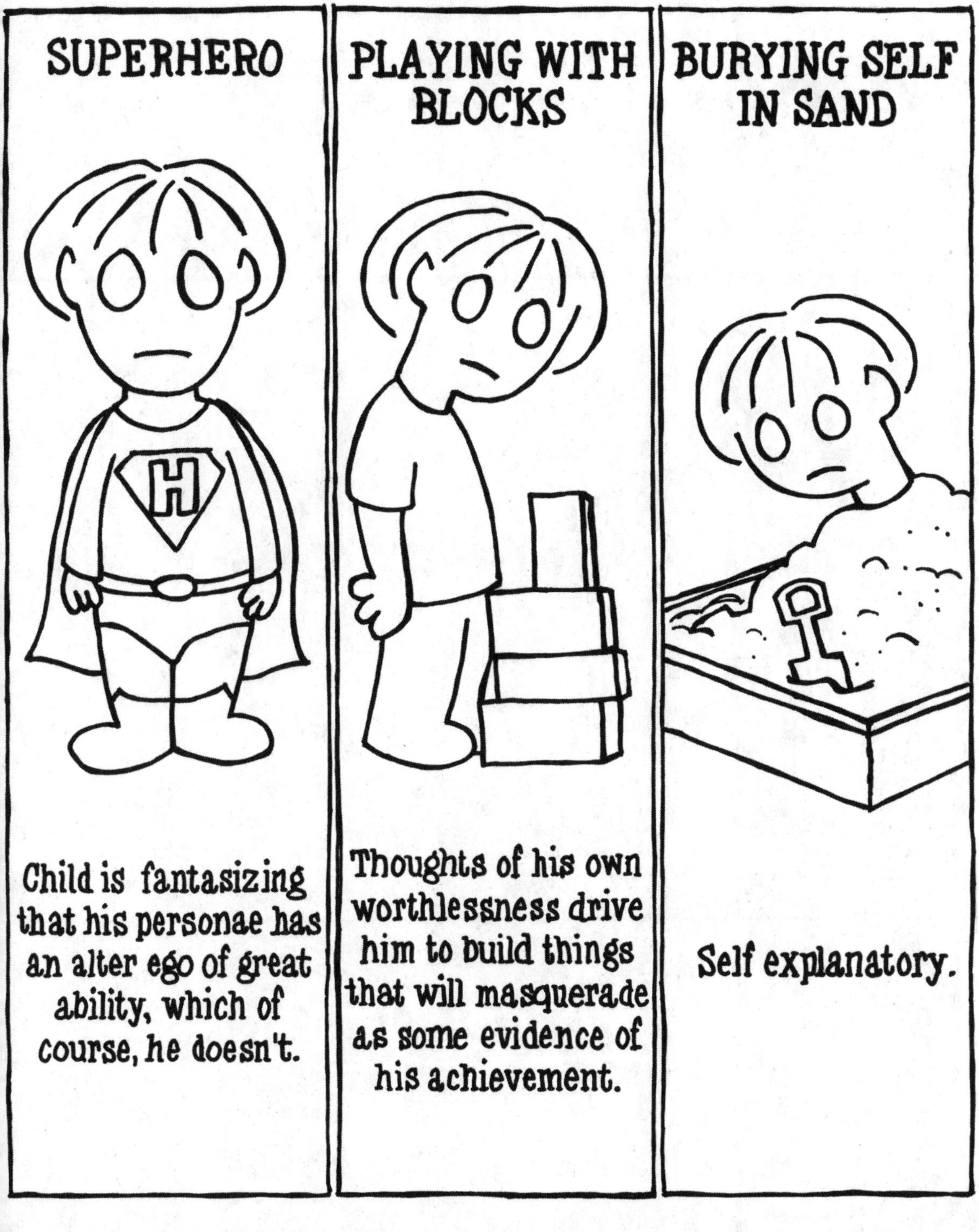
SUPERHERO
Child is fantasizing that his personae has an alter ego of great ability, which of course, he doesn't.
H
PLAYING WITH BLOCKS
Thoughts of his own worthlessness drive him to build things that will masquerade as some evidence of his achievement.
BURYING SELF IN SAND
Self explanatory.

WHAT I WAS THINKING THE NIGHT BEFORE EACH SCHOOL YEAR BEGAN

This year is going to be different.
This is the year things will change.
This year people are gonna think I'm cool.
This year I'm going to make friends.
This year I will get good grades.
This year I'll be on a team or something.
This year I'm gonna wear cool clothes.
This will be the best year of my life...

CHAPTER 2:
I went to school.

What I learned

1. I learned to recite the Pledge of Allegiance.

2. Australia has Kangaroos.

3. If you shrank the Earth to the size of a ball bearing, it would be more perfectly round than a ball bearing.

4. Most Sharks attack in 10 or 15 feet of water

5. Louis Braille invented Braille.

6. $8 \times 7 = 56$

7. The Penis is useful for Procreation.

in grade school

8. 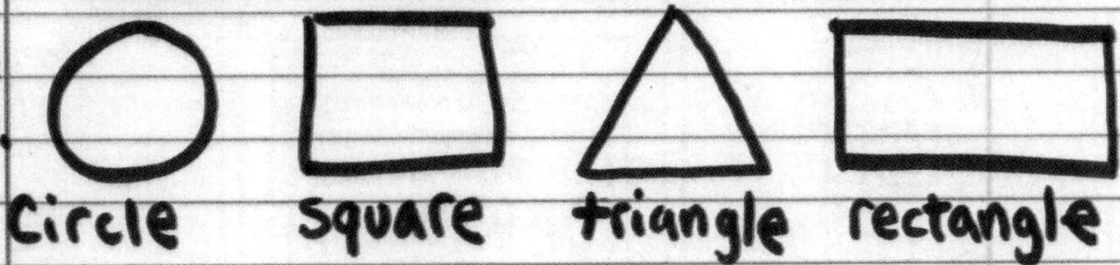
circle
square
triangle
rectangle

9. Cavemen and Dinosaurs did not live at the same time.

10. 9x9 = 81

11. South Africa is located in the Southern Hemisphere.

12. Treat people the way you want to be treated, even though they probably won't hold up their end of the bargain.

SO HOW DO YOU BECOME AN OUTSIDER?

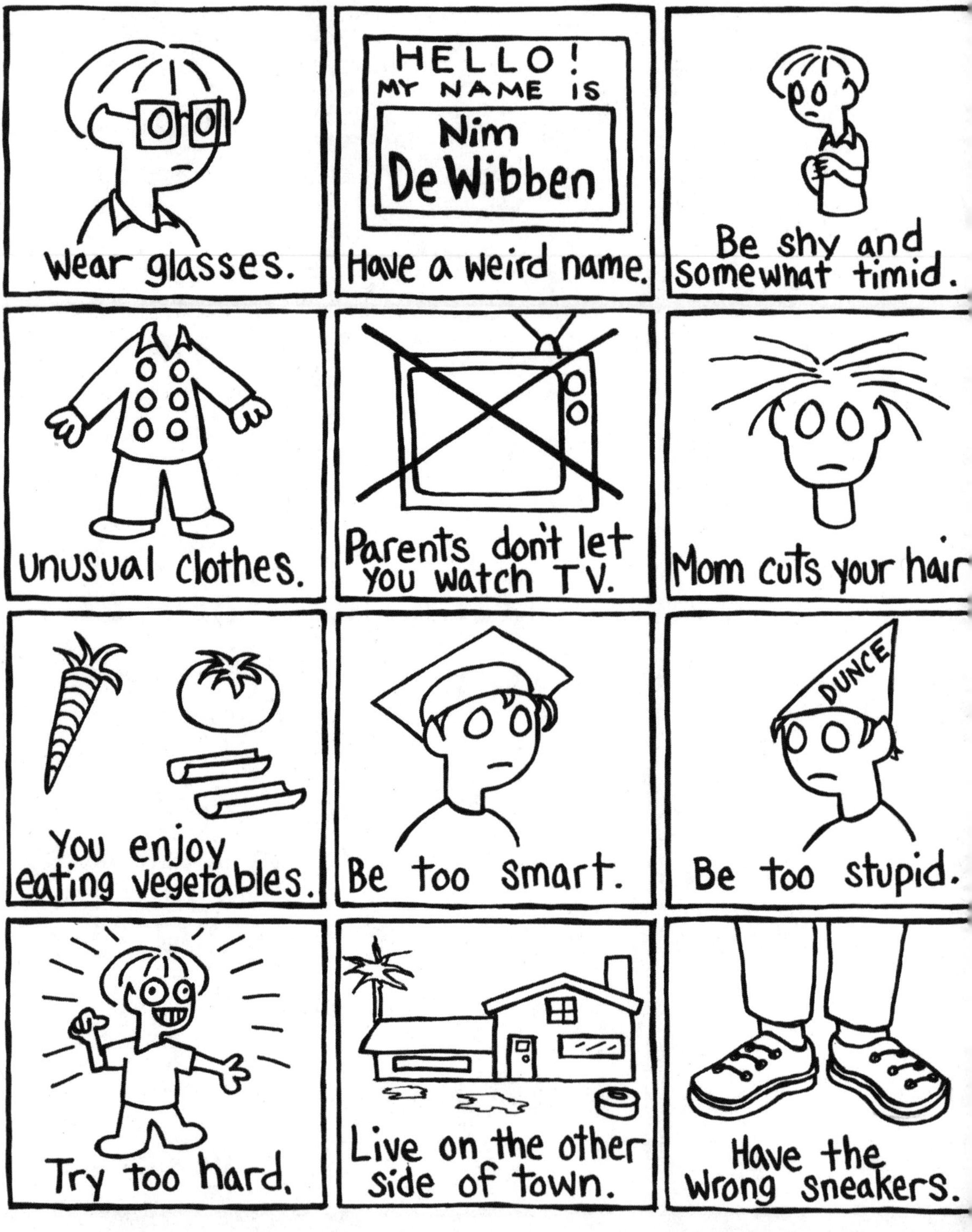
Wear glasses.
HELLO! MY NAME IS
Nim DeWibben
Have a weird name.
Be shy and somewhat timid.
Unusual clothes.
Parents don't let you watch TV.
Mom cuts your hair
DUNCE
You enjoy eating vegetables.
Be too smart.
Be too stupid.
Try too hard.
Live on the other side of town.
Have the wrong sneakers.

There are a variety of ways you can become a target of great derision, hatred and scorn. Any one of these will start you off, and you'll be on your way!!!

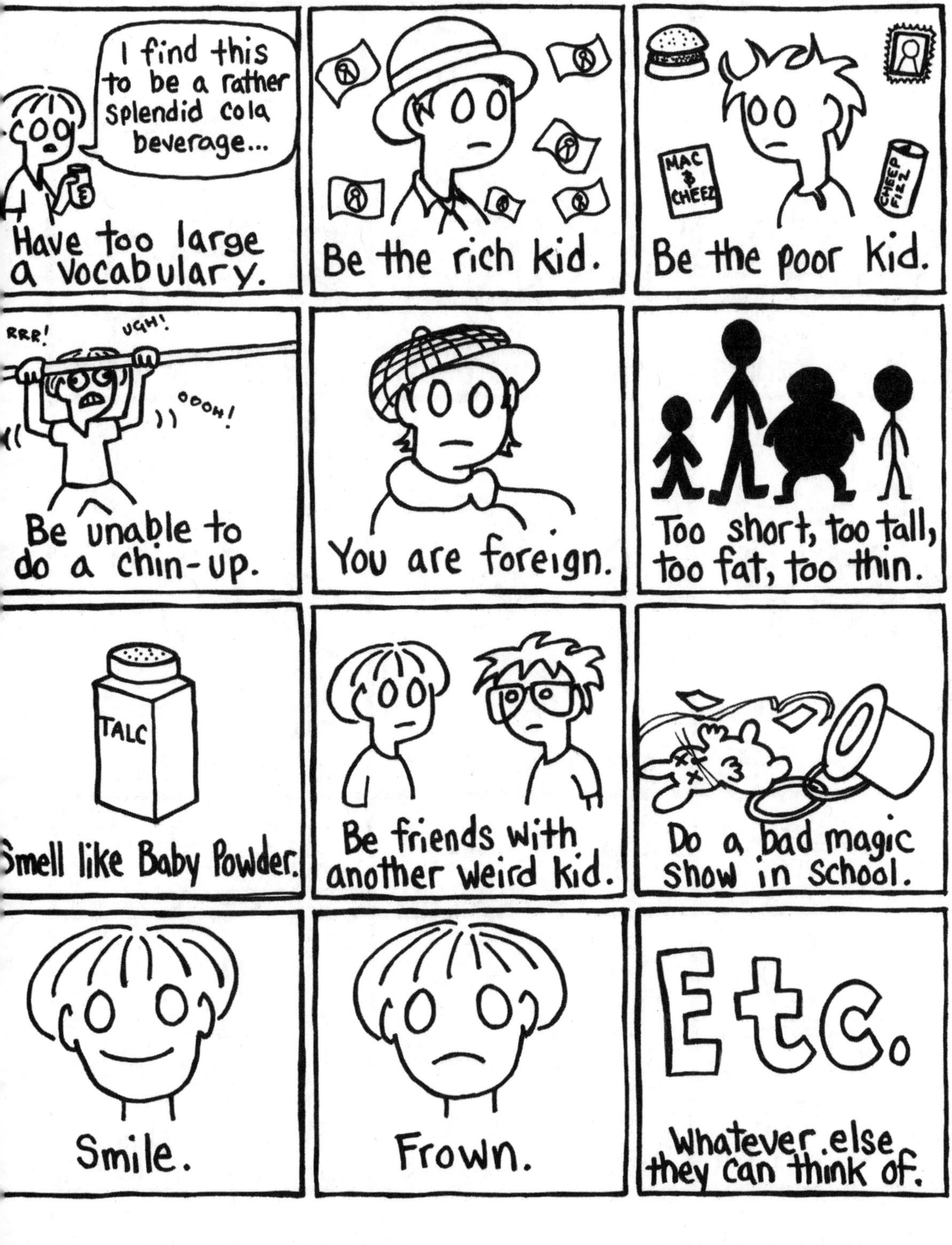
I find this to be a rather splendid cola beverage...
Have too large a vocabulary.
Be the rich kid.
MAC & CHEEZ
CHEEP FIZZ
Be the poor kid.
RRR!
UGH!
OOOH!
Be unable to do a chin-up.
You are foreign.
Too short, too tall, too fat, too thin.
TALC
Smell like Baby Powder.
Be friends with another weird kid.
Do a bad magic show in school.
Smile.
Frown.
Etc.
Whatever else they can think of.

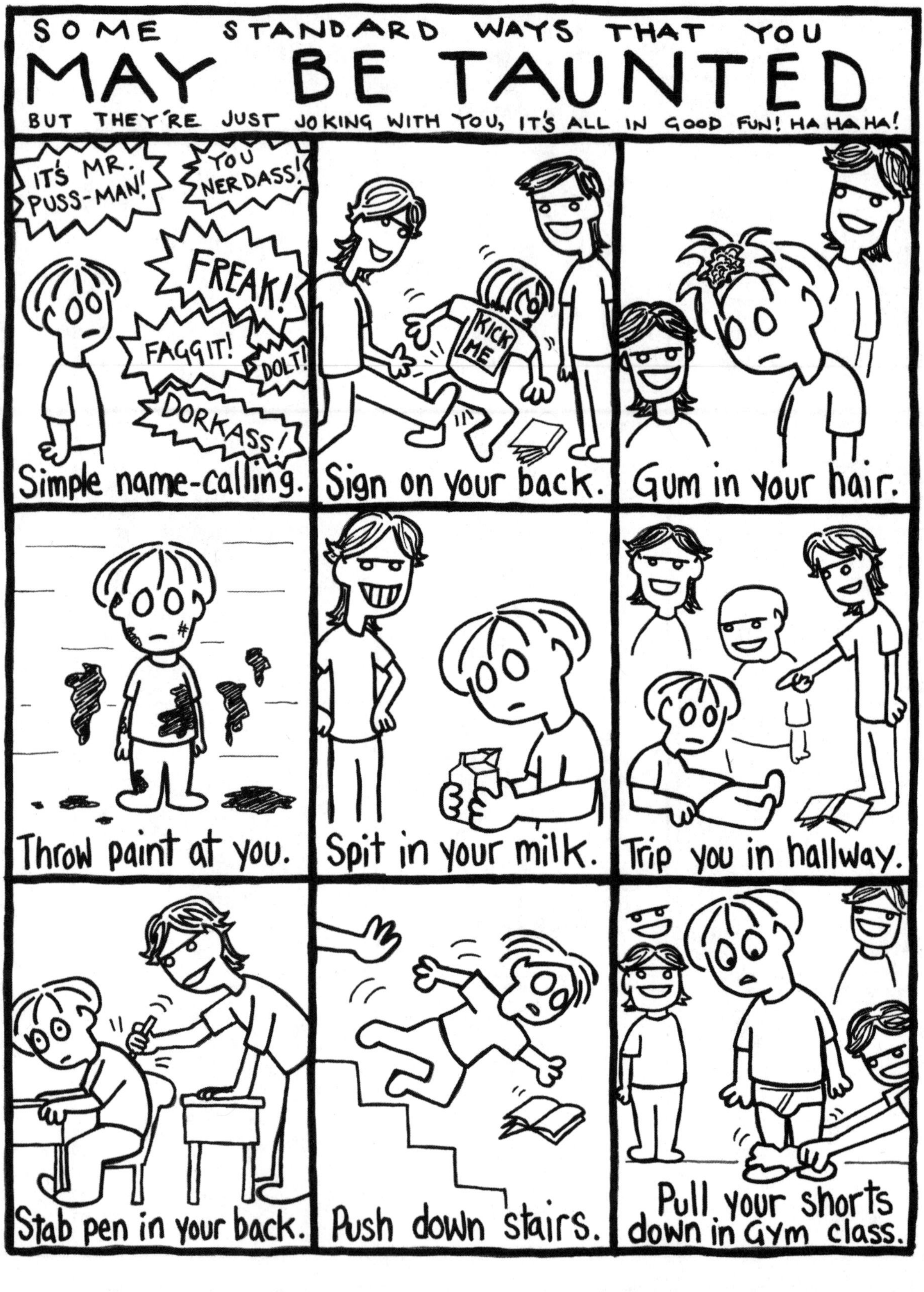
SOME STANDARD WAYS THAT YOU
MAY BE TAUNTED
BUT THEY'RE JUST JOKING WITH YOU, IT'S ALL IN GOOD FUN! HA HA HA!
IT'S MR. PUSS-MAN!
YOU NERDASS!
FREAK!
FAGGIT!
DOLT!
DORKASS!
Simple name-calling.
KICK ME
Sign on your back.
Gum in your hair.
Throw paint at you.
Spit in your milk.
Trip you in hallway.
Stab pen in your back.
Push down stairs.
Pull your shorts down in Gym class.

WHAT IS A BULLY ANYWAY?

All proper definitions aside, a bully is basically a person who derives some sort of pleasure and/or self-satisfaction from making your life miserable.

WHAT THIS MEANS TO YOU: Depending on your own disposition and general self-image, a bully's impact can range from a mere nuisance to greatly reinforcing and magnifying your inherent self-doubts in ways that you won't comprehend until you begin therapy some years later.

It is worthy to note however, that most bullies, are at heart, cowards. The phrase "Pick on someone your own size" was probably created to expose this paradox: For all the bravado and machismo most bullies try to project, they still for the most part only mess with lone targets, half their size, and when they have their friends around.

At a young age, it's a very difficult concept to grasp that "the tough kids may not be so tough after all". Many adults will likely try to explain this to you, but it won't really sink in, as you don't really care one way or the other if the guy who is punching you in the face is a coward while he is in the act of punching you in the face.

Nevertheless, you will likely one day understand that the actions bullies took against your youthful self were little more than pathetic attempts on their part to feel powerful and dominant. It didn't have much to do with you.

However, chances are you will realize this long after it is of any use to you, so you will probably try to pass this fact on to your own children, who in turn won't listen to you, and the cycle can begin anew.

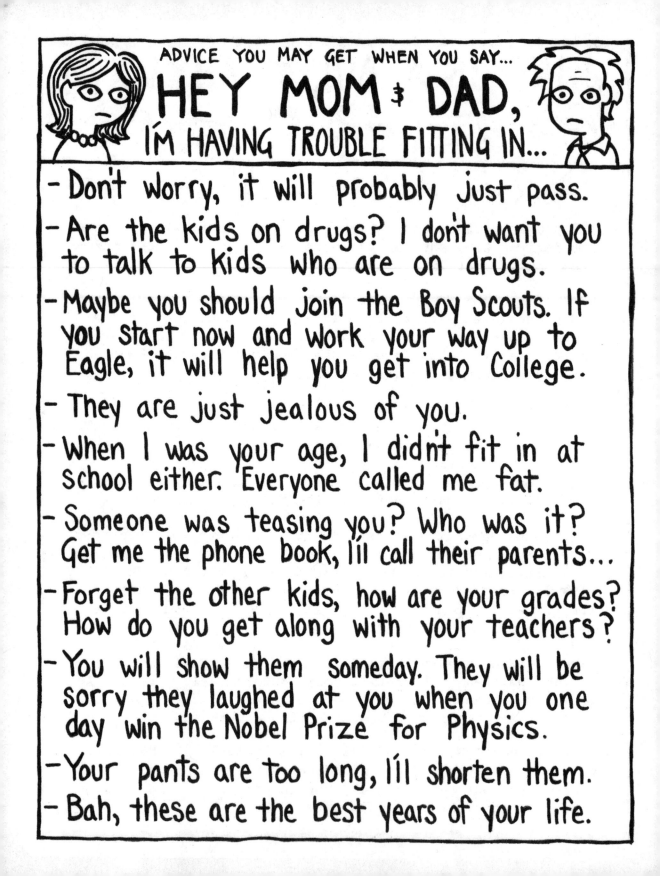

ADVICE YOU MAY GET WHEN YOU SAY...

HEY MOM & DAD,
I'M HAVING TROUBLE FITTING IN...

- Don't worry, it will probably just pass.
- Are the kids on drugs? I don't want you to talk to kids who are on drugs.
- Maybe you should join the Boy Scouts. If you start now and work your way up to Eagle, it will help you get into College.
- They are just jealous of you.
- When I was your age, I didn't fit in at school either. Everyone called me fat.
- Someone was teasing you? Who was it? Get me the phone book, I'll call their parents...
- Forget the other kids, how are your grades? How do you get along with your teachers?
- You will show them someday. They will be sorry they laughed at you when you one day win the Nobel Prize for Physics.
- Your pants are too long, I'll shorten them.
- Bah, these are the best years of your life.

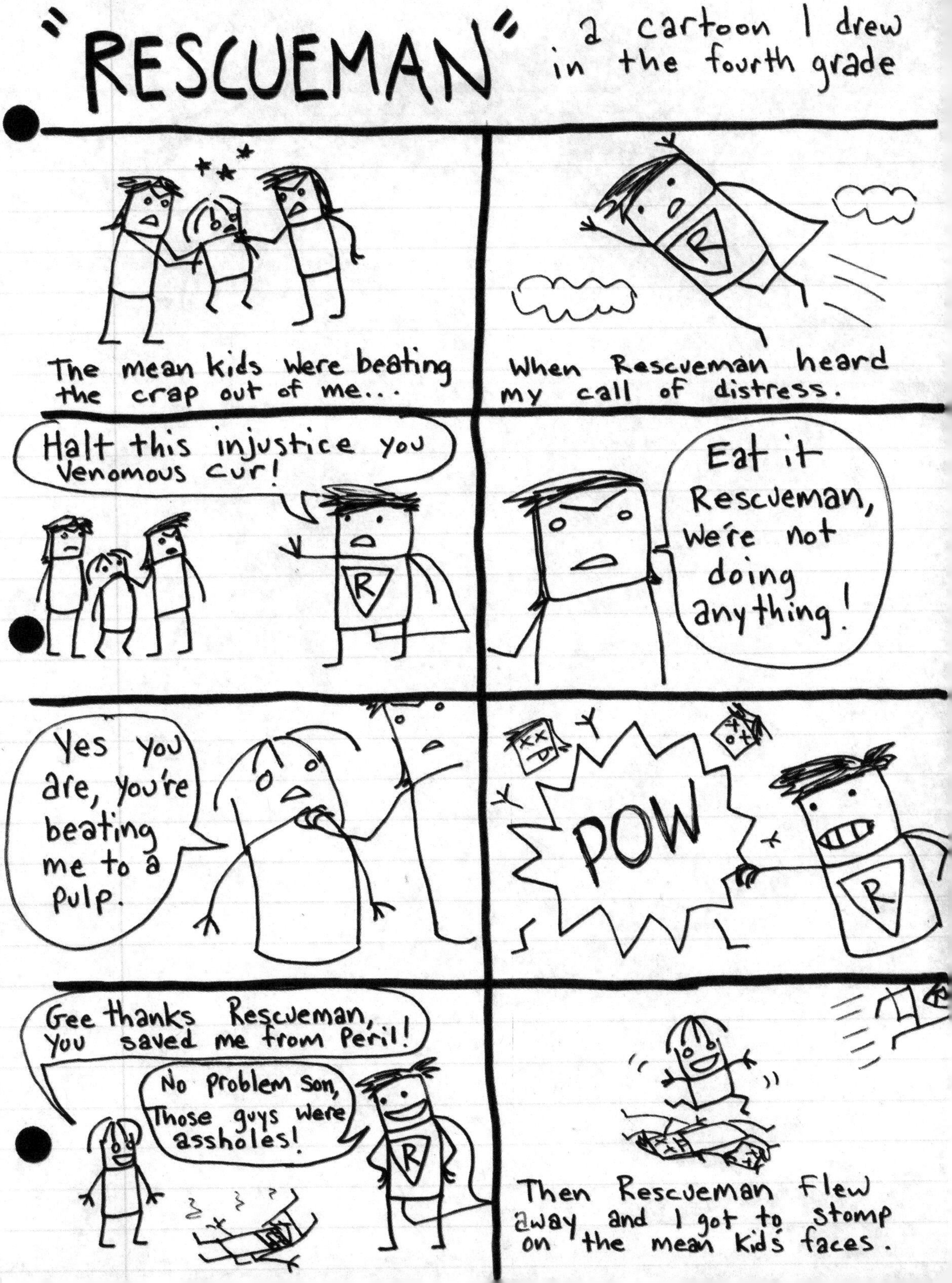
"RESCUEMAN" a cartoon I drew in the fourth grade
The mean kids were beating the crap out of me...
When Rescueman heard my call of distress.
Halt this injustice you Venomous cur!
Eat it Rescueman, we're not doing anything!
Yes you are, you're beating me to a pulp.
POW
Gee thanks Rescueman, you saved me from Peril!
No problem son, Those guys were assholes!
Then Rescueman flew away and I got to stomp on the mean kids faces.

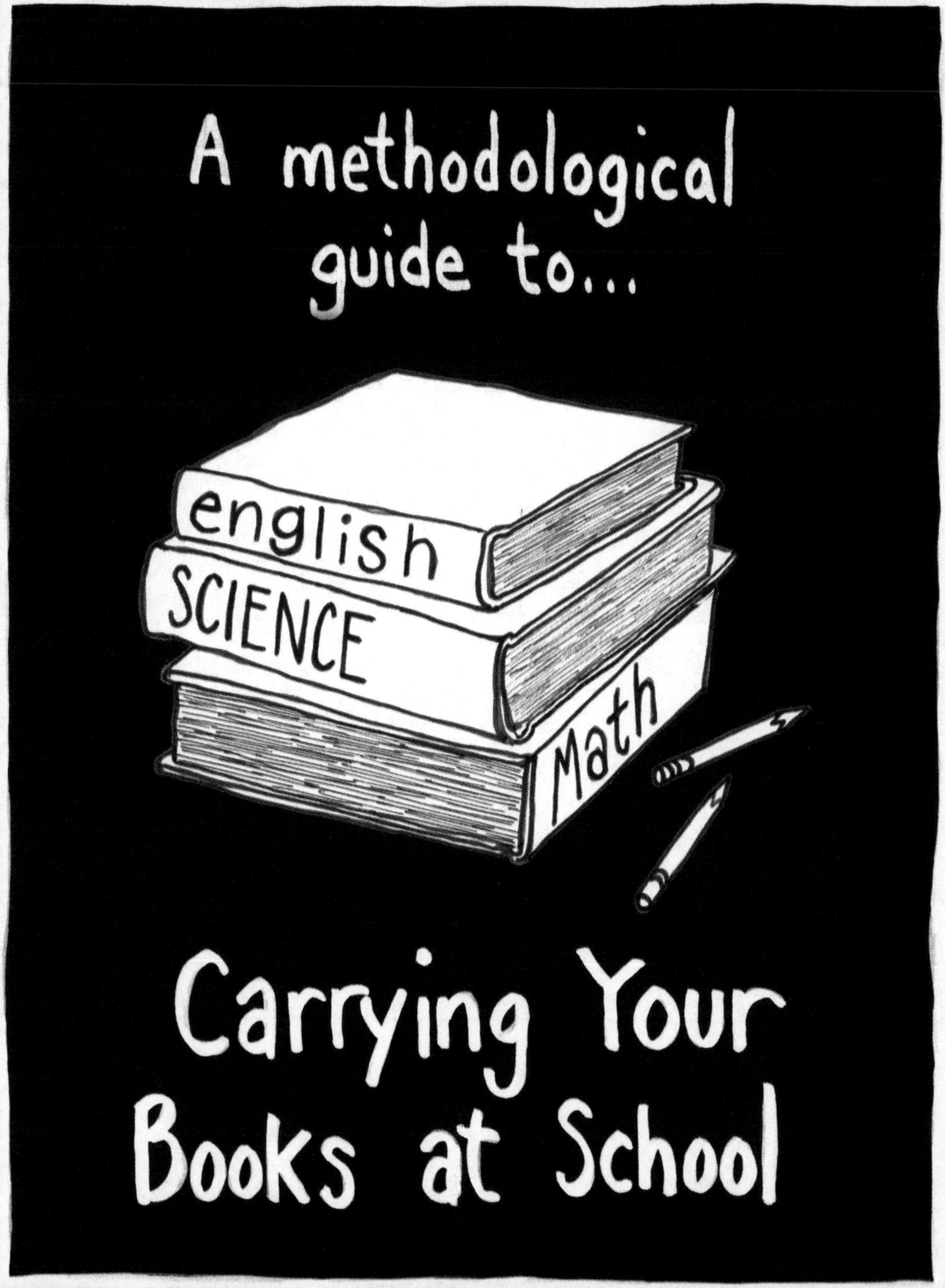
A methodological guide to...
english
SCIENCE
Math
Carrying Your Books at School

Method 1: SHOULDER BAG

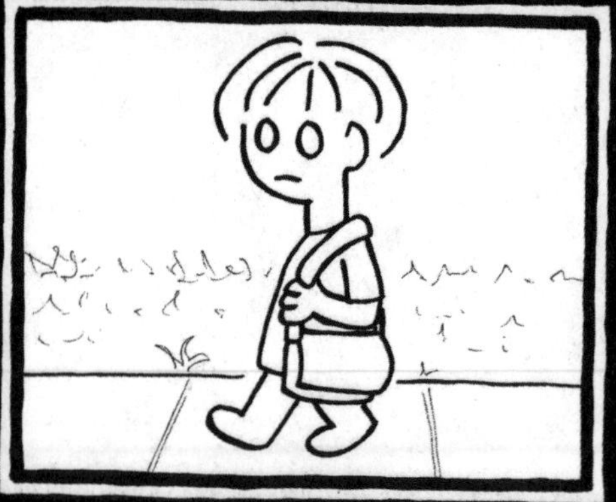

PROS: Simple, reasonably comfortable, logical. Easy access to your stuff.

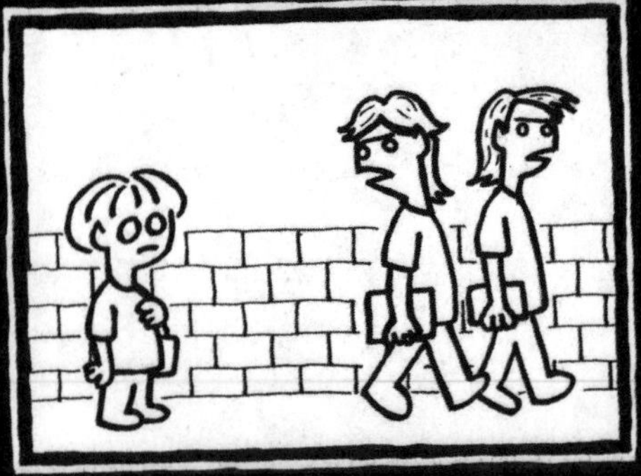

CONS: Schoolmates will say it looks like a purse. You will be subject to such taunts as "Bookbag Baby", "Bag Fag" and "Bag, Bag, Douchebag ".

Method 2: UNDER ONE ARM

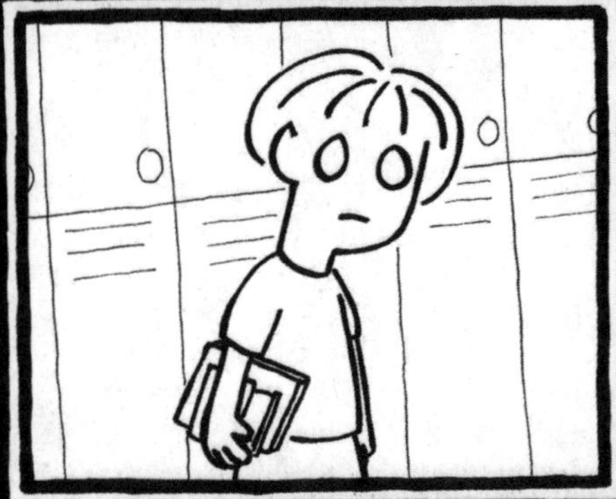

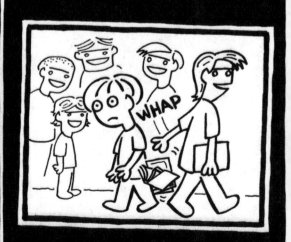

PROS: This is the way most of the big kids carry their books. It's fine if you don't have much to carry. Easiest method to strut with.

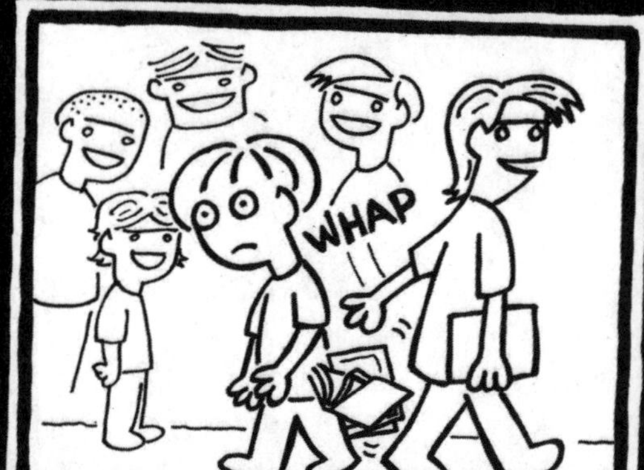
WHAP

CONS: You are now a target to get your books dumped.

Method 3: UNDER BOTH ARMS

PROS: This will help with weight distribution for heavy loads of books.

CONS: You are now a "2 for 1" target for getting your books dumped.

Method 4: THE STACK

PROS: I suppose you can carry a lot of books this way... fewer visits to your locker?

CONS: You really have got to be kidding .

Method 5: AGAINST CHEST

PROS: Creates temporary, false belief that your books will not be dumped today.

CONS: Your adversaries may be annoyed that you have made it less convenient for them to dump your books. They may be more aggressive as they shove you and pry your arms apart so they can dump your books.

Method 6: NO BOOKS AT ALL

PROS: No books to dump. Being bookless may make you look like kind of a badass.

CONS: You will probably fail all your classes.

ASIDE: You may find this to be a worthwhile trade off.

Method 7: BACKPACK, OVER BOTH SHOULDERS

(NOTE HANGING LOOP)

PROS: Sort of traditional, comfortable. Arms free.

CONS: If they yank the black hanging loop thing on your bag as you walk by, it will be rather easy for them to knock you on your ass.

Method 8: BACKPACK, OVER ONE SHOULDER

PROS: Everybody does it.   CONS: Everybody does it.

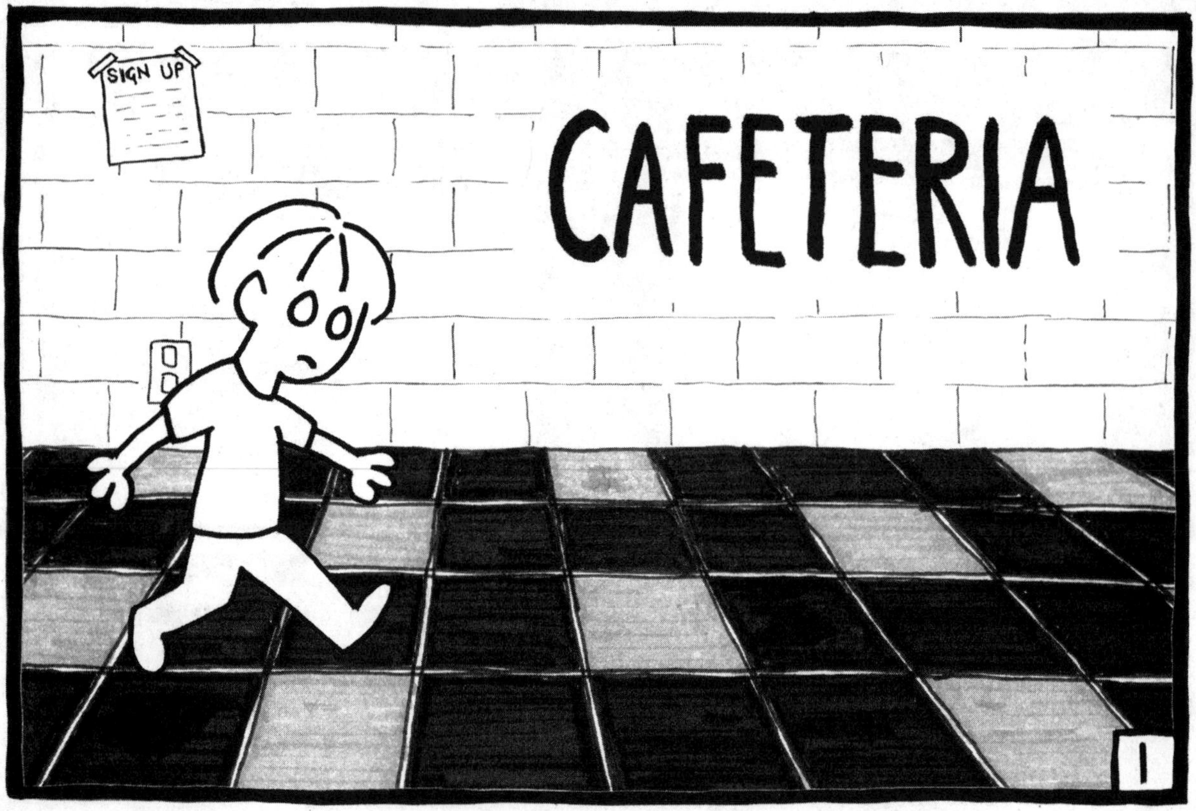
SIGN UP
CAFETERIA
1

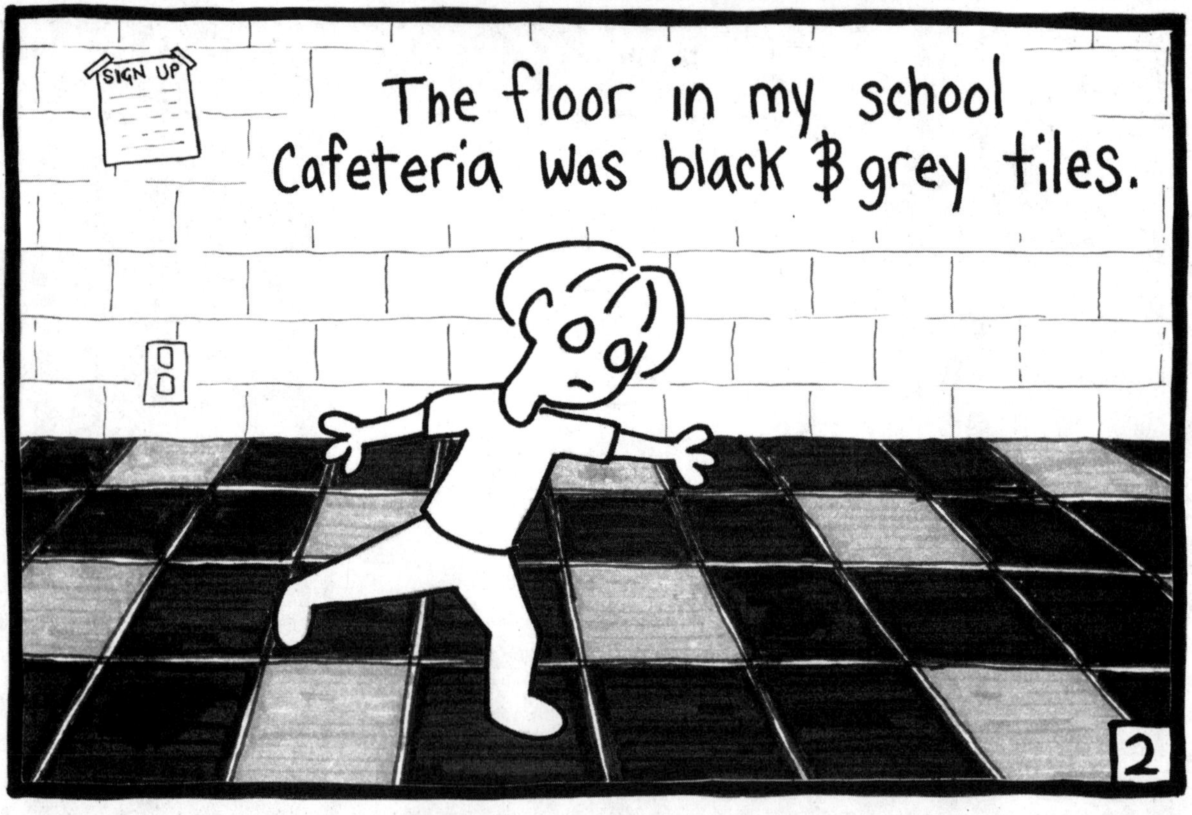
SIGN UP
The floor in my school Cafeteria was black & grey tiles.
2

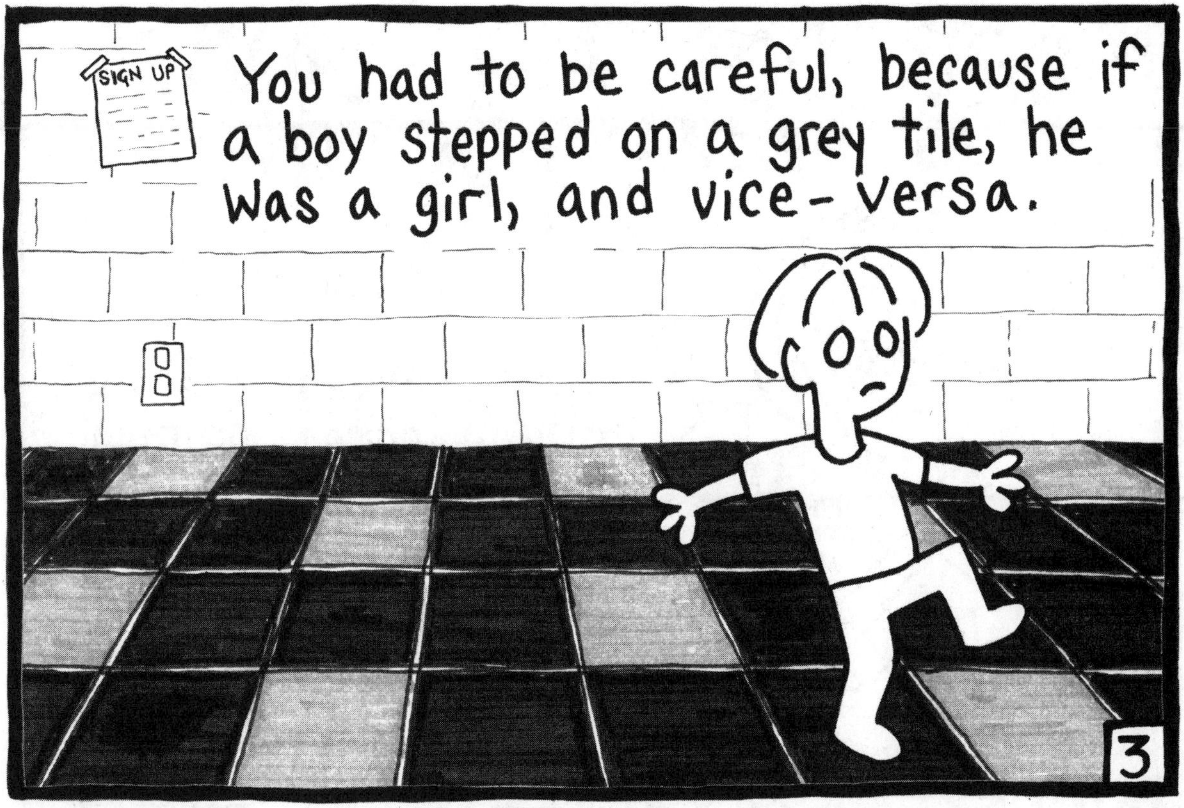
SIGN UP
You had to be careful, because if a boy stepped on a grey tile, he was a girl, and vice-versa.
3

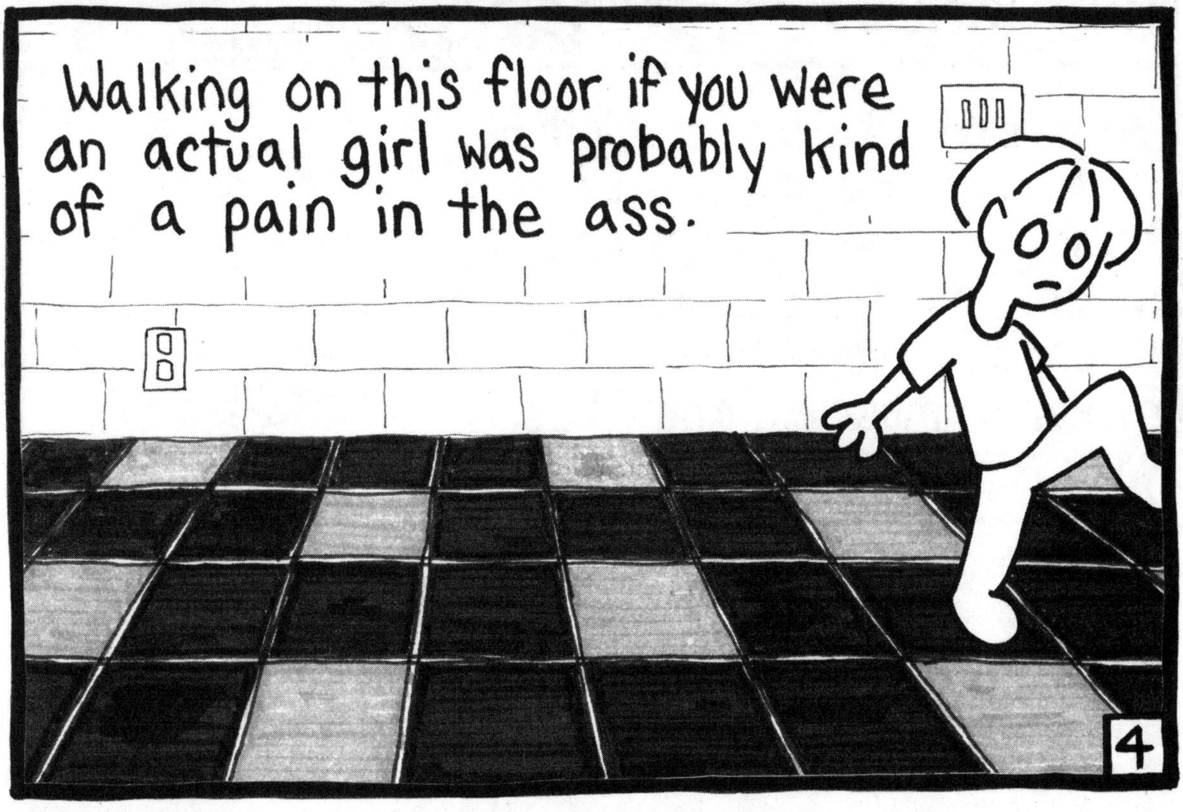
Walking on this floor if you were an actual girl was probably kind of a pain in the ass.
4

MORE DO'S AND DONT'S...

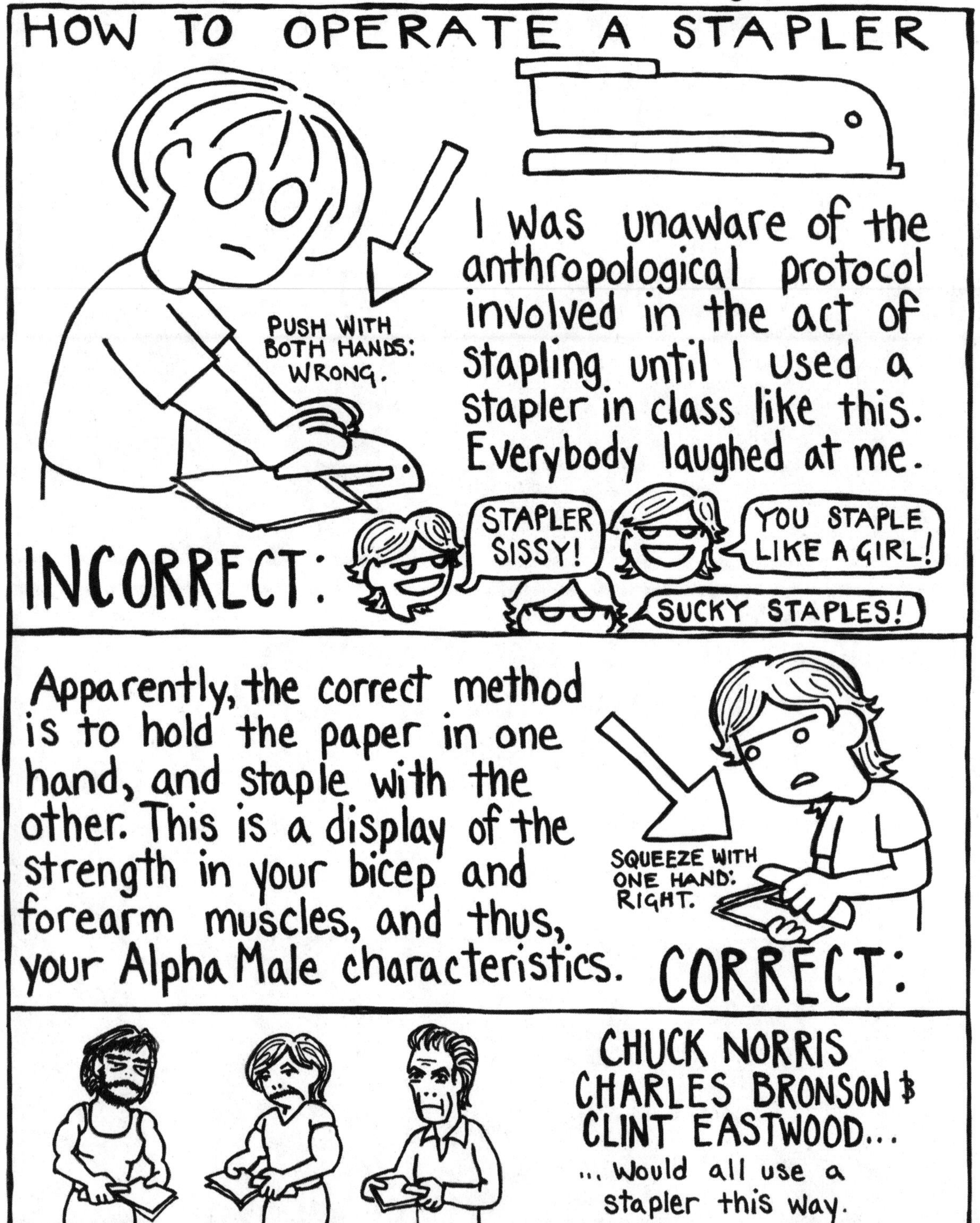
HOW TO OPERATE A STAPLER
I was unaware of the anthropological protocol involved in the act of stapling until I used a stapler in class like this. Everybody laughed at me.
PUSH WITH BOTH HANDS: WRONG.
INCORRECT:
STAPLER SISSY!
YOU STAPLE LIKE A GIRL!
SUCKY STAPLES!
Apparently, the correct method is to hold the paper in one hand, and staple with the other. This is a display of the strength in your bicep and forearm muscles, and thus, your Alpha Male characteristics.
SQUEEZE WITH ONE HAND: RIGHT.
CORRECT:
CHUCK NORRIS CHARLES BRONSON & CLINT EASTWOOD...
...would all use a stapler this way.

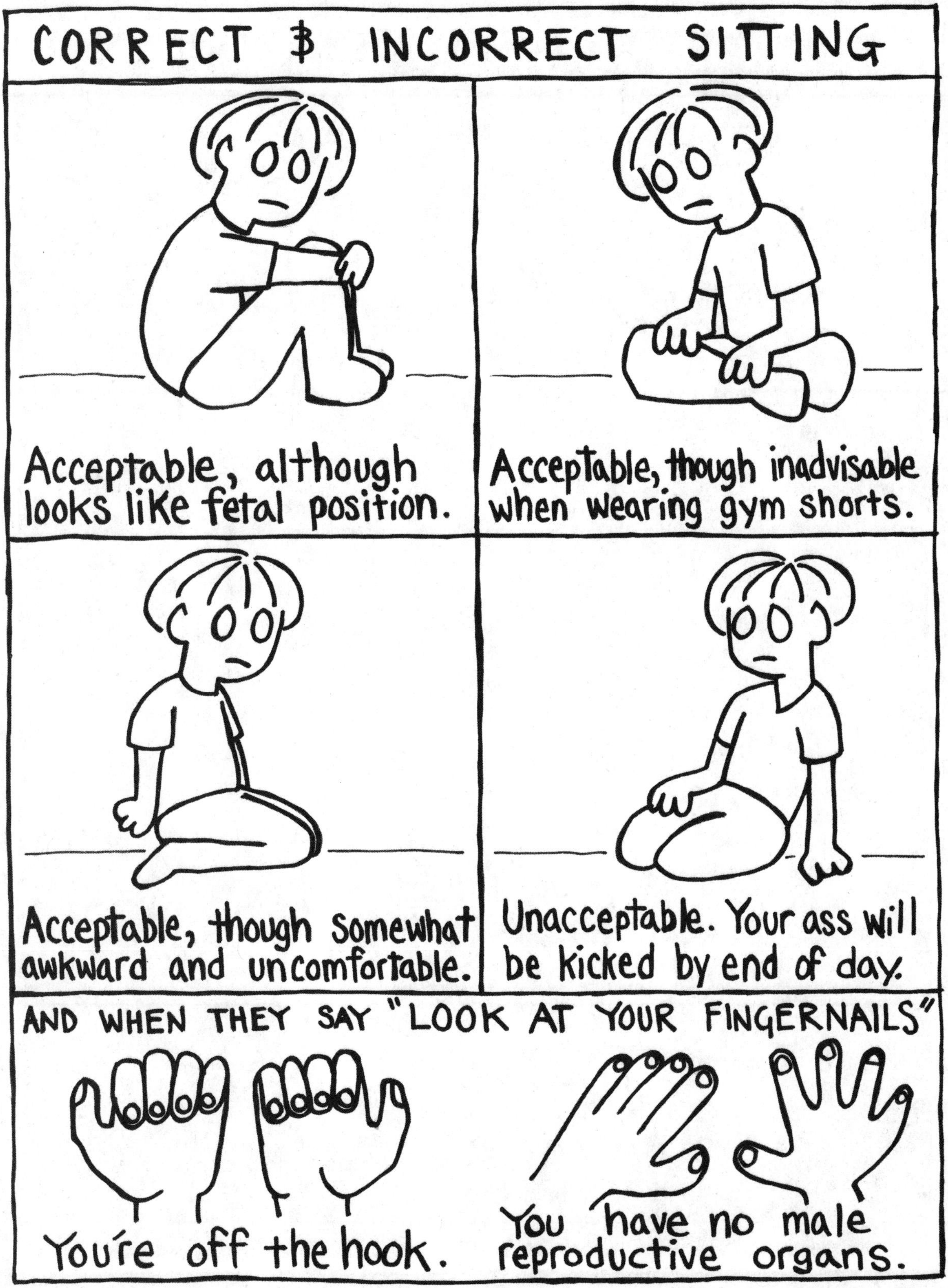
CORRECT & INCORRECT SITTING
Acceptable, although looks like fetal position.
Acceptable, though inadvisable when wearing gym shorts.
Acceptable, though somewhat awkward and uncomfortable.
Unacceptable. Your ass will be kicked by end of day.
AND WHEN THEY SAY "LOOK AT YOUR FINGERNAILS"
You're off the hook.
You have no male reproductive organs.

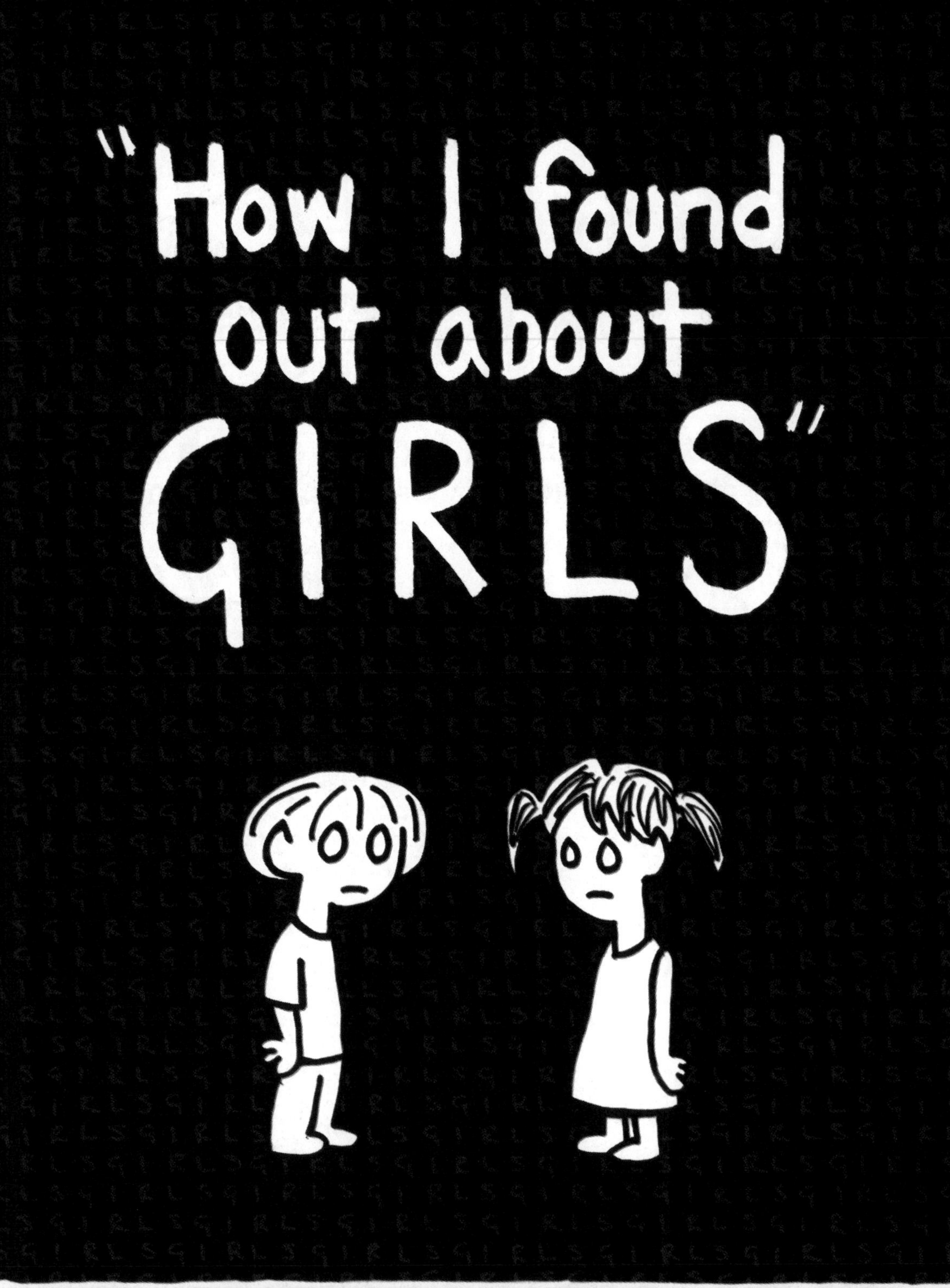
"How I found out about GIRLS"

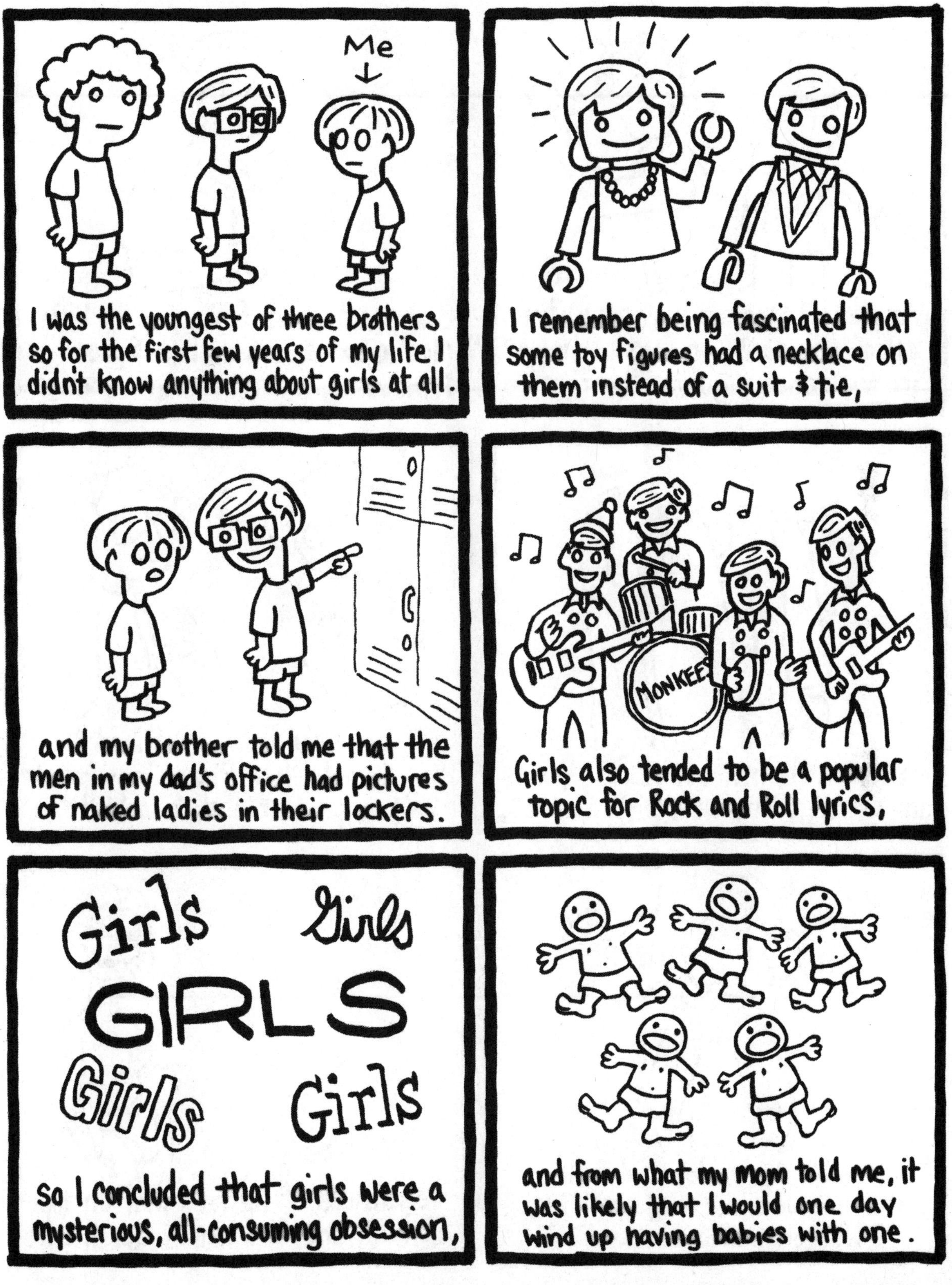
Me
I was the youngest of three brothers so for the first few years of my life I didn't know anything about girls at all.
I remember being fascinated that some toy figures had a necklace on them instead of a suit & tie,
and my brother told me that the men in my dad's office had pictures of naked ladies in their lockers.
MONKEES
Girls also tended to be a popular topic for Rock and Roll lyrics,
Girls
Girls
GIRLS
Girls
Girls
so I concluded that girls were a mysterious, all-consuming obsession,
and from what my mom told me, it was likely that I would one day wind up having babies with one.

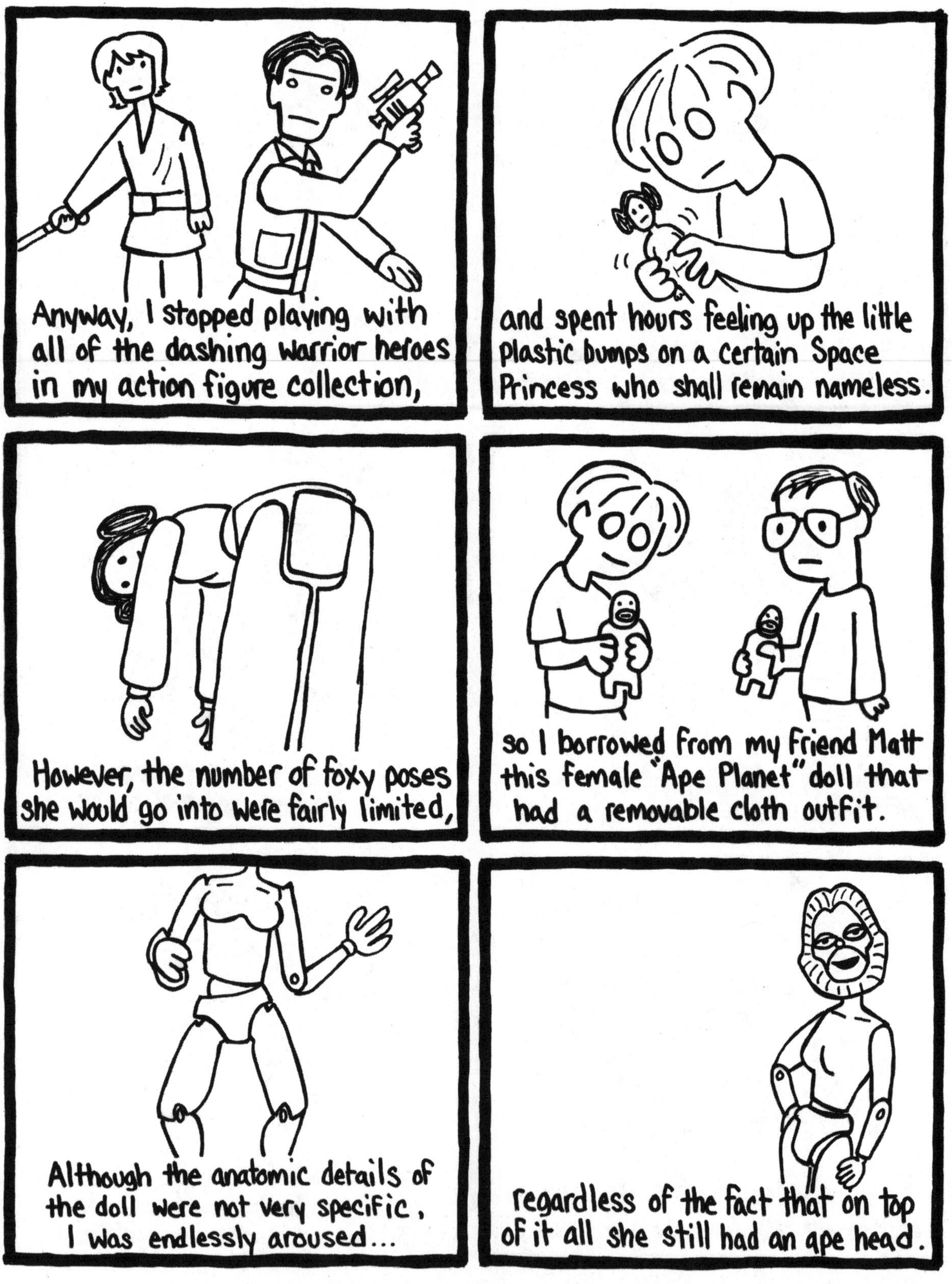
Anyway, I stopped playing with all of the dashing warrior heroes in my action figure collection,
and spent hours feeling up the little plastic bumps on a certain Space Princess who shall remain nameless.
However, the number of foxy poses she would go into were fairly limited,
so I borrowed from my friend Matt this female "Ape Planet" doll that had a removable cloth outfit.
Although the anatomic details of the doll were not very specific, I was endlessly aroused...
regardless of the fact that on top of it all she still had an ape head.

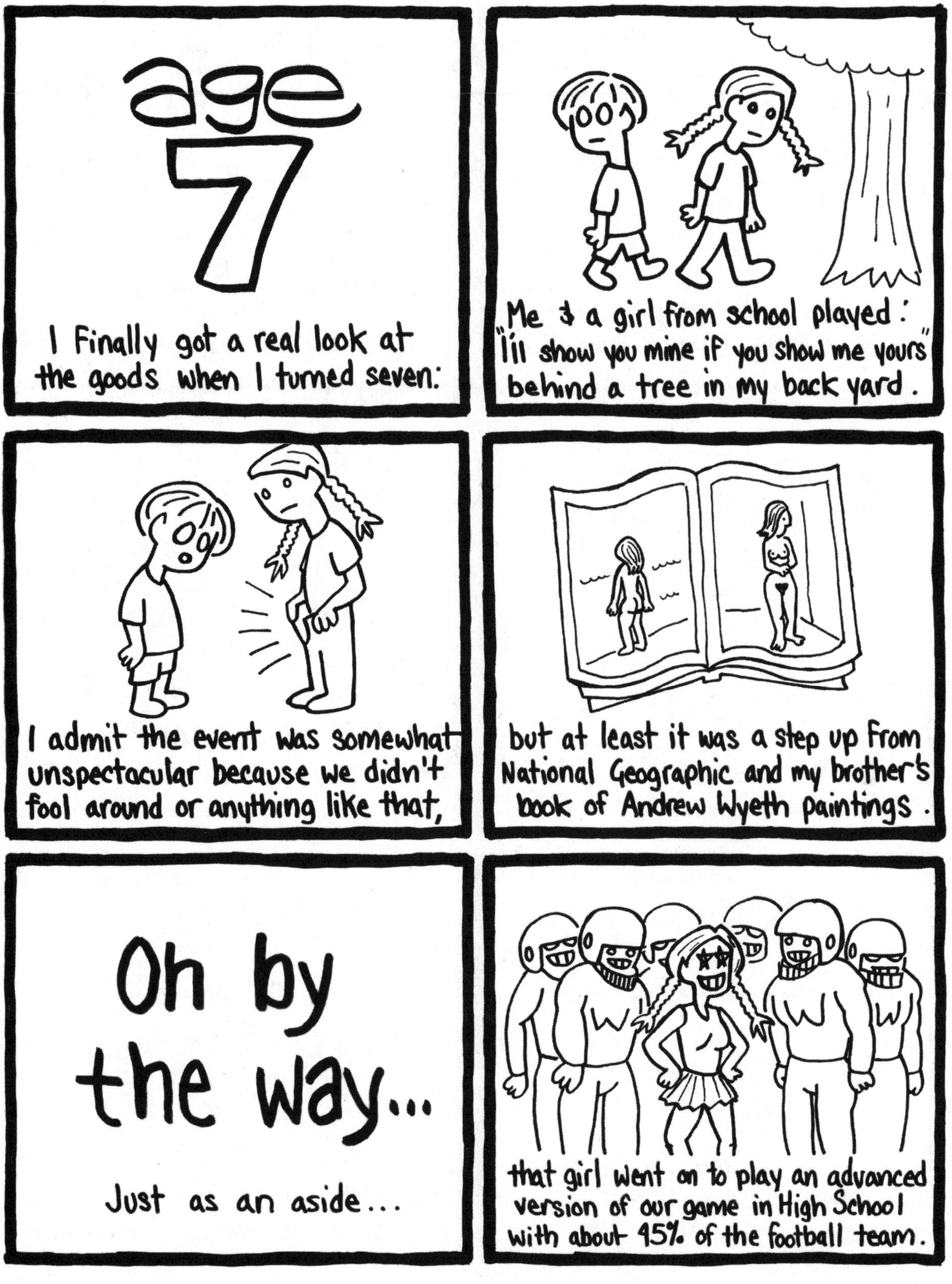
age 7
I Finally got a real look at the goods when I turned seven:
Me & a girl from school played: "I'll show you mine if you show me yours" behind a tree in my back yard.
I admit the event was somewhat unspectacular because we didn't fool around or anything like that,
but at least it was a step up from National Geographic and my brother's book of Andrew Wyeth paintings.
Oh by the way...
Just as an aside...
that girl went on to play an advanced version of our game in High School with about 45% of the football team.

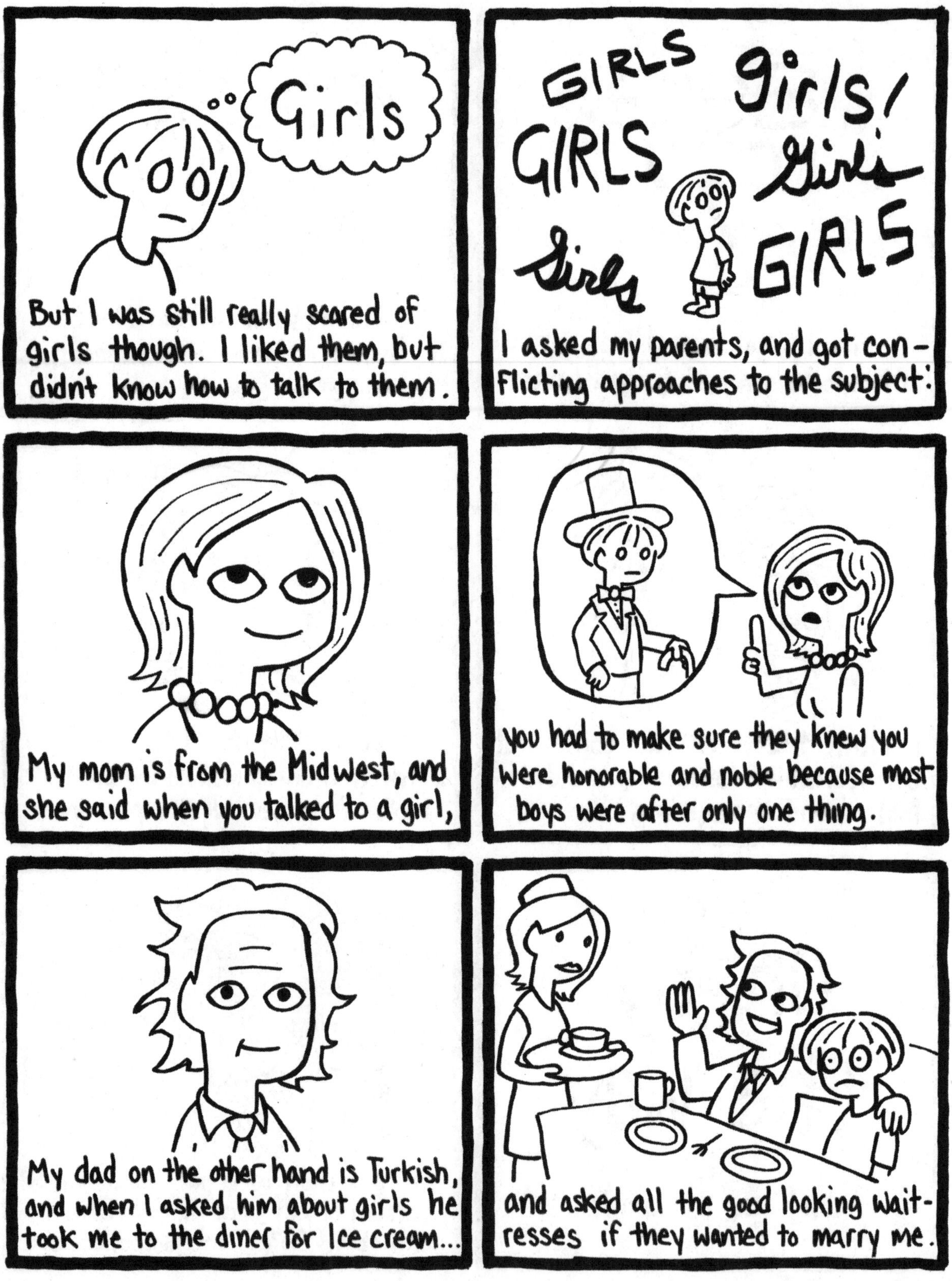
Girls
But I was still really scared of girls though. I liked them, but didn't know how to talk to them.
GIRLS girls! GIRLS Girls Girls GIRLS
I asked my parents, and got con-flicting approaches to the subject:
My mom is from the Midwest, and she said when you talked to a girl,
you had to make sure they knew you were honorable and noble because most boys were after only one thing.
My dad on the other hand is Turkish, and when I asked him about girls he took me to the diner for Ice cream...
and asked all the good looking wait-resses if they wanted to marry me.

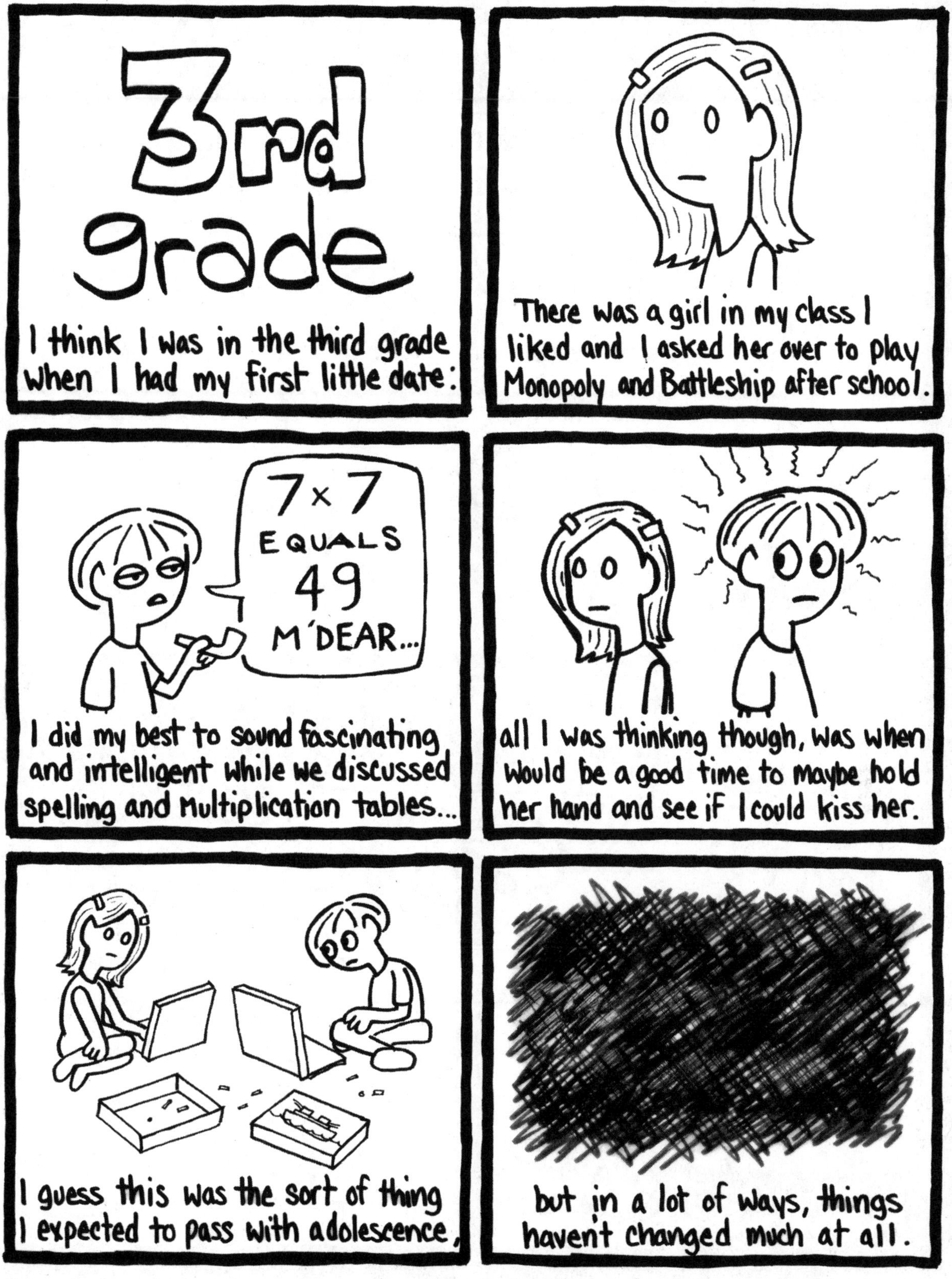
3rd grade
I think I was in the third grade when I had my first little date:
There was a girl in my class I liked and I asked her over to play Monopoly and Battleship after school.
7×7 EQUALS 49 M'DEAR...
I did my best to sound fascinating and intelligent while we discussed spelling and multiplication tables...
all I was thinking though, was when would be a good time to maybe hold her hand and see if I could kiss her.
I guess this was the sort of thing I expected to pass with adolescence,
but in a lot of ways, things haven't changed much at all.

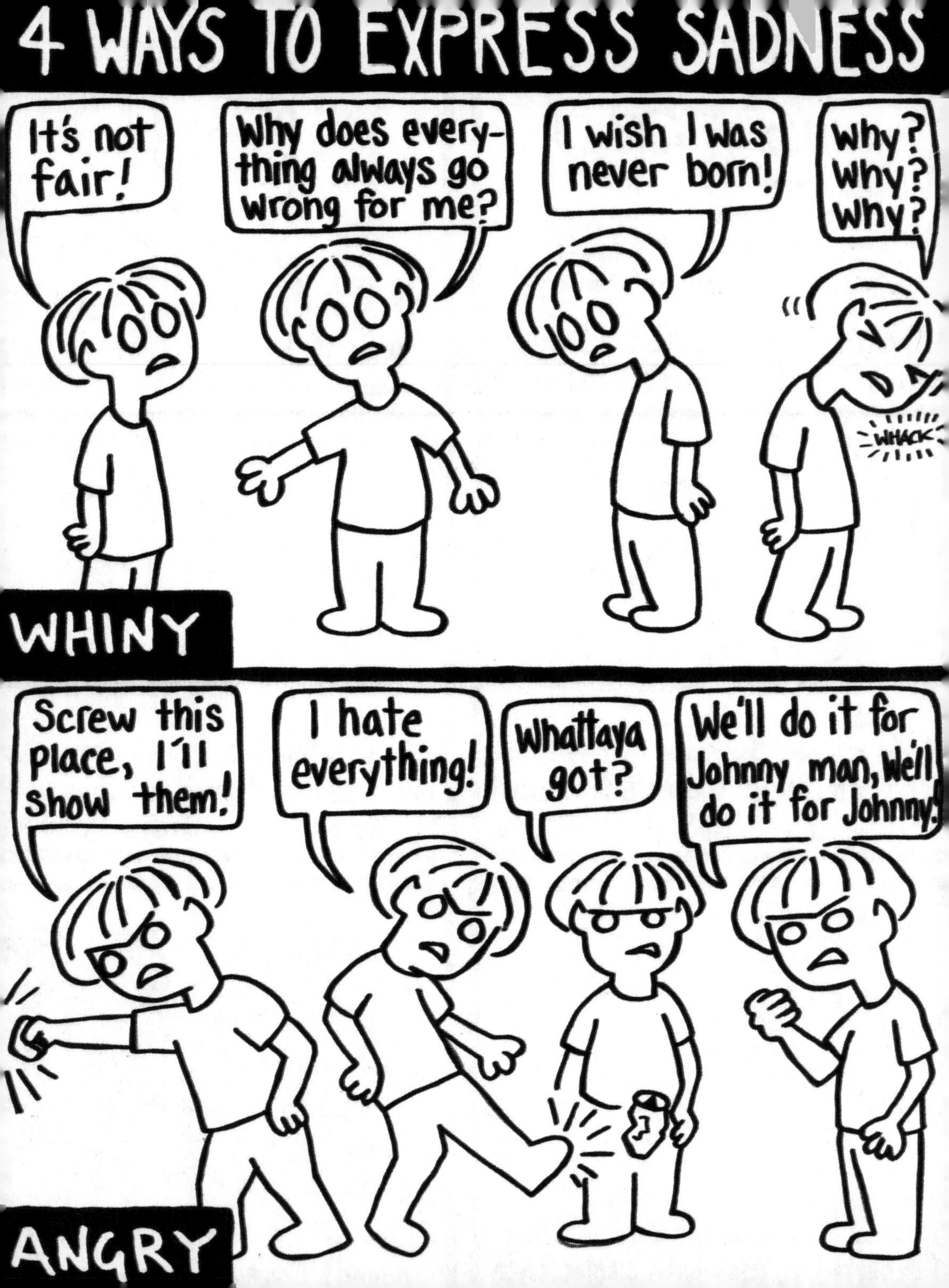
4 WAYS TO EXPRESS SADNESS
It's not fair!
Why does everything always go wrong for me?
I wish I was never born!
Why? Why? Why?
WHACK
WHINY
Screw this place, I'll show them!
I hate everything!
Whattaya got?
We'll do it for Johnny man, We'll do it for Johnny!
ANGRY

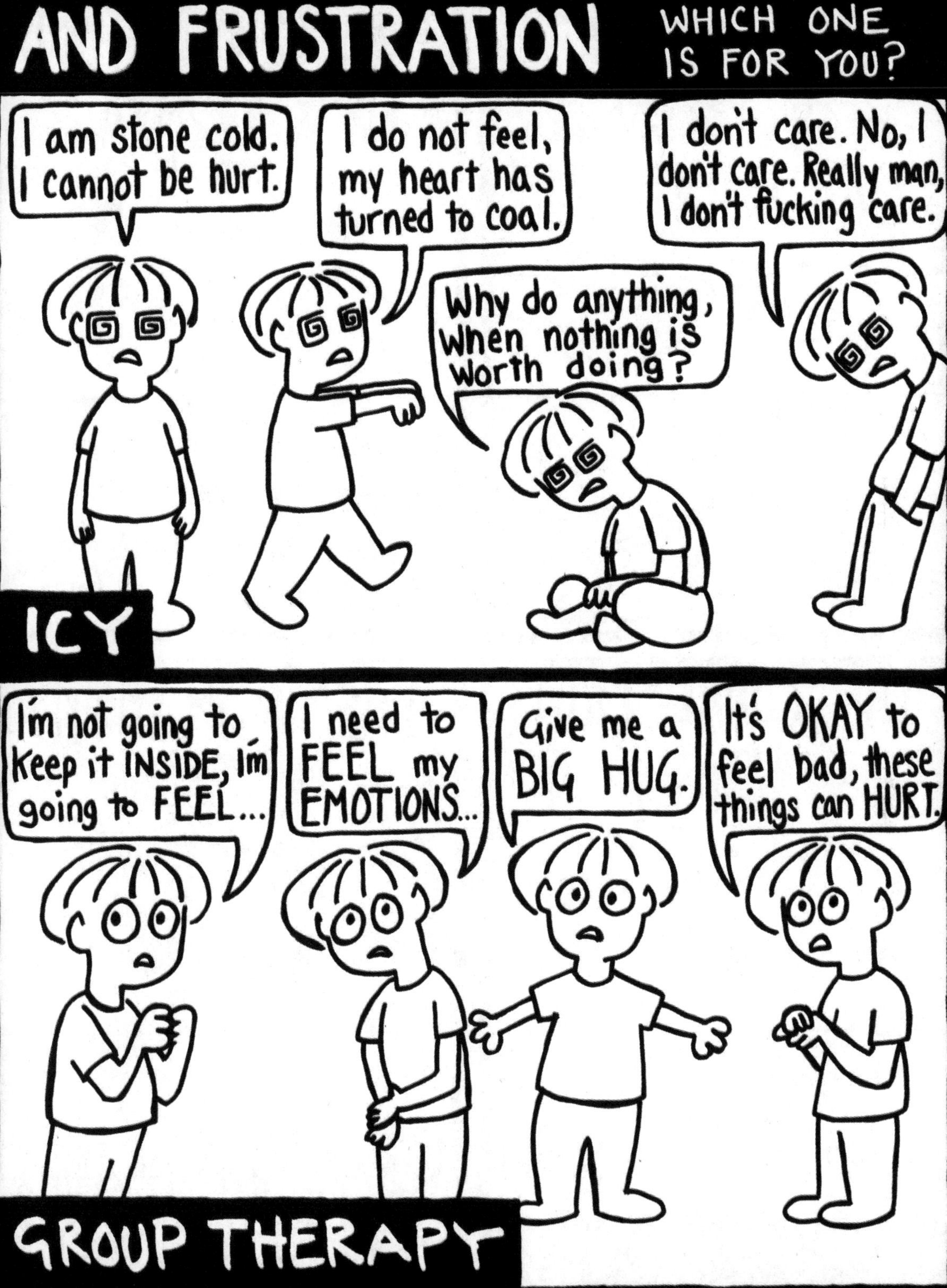
AND FRUSTRATION
WHICH ONE IS FOR YOU?
I am stone cold. I cannot be hurt.
I do not feel, my heart has turned to coal.
Why do anything, when nothing is worth doing?
I don't care. No, I don't care. Really man, I don't fucking care.
ICY
I'm not going to keep it INSIDE, I'm going to FEEL...
I need to FEEL my EMOTIONS...
Give me a BIG HUG.
It's OKAY to feel bad, these things can HURT.
GROUP THERAPY

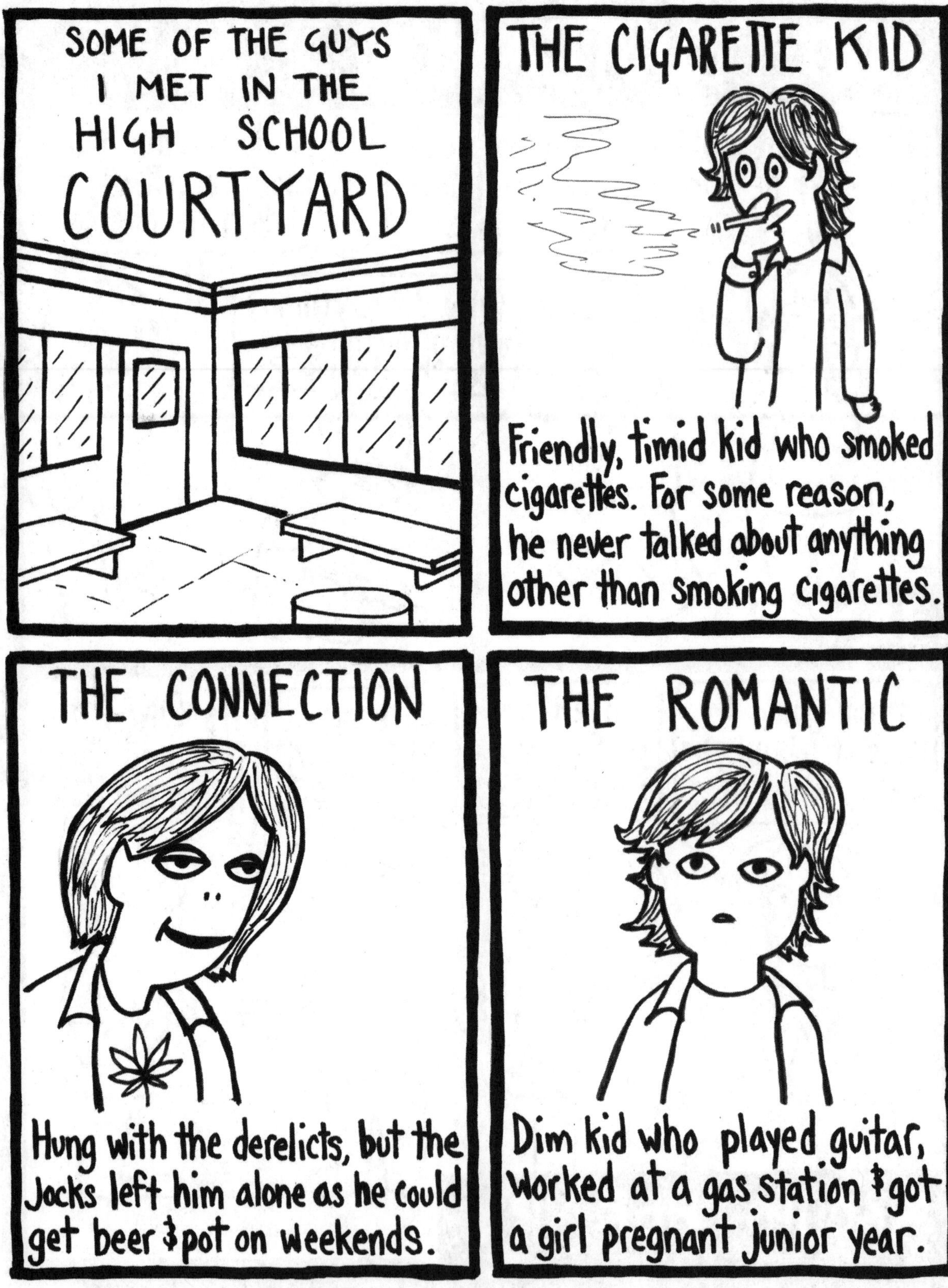
SOME OF THE GUYS I MET IN THE HIGH SCHOOL COURTYARD
THE CIGARETTE KID
Friendly, timid kid who smoked cigarettes. For some reason, he never talked about anything other than smoking cigarettes.
THE CONNECTION
Hung with the derelicts, but the Jocks left him alone as he could get beer $ pot on weekends.
THE ROMANTIC
Dim kid who played guitar, worked at a gas station $ got a girl pregnant junior year.

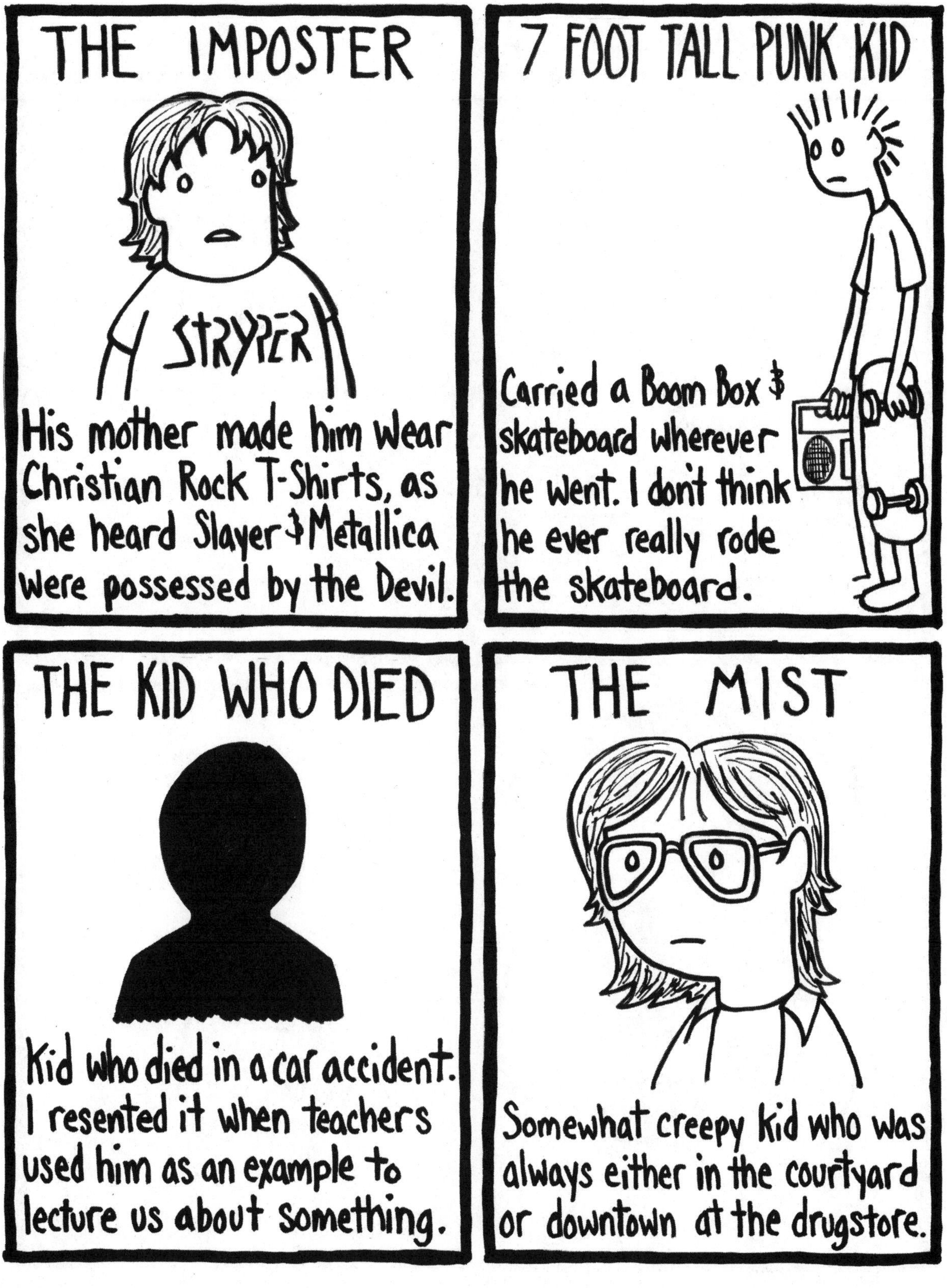
THE IMPOSTER
STRYPER
His mother made him wear Christian Rock T-Shirts, as she heard Slayer & Metallica were possessed by the Devil.
7 FOOT TALL PUNK KID
Carried a Boom Box & skateboard wherever he went. I don't think he ever really rode the skateboard.
THE KID WHO DIED
Kid who died in a car accident. I resented it when teachers used him as an example to lecture us about something.
THE MIST
Somewhat creepy kid who was always either in the courtyard or downtown at the drugstore.

SHADOW

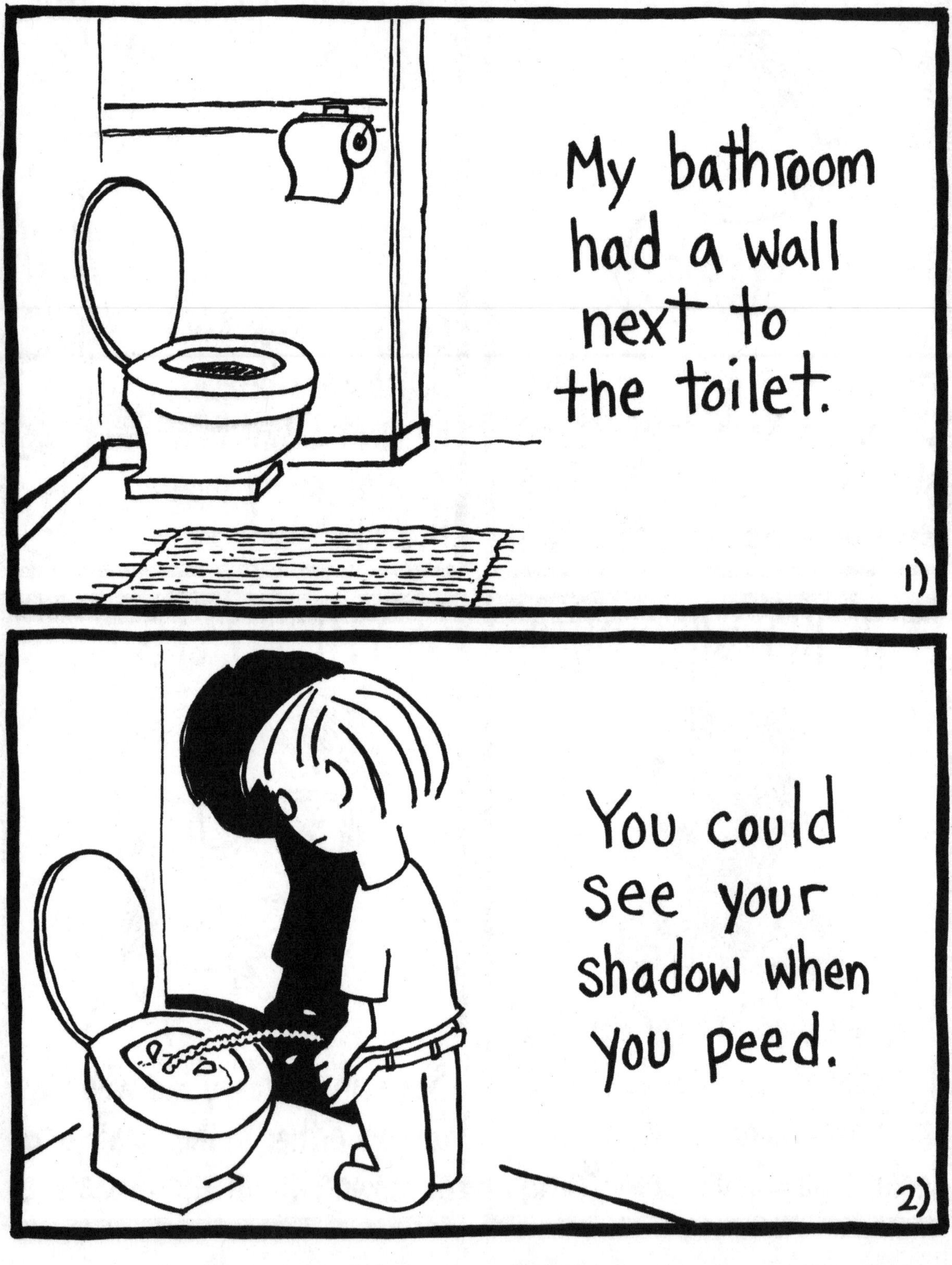
My bathroom had a wall next to the toilet.
1)
You could see your shadow when you peed.
2)

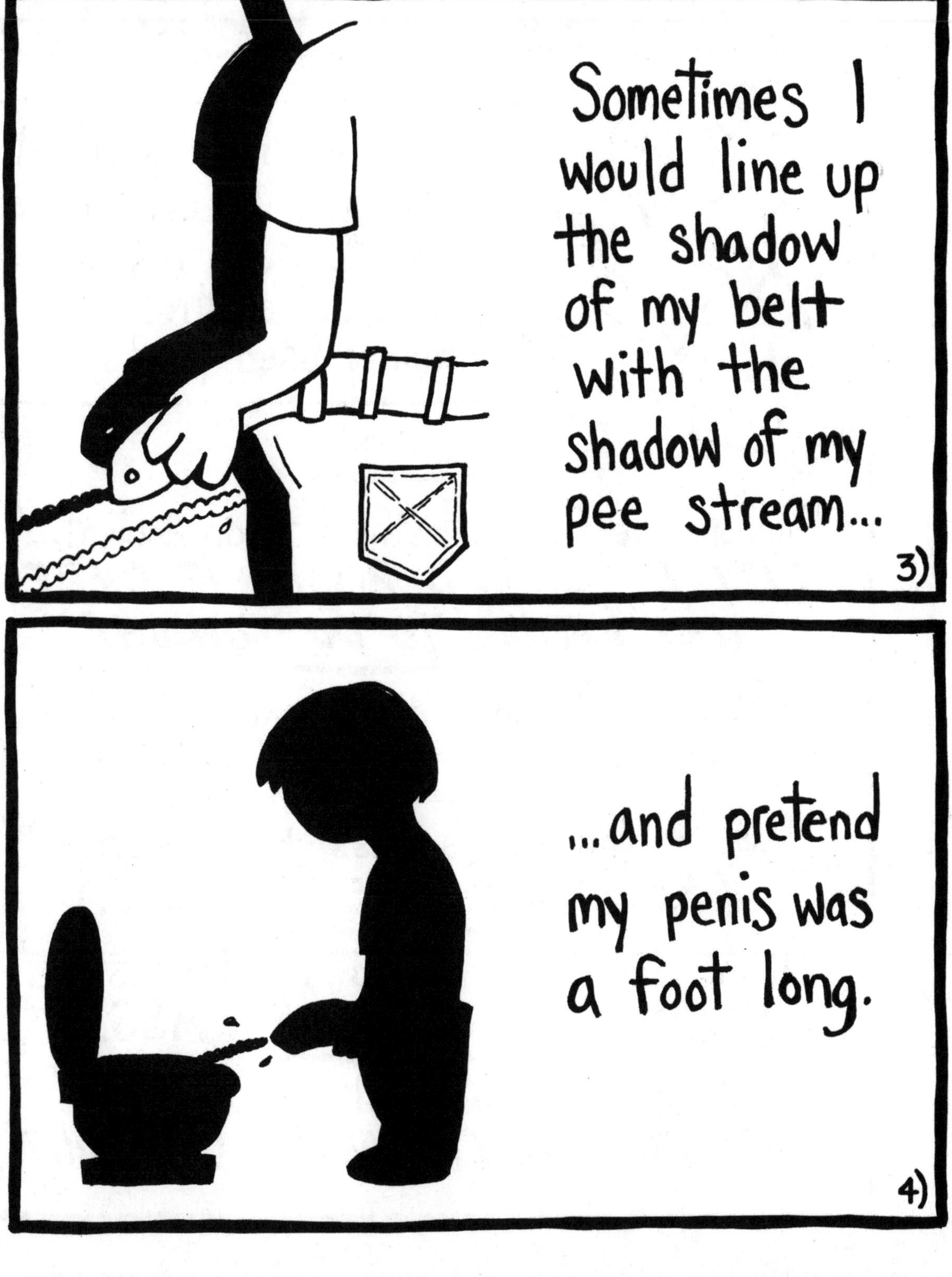
Sometimes I would line up the shadow of my belt with the shadow of my pee stream...
3)
...and pretend my penis was a foot long.
4)

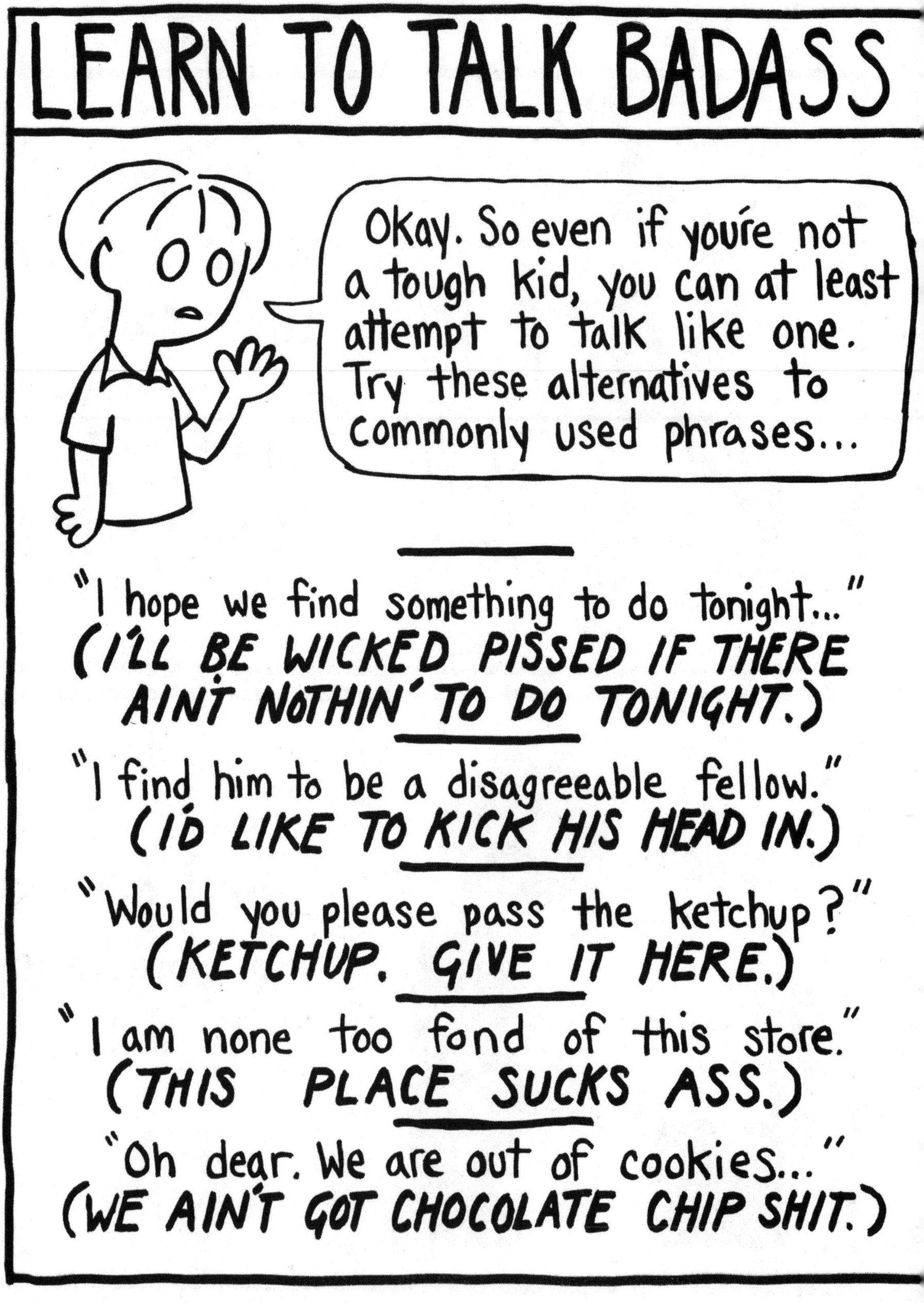
LEARN TO TALK BADASS
Okay. So even if you're not a tough kid, you can at least attempt to talk like one. Try these alternatives to commonly used phrases...
"I hope we find something to do tonight..."
(I'LL BE WICKED PISSED IF THERE AIN'T NOTHIN' TO DO TONIGHT.)
"I find him to be a disagreeable fellow."
(I'D LIKE TO KICK HIS HEAD IN.)
"Would you please pass the ketchup?"
(KETCHUP. GIVE IT HERE.)
"I am none too fond of this store."
(THIS PLACE SUCKS ASS.)
"Oh dear. We are out of cookies..."
(WE AIN'T GOT CHOCOLATE CHIP SHIT.)

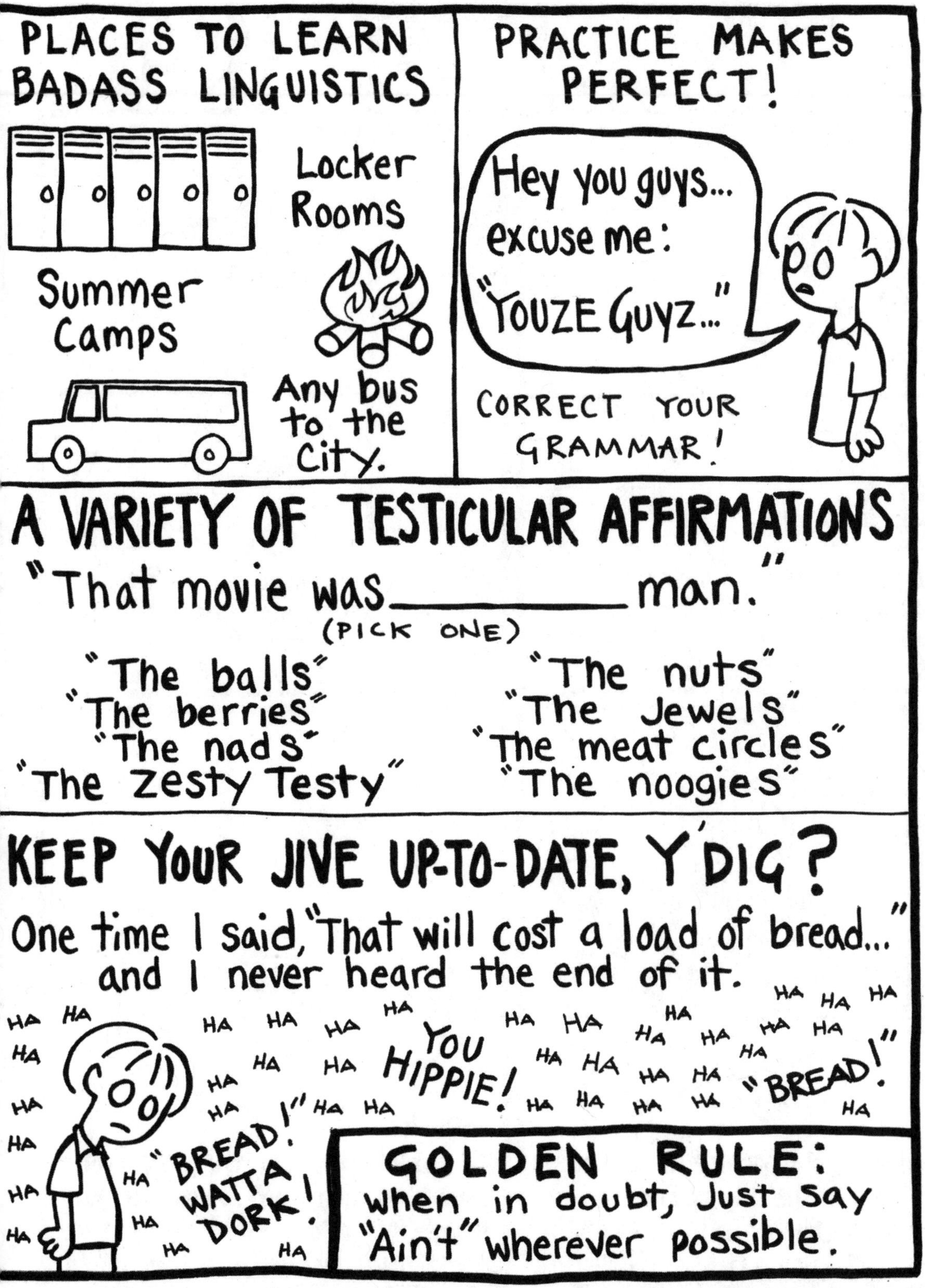
PLACES TO LEARN BADASS LINGUISTICS
Locker Rooms
Summer Camps
Any bus to the City.
PRACTICE MAKES PERFECT!
Hey you guys... excuse me: "YOUZE GUYZ..."
CORRECT YOUR GRAMMAR!
A VARIETY OF TESTICULAR AFFIRMATIONS
"That movie was ________ man."
(PICK ONE)
"The balls"
"The berries"
"The nads"
"The zesty Testy"
"The nuts"
"The Jewels"
"The meat circles"
"The noogies"
KEEP YOUR JIVE UP-TO-DATE, Y'DIG?
One time I said, "That will cost a load of bread..." and I never heard the end of it.
HA HA HA HA HA HA HA HA HA HA HA HA HA HA HA HA HA HA HA HA HA HA
YOU HIPPIE!
"BREAD!"
"BREAD!" WATTA DORK!
GOLDEN RULE: when in doubt, Just say "Ain't" wherever possible.

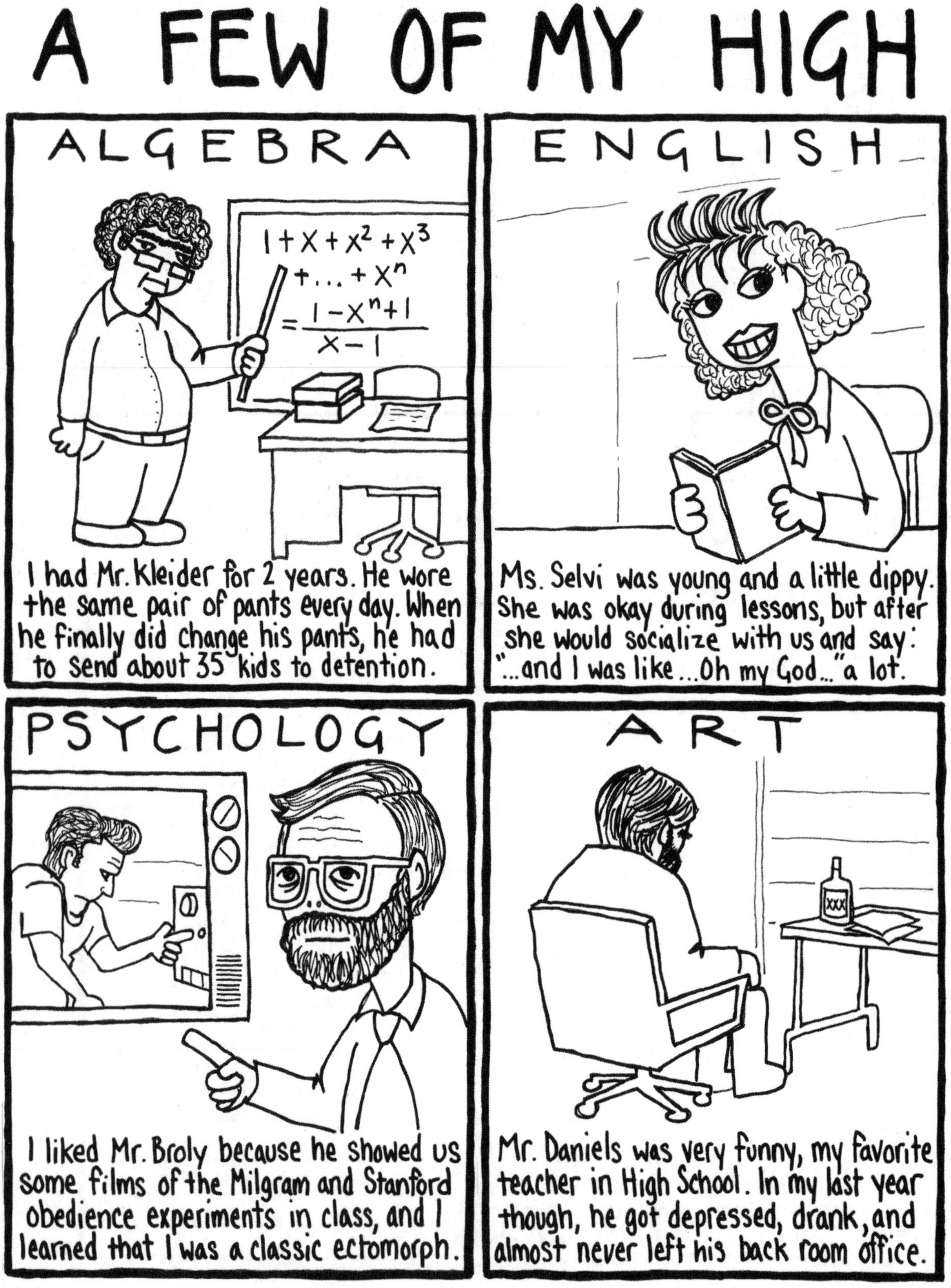
A FEW OF MY HIGH
ALGEBRA
1+X+X^2+X^3 +...+X^n = (1-X^n+1)/(X-1)
I had Mr. Kleider for 2 years. He wore the same pair of pants every day. When he finally did change his pants, he had to send about 35 kids to detention.
ENGLISH
Ms. Selvi was young and a little dippy. She was okay during lessons, but after she would socialize with us and say: "...and I was like ...Oh my God..." a lot.
PSYCHOLOGY
I liked Mr. Broly because he showed us some films of the Milgram and Stanford obedience experiments in class, and I learned that I was a classic ectomorph.
ART
XXX
Mr. Daniels was very funny, my favorite teacher in High School. In my last year though, he got depressed, drank, and almost never left his back room office.

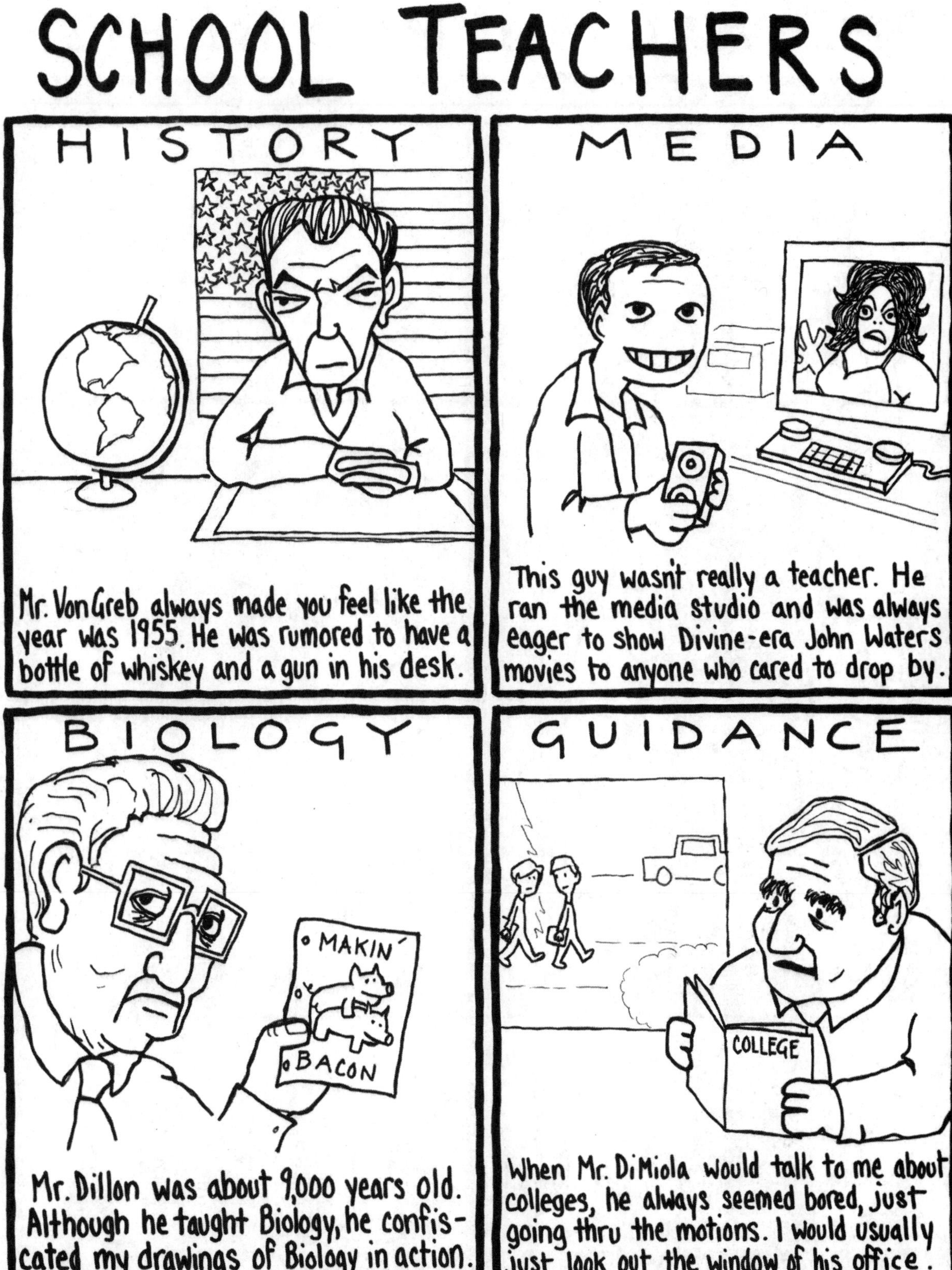
SCHOOL TEACHERS
HISTORY
Mr. VonGreb always made you feel like the year was 1955. He was rumored to have a bottle of whiskey and a gun in his desk.
MEDIA
This guy wasn't really a teacher. He ran the media studio and was always eager to show Divine-era John Waters movies to anyone who cared to drop by.
BIOLOGY
MAKIN'
BACON
Mr. Dillon was about 9,000 years old. Although he taught Biology, he confis-cated my drawings of Biology in action.
GUIDANCE
COLLEGE
When Mr. DiMiola would talk to me about colleges, he always seemed bored, just going thru the motions. I would usually just look out the window of his office.

SOME WALKS I HAD IN HIGH

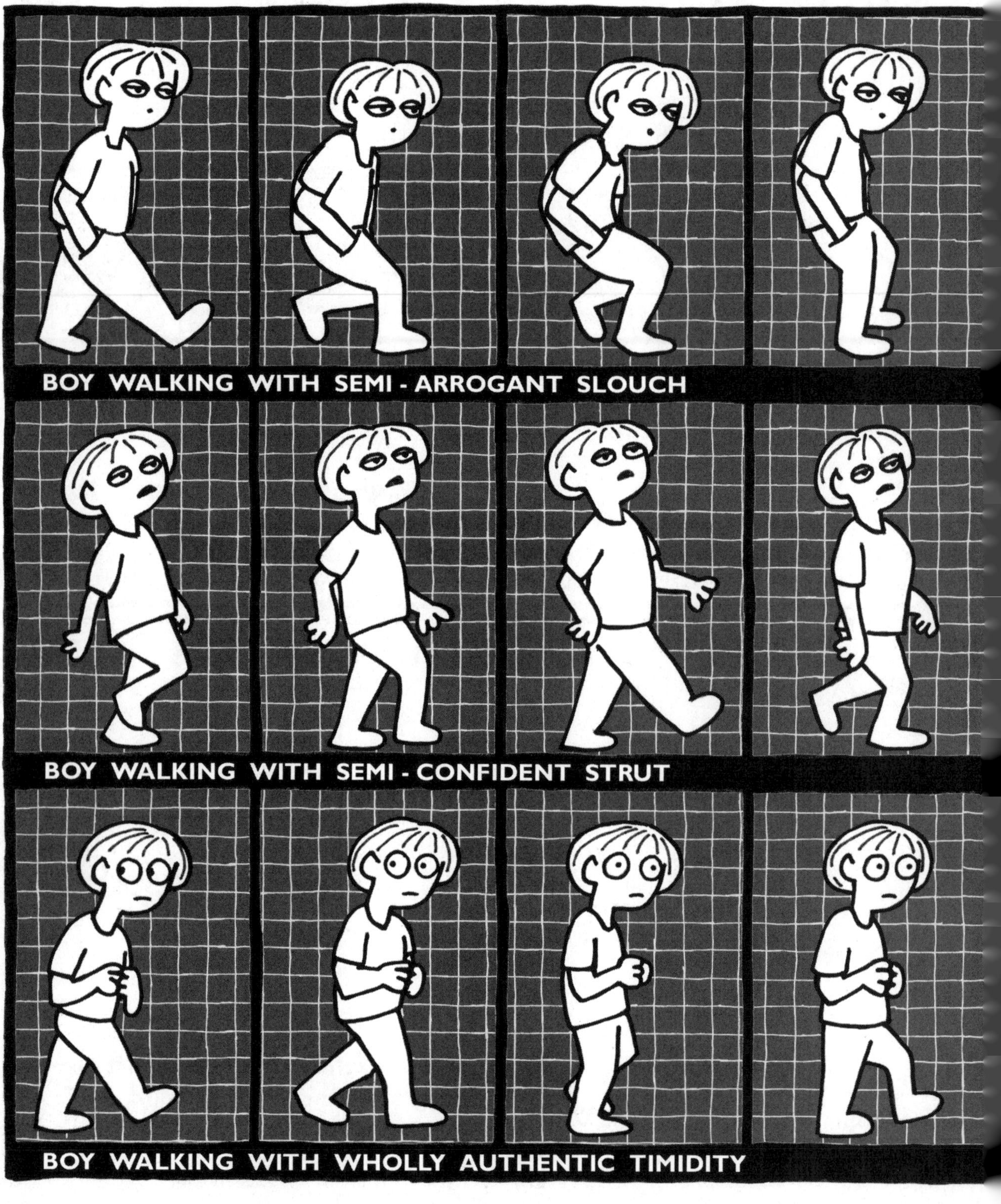

BOY WALKING WITH SEMI-ARROGANT SLOUCH
BOY WALKING WITH SEMI-CONFIDENT STRUT
BOY WALKING WITH WHOLLY AUTHENTIC TIMIDITY

SCHOOL

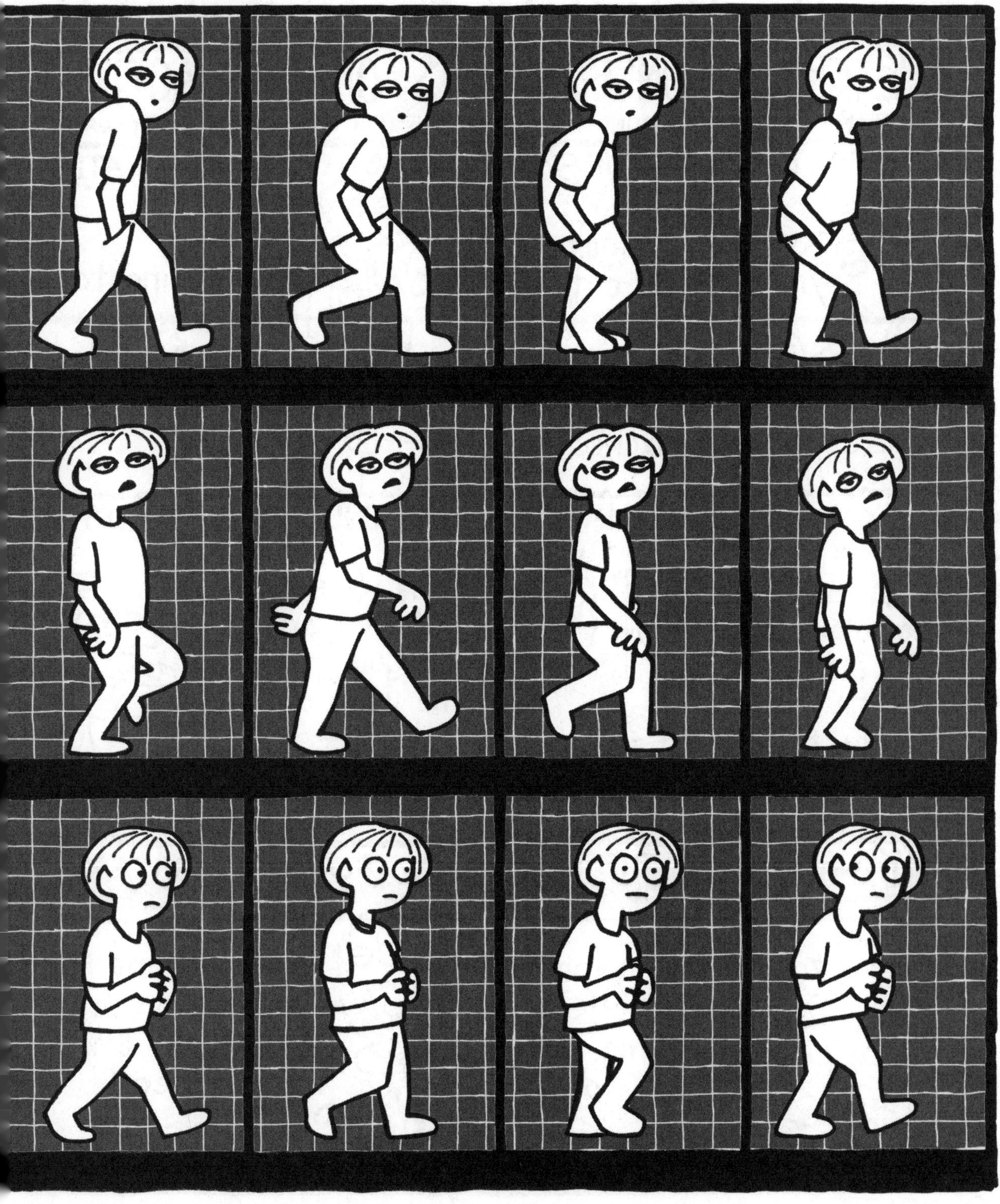

MY MOM WORRIED

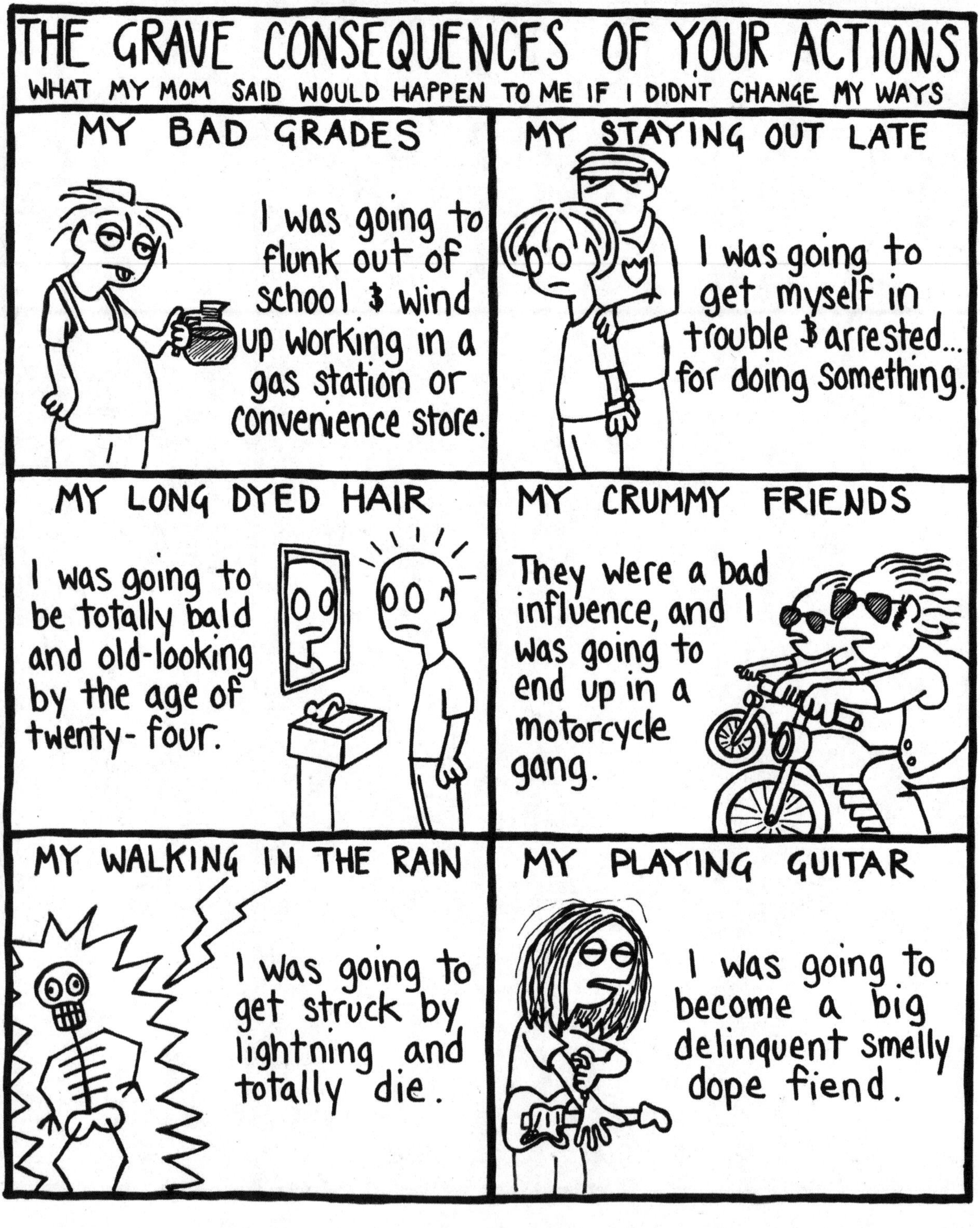

THE GRAVE CONSEQUENCES OF YOUR ACTIONS
WHAT MY MOM SAID WOULD HAPPEN TO ME IF I DIDN'T CHANGE MY WAYS
MY BAD GRADES
I was going to flunk out of school $ wind up working in a gas station or convenience store.
MY STAYING OUT LATE
I was going to get myself in trouble $ arrested... for doing something.
MY LONG DYED HAIR
I was going to be totally bald and old-looking by the age of twenty-four.
MY CRUMMY FRIENDS
They were a bad influence, and I was going to end up in a motorcycle gang.
MY WALKING IN THE RAIN
I was going to get struck by lightning and totally die.
MY PLAYING GUITAR
I was going to become a big delinquent smelly dope fiend.

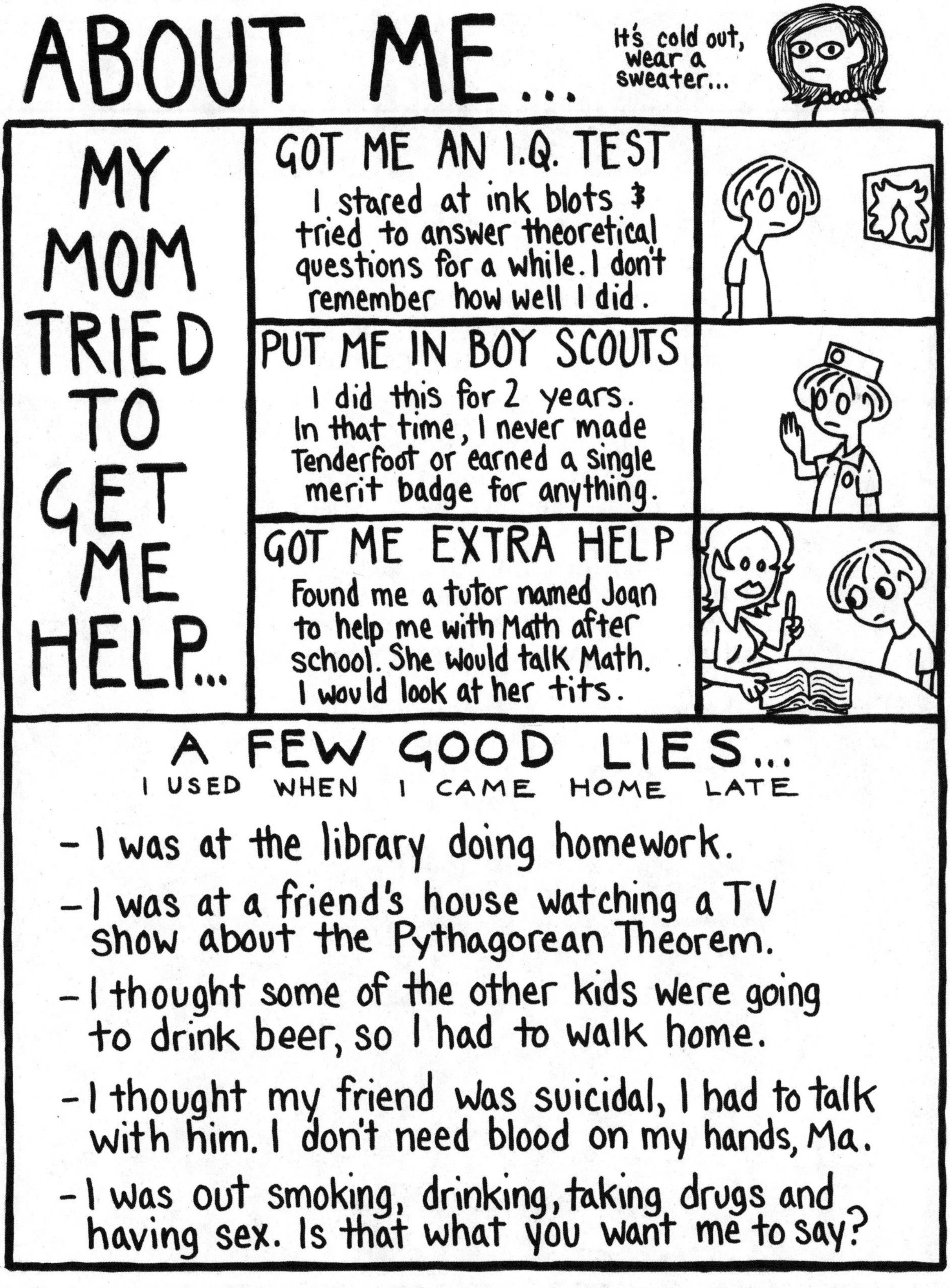
ABOUT ME...
It's cold out, wear a sweater...
MY MOM TRIED TO GET ME HELP...
GOT ME AN I.Q. TEST
I stared at ink blots & tried to answer theoretical questions for a while. I don't remember how well I did.
PUT ME IN BOY SCOUTS
I did this for 2 years. In that time, I never made Tenderfoot or earned a single merit badge for anything.
GOT ME EXTRA HELP
Found me a tutor named Joan to help me with Math after school. She would talk Math. I would look at her tits.
A FEW GOOD LIES...
I USED WHEN I CAME HOME LATE
- I was at the library doing homework.
- I was at a friend's house watching a TV show about the Pythagorean Theorem.
- I thought some of the other kids were going to drink beer, so I had to walk home.
- I thought my friend was suicidal, I had to talk with him. I don't need blood on my hands, Ma.
- I was out smoking, drinking, taking drugs and having sex. Is that what you want me to say?

SOME OF MY SHITTY TEENAGE POETRY

IN THE DARK

Hark, Hark,
I am lost, here in the dark.
There is no flame, there is no spark,
I see no point, I make no mark.

Laughter is scarce, laughter is stark,
It's very lonely, here in the dark.
I am in pain, pain patriarch,
stung by a bee, bit by a shark.

Rain falls, falls from the dark,
raining more, than Noah's Ark.
Afraid to go, scared to embark,
upon this journey, here thru the dark.

There is no light, there is no lark,
the hellhounds growl, the hellhounds bark.
I feel so small, small like a quark,
maybe I'll die, here in the dark.

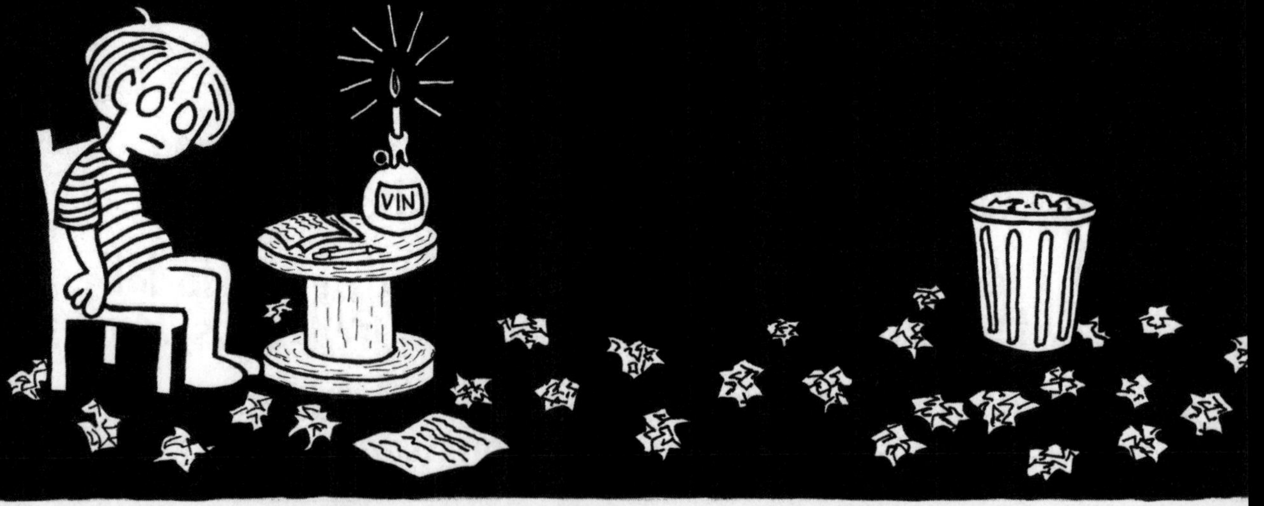

PHONE , ALONE !

I sit here, like a stone. I sit here, by the phone.
My despair, it has grown, as I know I'm alone.
I try to call people, but no one is home.
And no one calls me, because I'm not known.
I thought I knew people, I thought friends I had sown,
but me, they disown. Me, they postpone.

You mock me, you phone! Mock me with the drone,
of the cruel cruel dial tone, tells me I'm alone.
In my heart, there's a hole, like the hole in ozone,
as I hang up this black-hearted beast called my phone.
In my castle of sorrows, I sit on my throne,
and I weep, and I moan.

Phone. Alone.

TIME

Time, it is passing, yes passing, too fast.
Time, it reminds me, that life will not last.
One breath, and the days, they are passing, en masse,
one blink, and the present, has become my past.

It seems, only yesterday, that my life began,
but in my reflection, I now see a man.
Though I don't want a lie, I can't bear the truth,
that I, plain and simple, no more have my youth.

Time! You have tricked me! I swung, and you ducked!
Youth gone! Gone forever! Time passing, you suck!
I give up, and time tries. I shower, and time dries.
I walk, and time flies, I listen, and time lies.

Now my days diminish, with speed and with strife,
from the sack, which was full, of the days of my life.
A thief's crafty hand has stolen what's mine.
The act was a crime. The thief, it was time.

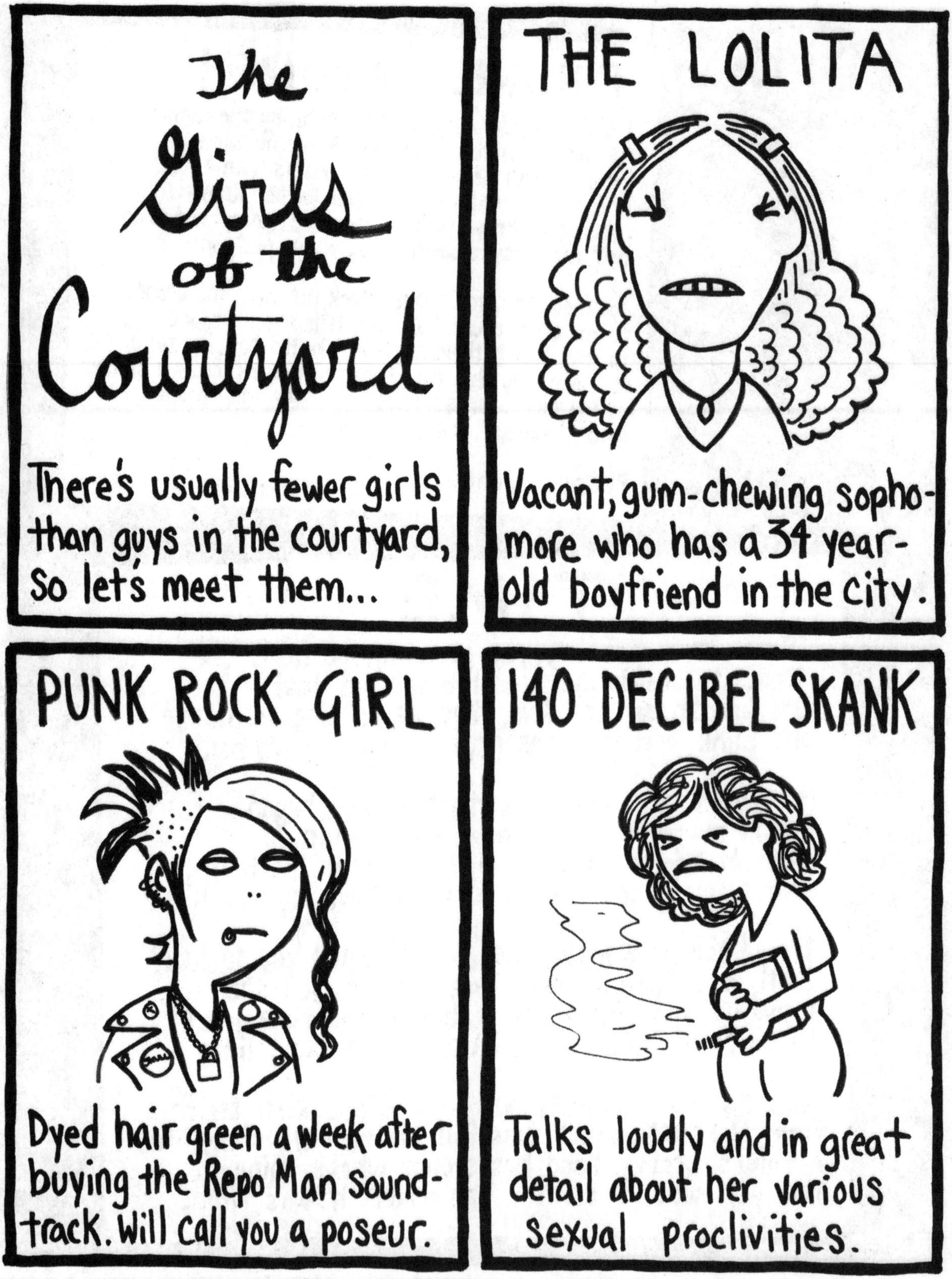
The Girls of the Courtyard
There's usually fewer girls than guys in the courtyard, so let's meet them...
THE LOLITA
Vacant, gum-chewing sophomore who has a 34 year-old boyfriend in the city.
PUNK ROCK GIRL
Dyed hair green a week after buying the Repo Man soundtrack. Will call you a poseur.
140 DECIBEL SKANK
Talks loudly and in great detail about her various sexual proclivities.

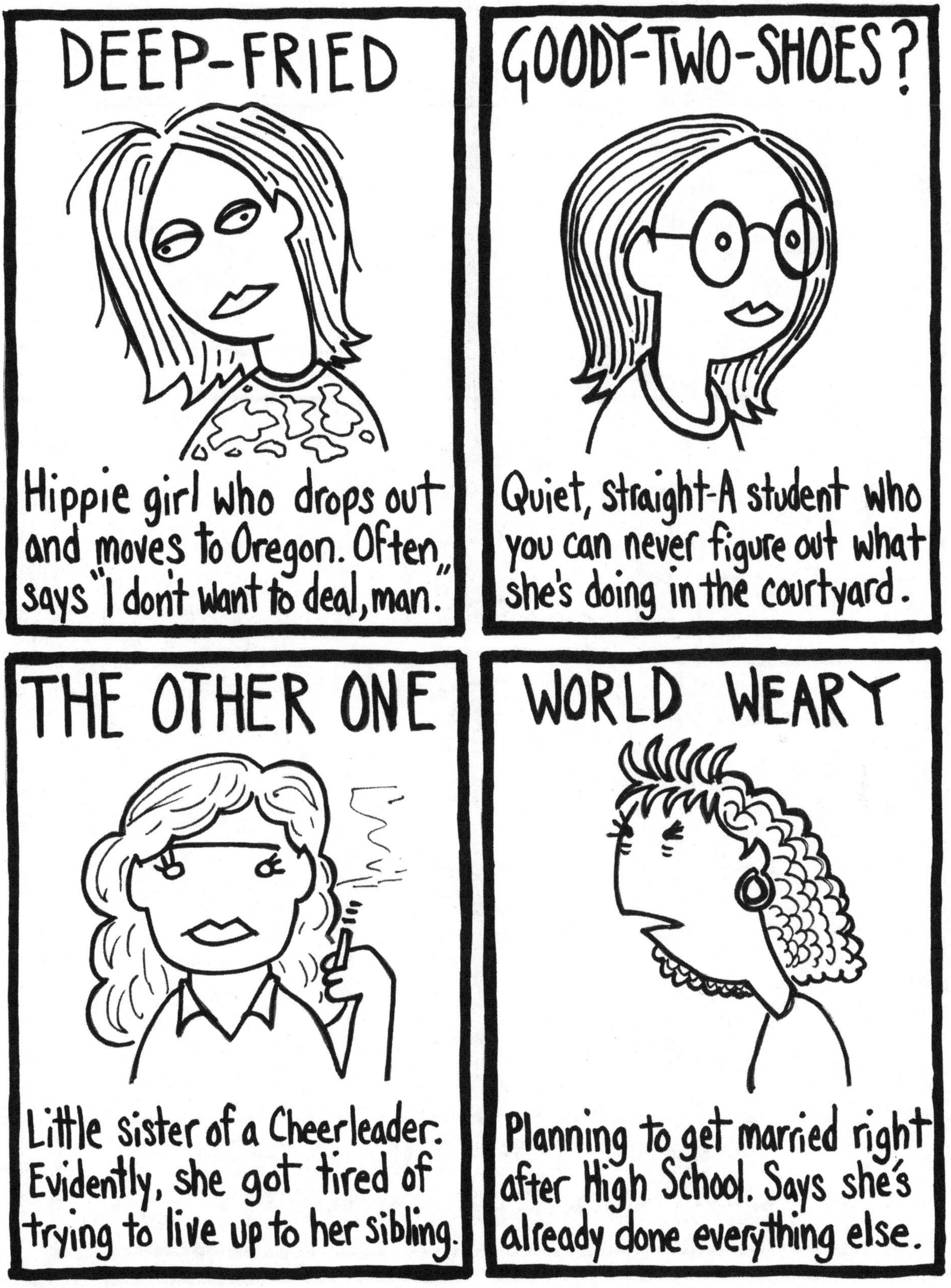
DEEP-FRIED
Hippie girl who drops out and moves to Oregon. Often, says "I don't want to deal, man."
GOODY-TWO-SHOES?
Quiet, straight-A student who you can never figure out what she's doing in the courtyard.
THE OTHER ONE
Little sister of a Cheerleader. Evidently, she got tired of trying to live up to her sibling.
WORLD WEARY
Planning to get married right after High School. Says she's already done everything else.

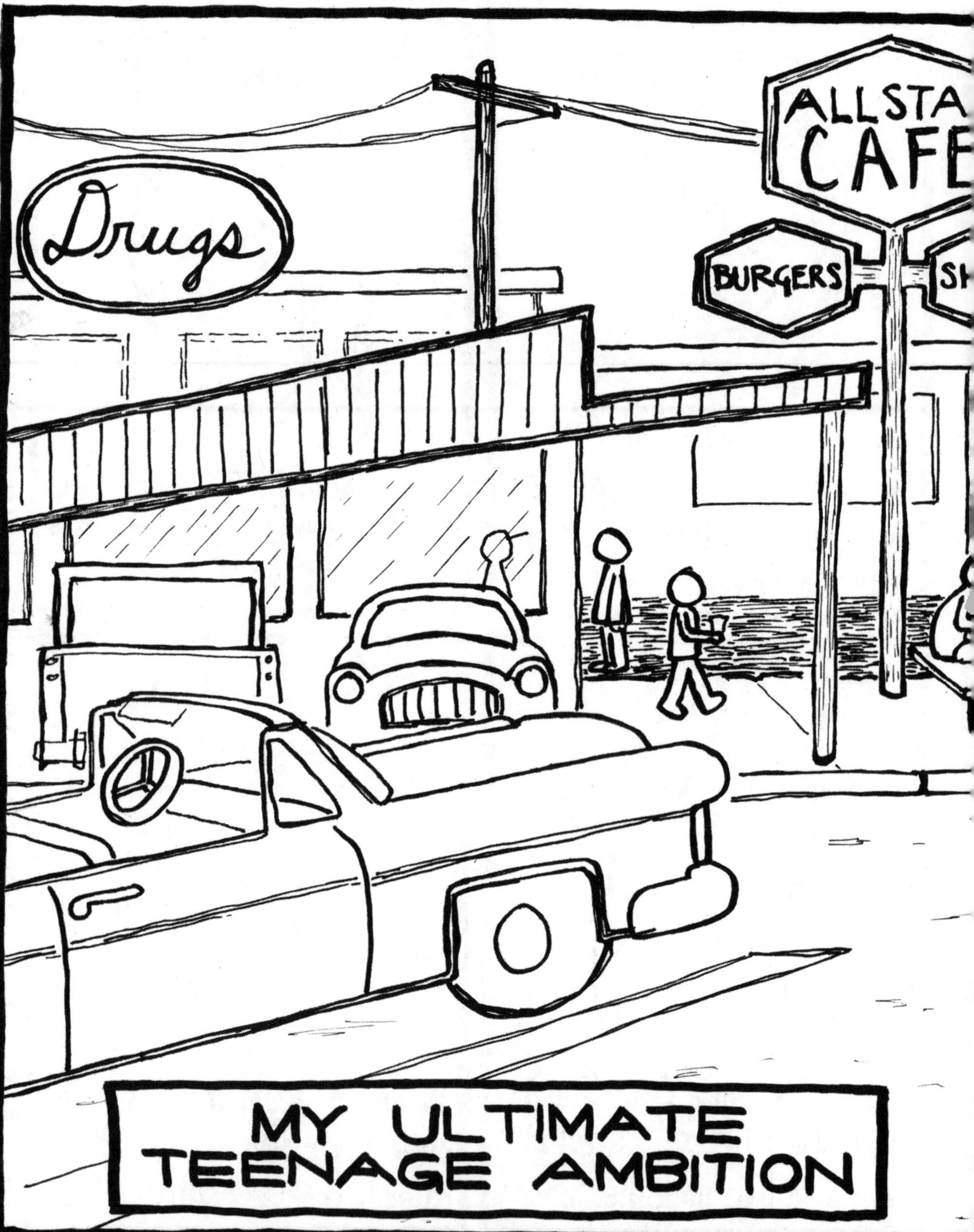
Drugs
ALLSTA
CAFE
BURGERS
MY ULTIMATE TEENAGE AMBITION

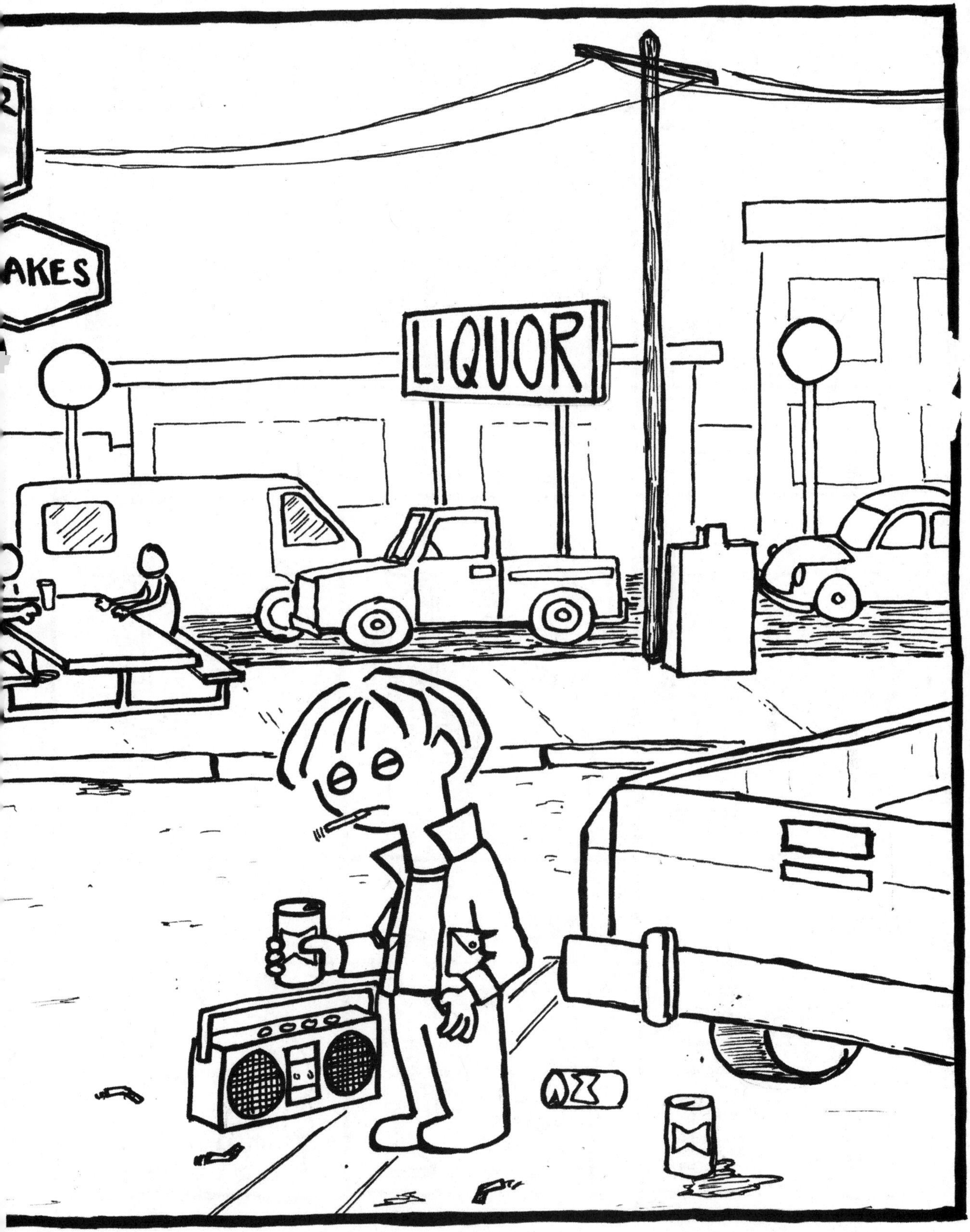
AKES
LIQUOR

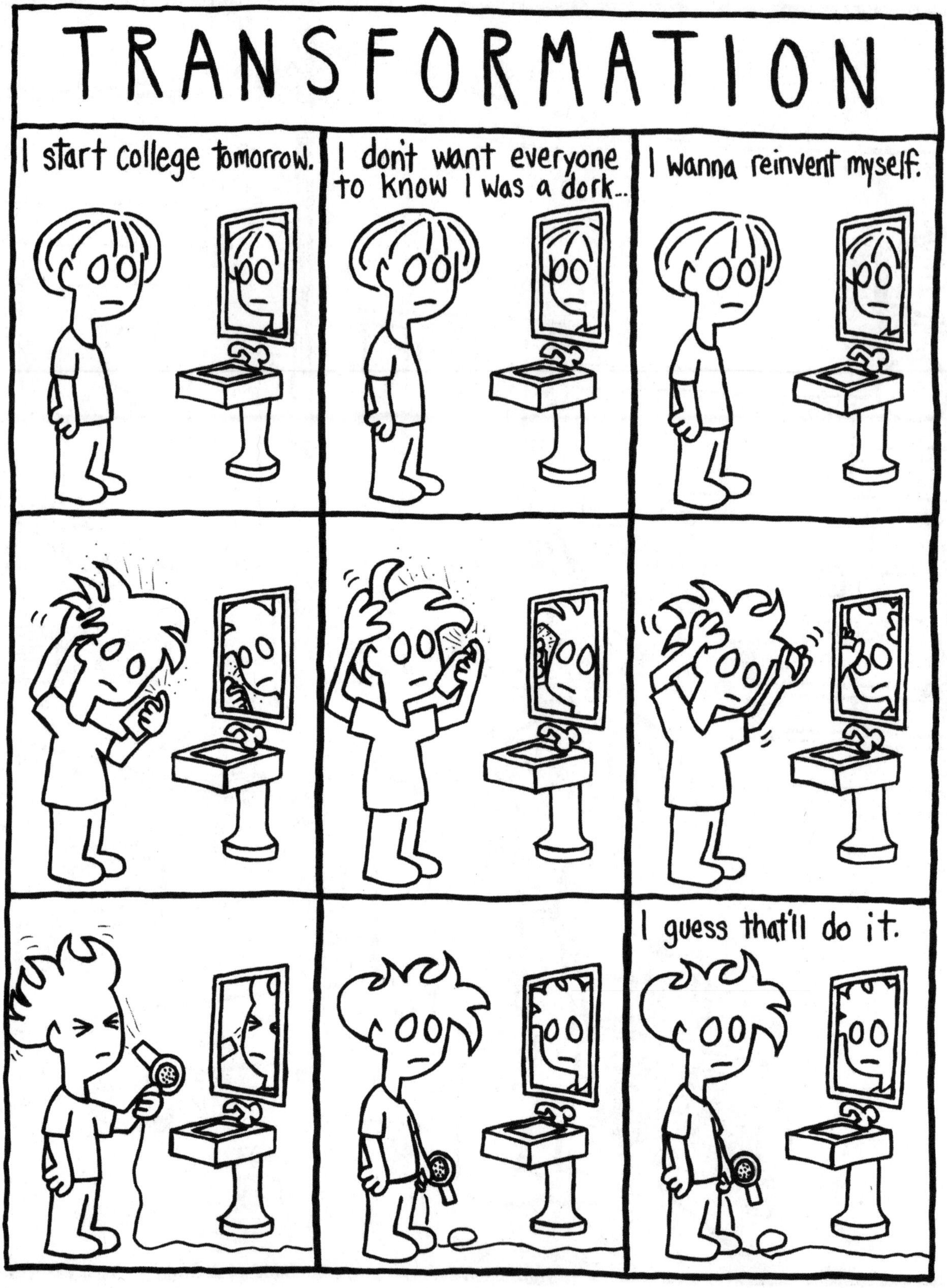
TRANSFORMATION
I start college tomorrow.
I don't want everyone to know I was a dork...
I wanna reinvent myself.
I guess that'll do it.

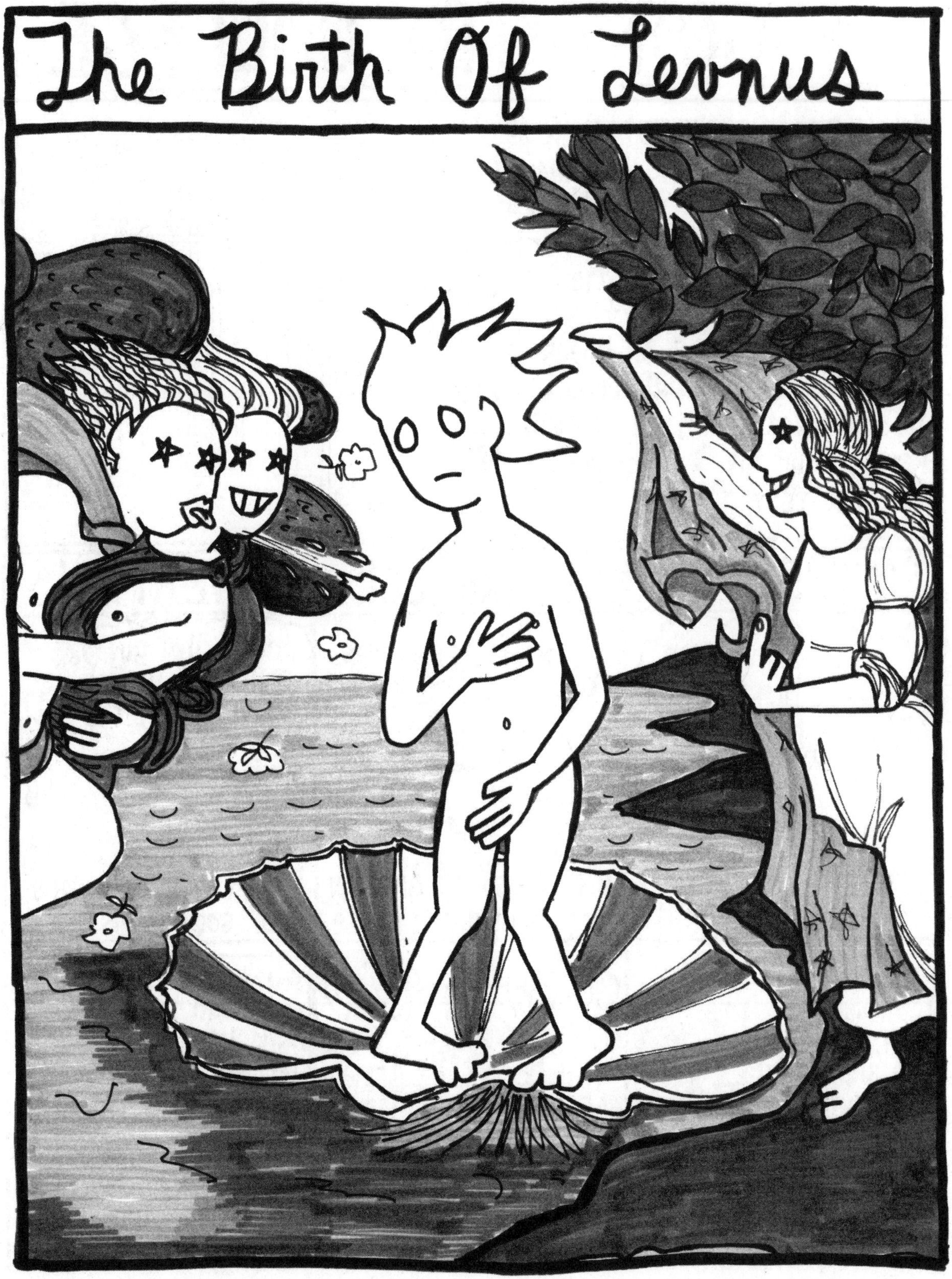
The Birth Of Levnus

GOING TO COLLEGE

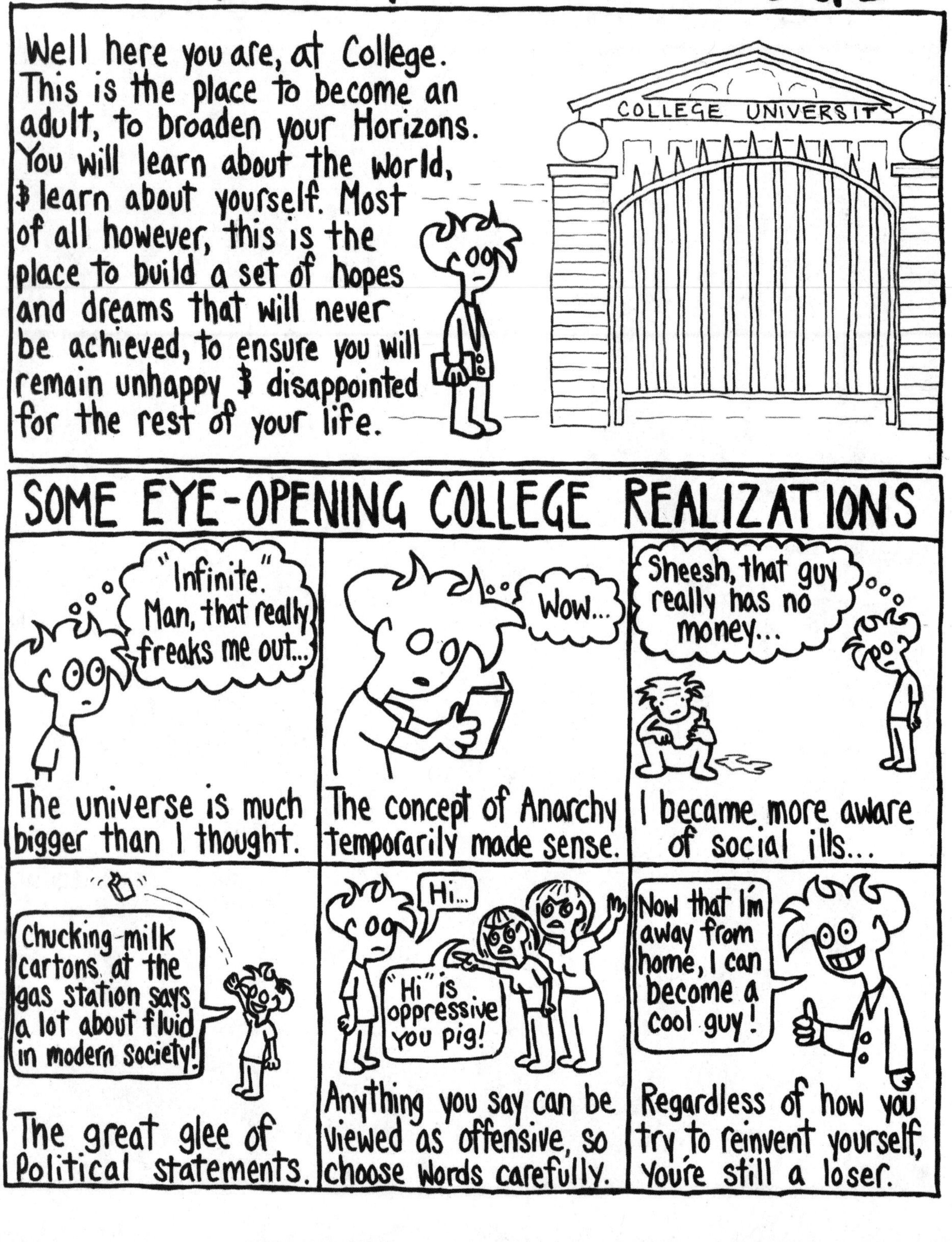
Well here you are, at College. This is the place to become an adult, to broaden your Horizons. You will learn about the world, $ learn about yourself. Most of all however, this is the place to build a set of hopes and dreams that will never be achieved, to ensure you will remain unhappy $ disappointed for the rest of your life.
COLLEGE UNIVERSITY
SOME EYE-OPENING COLLEGE REALIZATIONS
"Infinite." Man, that really freaks me out...
The universe is much bigger than I thought.
Wow...
The concept of Anarchy temporarily made sense.
Sheesh, that guy really has no money...
I became more aware of social ills...
Chucking milk cartons at the gas station says a lot about fluid in modern society!
The great glee of Political statements.
Hi...
"Hi" is oppressive you pig!
Anything you say can be viewed as offensive, so choose words carefully.
Now that I'm away from home, I can become a cool guy!
Regardless of how you try to reinvent yourself, You're still a loser.

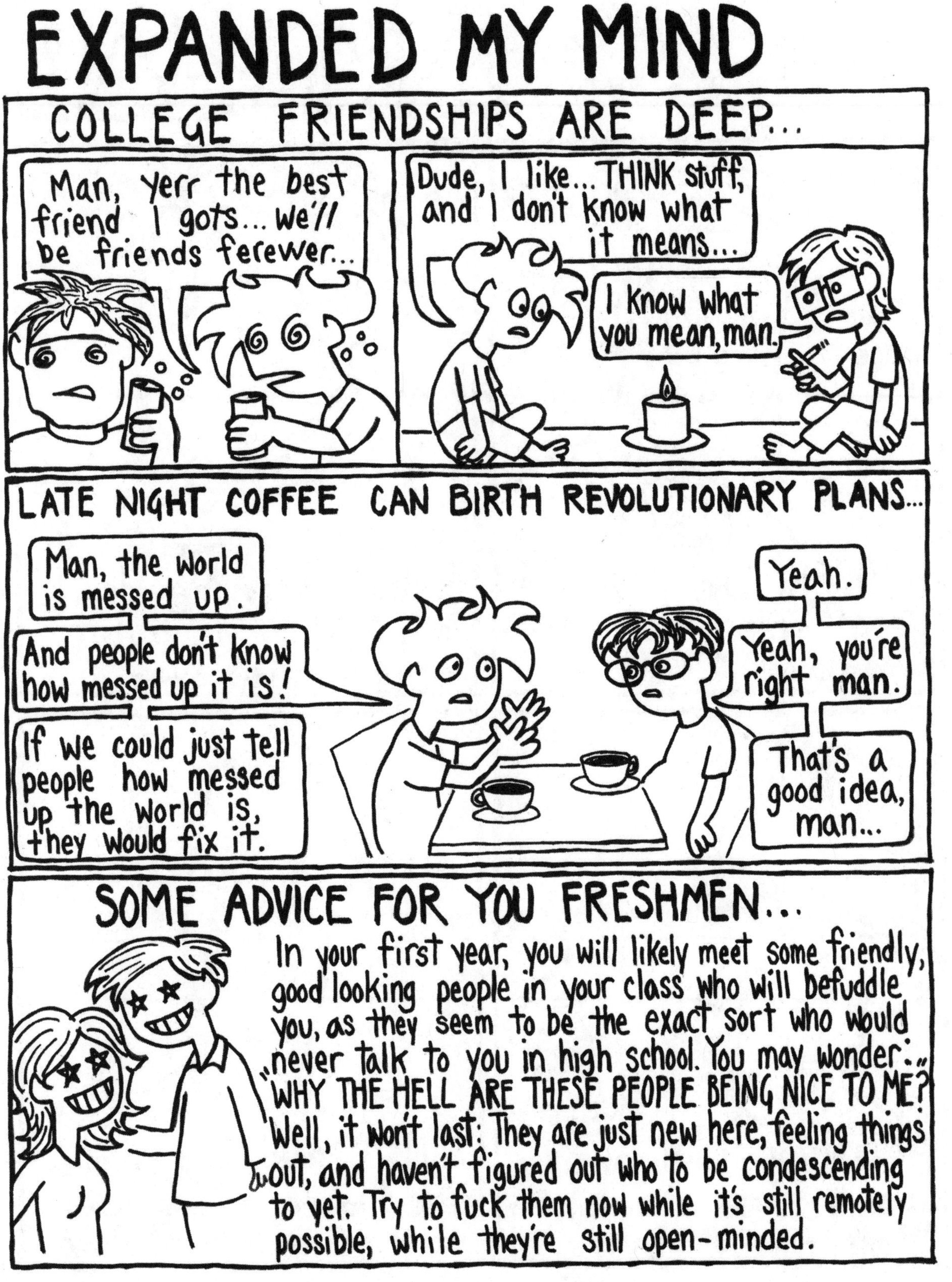
EXPANDED MY MIND
COLLEGE FRIENDSHIPS ARE DEEP...
Man, yerr the best friend I gots... we'll be friends ferewer...
Dude, I like... THINK stuff, and I don't know what it means...
I know what you mean, man.
LATE NIGHT COFFEE CAN BIRTH REVOLUTIONARY PLANS...
Man, the world is messed up.
And people don't know how messed up it is!
If we could just tell people how messed up the world is, they would fix it.
Yeah.
Yeah, you're right man.
That's a good idea, man...
SOME ADVICE FOR YOU FRESHMEN...
In your first year, you will likely meet some friendly, good looking people in your class who will befuddle you, as they seem to be the exact sort who would never talk to you in high school. You may wonder: "WHY THE HELL ARE THESE PEOPLE BEING NICE TO ME?" Well, it won't last: They are just new here, feeling things out, and haven't figured out who to be condescending to yet. Try to fuck them now while it's still remotely possible, while they're still open-minded.

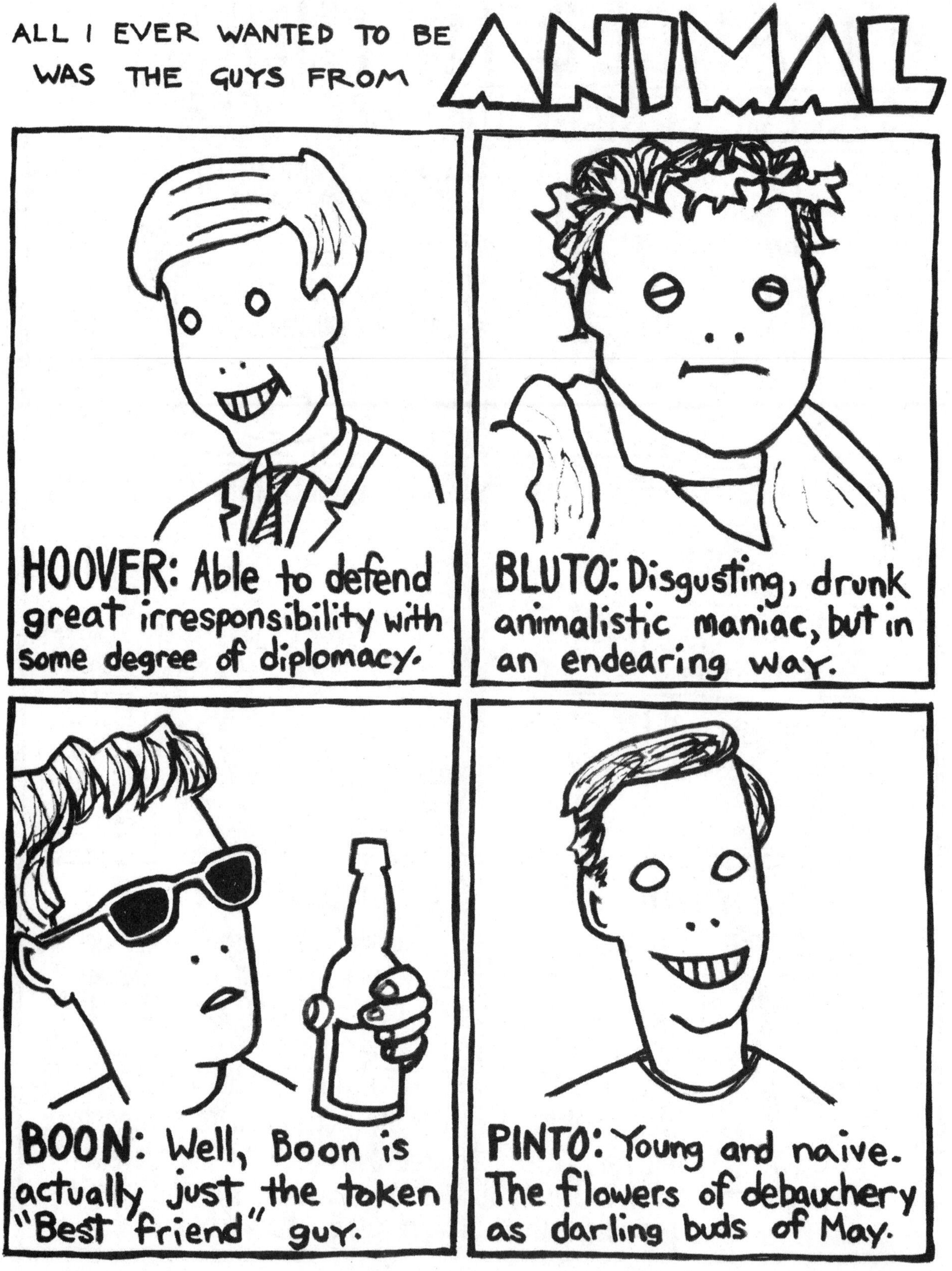
ALL I EVER WANTED TO BE WAS THE GUYS FROM
ANIMAL
HOOVER: Able to defend great irresponsibility with some degree of diplomacy.
BLUTO: Disgusting, drunk animalistic maniac, but in an endearing way.
BOON: Well, Boon is actually just the token "Best friend" guy.
PINTO: Young and naive. The flowers of debauchery as darling buds of May.

HOUSE ALL ROLLED INTO ONE.

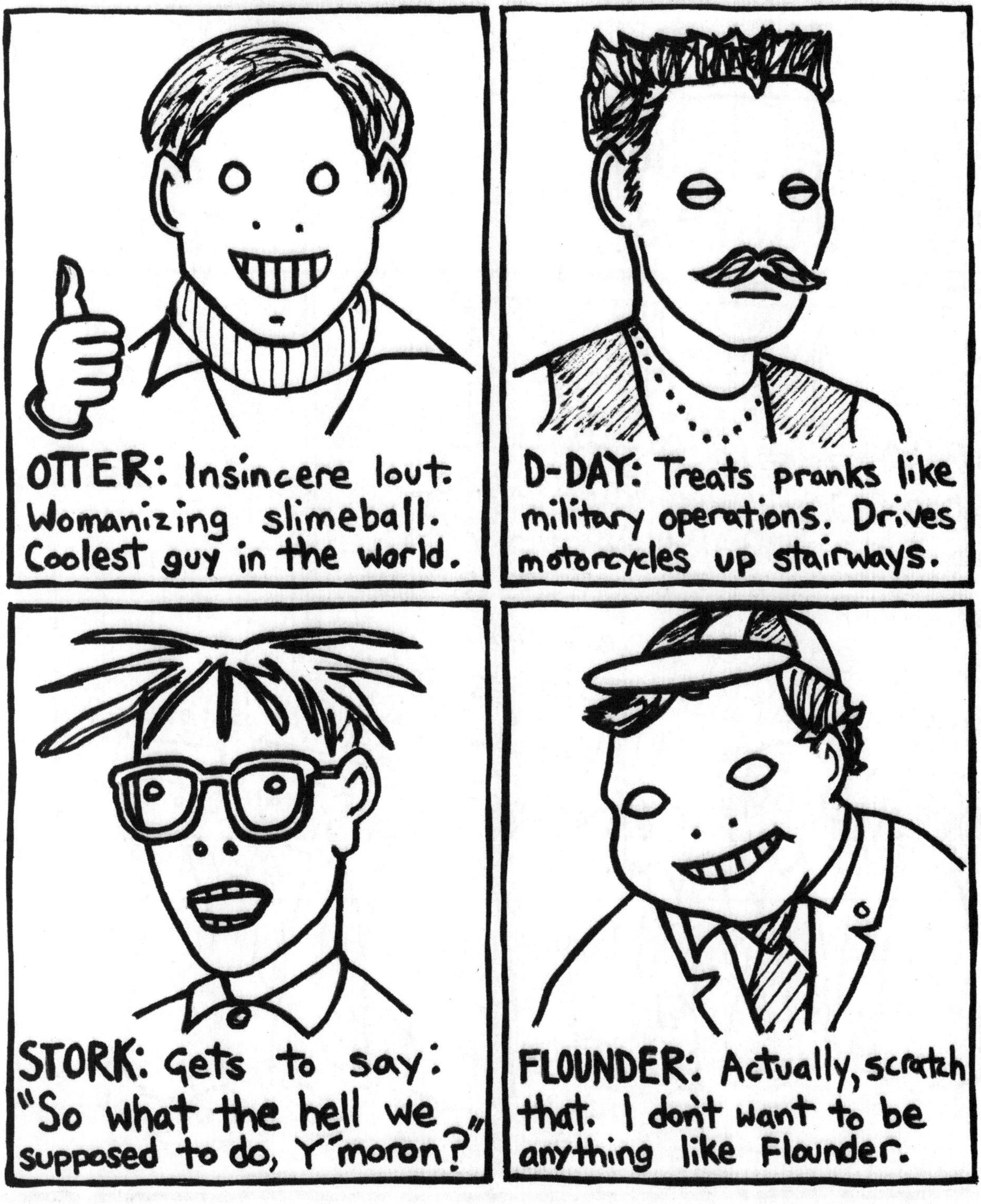
OTTER: Insincere lout. Womanizing slimeball. Coolest guy in the world.
D-DAY: Treats pranks like military operations. Drives motorcycles up stairways.
STORK: Gets to say: "So what the hell we supposed to do, Y'moron?"
FLOUNDER: Actually, scratch that. I don't want to be anything like Flounder.

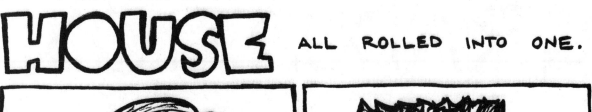

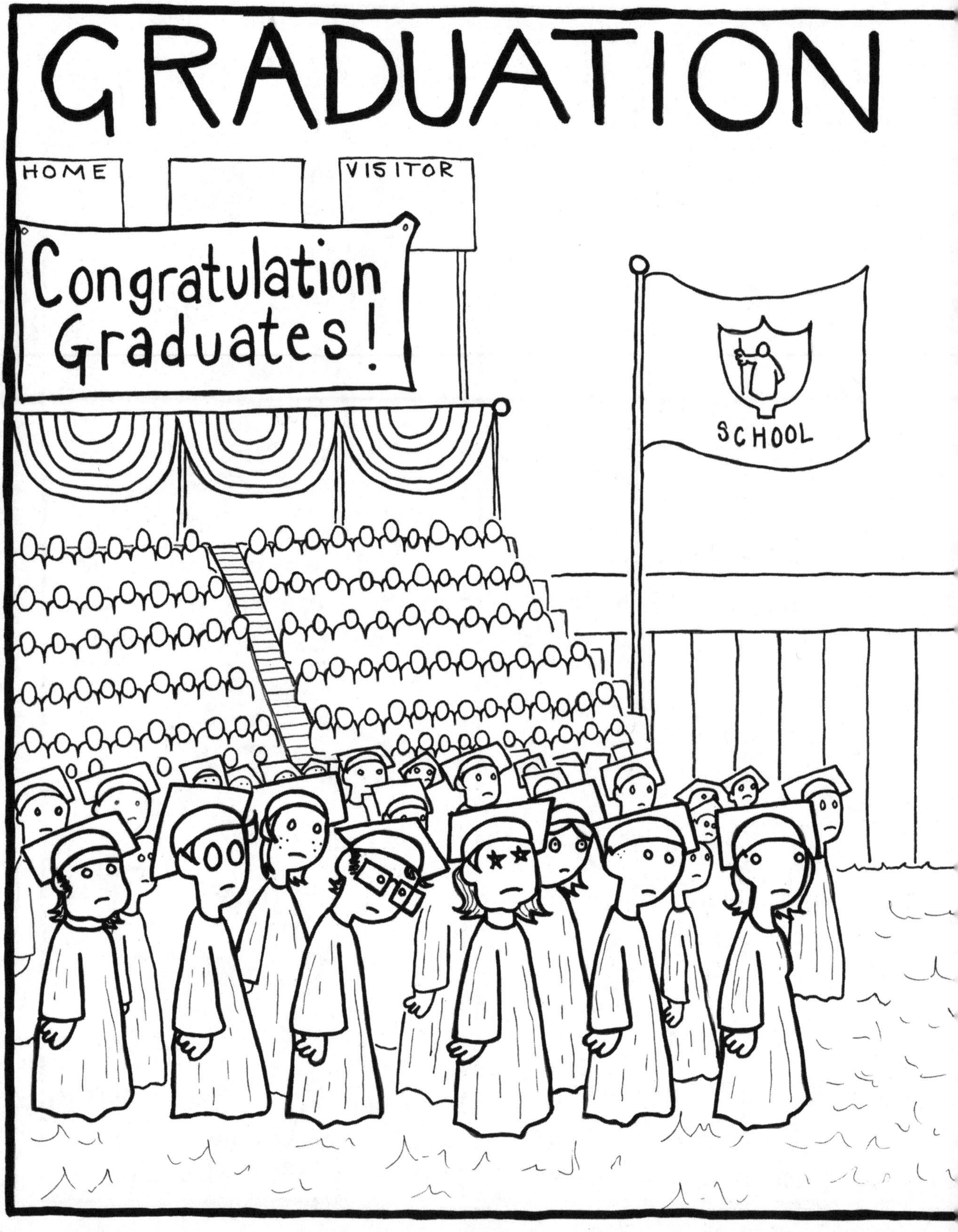
GRADUATION
HOME
VISITOR
Congratulation Graduates!
SCHOOL

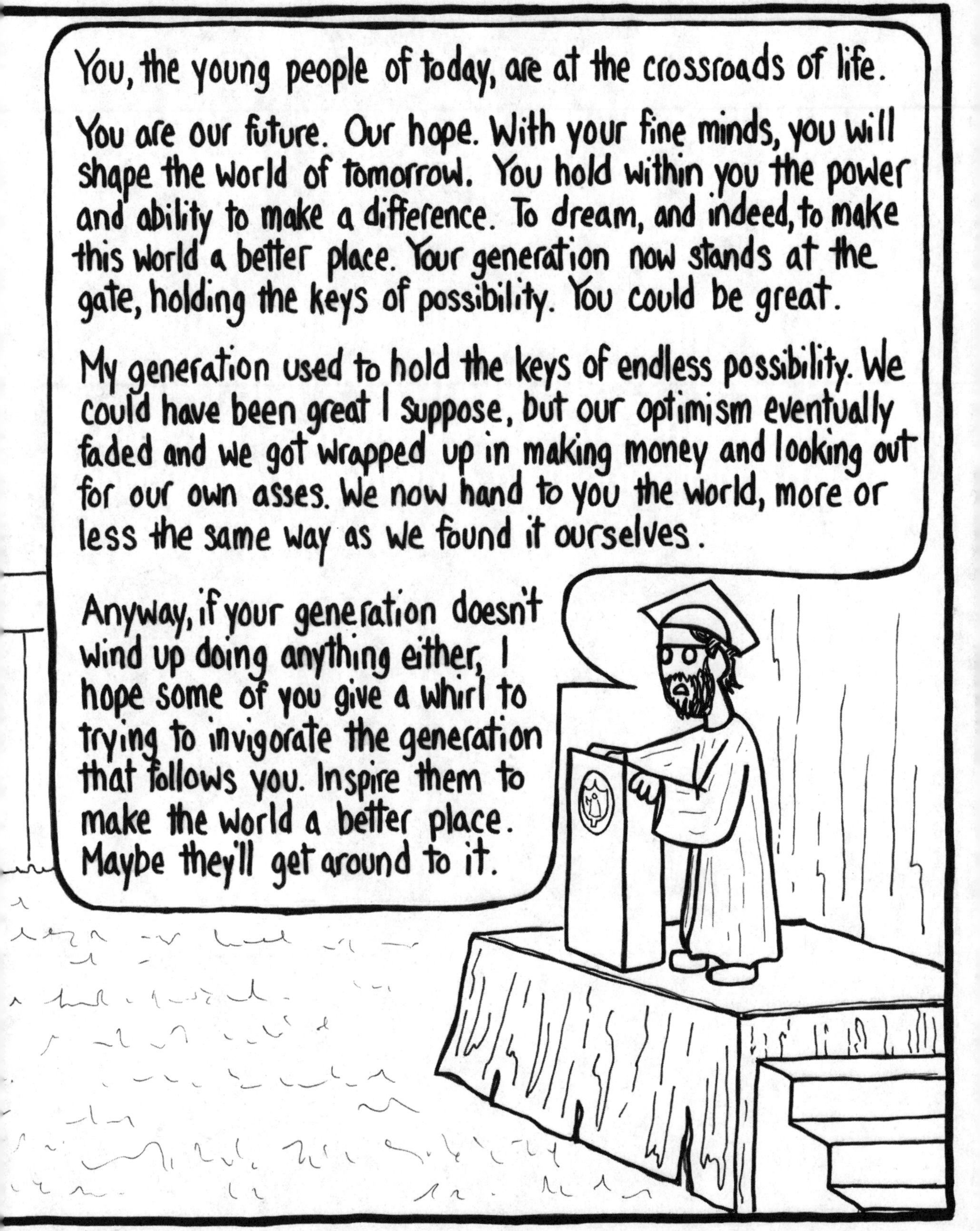
You, the young people of today, are at the crossroads of life.
You are our future. Our hope. With your fine minds, you will shape the world of tomorrow. You hold within you the power and ability to make a difference. To dream, and indeed, to make this world a better place. Your generation now stands at the gate, holding the keys of possibility. You could be great.
My generation used to hold the keys of endless possibility. We could have been great I suppose, but our optimism eventually faded and we got wrapped up in making money and looking out for our own asses. We now hand to you the world, more or less the same way as we found it ourselves.
Anyway, if your generation doesn't wind up doing anything either, I hope some of you give a whirl to trying to invigorate the generation that follows you. Inspire them to make the world a better place. Maybe they'll get around to it.

You probably have noticed that so far, there has been something of a narrative in this book. You will also probably notice that from here, the narrative kind of stops .

There is a perfectly logical reason for this: When I was growing up, it usually felt like I was following some kind of movie script, and I thought that something dramatic and important was coming. I thought something was going to happen.

Then when I reached adulthood, I found out nothing did.

CHAPTER 3:
I sort of became an adult.

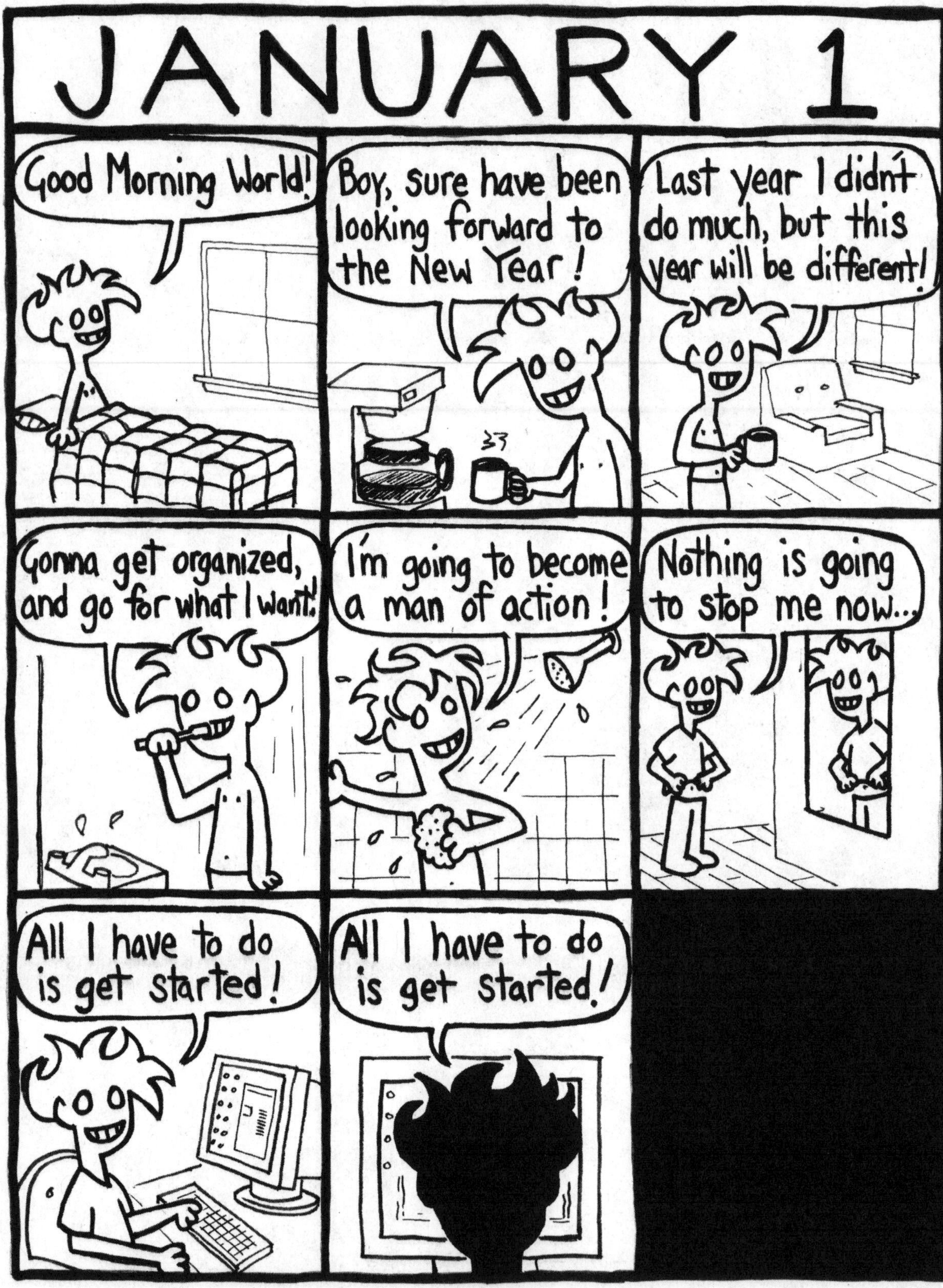
JANUARY 1
Good Morning World!
Boy, sure have been looking forward to the New Year!
Last year I didn't do much, but this year will be different!
Gonna get organized, and go for what I want!
I'm going to become a man of action!
Nothing is going to stop me now...
All I have to do is get started!
All I have to do is get started!

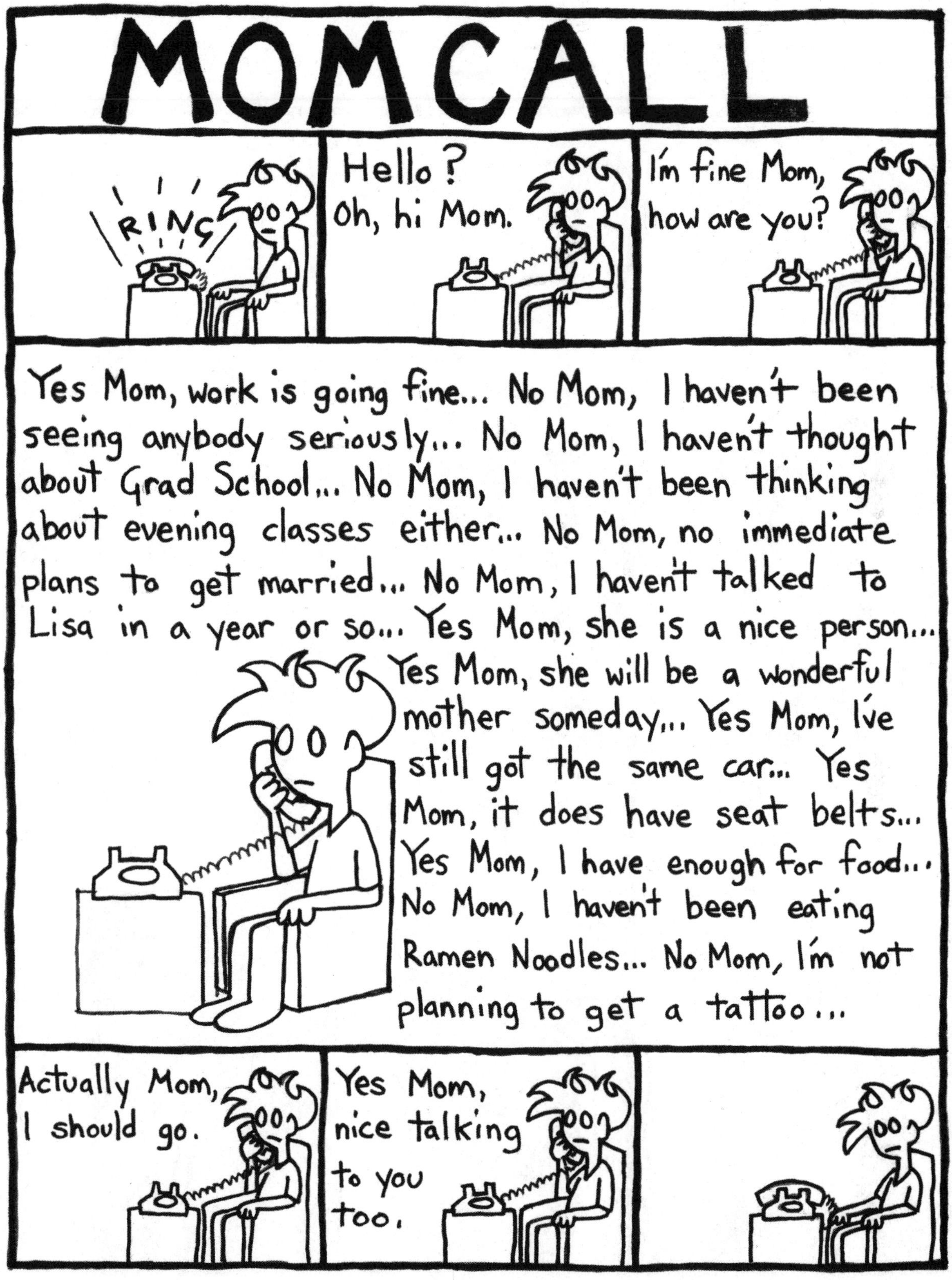
MOMCALL
RING
Hello? Oh, hi Mom.
I'm fine Mom, how are you?
Yes Mom, work is going fine... No Mom, I haven't been seeing anybody seriously... No Mom, I haven't thought about Grad School... No Mom, I haven't been thinking about evening classes either... No Mom, no immediate plans to get married... No Mom, I haven't talked to Lisa in a year or so... Yes Mom, she is a nice person... Yes Mom, she will be a wonderful mother someday... Yes Mom, I've still got the same car... Yes Mom, it does have seat belts... Yes Mom, I have enough for food... No Mom, I haven't been eating Ramen Noodles... No Mom, I'm not planning to get a tattoo...
Actually Mom, I should go.
Yes Mom, nice talking to you too.

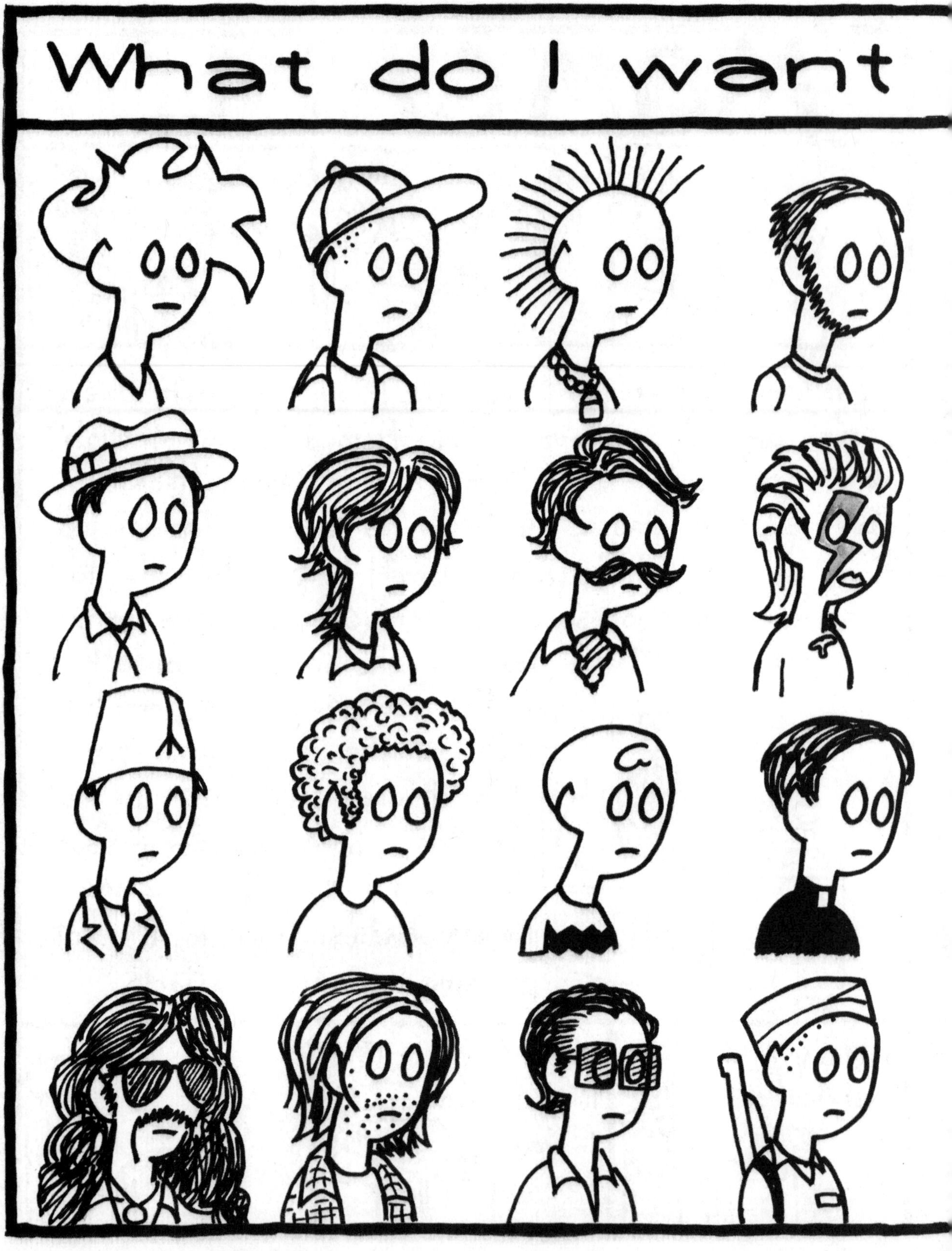
What do I want

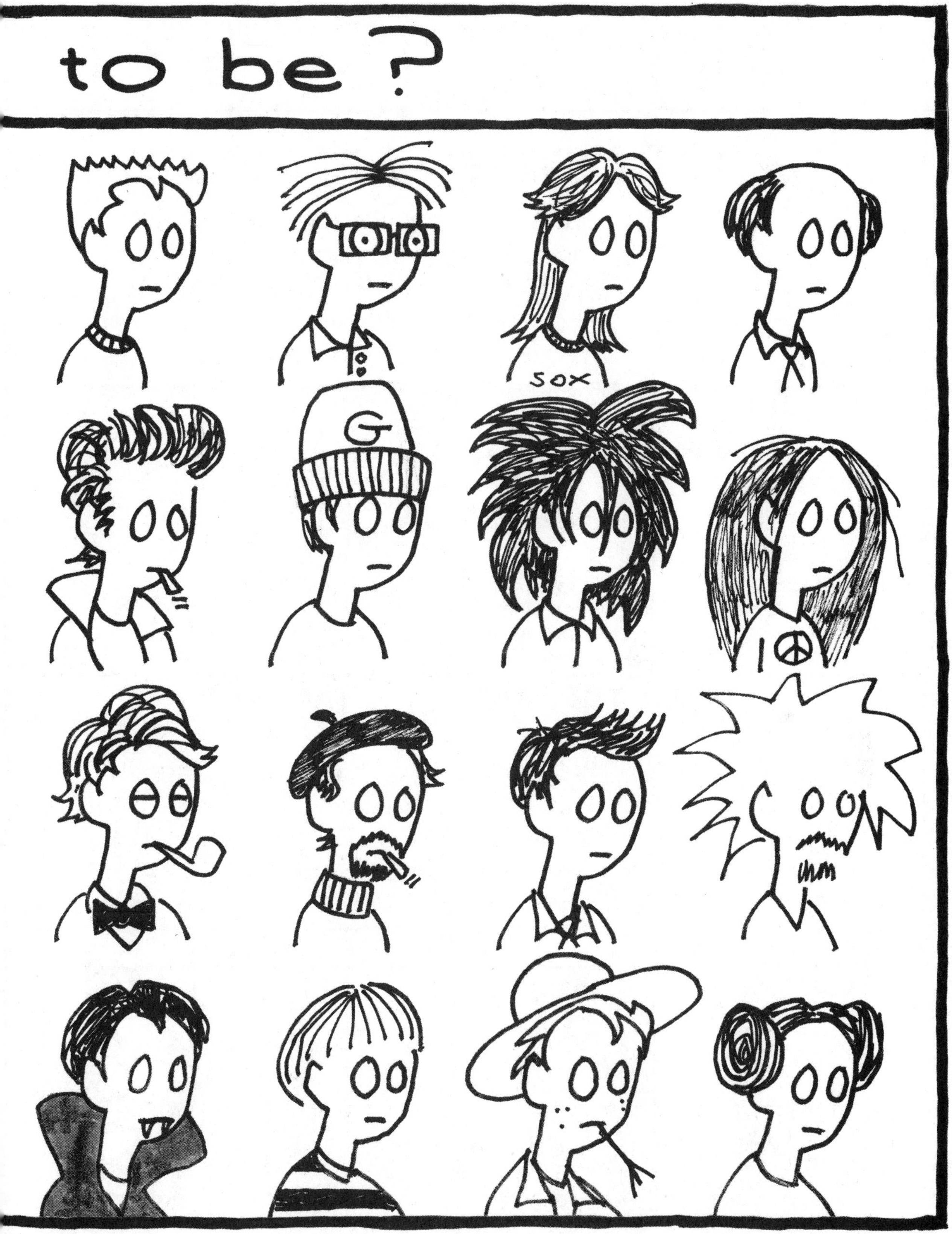
to be?
SOX

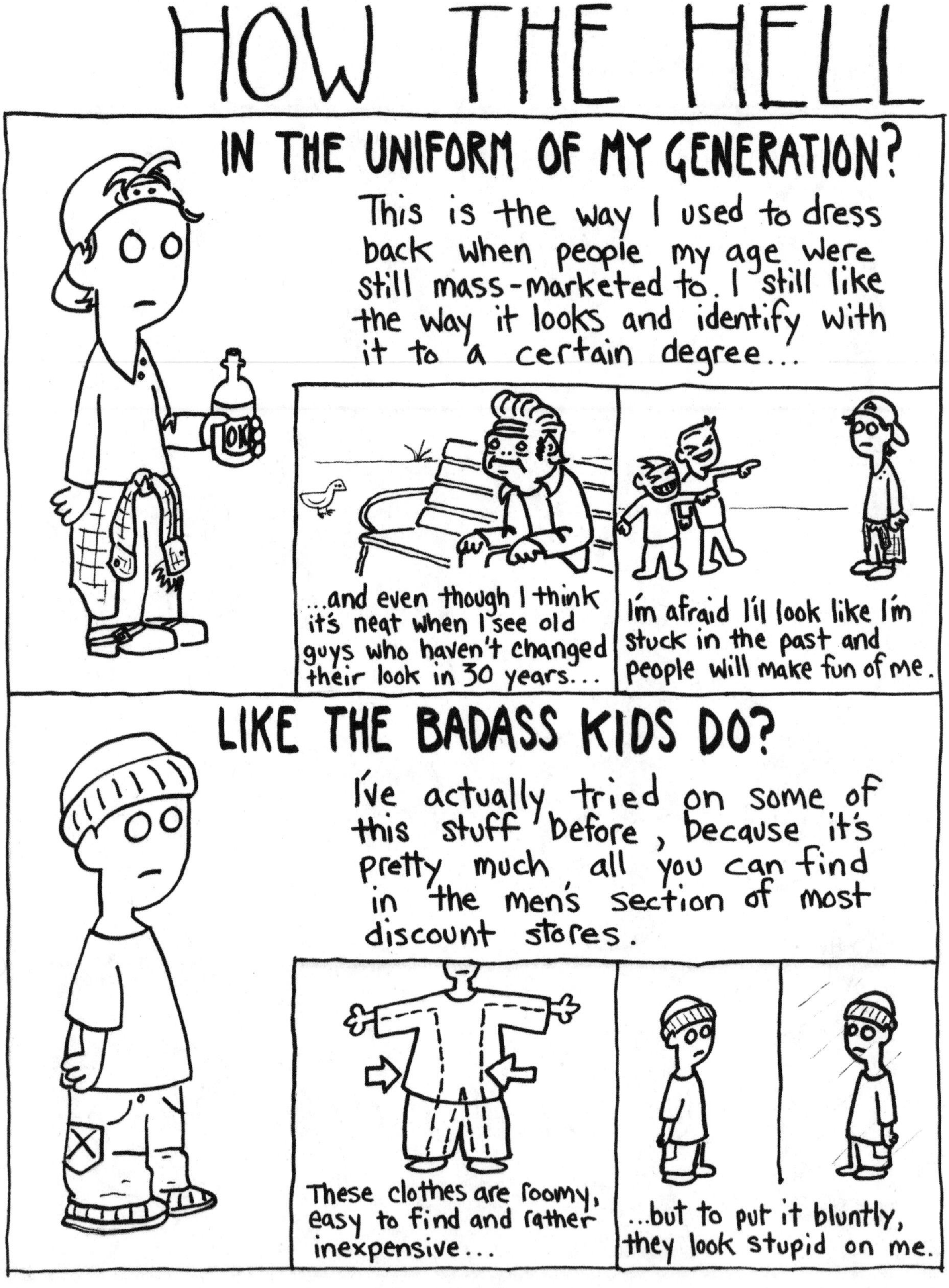
HOW THE HELL
IN THE UNIFORM OF MY GENERATION?
This is the way I used to dress back when people my age were still mass-marketed to. I still like the way it looks and identify with it to a certain degree...
OK
...and even though I think it's neat when I see old guys who haven't changed their look in 30 years...
I'm afraid I'll look like I'm stuck in the past and people will make fun of me.
LIKE THE BADASS KIDS DO?
I've actually tried on some of this stuff before, because it's pretty much all you can find in the men's section of most discount stores.
These clothes are roomy, easy to find and rather inexpensive...
...but to put it bluntly, they look stupid on me.

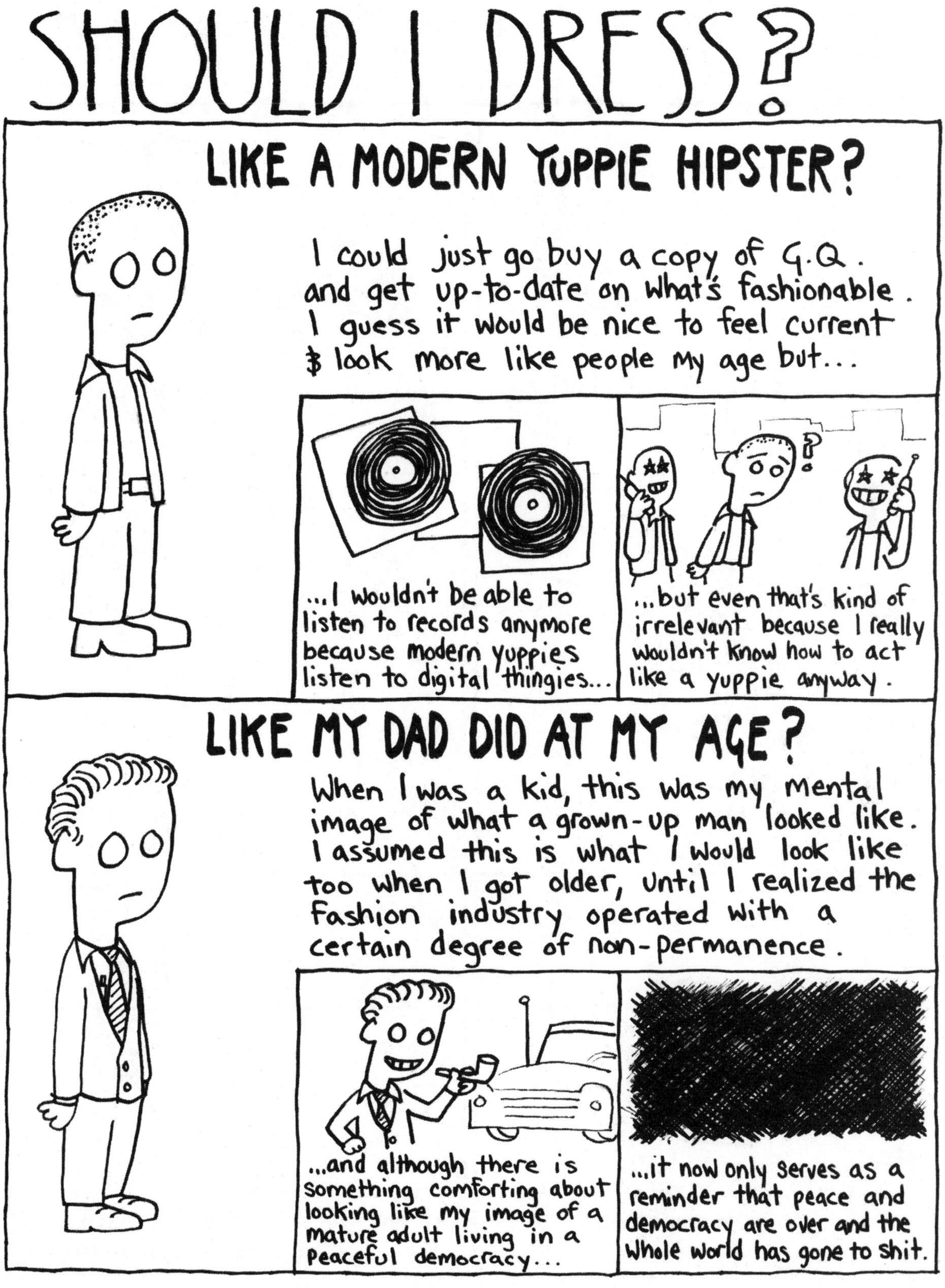
SHOULD I DRESS?
LIKE A MODERN YUPPIE HIPSTER?
I could just go buy a copy of G.Q. and get up-to-date on what's fashionable. I guess it would be nice to feel current $ look more like people my age but...
...I wouldn't be able to listen to records anymore because modern yuppies listen to digital thingies...
...but even that's kind of irrelevant because I really wouldn't know how to act like a yuppie anyway.
LIKE MY DAD DID AT MY AGE?
When I was a kid, this was my mental image of what a grown-up man looked like. I assumed this is what I would look like too when I got older, until I realized the fashion industry operated with a certain degree of non-permanence.
...and although there is something comforting about looking like my image of a mature adult living in a peaceful democracy...
...it now only serves as a reminder that peace and democracy are over and the whole world has gone to shit.

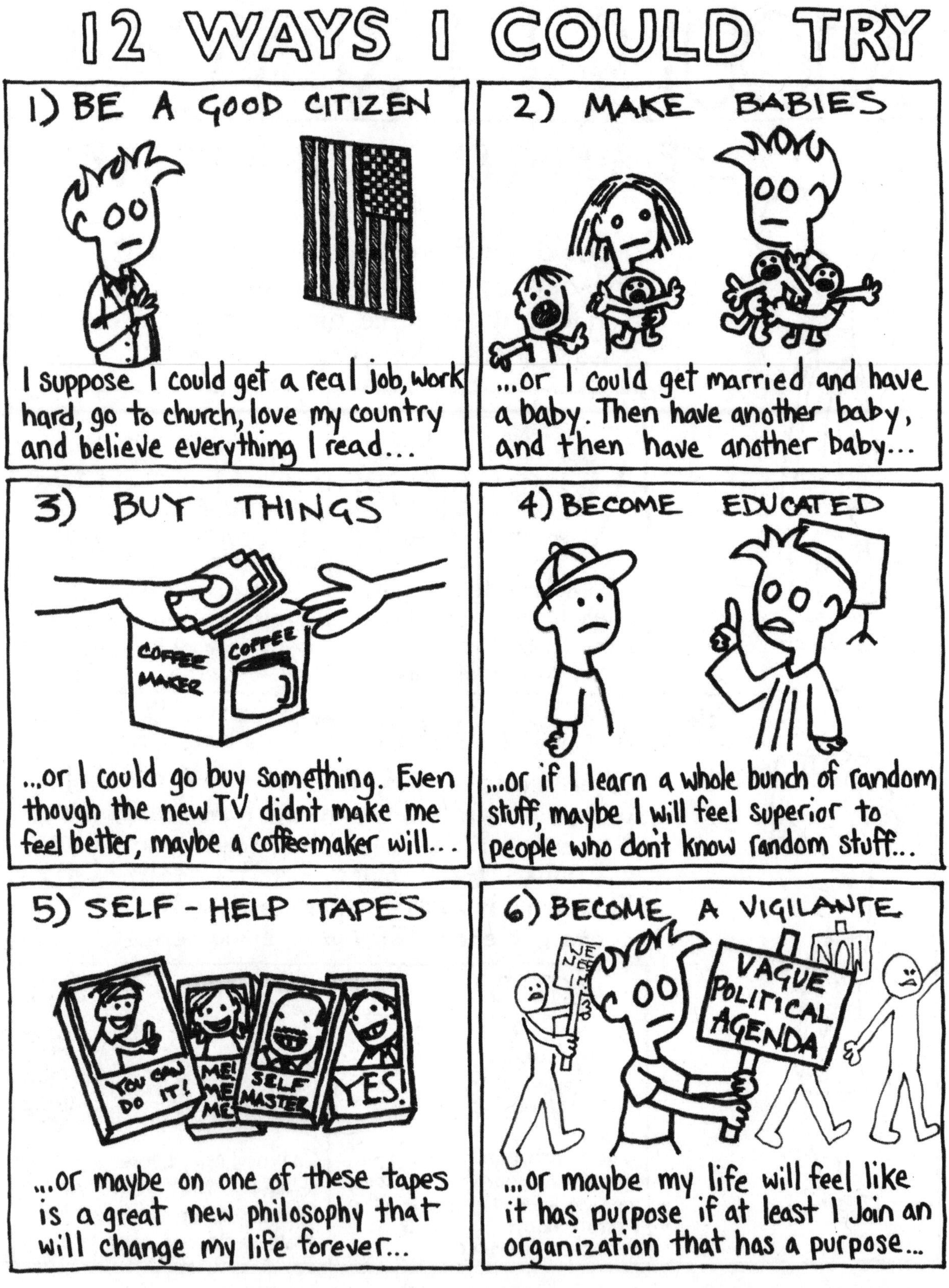
12 WAYS I COULD TRY
1) BE A GOOD CITIZEN
I suppose I could get a real job, work hard, go to church, love my country and believe everything I read...
2) MAKE BABIES
...or I could get married and have a baby. Then have another baby, and then have another baby...
3) BUY THINGS
COFFEE MAKER
COFFEE
...or I could go buy something. Even though the new TV didnt make me feel better, maybe a coffeemaker will...
4) BECOME EDUCATED
...or if I learn a whole bunch of random stuff, maybe I will feel superior to people who dont know random stuff...
5) SELF-HELP TAPES
YOU CAN DO IT!
ME! ME ME
SELF MASTER
YES!
...or maybe on one of these tapes is a great new philosophy that will change my life forever...
6) BECOME A VIGILANTE
NOW
VAGUE POLITICAL AGENDA
...or maybe my life will feel like it has purpose if at least I Join an organization that has a purpose...

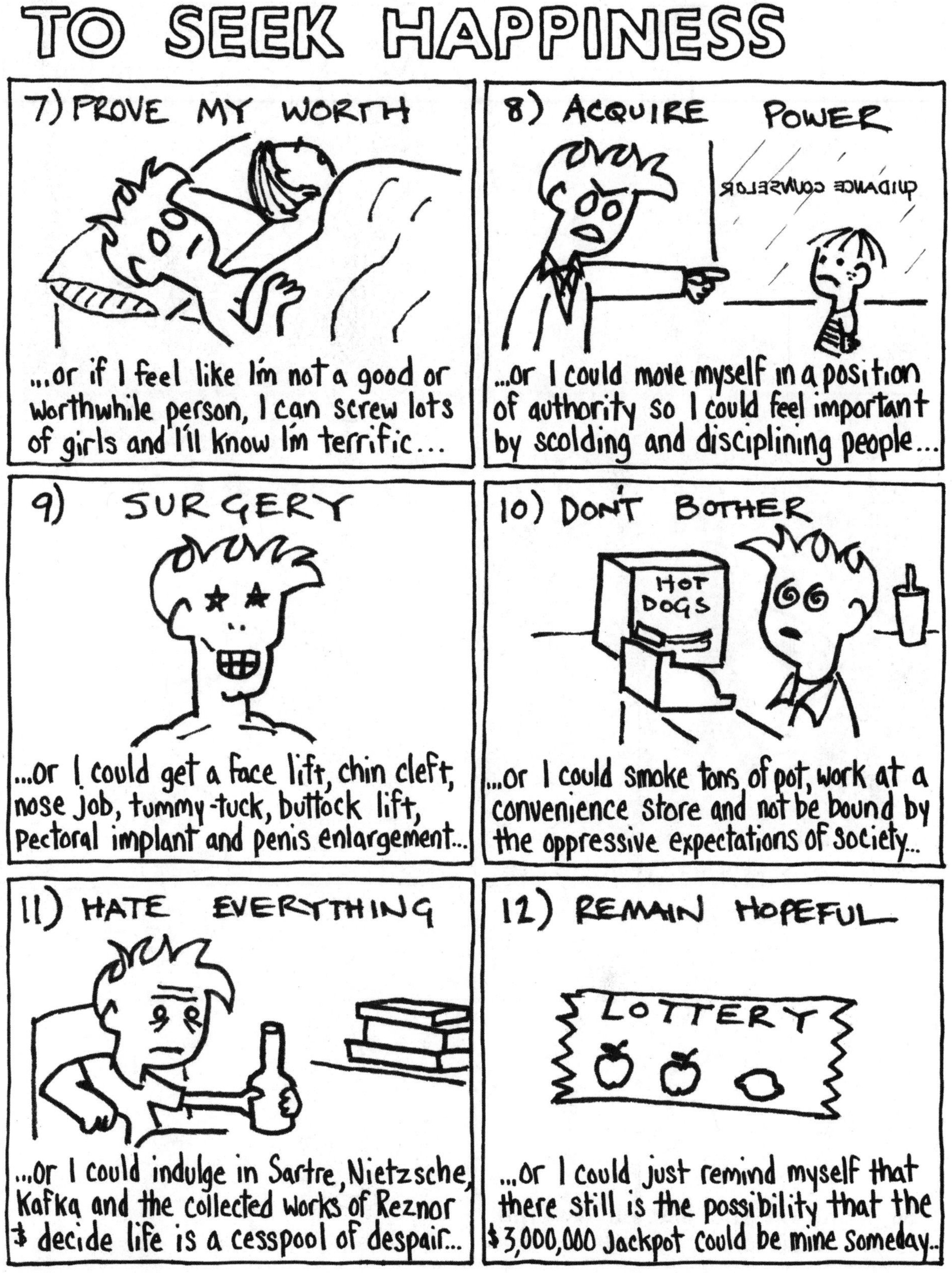
TO SEEK HAPPINESS
7) PROVE MY WORTH
...or if I feel like I'm not a good or worthwhile person, I can screw lots of girls and I'll know I'm terrific...
8) ACQUIRE POWER
GUIDANCE COUNSELOR
...or I could move myself in a position of authority so I could feel important by scolding and disciplining people...
9) SURGERY
...or I could get a face lift, chin cleft, nose job, tummy-tuck, buttock lift, pectoral implant and penis enlargement...
10) DON'T BOTHER
HOT DOGS
...or I could smoke tons of pot, work at a convenience store and not be bound by the oppressive expectations of society...
11) HATE EVERYTHING
...or I could indulge in Sartre, Nietzsche, Kafka and the collected works of Reznor & decide life is a cesspool of despair...
12) REMAIN HOPEFUL
LOTTERY
...or I could just remind myself that there still is the possibility that the $3,000,000 Jackpot could be mine someday...

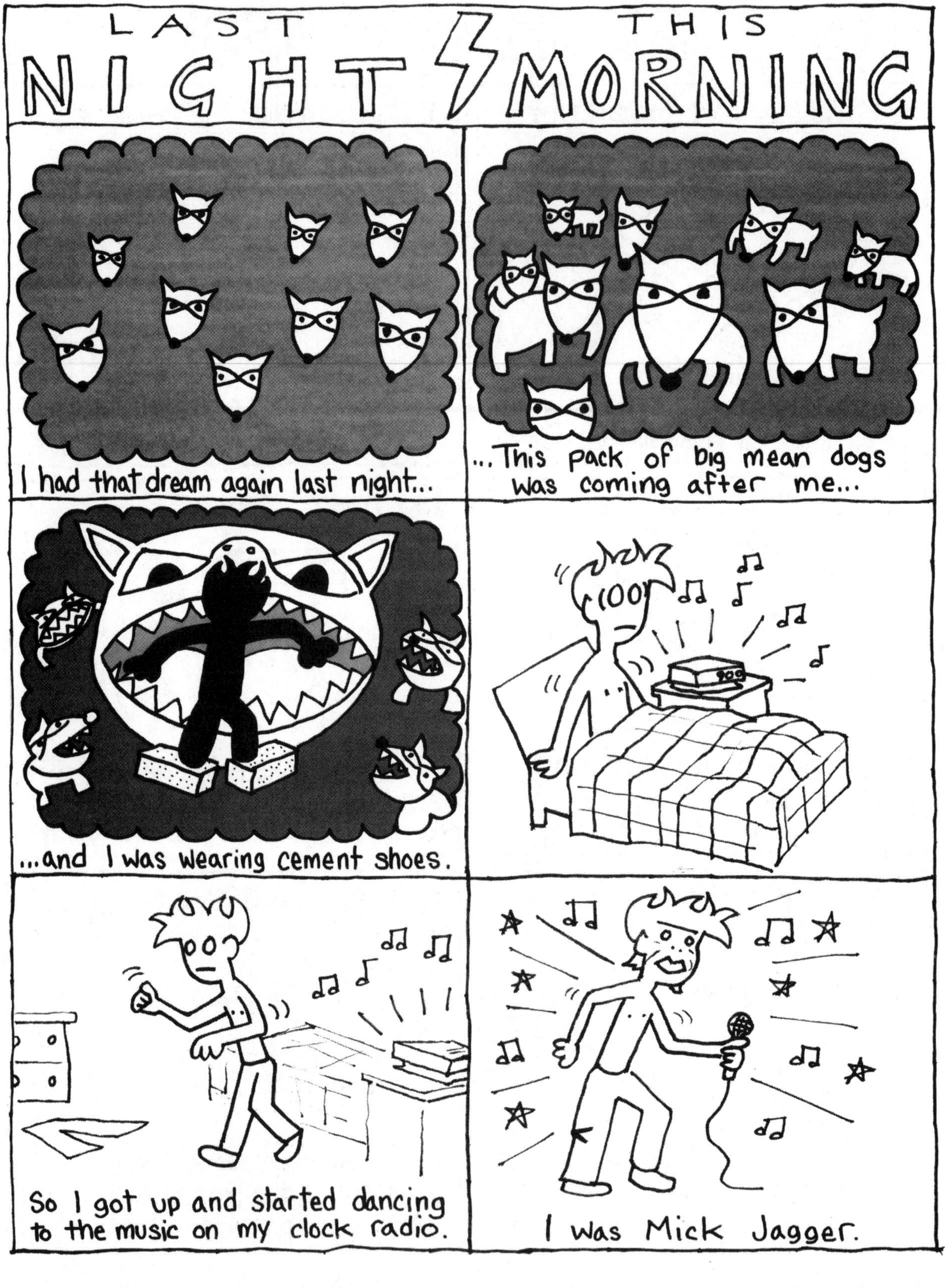
LAST NIGHT
THIS MORNING
I had that dream again last night...
...This pack of big mean dogs was coming after me...
...and I was wearing cement shoes.
So I got up and started dancing to the music on my clock radio.
I was Mick Jagger.

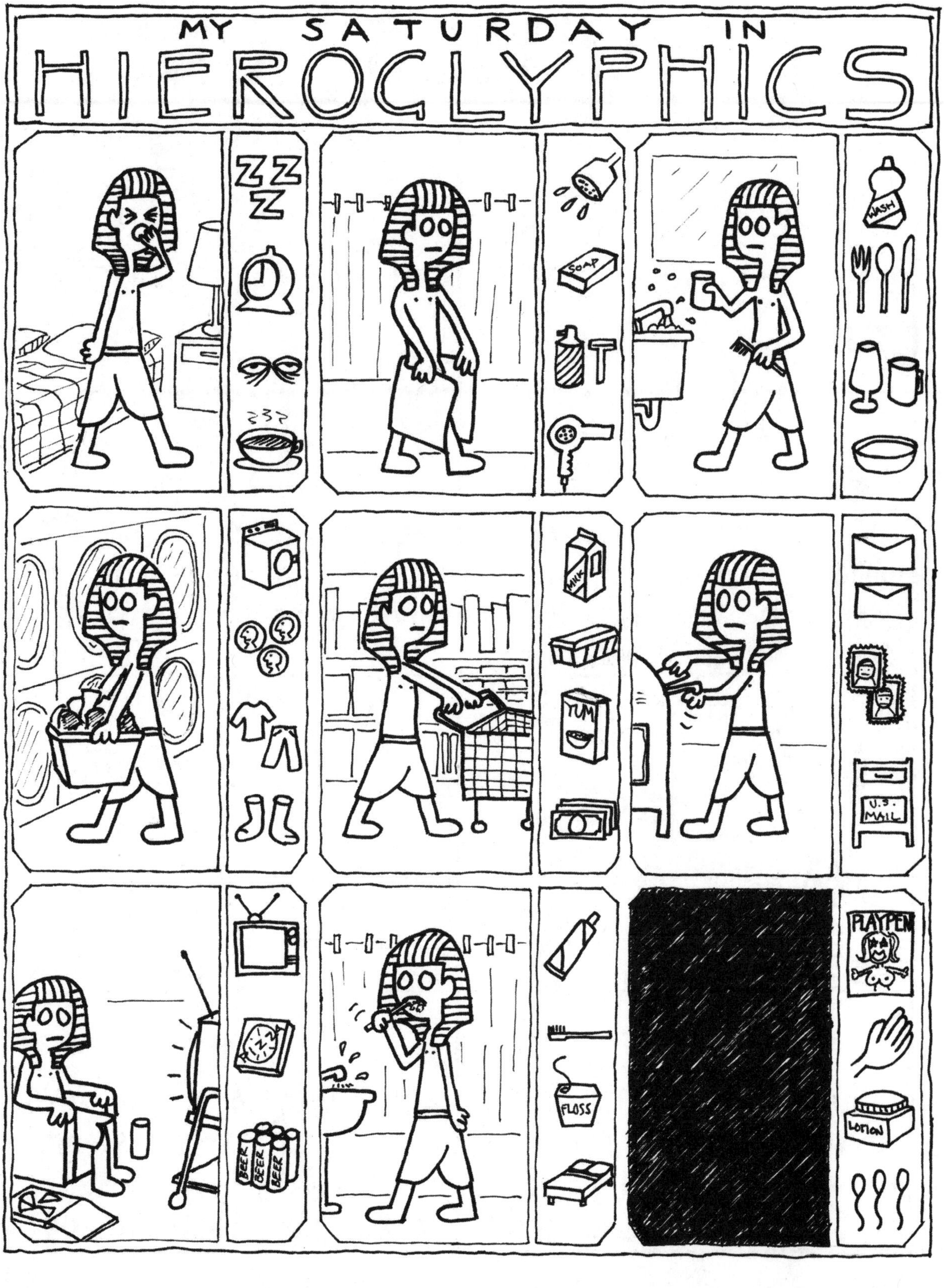
MY SATURDAY IN
HIEROGLYPHICS
WASH
SOAP
MILK
YUM
U.S. MAIL
BEER
BEER
BEER
FLOSS
PLAYPEN
LOTION

THE VARIOUS KINDS

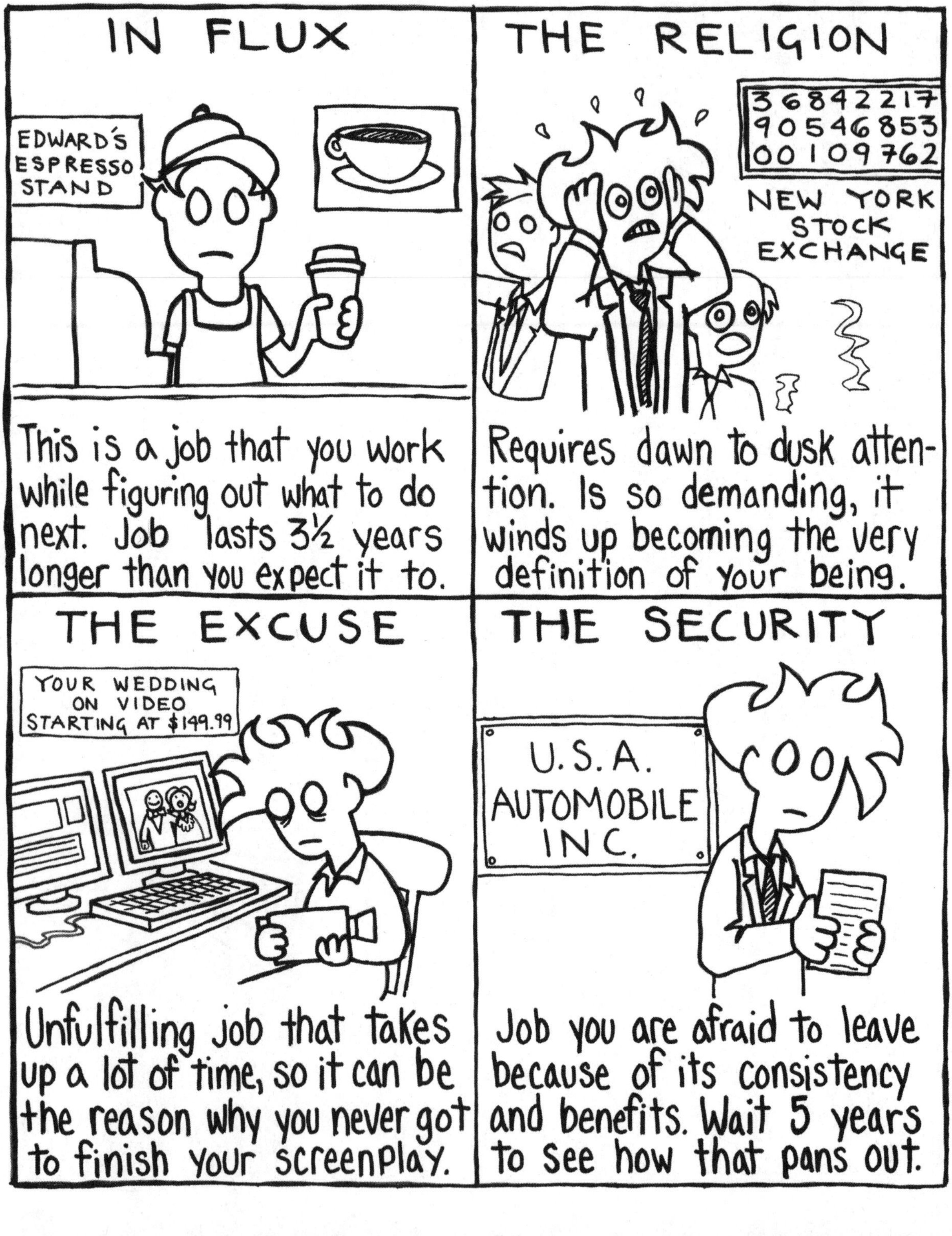

IN FLUX
EDWARD'S ESPRESSO STAND
This is a job that you work while figuring out what to do next. Job lasts 3½ years longer than you expect it to.
THE RELIGION
36842217
90546853
00109762
NEW YORK STOCK EXCHANGE
Requires dawn to dusk attention. Is so demanding, it winds up becoming the very definition of your being.
THE EXCUSE
YOUR WEDDING ON VIDEO STARTING AT $149.99
Unfulfilling job that takes up a lot of time, so it can be the reason why you never got to finish your screenplay.
THE SECURITY
U.S.A. AUTOMOBILE INC.
Job you are afraid to leave because of its consistency and benefits. Wait 5 years to see how that pans out.

OF JOBS YOU CAN GET

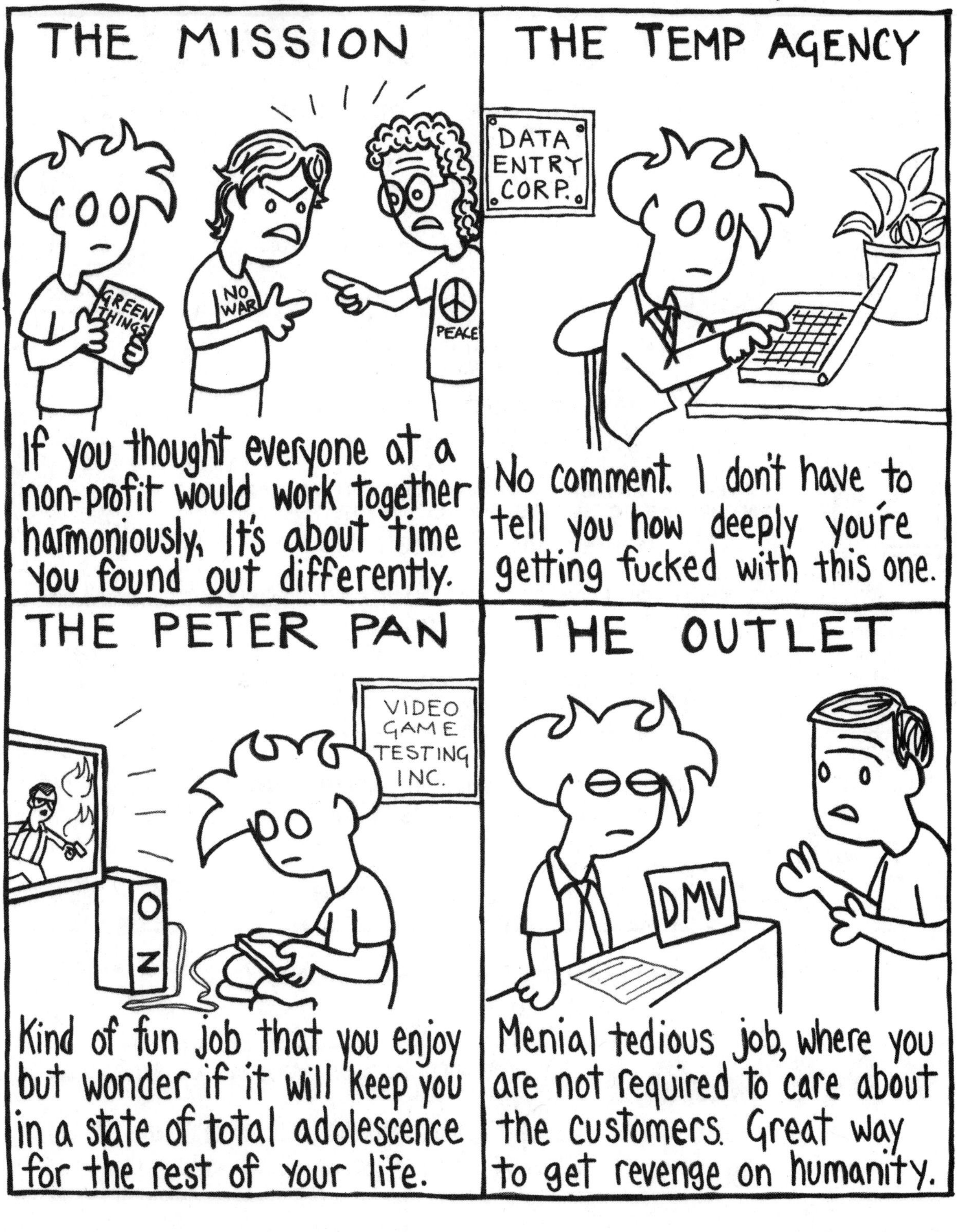

THE MISSION
GREEN THINGS
NO WAR
PEACE
If you thought everyone at a non-profit would work together harmoniously, It's about time you found out differently.
THE TEMP AGENCY
DATA ENTRY CORP.
No comment. I don't have to tell you how deeply you're getting fucked with this one.
THE PETER PAN
VIDEO GAME TESTING INC.
ON
Kind of fun job that you enjoy but wonder if it will keep you in a state of total adolescence for the rest of your life.
THE OUTLET
DMV
Menial tedious job, where you are not required to care about the customers. Great way to get revenge on humanity.

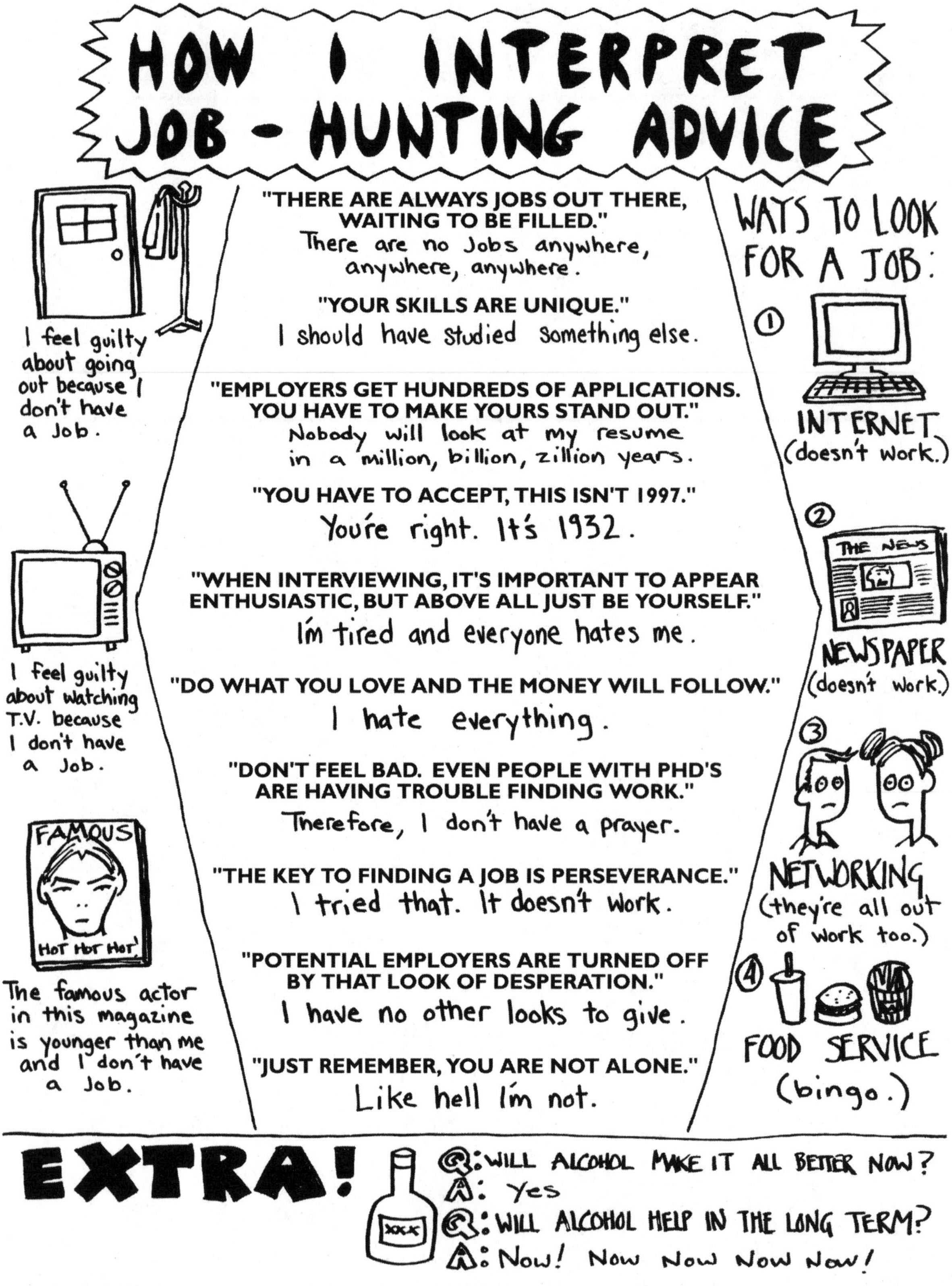
HOW I INTERPRET JOB-HUNTING ADVICE
"THERE ARE ALWAYS JOBS OUT THERE, WAITING TO BE FILLED."
There are no Jobs anywhere, anywhere, anywhere.
"YOUR SKILLS ARE UNIQUE."
I should have studied something else.
"EMPLOYERS GET HUNDREDS OF APPLICATIONS. YOU HAVE TO MAKE YOURS STAND OUT."
Nobody will look at my resume in a million, billion, zillion years.
"YOU HAVE TO ACCEPT, THIS ISN'T 1997."
You're right. It's 1932.
"WHEN INTERVIEWING, IT'S IMPORTANT TO APPEAR ENTHUSIASTIC, BUT ABOVE ALL JUST BE YOURSELF."
I'm tired and everyone hates me.
"DO WHAT YOU LOVE AND THE MONEY WILL FOLLOW."
I hate everything.
"DON'T FEEL BAD. EVEN PEOPLE WITH PHD'S ARE HAVING TROUBLE FINDING WORK."
Therefore, I don't have a prayer.
"THE KEY TO FINDING A JOB IS PERSEVERANCE."
I tried that. It doesn't work.
"POTENTIAL EMPLOYERS ARE TURNED OFF BY THAT LOOK OF DESPERATION."
I have no other looks to give.
"JUST REMEMBER, YOU ARE NOT ALONE."
Like hell I'm not.
I feel guilty about going out because I don't have a Job.
I feel guilty about watching T.V. because I don't have a Job.
FAMOUS
HOT HOT HOT
The famous actor in this magazine is younger than me and I don't have a Job.
WAYS TO LOOK FOR A JOB:
① INTERNET (doesn't work.)
② THE NEWS
NEWSPAPER (doesn't work.)
③ NETWORKING (they're all out of work too.)
④ FOOD SERVICE (bingo.)
EXTRA!
XXX
Q: WILL ALCOHOL MAKE IT ALL BETTER NOW?
A: Yes
Q: WILL ALCOHOL HELP IN THE LONG TERM?
A: Now! Now Now Now Now!

THANK YOU FOR THE JOB INTERVIEW

November 5, 2008

Dear Mr. Fucking Dickhead,

I would like to thank you for wasting my time while meeting with me last week. It was indeed a pleasure to know life at your company is Hell on Earth, and everyone there including you is an incomprehensible asshole. Having met with you, I am even more excited about the idea of getting lost at sea so I can spend the rest of my life living on a desert island. I sincerely hope that your company will forget about me, as I am doing my best to forget about you with a bottle of cheap whiskey and a Beavis And Butthead DVD. While I am confident that I will think of you for the rest of my life every time I give someone the finger, I also feel that I will think of your face in my toilet from now on when I shit.

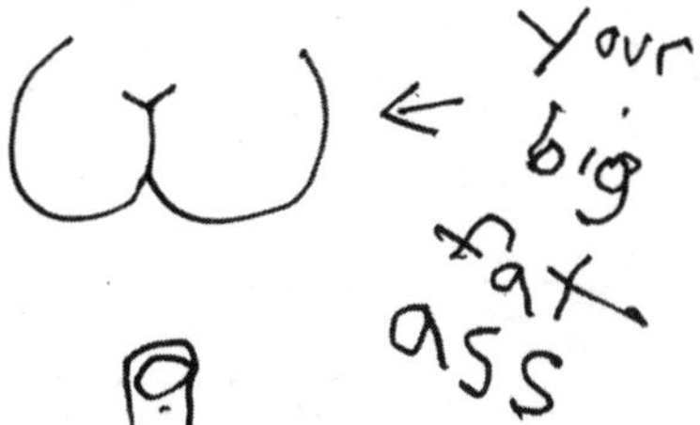
Your big fat ass

Thank you for your consideration.
Sincerely,

Applicant

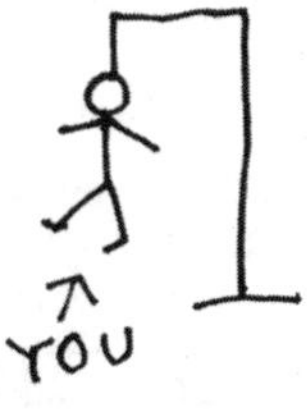
YOU

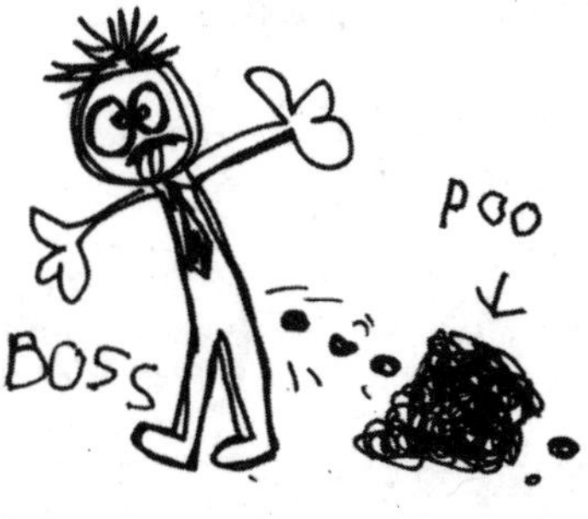
BOSS
POO

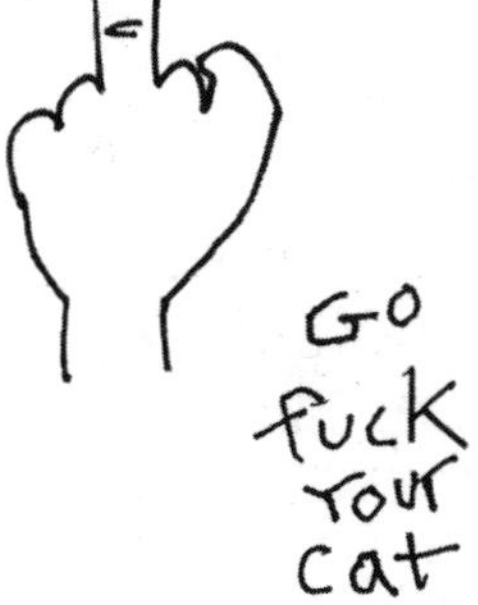
GO fuck Your cat

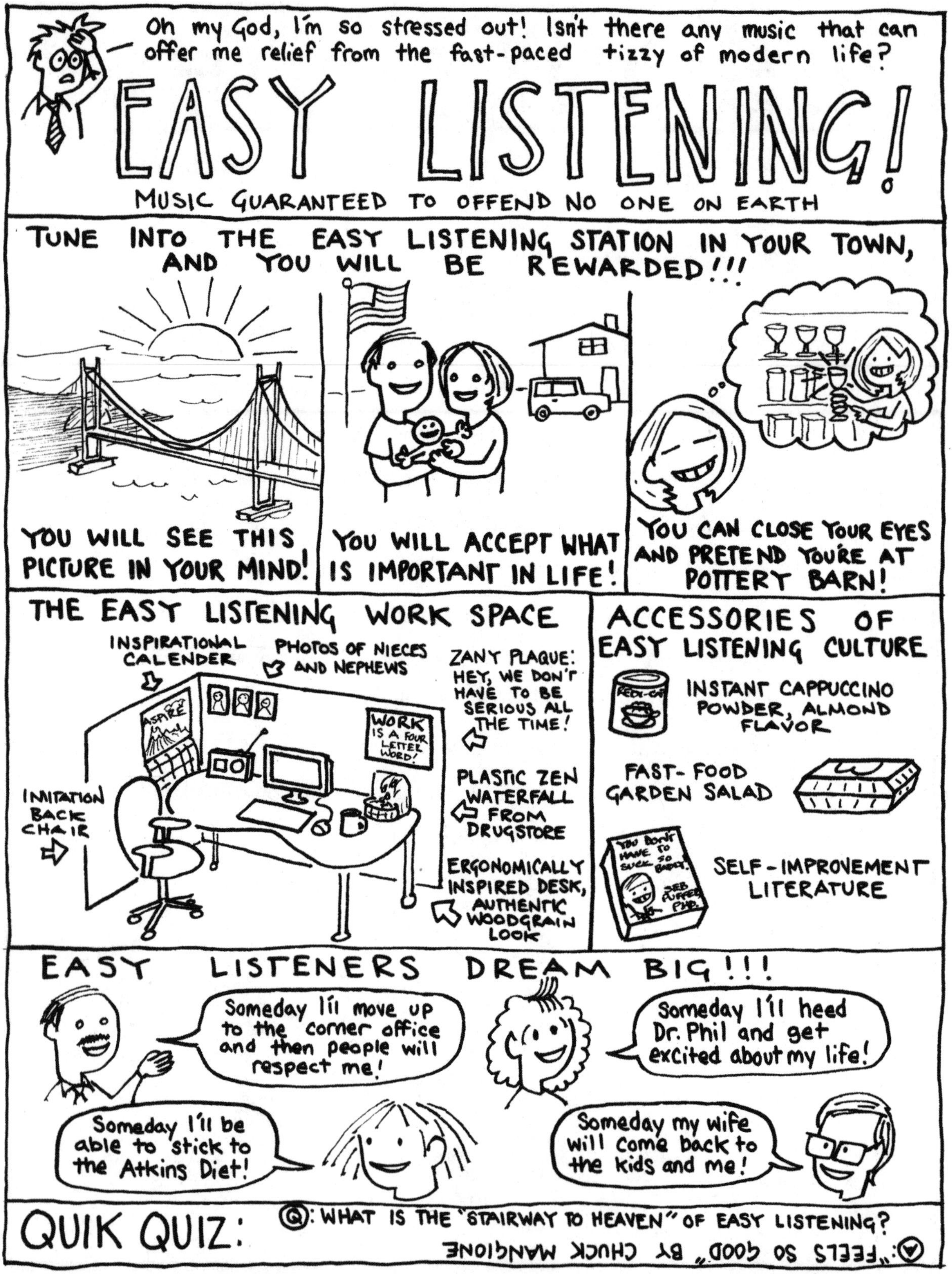
Oh my God, I'm so stressed out! Isn't there any music that can offer me relief from the fast-paced tizzy of modern life?
EASY LISTENING!
MUSIC GUARANTEED TO OFFEND NO ONE ON EARTH
TUNE INTO THE EASY LISTENING STATION IN YOUR TOWN, AND YOU WILL BE REWARDED!!!
YOU WILL SEE THIS PICTURE IN YOUR MIND!
YOU WILL ACCEPT WHAT IS IMPORTANT IN LIFE!
YOU CAN CLOSE YOUR EYES AND PRETEND YOU'RE AT POTTERY BARN!
THE EASY LISTENING WORK SPACE
INSPIRATIONAL CALENDER
PHOTOS OF NIECES AND NEPHEWS
ZANY PLAQUE: HEY, WE DON'T HAVE TO BE SERIOUS ALL THE TIME!
ASPIRE
WORK IS A FOUR LETTER WORD!
PLASTIC ZEN WATERFALL FROM DRUGSTORE
IMITATION BACK CHAIR
ERGONOMICALLY INSPIRED DESK, AUTHENTIC WOODGRAIN LOOK
ACCESSORIES OF EASY LISTENING CULTURE
INSTANT CAPPUCCINO POWDER, ALMOND FLAVOR
FAST-FOOD GARDEN SALAD
YOU DON'T HAVE TO SUCK SO BADLY
SEB PUFFER PHD.
SELF-IMPROVEMENT LITERATURE
EASY LISTENERS DREAM BIG!!!
Someday I'll move up to the corner office and then people will respect me!
Someday I'll heed Dr. Phil and get excited about my life!
Someday I'll be able to stick to the Atkins Diet!
Someday my wife will come back to the kids and me!
QUIK QUIZ:
Q: WHAT IS THE "STAIRWAY TO HEAVEN" OF EASY LISTENING?
A: "FEELS SO GOOD" BY CHUCK MANGIONE

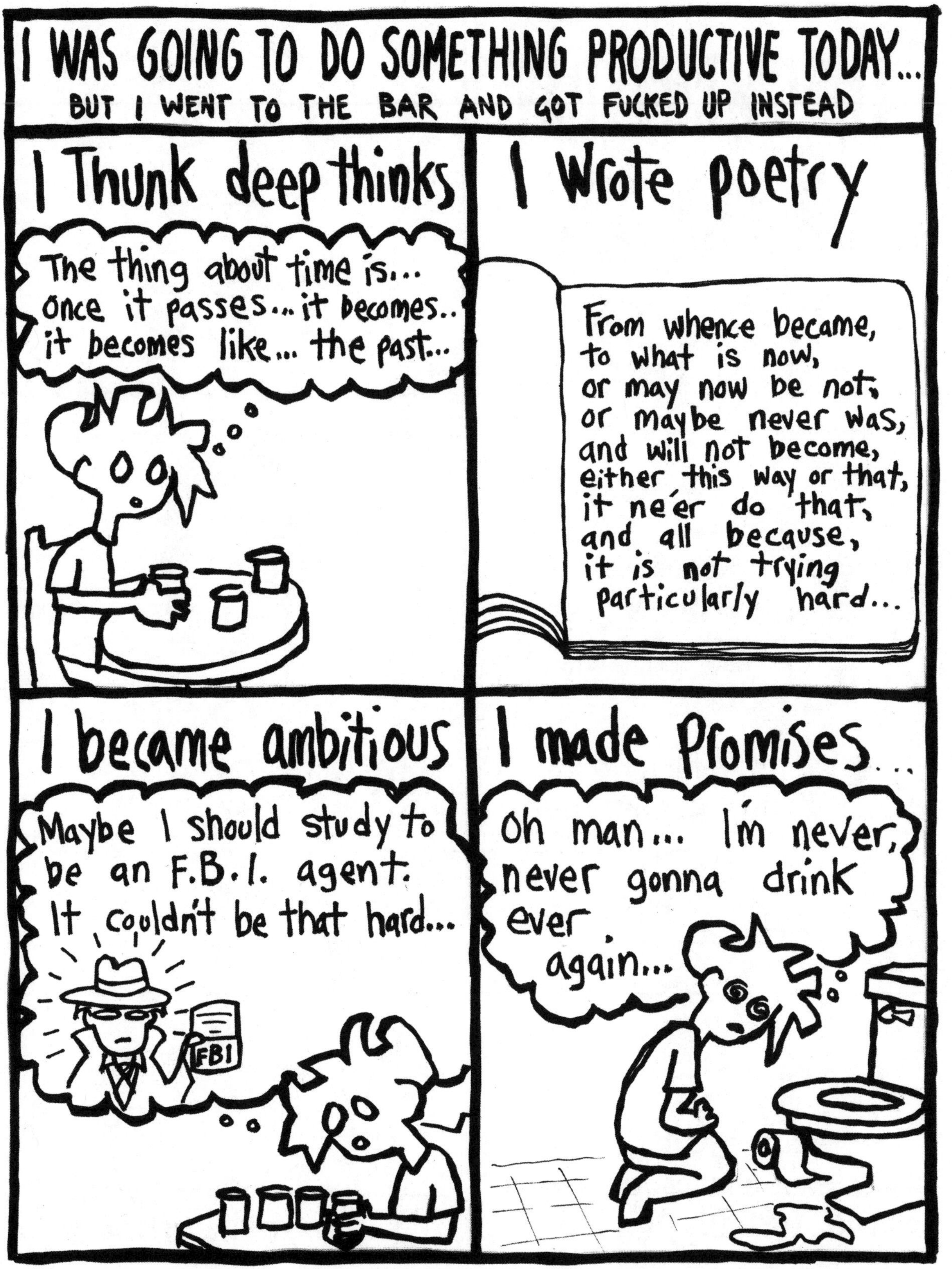
I WAS GOING TO DO SOMETHING PRODUCTIVE TODAY...
BUT I WENT TO THE BAR AND GOT FUCKED UP INSTEAD
I Thunk deep thinks
The thing about time is... once it passes... it becomes.. it becomes like... the past...
I Wrote poetry
From whence became, to what is now, or may now be not, or maybe never was, and will not become, either this way or that, it ne'er do that, and all because, it is not trying particularly hard...
I became ambitious
Maybe I should study to be an F.B.I. agent. It couldn't be that hard...
FBI
I made Promises...
Oh man... I'm never, never gonna drink ever again...

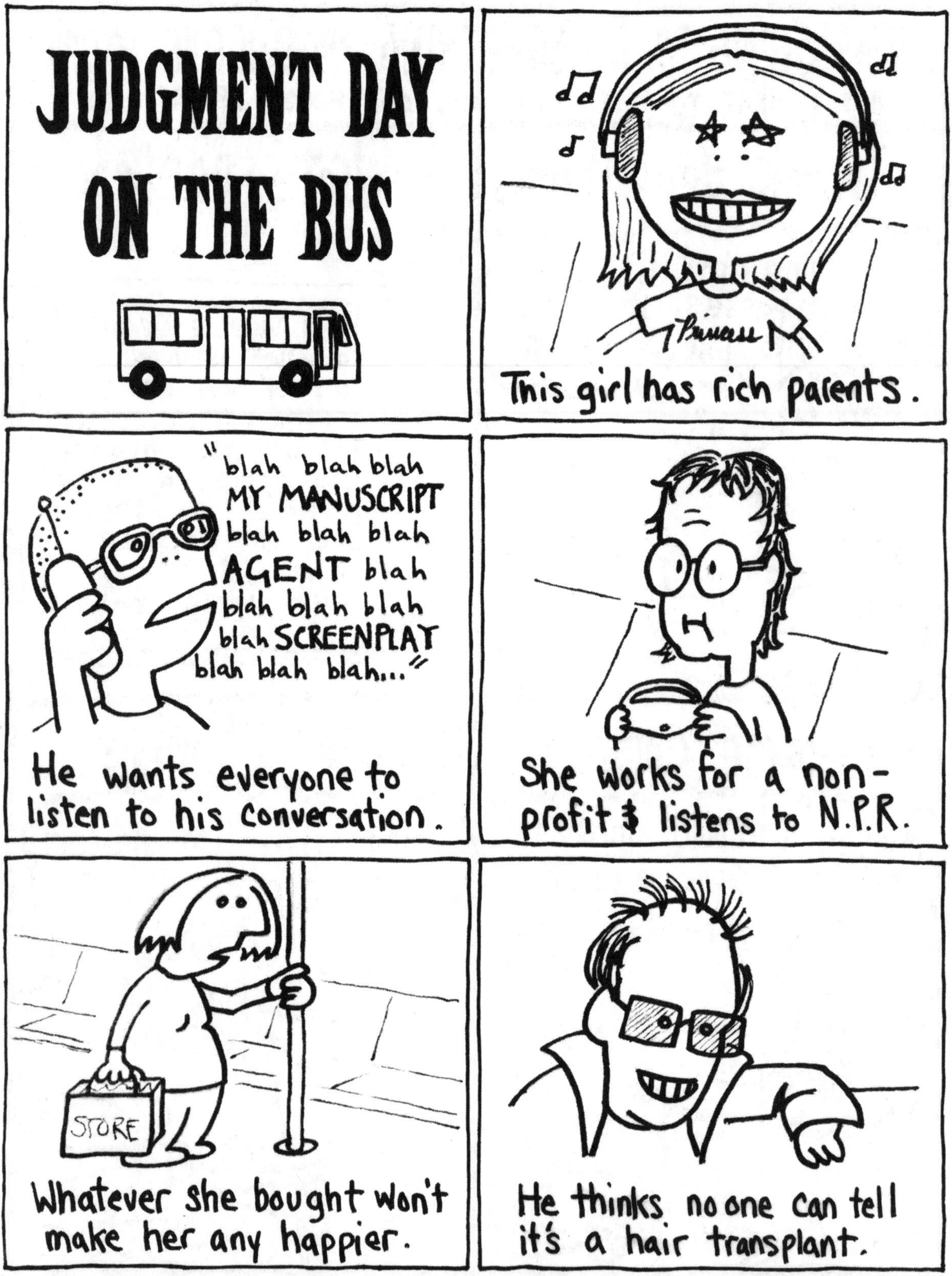
JUDGMENT DAY ON THE BUS
This girl has rich parents.
"blah blah blah MY MANUSCRIPT blah blah blah AGENT blah blah blah blah blah SCREENPLAY blah blah blah..."
He wants everyone to listen to his conversation.
She works for a non-profit $ listens to N.P.R.
STORE
Whatever she bought won't make her any happier.
He thinks no one can tell it's a hair transplant.

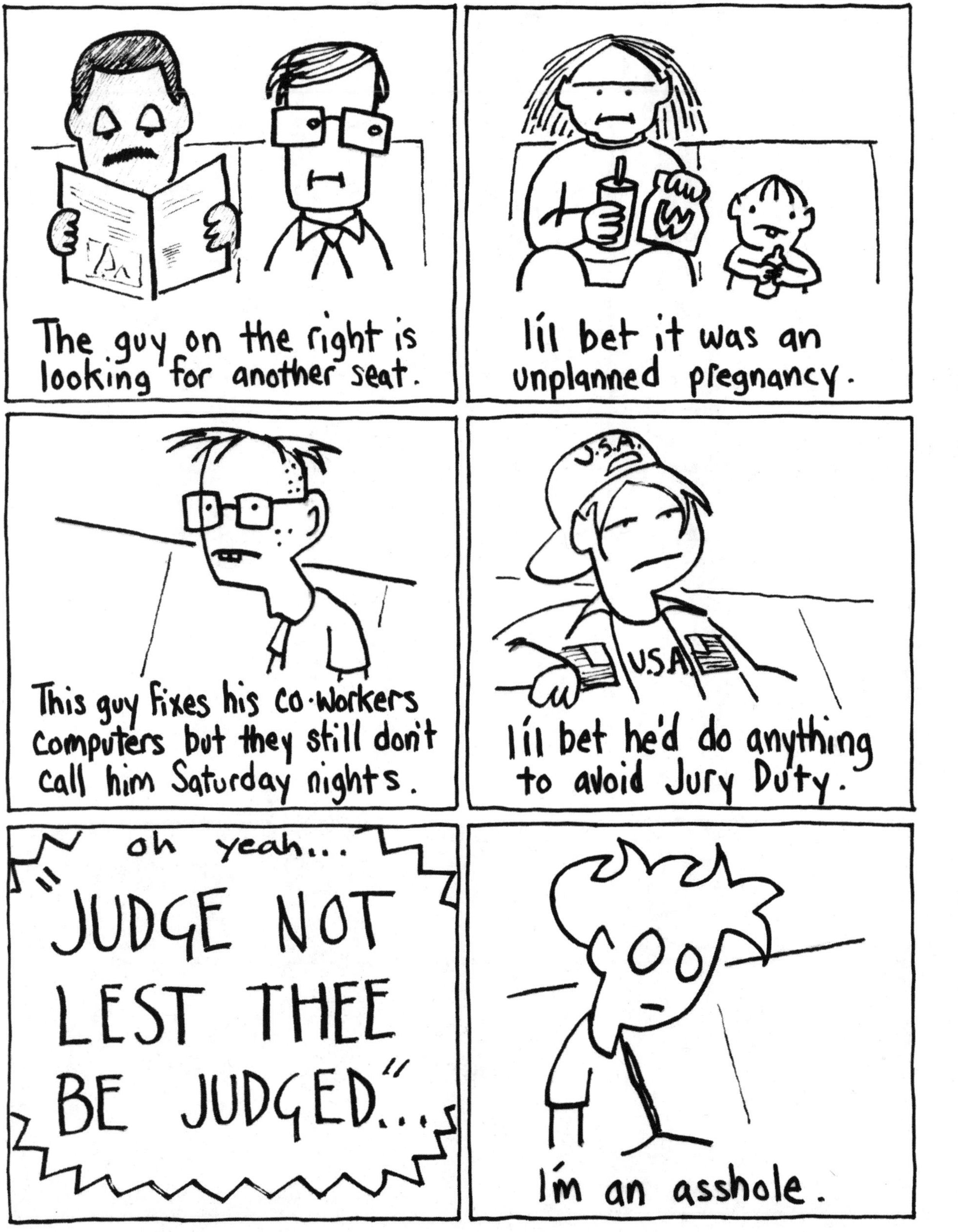
The guy on the right is looking for another seat.
Lil bet it was an unplanned pregnancy.
This guy fixes his co-workers computers but they still don't call him Saturday nights.
U.S.A.
USA
Lil bet he'd do anything to avoid Jury Duty.
oh yeah...
"JUDGE NOT LEST THEE BE JUDGED"...
I'm an asshole.

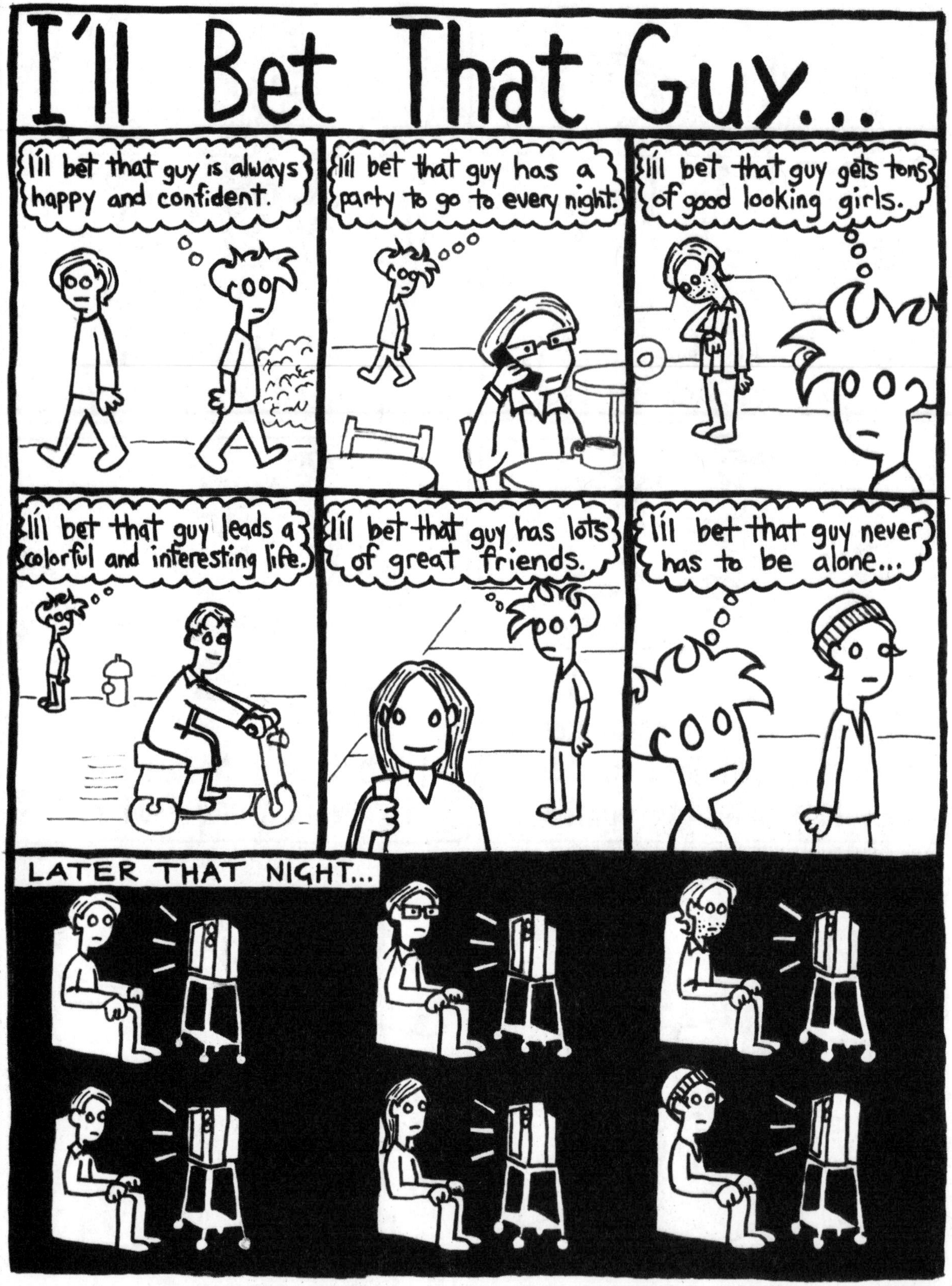
I'll Bet That Guy...
I'll bet that guy is always happy and confident.
I'll bet that guy has a party to go to every night.
I'll bet that guy gets tons of good looking girls.
I'll bet that guy leads a colorful and interesting life.
I'll bet that guy has lots of great friends.
I'll bet that guy never has to be alone...
LATER THAT NIGHT...

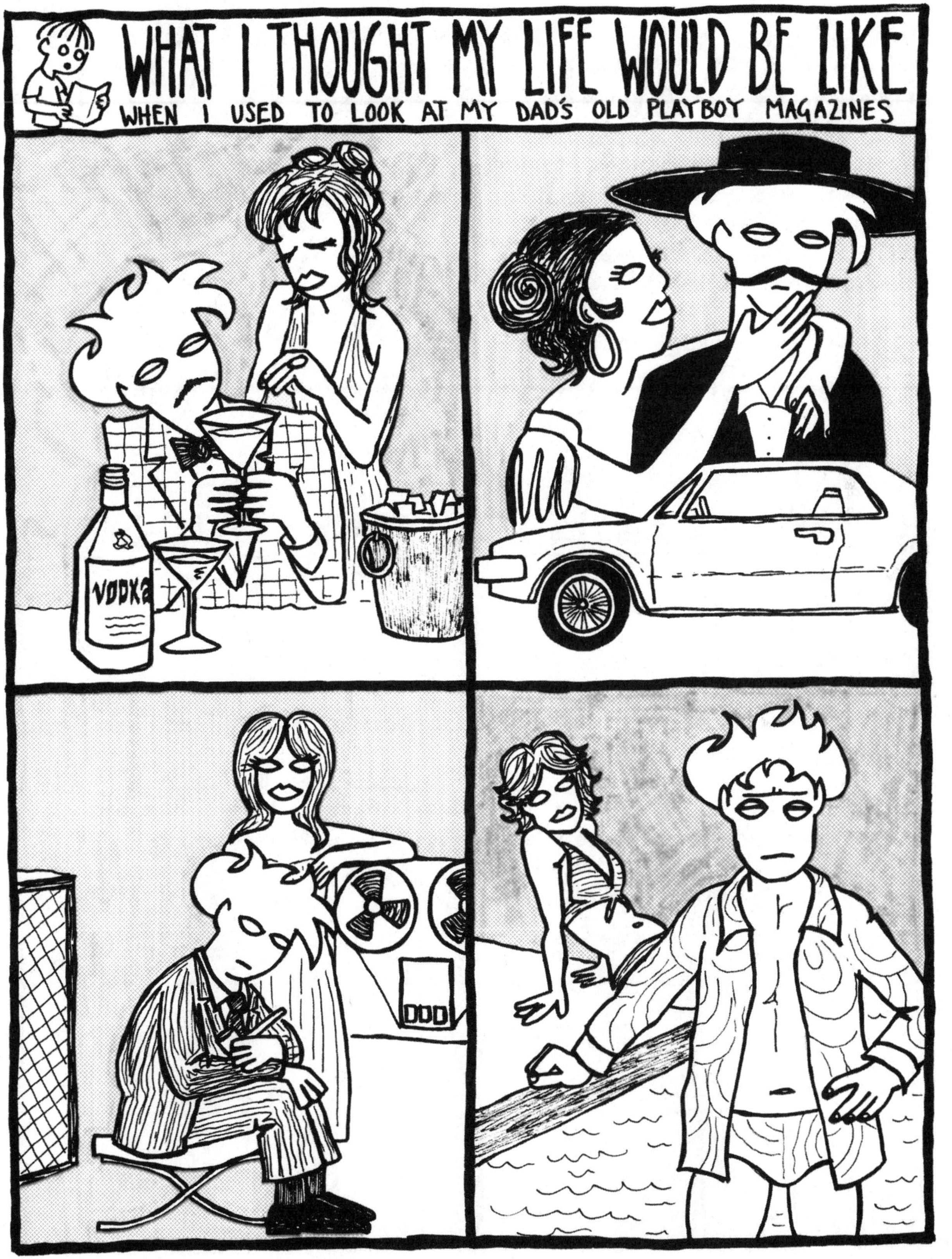
WHAT I THOUGHT MY LIFE WOULD BE LIKE
WHEN I USED TO LOOK AT MY DAD'S OLD PLAYBOY MAGAZINES
VODKA

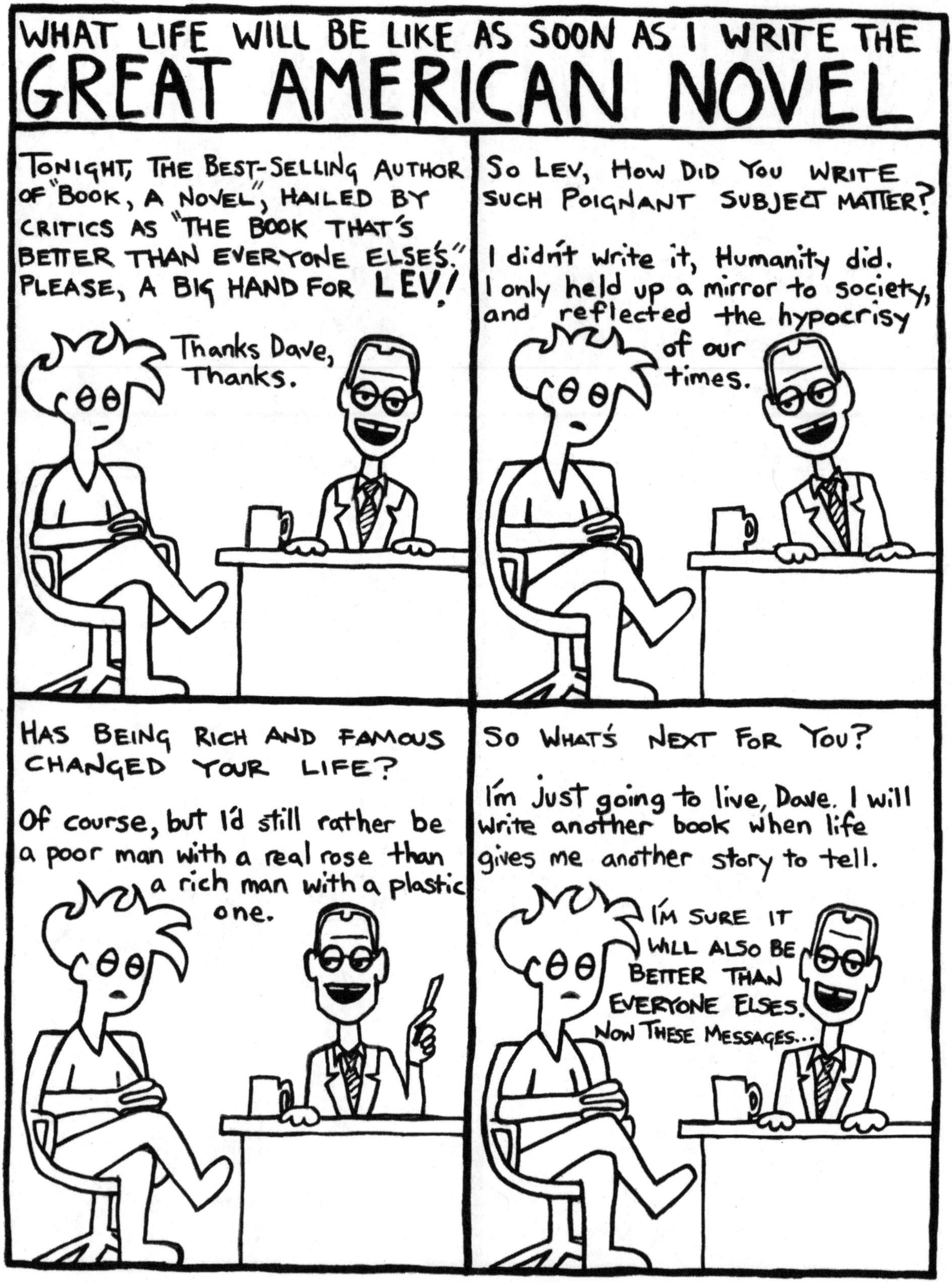
WHAT LIFE WILL BE LIKE AS SOON AS I WRITE THE
GREAT AMERICAN NOVEL
TONIGHT, THE BEST-SELLING AUTHOR OF "BOOK, A NOVEL", HAILED BY CRITICS AS "THE BOOK THAT'S BETTER THAN EVERYONE ELSE'S." PLEASE, A BIG HAND FOR LEV!
Thanks Dave, Thanks.
SO LEV, HOW DID YOU WRITE SUCH POIGNANT SUBJECT MATTER?
I didn't write it, Humanity did. I only held up a mirror to society, and reflected the hypocrisy of our times.
HAS BEING RICH AND FAMOUS CHANGED YOUR LIFE?
Of course, but I'd still rather be a poor man with a real rose than a rich man with a plastic one.
SO WHAT'S NEXT FOR YOU?
I'm just going to live, Dave. I will write another book when life gives me another story to tell.
I'M SURE IT WILL ALSO BE BETTER THAN EVERYONE ELSES. NOW THESE MESSAGES...

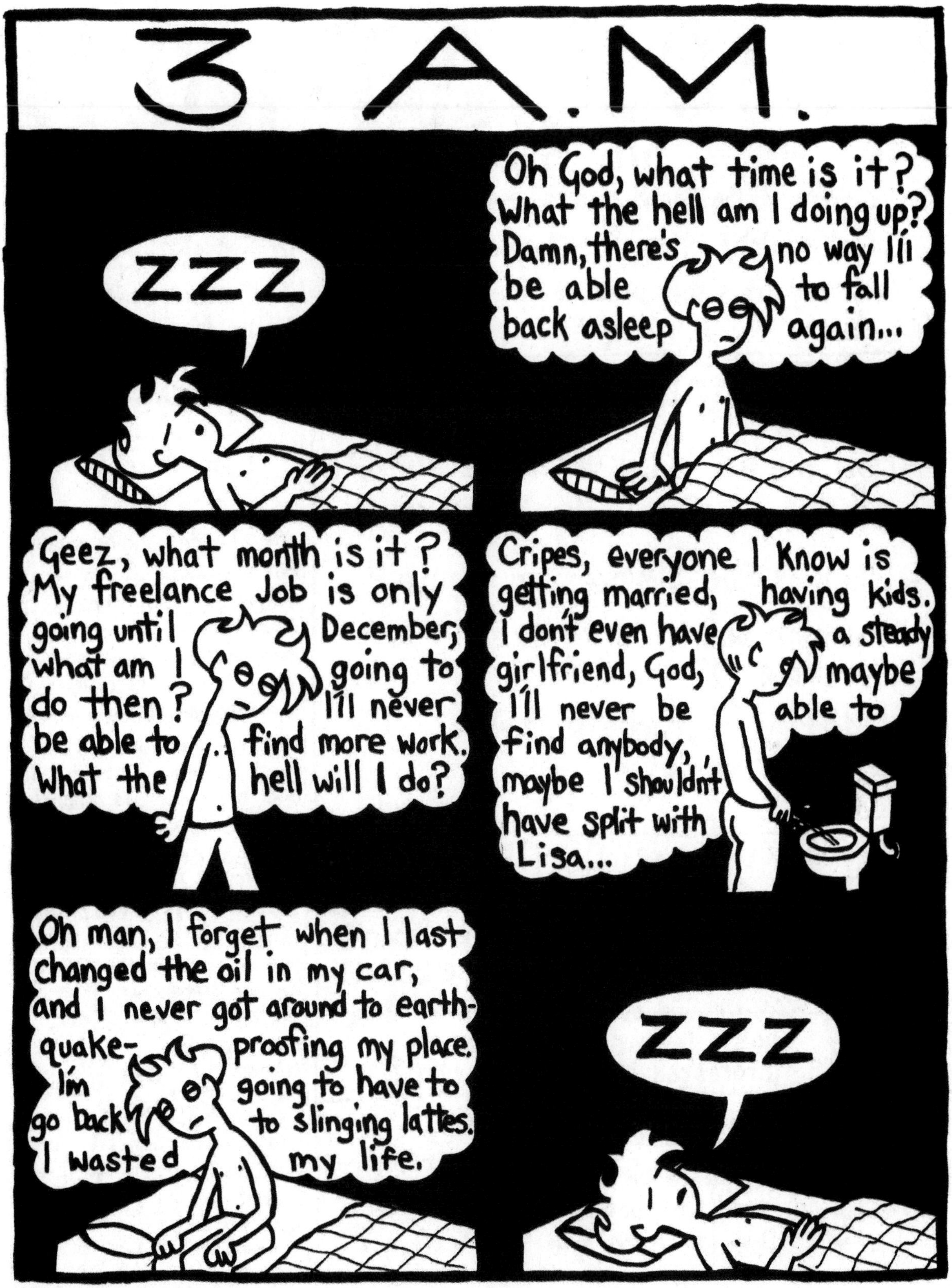
3 A.M.
ZZZ
Oh God, what time is it? What the hell am I doing up? Damn, there's no way I'll be able to fall back asleep again...
Geez, what month is it? My freelance Job is only going until December, what am I going to do then? I'll never be able to find more work. What the hell will I do?
Cripes, everyone I Know is getting married, having kids. I don't even have a steady girlfriend, God, maybe I'll never be able to find anybody, maybe I shouldn't have split with Lisa...
Oh man, I forget when I last changed the oil in my car, and I never got around to earth-quake-proofing my place. I'm going to have to go back to slinging lattes. I wasted my life.
ZZZ

ISOLATION

SO HOW DID YOU GET ISOLATED?

- ☐ Girlfriend/Boyfriend dumped me.
- ☐ Lost my Job/working from home.
- ☐ Nobody likes me because I'm depressed all the time.
- ☐ Got a bag of primo weed.
- ☐ Decided to forsake Deity.
- ☐ Nobody likes me because I'm happy all the time.

BURNING ISOLATION QUESTIONS:

- How the hell did it get to be 1 P.M.?
- Did I Just eat all those crackers?
- When is the Simpsons on again?
- I wonder which of my exes was the love of my life?
- Didn't I masturbate twice already today?

MAYBE YOU SHOULD CALL HOME...

MOM WILL SAY... - "Make sure you get plenty of fiber."
- "Maybe you should take a class."
- "You should call Mrs. Gleason's son, he's a lawyer. Weren't you once interested in being a lawyer?"

DAD WILL SAY... - "Keep your chin up."
(within a week however, he will send you books by Bill Gates, Donald Trump and Sam Walton)

PREDOMINANT ISOLATION THOUGHTS...

There's no one here but me. There's no one here but me me me.

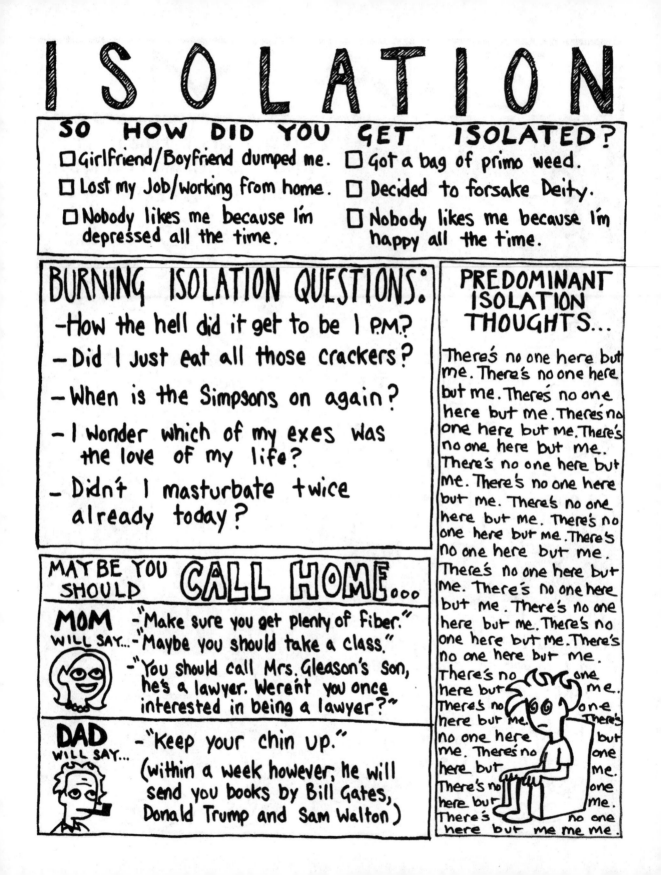

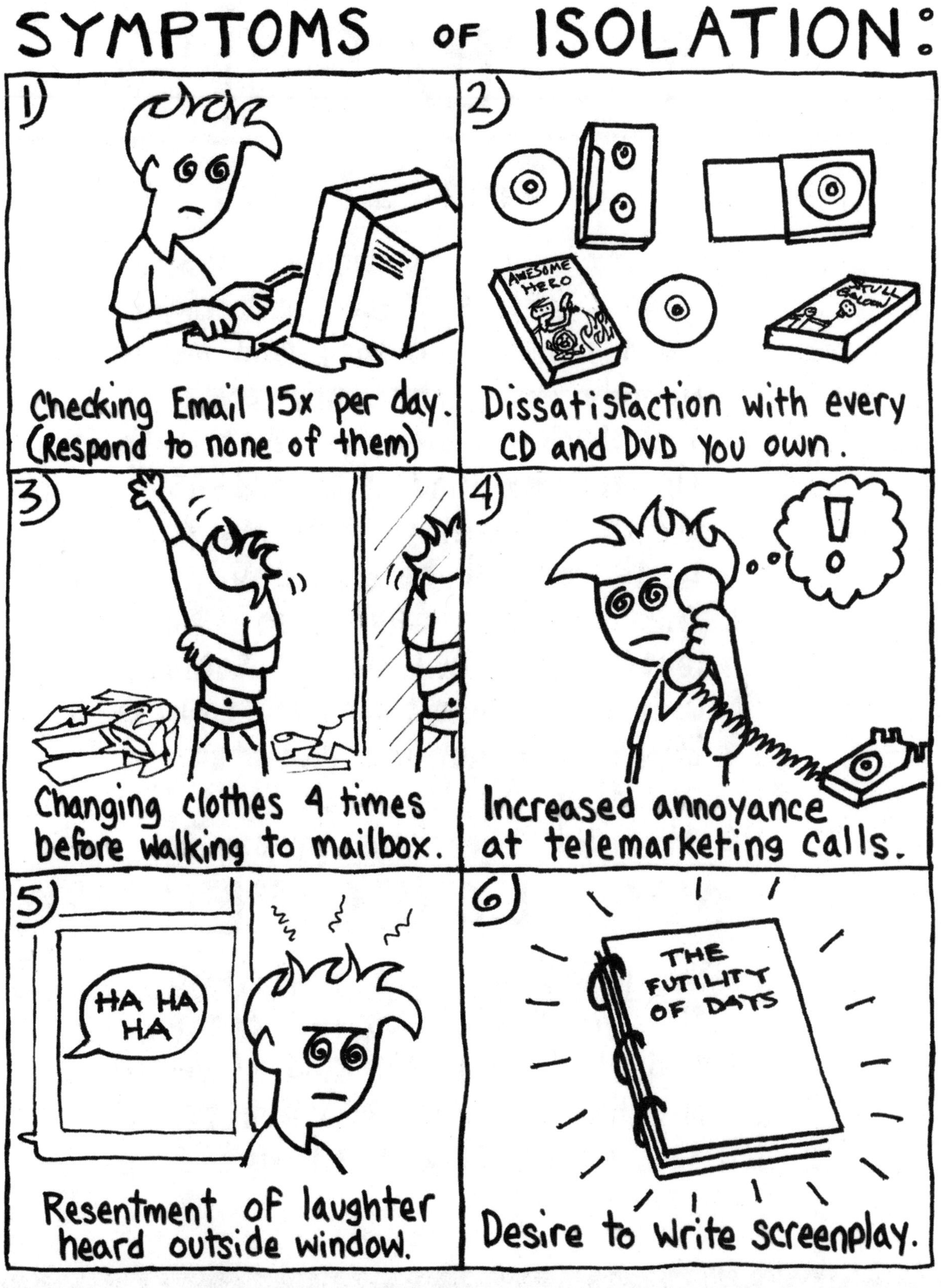
SYMPTOMS OF ISOLATION:
1)
Checking Email 15x per day. (Respond to none of them)
2)
AWESOME HERO
SKULL SALOON
Dissatisfaction with every CD and DVD you own.
3)
Changing clothes 4 times before walking to mailbox.
4)
!
Increased annoyance at telemarketing calls.
5)
HA HA HA
Resentment of laughter heard outside window.
6)
THE FUTILITY OF DAYS
Desire to write screenplay.

29 REASONS

MY CAREER:

1. I don't want to brown-nose.
2. I saw "Office Space" last night.
3. I'd try harder if they paid me more.
4. Nobody would notice anyway.
5. If I slack off and get away with it, I'll feel like kind of a bad-ass.
6. My shirt doesn't go with my pants, so I'm not all here today.
7. This job fuels Capitalism, which causes great evil in our society.
8. Don't want to outshine my coworkers.
9. Effort may get me promoted, and then I'd be stuck here.
10. How did I get here anyway?

MY LOVELIFE:

1. She probably has a boyfriend.
2. She probably thinks I'm creepy.
3. I don't know what kind of person she likes, I won't know how to act.
4. I'll just screw it all up.

NOT TO EXPEND ANY EFFORT TODAY

5. I'll talk to her some other time.

6. I may smell bad.

7. Even if she doesn't hate me, her friends probably will.

8. I may move to Europe anyway.

9. I can't strike out if I don't go up and talk to her, right?

10. Someone laughed at me in the 9th grade.

MY CREATIVE ENDEAVORS

1) I don't have a good enough idea.

2. I don't have enough time.

3. I'm not hungry, but I could eat another bowl of Cheerios.

4. I'll work on it later.

5. I'll work on it tomorrow.

6. I'll work on it as soon as I finish reading the Mötley Crüe book.

7. I'm not sure I really, totally, 100\% feel like it.

8. My idea won't save the world, so I'll wait until I get an idea that will.

9. Fuck it.

EVEN MY THERAPIST

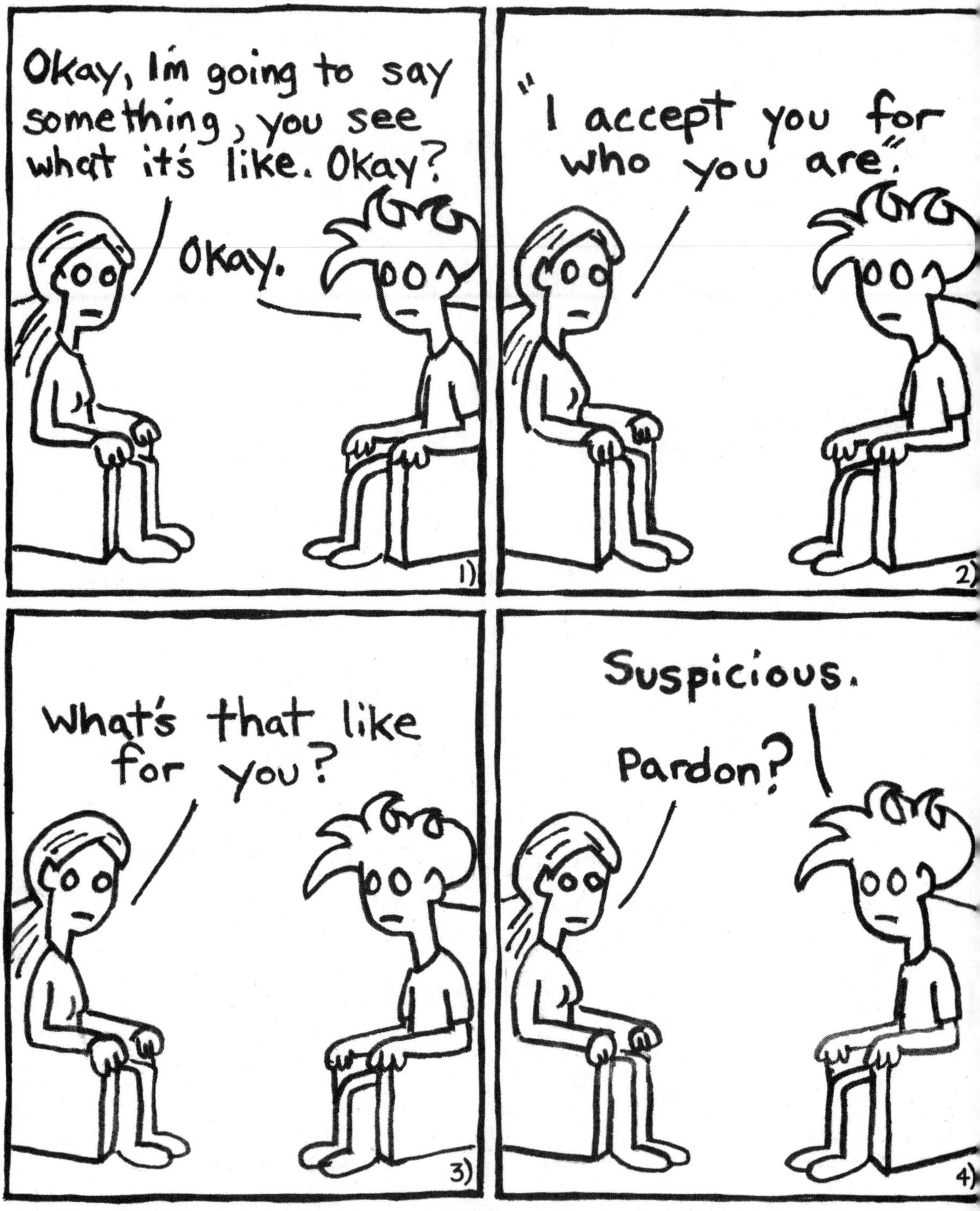
Okay, I'm going to say something, you see what it's like. Okay?
Okay.
"I accept you for who you are."
What's that like for you?
Suspicious.
Pardon?

THINKS I'M A PAIN IN THE ASS

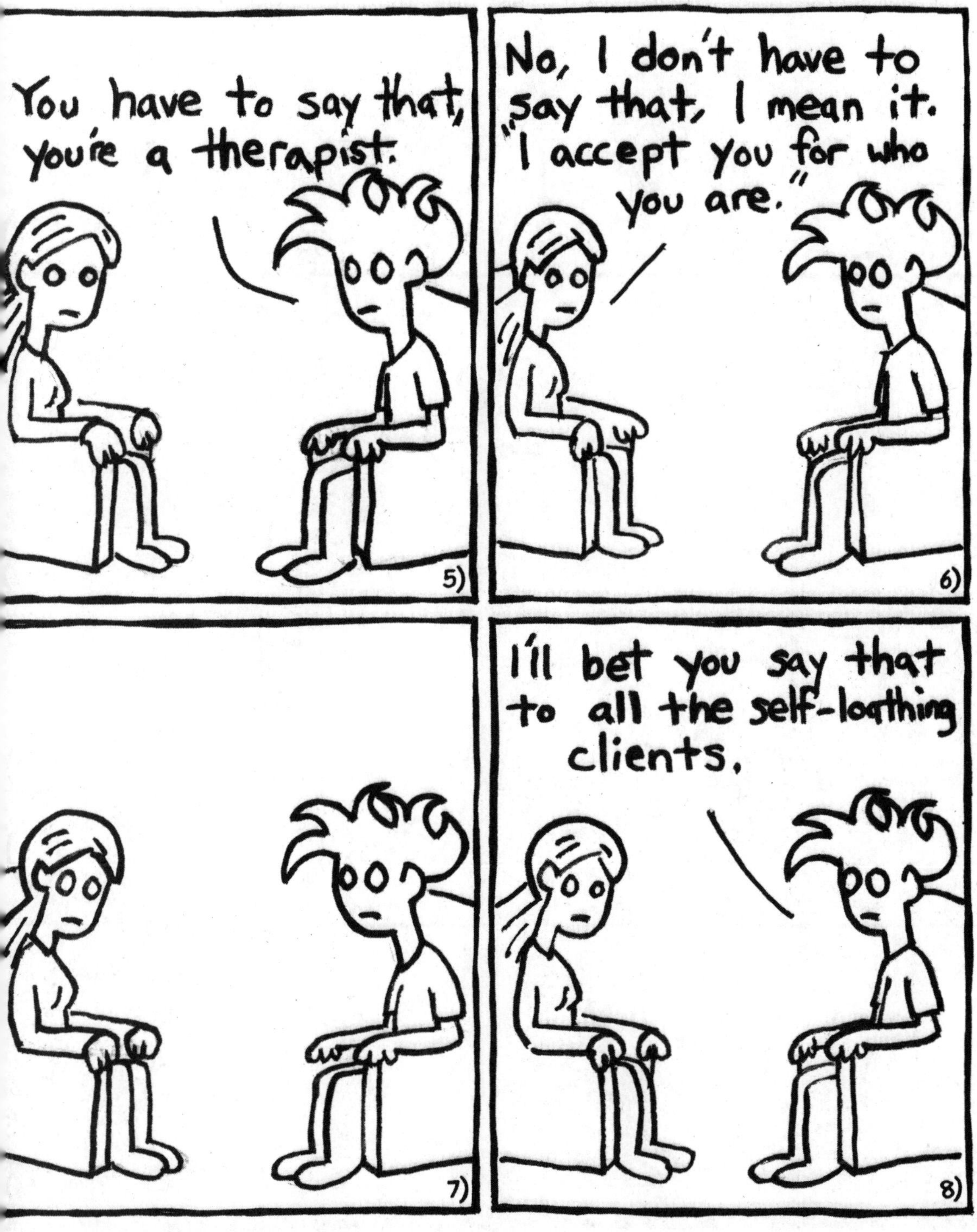
You have to say that, you're a therapist.
No, I don't have to say that, I mean it. "I accept you for who you are."
I'll bet you say that to all the self-loathing clients.
5)
6)
7)
8)

PARTY ANIMAL

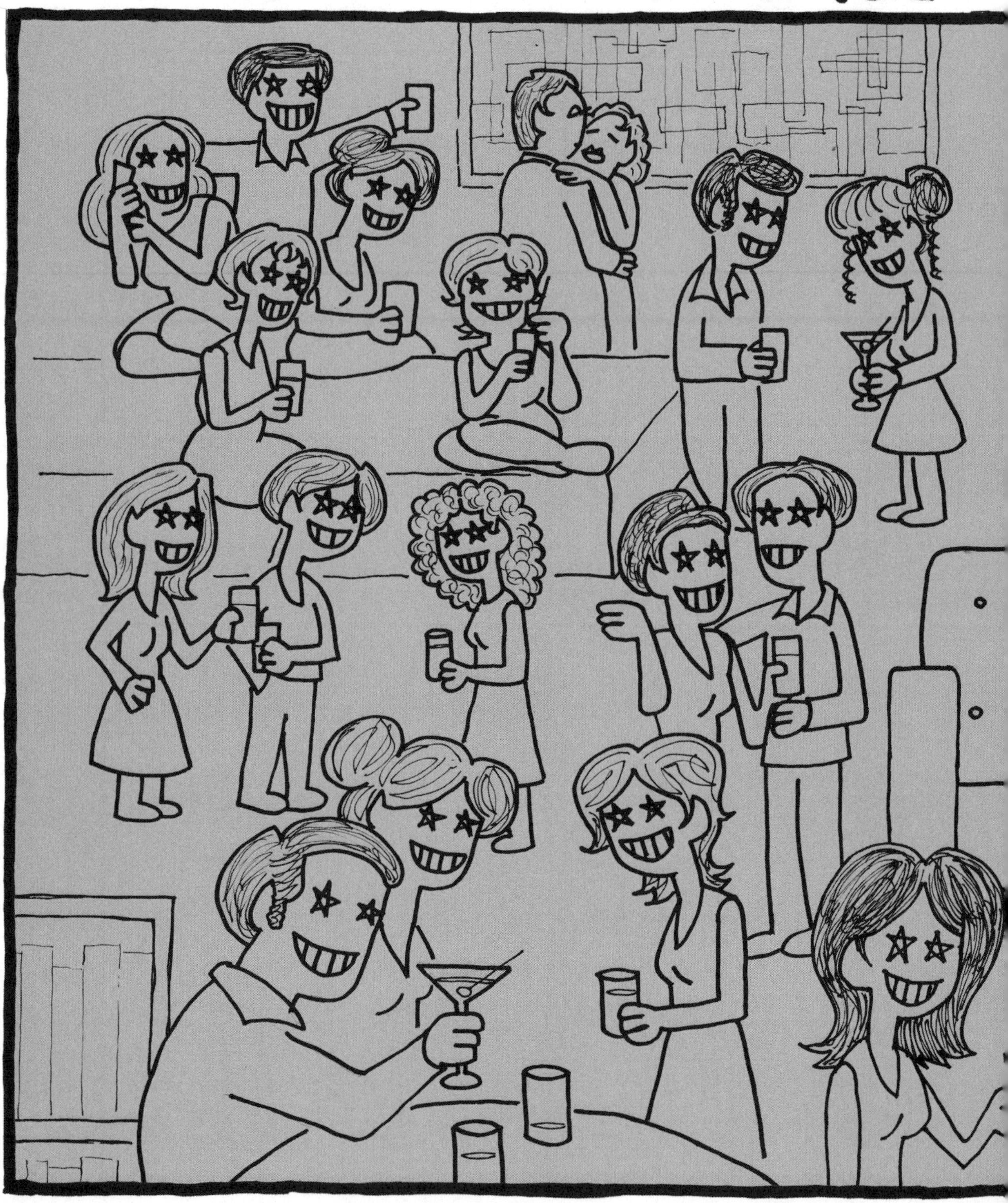

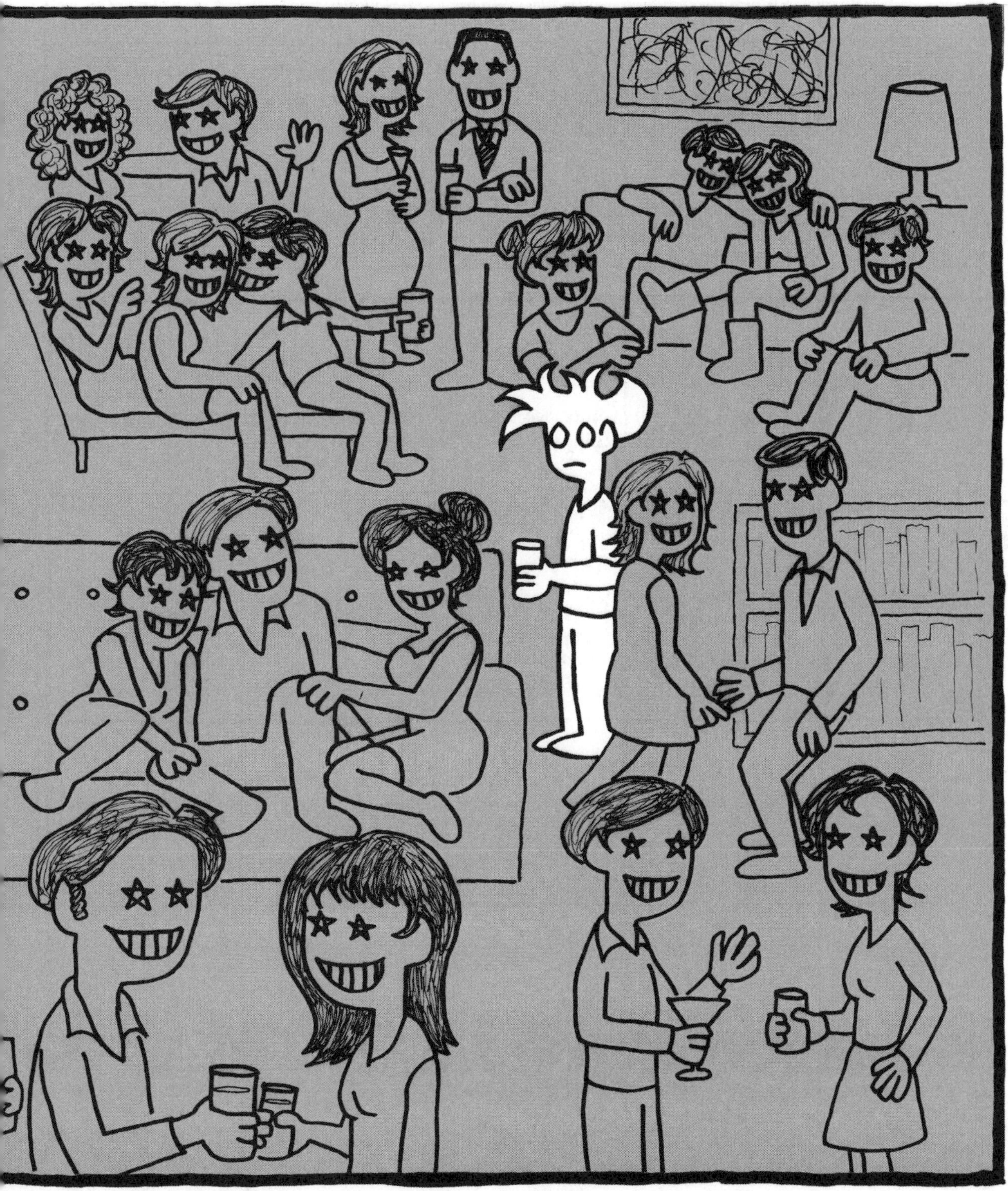

4 STAGES OF MALE INEBRIATION

	1-2 DRINKS	3-4 DRINKS	5-6 DRINKS	7-8 DRINKS
BODY LANGUAGE 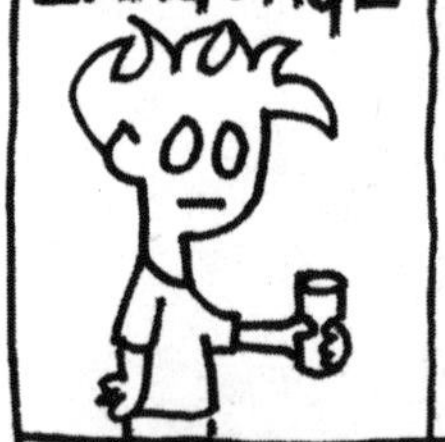	"I am going to walk around the bar smiling to show that I am the friendly, Jovial type."	"I am going to slouch against this wall here to show that I am the dark $ mysterious type."	"I am going to sit alone at the bar and write in my notebook to show that I'm the Great American Author type."	"...gonna put my hand under my chin to hold my goddamn head up... yeah..."
CONVERSATION TOPICS 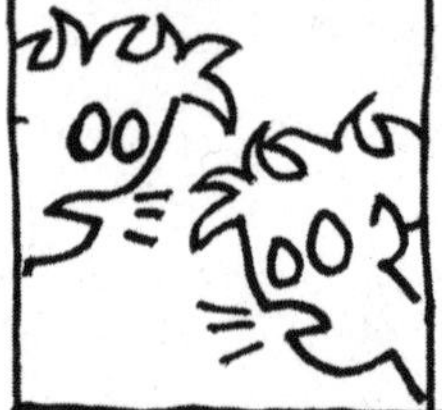	"Hi, what's your name? Where do you live? What do you do?"	"Where did you go to school? Do you like your Job? What was your name again?"	"Where did you grow up? Do your folks still live there? Your name slipped my mind, what was it?"	"Uhhh... don' go away... I'll be right back Dina... no... Amy... umm... What was your name again?"
PICK-UP METHODS 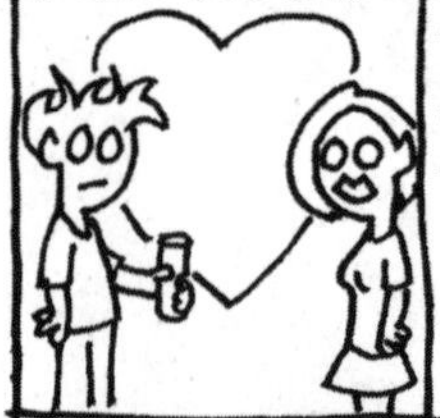	-INDIRECT- "I'm not trying to pick you up or anything, I Just thought you looked really interesting..."	-BRAGGART- "I went to the same high school as the Bass player of 'The Extreme'. Oh... you never heard of them? Oh. Never mind."	-COMPLIMENTS- "Hey, you know if you were a Prostitute, you'd be worth at least 300 bucks."	-MODESTY- "Mmph... I'm no good,... I'm a worthless piece of crap... you really wanna talk to me..., nah, you don't..."
NIGGLING THOUGHTS 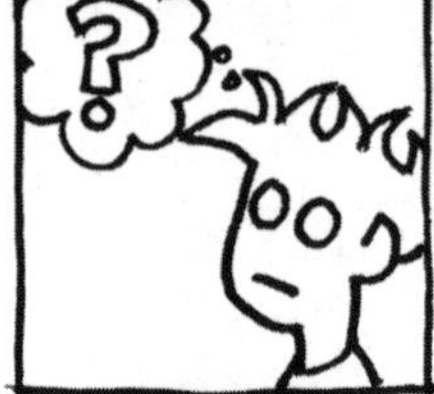	"Does my hair look okay? Does my shirt look okay?"	"I wonder why everyone else is having a better time than I am..."	"There's not enough honesty in the world, it's my duty to tell people if I think they're stupid..."	I hate everybody. I hate everybody. I hate everybody. I hate everybody. I hate everybody. I hate everybody. Nobody likes me.
VENT AGRESSION VIA... 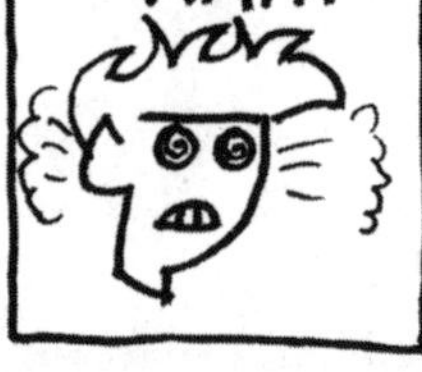	Chew on cocktail straws	Tear up bar napkins	Throw wet toilet paper on ceiling of bathroom.	Kick over newspaper boxes and curse self on way home.

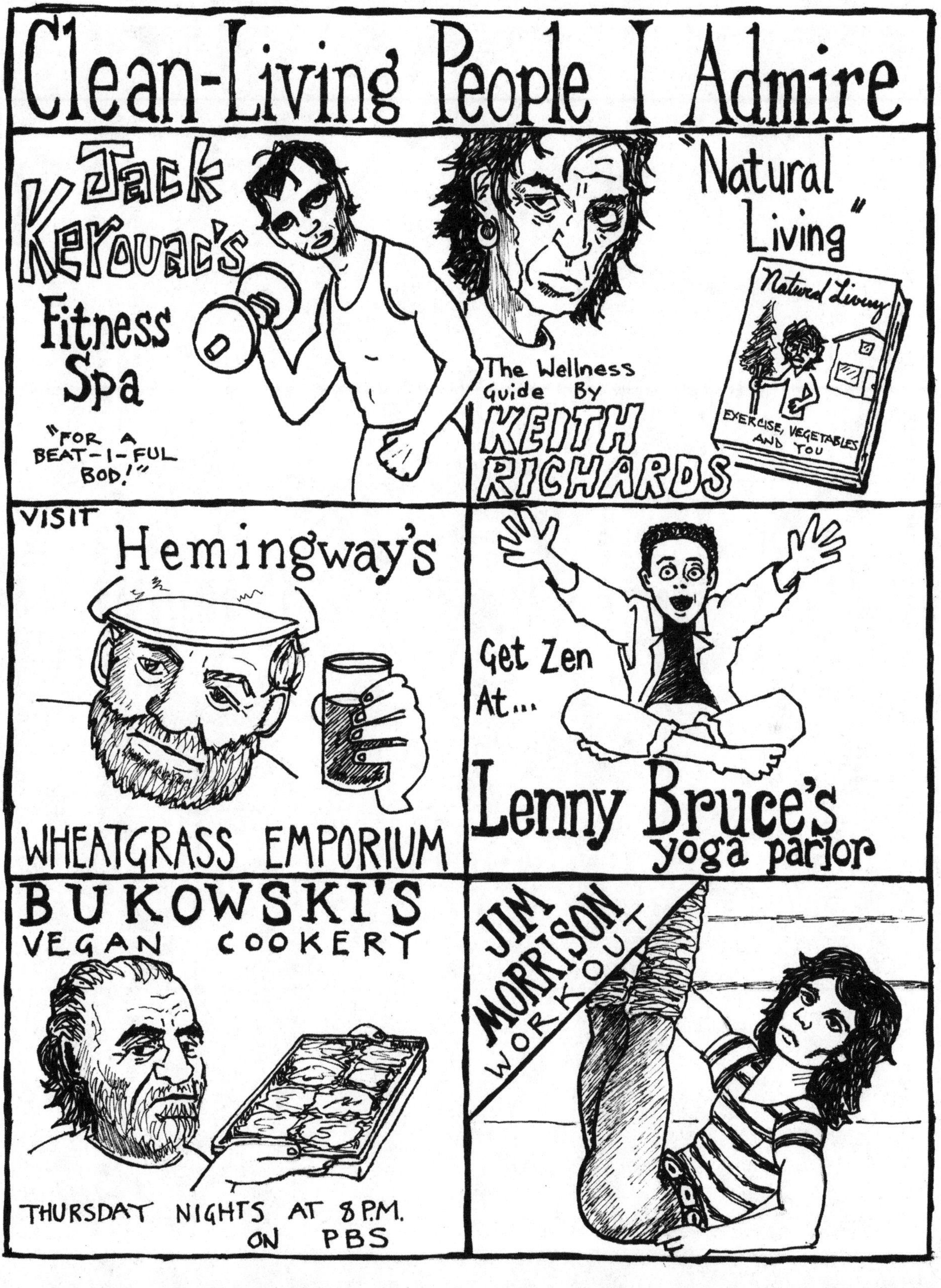
Clean-Living People I Admire
Jack Kerouac's
Fitness Spa
"For a beat-i-ful bod!"
"Natural Living"
Natural Living
Exercise, Vegetables and You
The Wellness Guide By
KEITH RICHARDS
VISIT
Hemingway's
WHEATGRASS EMPORIUM
Get Zen At...
Lenny Bruce's
yoga parlor
BUKOWSKI'S
VEGAN COOKERY
THURSDAY NIGHTS AT 8 P.M.
ON PBS
JIM MORRISON
WORKOUT

HOW TO COPE WITH DEPRESSION

(some advice I have gotten)

Tip #1 from MY CO-WORKER

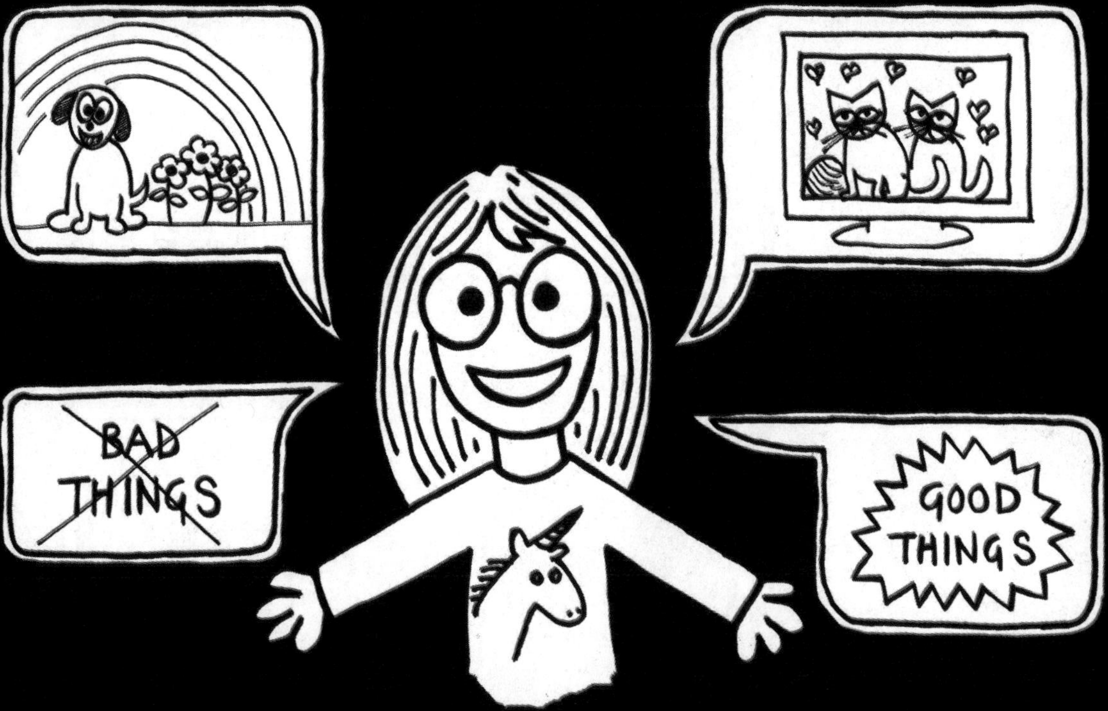
BAD THINGS
GOOD THINGS

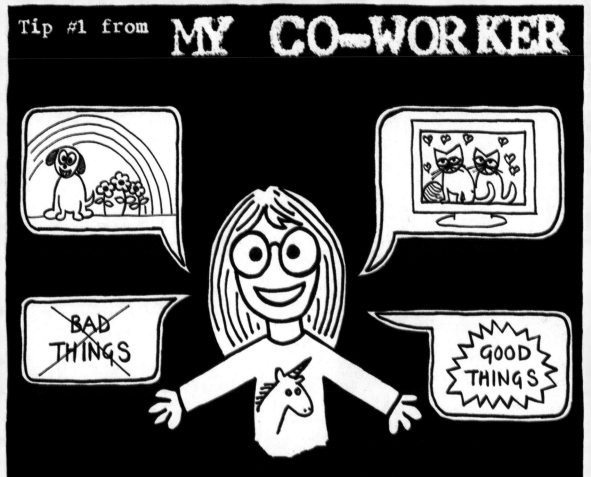

I don't remember how it came up, but one time I mentioned to a co-worker that I had been kind of bummed out, and her advice to me was that I shouldn't be sad, I should be happy. She said that I shouldn't think about bad things, but think about good things instead, and whenever she's sad, she thinks about flowers, rainbows and cute puppies and that tomorrow is going to be a sunny day. Then, for the next 2 months she forwarded me emails with pictures of kittens in them.

Tip #2 from MY PEERS

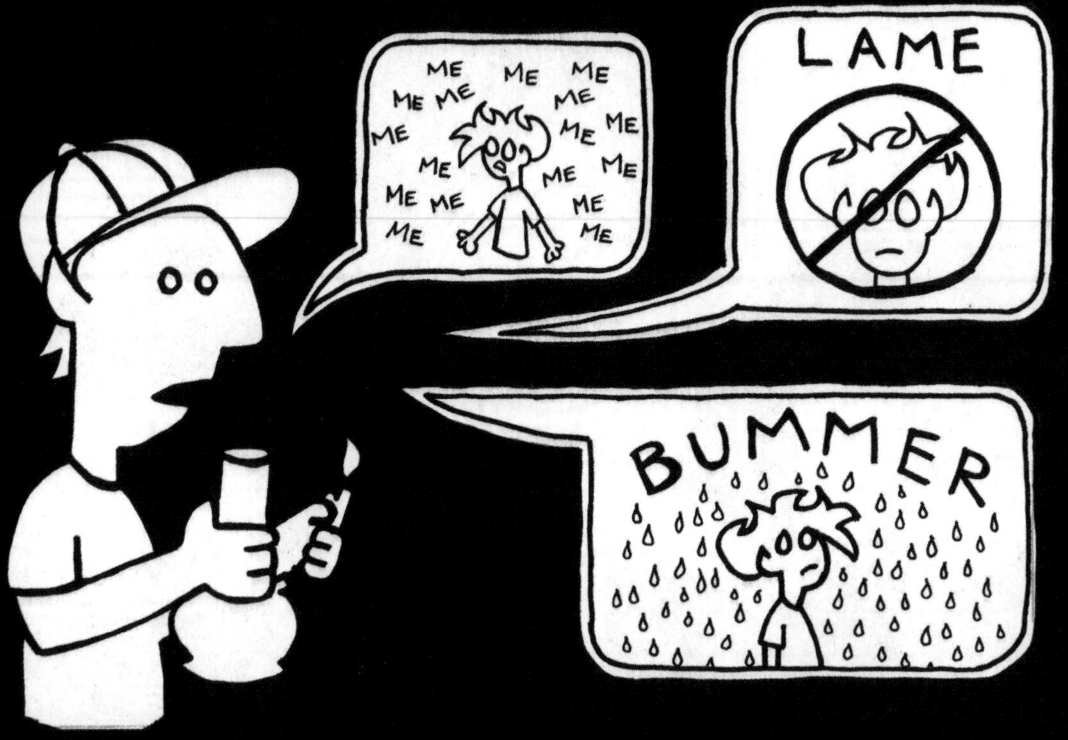
ME ME ME ME ME ME ME ME ME ME ME ME ME ME ME ME ME
LAME
BUMMER

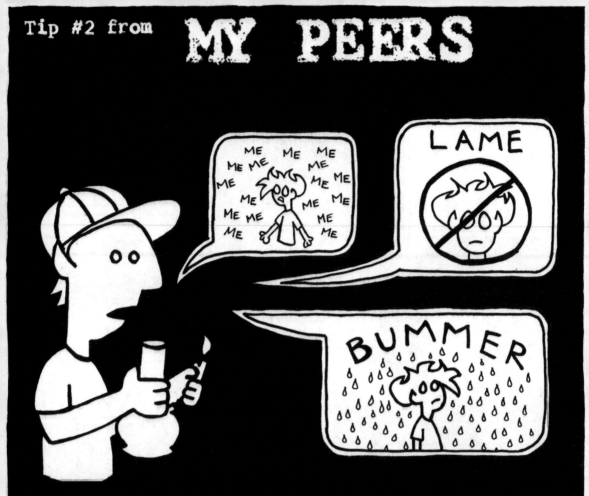

I also once said something similar to this guy I met at a party, and he told me that I had to just get over it, that I had to lighten up and get outside myself, and that talking to me was bringing him down. Then he said he didn't want me to be offended or anything but that I was really kind of a drag.

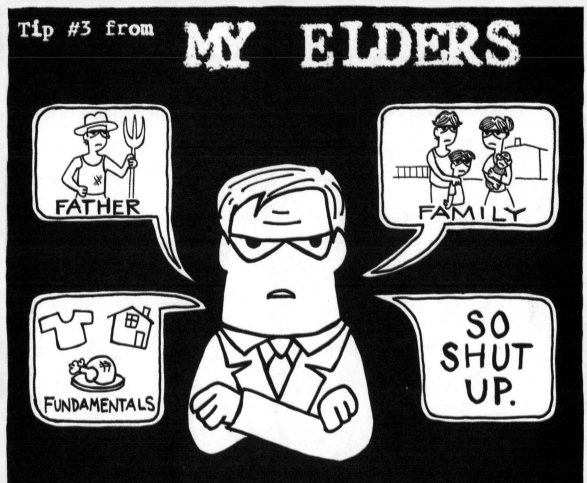

Tip #3 from **MY ELDERS**

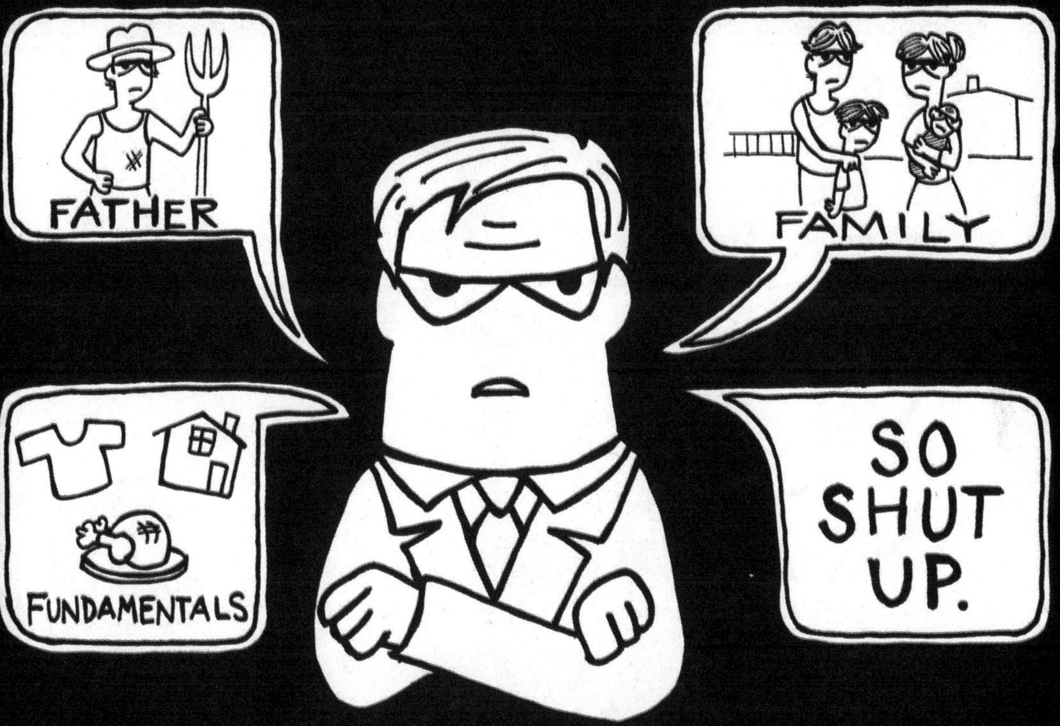
FATHER
FAMILY
FUNDAMENTALS
SO SHUT UP.

A teacher I had called me "Young Man", and said that I had no business being morose as I have clothes on my back, a roof over my head, and food on the table and that when he was a boy, his father worked three jobs and they were still struggling to get by, but he and his family were proud people and they had each other. Then he said that any troubles I think I have were insignificant in comparison, and so I should just buck up and stop talking nonsense.

Tip #4 from **MY FAMILY**

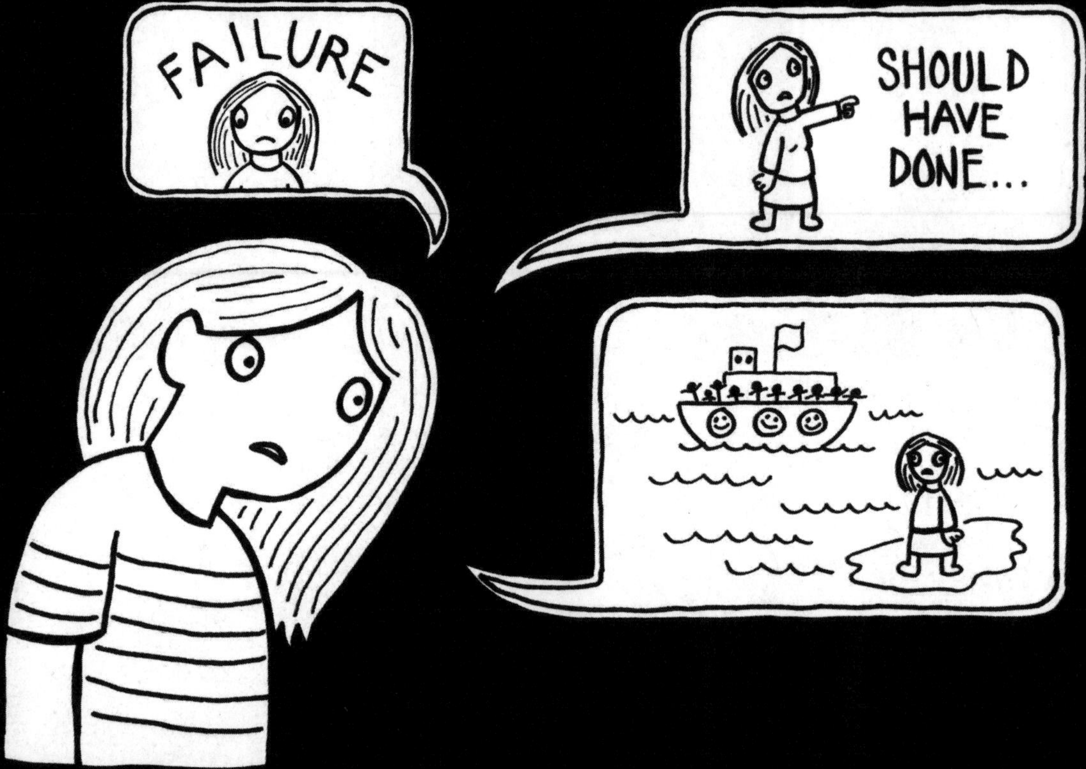
FAILURE
SHOULD HAVE DONE...

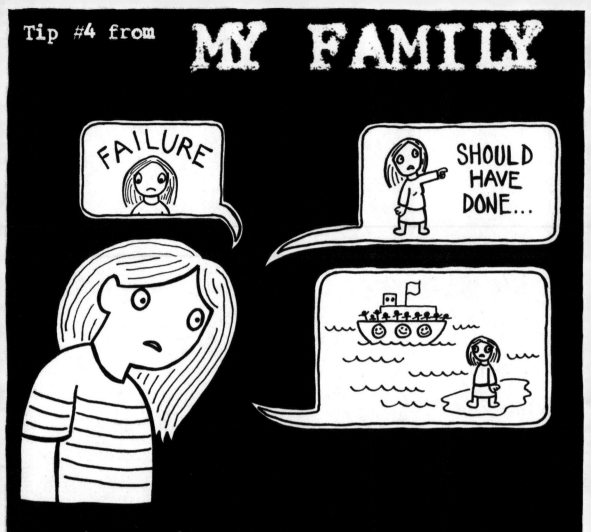

My sister said that she had been depressed too, and that she felt like she had wasted her life, and that she just thinks of all the things that she should have done, and now it's too late, and that her life feels meaningless, and that it was as if everyone else was on the happy boat that had left the shore and she was stranded on lonely island.

Tip #5 from

THIS GUY I KNEW IN HIGH SCHOOL

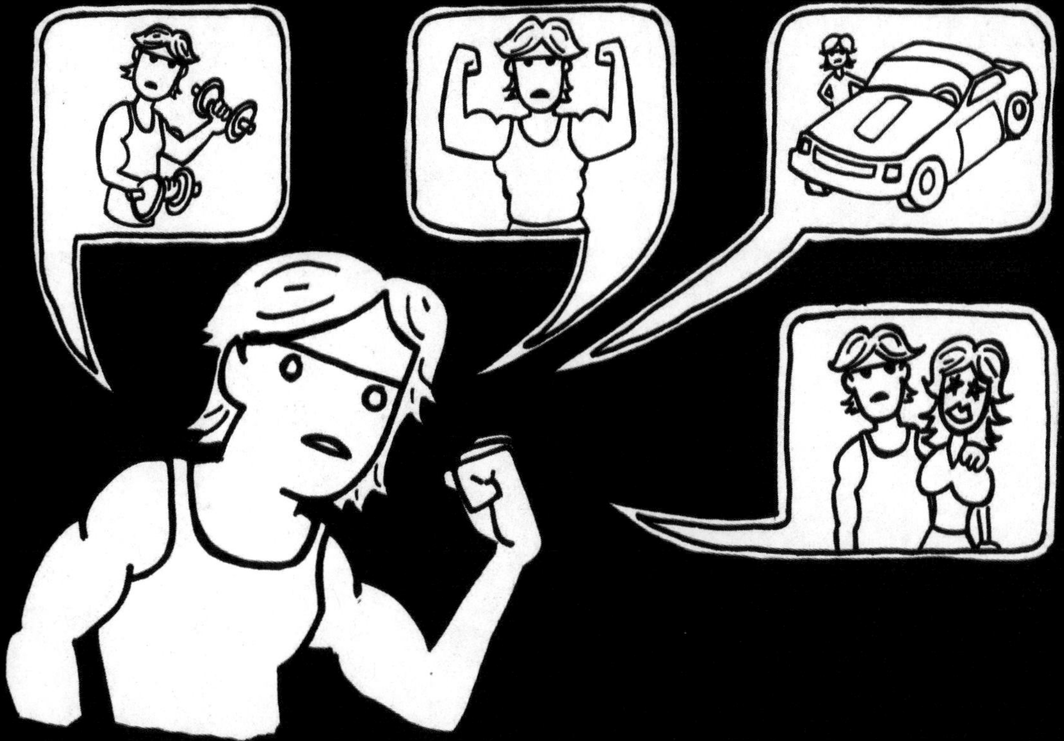

This guy I used to know in High School told me that if you're bummed, what you really had to do was lift weights, because if you lift weights, you get big, and then you can get a cool car, and then you can fuck chicks. He said that's what he did, that he used to be skinny, but then he started to lift weights, and after a few months, he was big. Then he got himself a Ford Mustang, and now he fucks chicks. Then he went over it again, he said that I should: A) Lift weights. B) Get big. C) Get a cool car. D) Fuck chicks. Then he said not to worry about it, that I was going to be all right.

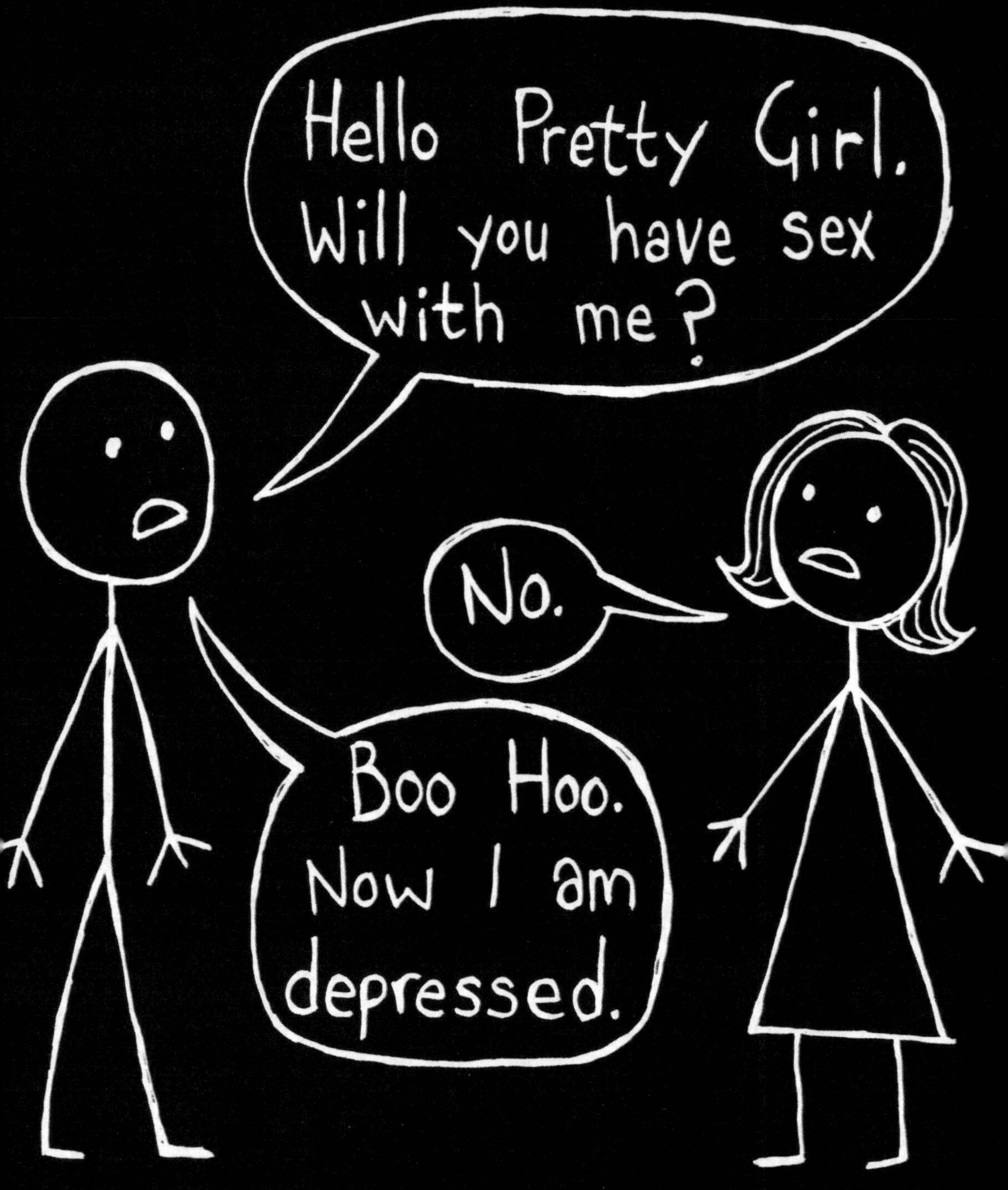
Hello Pretty Girl. Will you have sex with me?
No.
Boo Hoo. Now I am depressed.

CHAPTER 4:
I found love to be somewhat complicated.

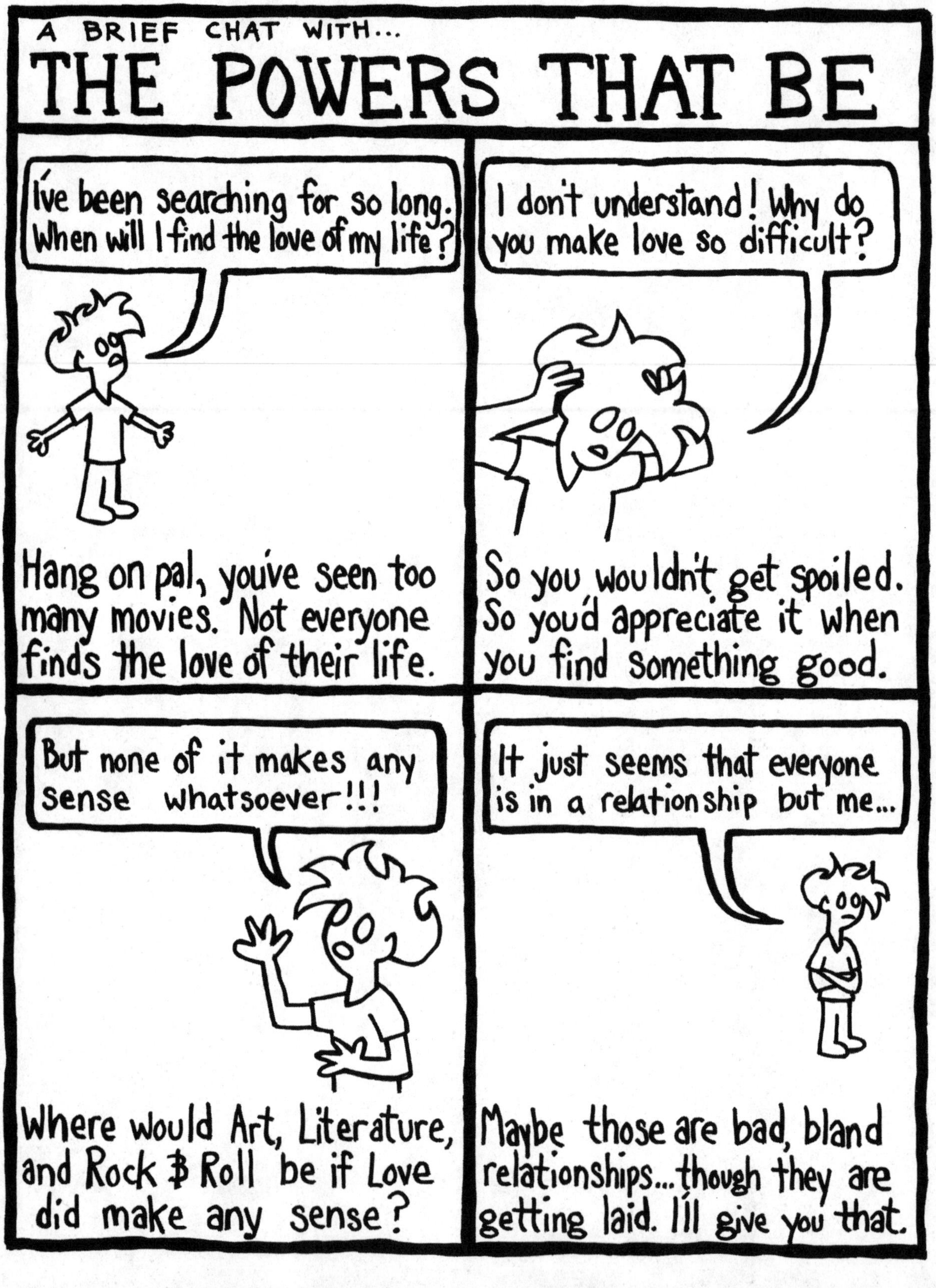
A BRIEF CHAT WITH...
THE POWERS THAT BE
I've been searching for so long. When will I find the love of my life?
Hang on pal, you've seen too many movies. Not everyone finds the love of their life.
I don't understand! Why do you make love so difficult?
So you wouldn't get spoiled. So you'd appreciate it when you find something good.
But none of it makes any sense whatsoever!!!
Where would Art, Literature, and Rock $ Roll be if Love did make any sense?
It just seems that everyone is in a relationship but me...
Maybe those are bad, bland relationships...though they are getting laid. I'll give you that.

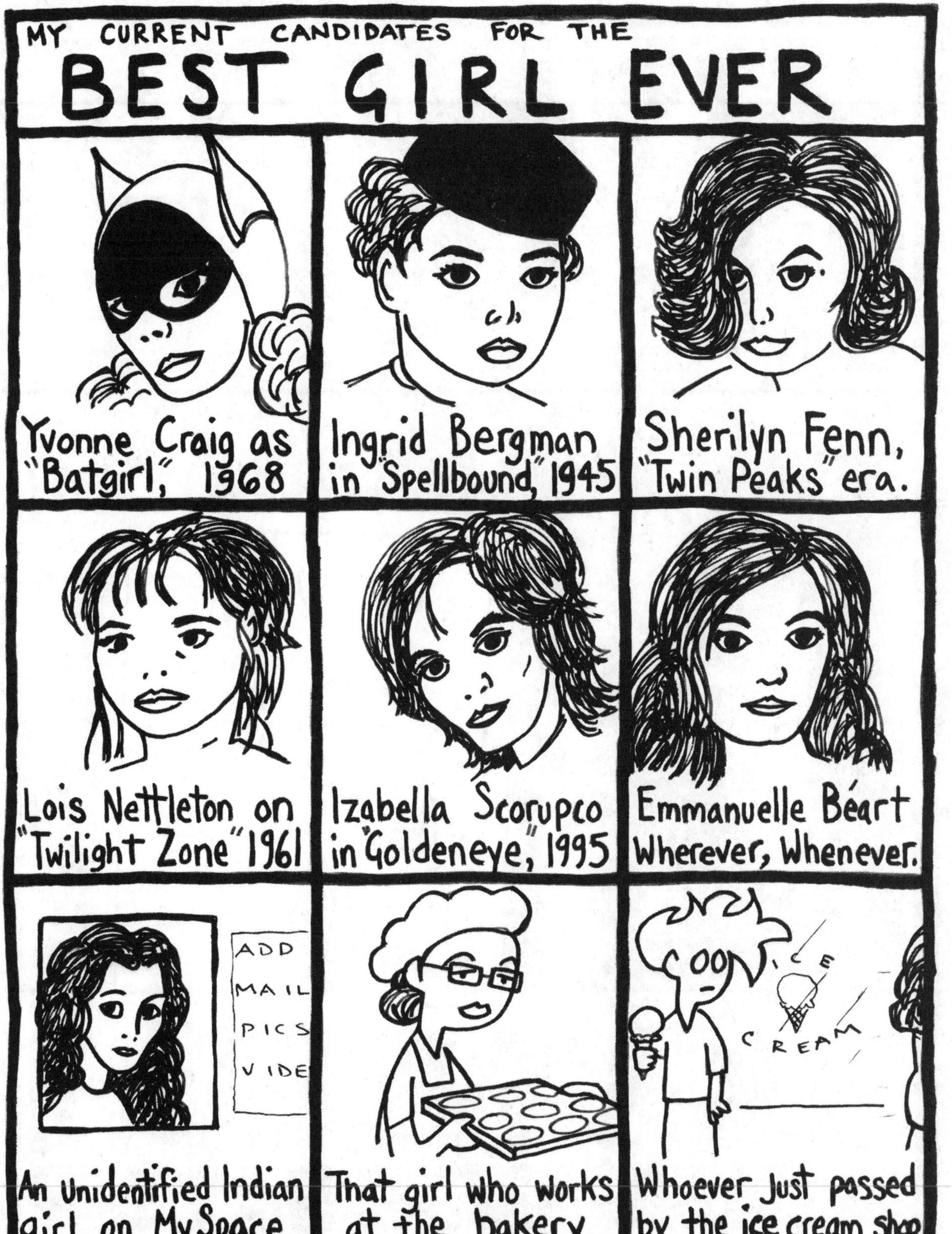

MY CURRENT CANDIDATES FOR THE
BEST GIRL EVER
Yvonne Craig as "Batgirl," 1968
Ingrid Bergman in "Spellbound," 1945
Sherilyn Fenn, "Twin Peaks" era.
Lois Nettleton on "Twilight Zone" 1961
Izabella Scorupco in "Goldeneye," 1995
Emmanuelle Béart Wherever, Whenever.
ADD
MAIL
PICS
VIDE
An unidentified Indian girl on MySpace
That girl who works at the bakery.
ICE CREAM
Whoever just passed by the ice cream shop.

MULTIPLE BOMB-OUT REPORT

A case by case study of erroneous and ineffective mating practices

SUBJECT:

NAME:

Lev

OCCUPATION:

Marginal

AESTHETIC STATUS:

Open to interpretation

NOTES:

Prone to Self-Loathing, Self-Analysis, Self-Examination, Self-Doubt, Self-Destruction, Self-Obsession.

CASE I

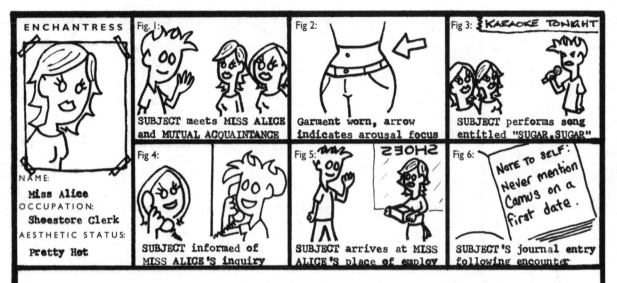

ENCHANTRESS

NAME:
Miss Alice
OCCUPATION:
Shoestore Clerk
AESTHETIC STATUS:
Pretty Hot

Fig. 1:
SUBJECT meets MISS ALICE and MUTUAL ACQUAINTANCE

Fig 2:
Garment worn, arrow indicates arousal focus

Fig 3: KARAOKE TONIGHT
SUBJECT performs song entitled "SUGAR, SUGAR"

Fig 4:
SUBJECT informed of MISS ALICE'S inquiry

Fig 5: SHOES
SUBJECT arrives at MISS ALICE'S place of employ

Fig 6:
NOTE TO SELF: Never mention Camus on a first date.
SUBJECT'S journal entry following encounter

APRIL 6, 9:03PM: SUBJECT first encountered MISS ALICE with MUTUAL ACQUAINTANCE during a self-described "Night On The Town" (fig 1). Upon this meeting, SUBJECT experienced feelings of want, stirred by the visual impact of her worn garments, which revealed her abdomen (fig 2). SUBJECT, MISS ALICE and MUTUAL ACQUAINTANCE gathered at a social club and consumed numerous intoxicating beverages and sang popular melodic compositions to a Japanese "Empty Orchestra" device (fig 3). SUBJECT and MISS ALICE proceeded to converse agreeably, and at the evening's conclusion, MISS ALICE inquired about the current romantic status of SUBJECT from MUTUAL ACQUAINTANCE.

APRIL 9, 11:58AM: MISS ALICE'S inquiry had been relayed to SUBJECT the night before (fig 4), and SUBJECT began a quest to augment his association with MISS ALICE into one of an amorous nature. SUBJECT visited MISS ALICE at her place of employ on her luncheon hour (fig 5), and suggested the two take a walk. Details of this encounter remain hazy, but it is suspected that due to the lack of intoxicants, SUBJECT was considerably less playful than at their first meeting and MISS ALICE's interest rapidly waned. MISS ALICE was quoted as saying "He was like, all serious and stuff. He totally creeped me out" (fig 6). Further advancements or associations between SUBJECT and MISS ALICE remain highly unlikely.

CASE 2

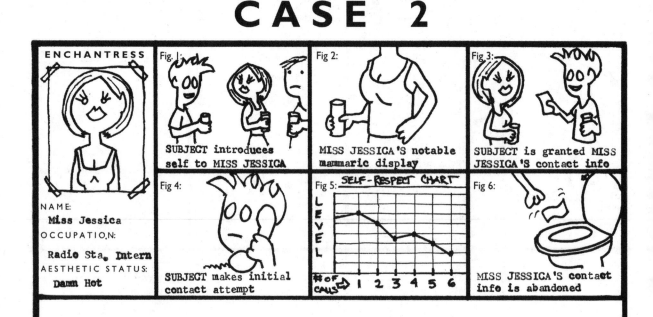

ENCHANTRESS

NAME:
Miss Jessica
OCCUPATION:
Radio Sta. Intern
AESTHETIC STATUS:
Damn Hot

Fig. 1: SUBJECT introduces self to MISS JESSICA

Fig 2: MISS JESSICA'S notable mammaric display

Fig 3: SUBJECT is granted MISS JESSICA'S contact info

Fig 4: SUBJECT makes initial contact attempt

Fig 5: SELF-RESPECT CHART — LEVEL / # OF CALLS ⟹ 1 2 3 4 5 6

Fig 6: MISS JESSICA'S contact info is abandoned

APRIL 24, 10:17PM: SUBJECT first approached MISS JESSICA at a large ceremonial gathering (fig 1). Although MISS JESSICA's bodily proportions differed significantly from MISS ALICE's, a similar appreciation in anatomic geometry was noted (fig 2). SUBJECT enjoyed a degree of success in laughter inducement from MISS JESSICA, with a rapid display of witty banter. Conversation continued for 24 minutes, and at 10:41PM SUBJECT requested and was granted MISS JESSICA's telephonic contact information (fig 3).

APRIL 27, 3:44PM: SUBJECT made attempt to contact MISS JESSICA, who did not answer. SUBJECT requested a return call on her automated message-recording device (fig 4).

APRIL 28, 1:32PM: MISS JESSICA had not yet responded, and over the next 3 days SUBJECT made several more efforts of contact. With each subsequent attempt, SUBJECT's disposition became markedly less glee oriented, documented in (fig 5).

MAY 1, 6:47PM: MISS JESSICA responded, and the two made plans to meet at 11:00AM the next morning.

MAY 2, 10:35AM: SUBJECT received message from MISS JESSICA cancelling the meeting. SUBJECT made attempt to return call and left message in turn. When no reply had been made from MISS JESSICA by 3:04PM, SUBJECT proceeded to dispose of MISS JESSICA's contact info in a ceramic waste transportal unit (fig 6).

CASE 3

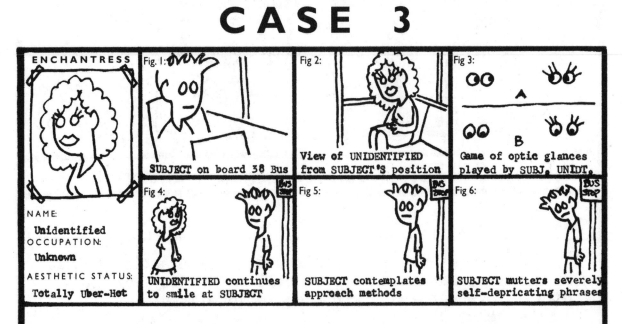

ENCHANTRESS

NAME:
Unidentified
OCCUPATION:
Unknown
AESTHETIC STATUS:
Totally Uber-Hot

Fig. 1: SUBJECT on board 38 Bus

Fig 2: View of UNIDENTIFIED from SUBJECT'S position

Fig 3: Game of optic glances played by SUBJ. UNIDT.

Fig 4: UNIDENTIFIED continues to smile at SUBJECT

Fig 5: SUBJECT contemplates approach methods

Fig 6: SUBJECT mutters severely self-depricating phrases

MAY 7, 3:10PM: Upon being relieved of his duties at his place of employ, SUBJECT boarded the 38 Geary bus and began the 25 minute ride to his domicile. Due to fatigue, SUBJECT's cerebral impulses were unfocused on any singular topic of contemplation or foment (fig 1). 10 minutes into the journey, SUBJECT chose to review his fellow bus passengers and became fixated upon UNIDENTI-FIED, who occupied a seat by the bus door (fig 2). UNIDENTIFIED became aware of SUBJECT's attention, and the two began to exchange a series of playful glances (fig 3). This pattern continued unabated until the announcement of bus arrival to the 6th Avenue stop, when the two proceeded to exit the vessel.

3:28PM: UNIDENTIFIED began to journey North on Geary Blvd, turning the occasional glance behind her to view the whereabouts of SUBJECT (fig 4). SUBJECT however, stood dormant at the bus stop, debating effective introductory sentences and therefore did not immediately proceed with his pursuit (fig 5).

3:29PM: Upon conclusion that the commonplace phrase 'Hi, what's your name?" would perhaps suffice, UNIDENTIFIED had already traveled 2 blocks North on Geary and SUBJECT concluded that the appropriate timeframe for romantic action had more than likely expired (fig 6).

Upon review of the above case, Dr. N. Strauss of the National Bombout Analysis Council concluded: "Jesus, this guy can be kind of a pussy sometimes."

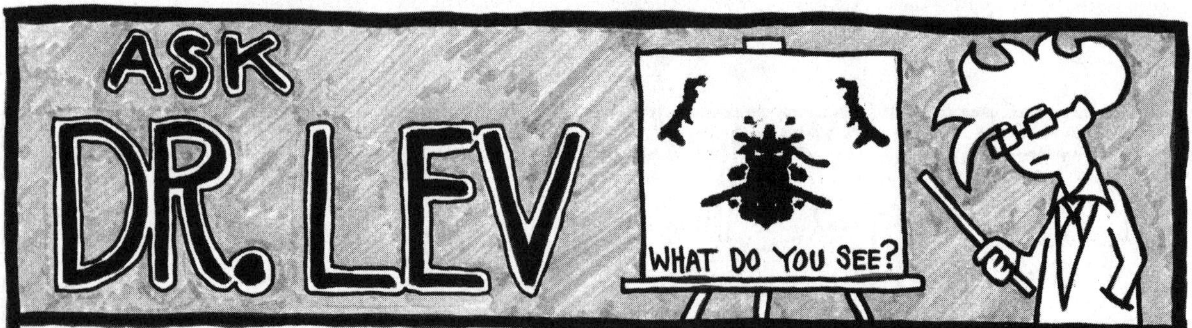
ASK
DR. LEV
WHAT DO YOU SEE?

"If you've got questions, he's got theories."

Dear Dr. Lev,

The girl I'm seeing says she needs space & wants to take things slow. She doesn't even call me her Boyfriend. I think I love her and I want her to love me. Can you help?

Sincerely,
Romeo Is Waiting

Dear Romeo Is Waiting,

Yeah sure, I can help. It would appear that you need to assert yourself more. Start by telling her you love her, maybe 25-30 times a day. Call her at work, send her text messages and emails, whatever methods at your disposal. When together, insist that she picks all the movies, restaurants and activities you attend. Compliments help too: Try taking a few days a week to follow her around wherever she goes and constantly tell her how beautiful and perfect she is.

Lastly, if she doesn't say the BF/GF labels, give her a T-shirt that says "I AM (your name here)'S GIRLFRIEND" in big red letters. Girls love that sort of thing.

-Dr. Lev

Dr. Lev

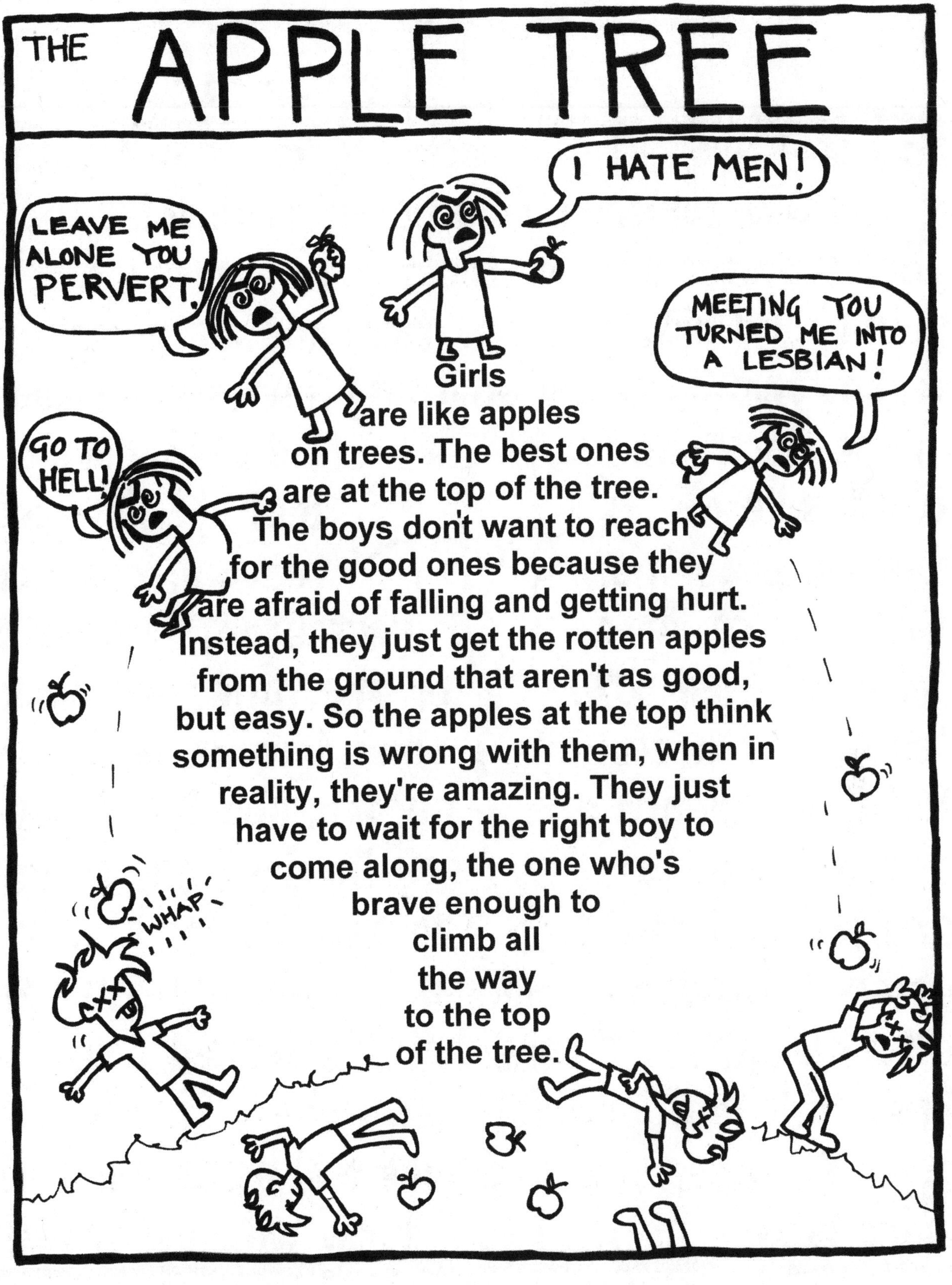
THE APPLE TREE
LEAVE ME ALONE YOU PERVERT!
I HATE MEN!
MEETING YOU TURNED ME INTO A LESBIAN!
GO TO HELL!
Girls
are like apples
on trees. The best ones
are at the top of the tree.
The boys don't want to reach
for the good ones because they
are afraid of falling and getting hurt.
Instead, they just get the rotten apples
from the ground that aren't as good,
but easy. So the apples at the top think
something is wrong with them, when in
reality, they're amazing. They just
have to wait for the right boy to
come along, the one who's
brave enough to
climb all
the way
to the top
of the tree.
WHAP

MY DA

So I saw this girl at a party the other night, and
if she was someone who hated small talk, and h
games, and maybe we could fall in love right the
public, and always smell good, and not complain
feeling that I can do anything, and say I'm good
in the world, and find it endearing i
and make me feel like I'm going
a moral opposition to veal, and not
when we're at a restaurant, and not s
coffee at least 50% of the time, and bonk
tell me I look cool when I drive, and neve
hanging out, and not talk about her ex-bo
sometimes, and say I'm dark and myster
and tell me I could be a model for a best s

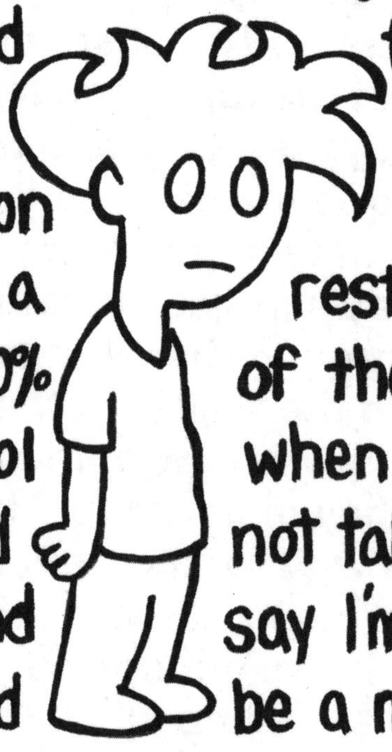

asion, and not get mad at me when I call her
attached, and not consider it a wasted day if w
knee-high leather boots somewhere in her clos
rules for poker, and make me feel better when I h
tried talking to her. I don't know why, but it was

RLING?

she was really cute, and so I started wondering
anging around in bars, and wasn't into playing
re, and maybe she would always hold my hand in
that I don't make much money, and give me the
looking, and make me feel like I'm the only guy
nstead of annoying that I like rotary telephones,
places, and not be a vegetarian but have
look around the room all the time
tay mad at me for too long, and make the
my brains out with great regularity, and
r answer her cell phone when we're
yfriends that often, and write me notes
ious even after she's known me a while,
elling dildo, and give me back rubs on occ-

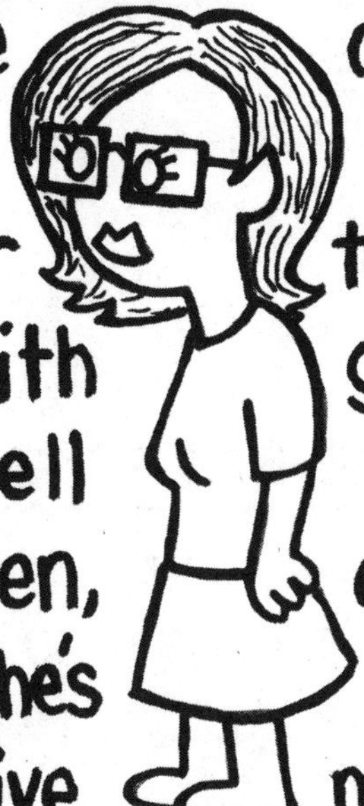

when I'm drunk, and not get scared off if I get
e don't get out of bed, and have a pair of those
et, and not get mad that I never remember the
ave a crappy day. Anyway, so then I went up and
awkward for some reason, so I just went home.

What would happen if I told the truth in...

MY PERSONALS AD

Hello! and welcome to internetdatez.com! The easy and fun way to connect with thousands of singles like yourself! Just create a profile by answering these questions, and you'll be on your way!

1. CHOOSE A PROFILE NAME:

"Morose Navelgazer"

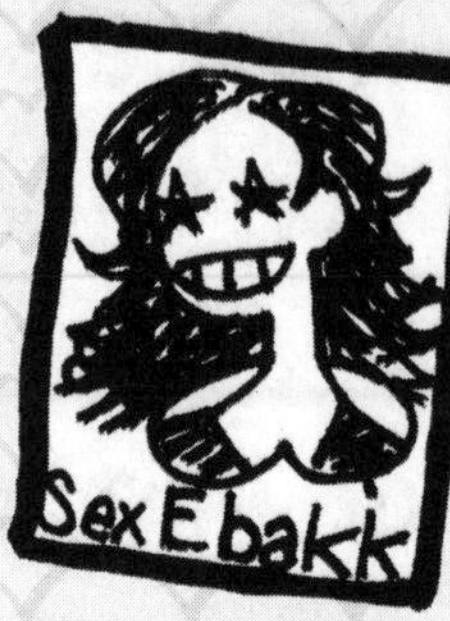
SexEbakk

2. YOUR AGE:

It depends who is asking.

3. WHY ARE YOU SIGNING UP AT INTERNETDATEZ.COM?

Call it a last resort.

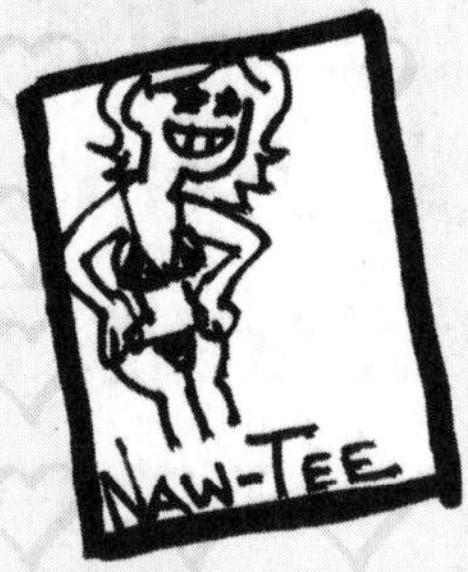
NAW-TEE

4. HOW DO YOU DESCRIBE YOURSELF?

Well evidently, I'm the sort of guy who resorts to personal ads: A lonely nerd that sucks at picking up girls.

5. IN MY BEDROOM YOU WILL FIND...

Empty wine bottles and a computer with 4GB of porn on the hard drive.

6. INCOME

You really don't want to know.

7. WHAT I'M LOOKING FOR IN A PERSON

I'd like to meet a girl with whom I have something in common, so someone who also hates everyone else on the planet.

8. HOBBIES?

I don't like hiking, biking, cooking or exploring, but if it increases my chances of getting laid, I'll say anything.

9. WHAT WOULD BE AN IDEAL FIRST DATE?

Going to a bar, scowling and cursing at everyone we see that's smiling and having a good time, and then going to my house to drink Vodka and listen to the Ramones.

10. CLOSING COMMENTS?

Are you the one, or rather, are you the one that will put up with me?

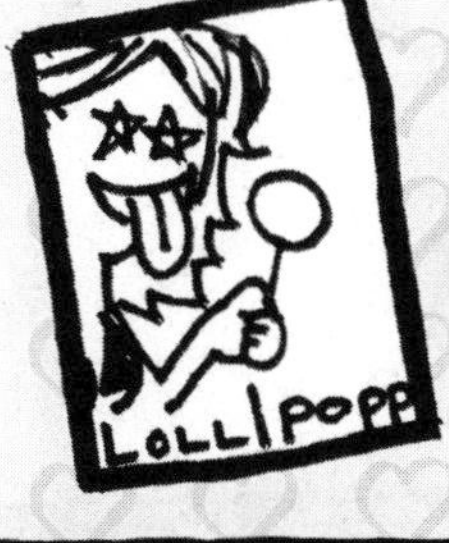
LOLLIPOPP

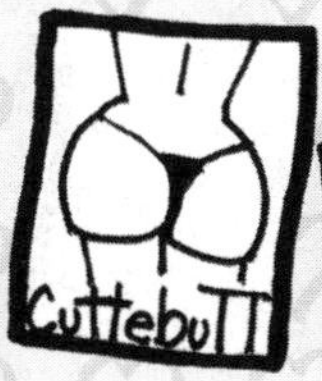
CutteBuTT

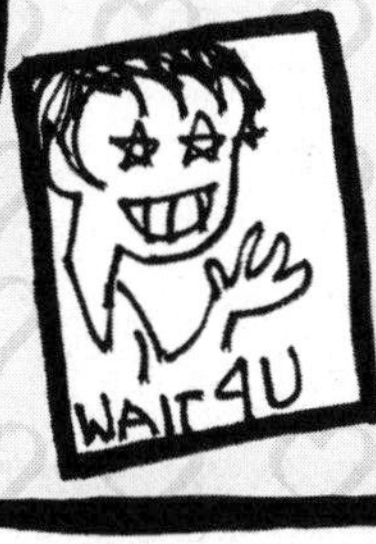
WAIT4U

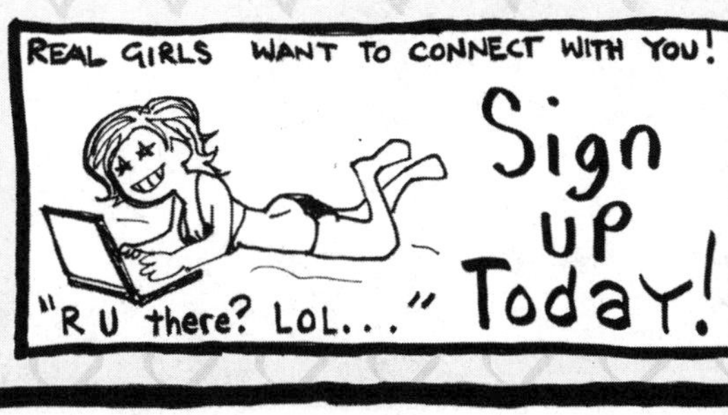
REAL GIRLS WANT TO CONNECT WITH YOU!
Sign up Today!
"R U there? LOL..."

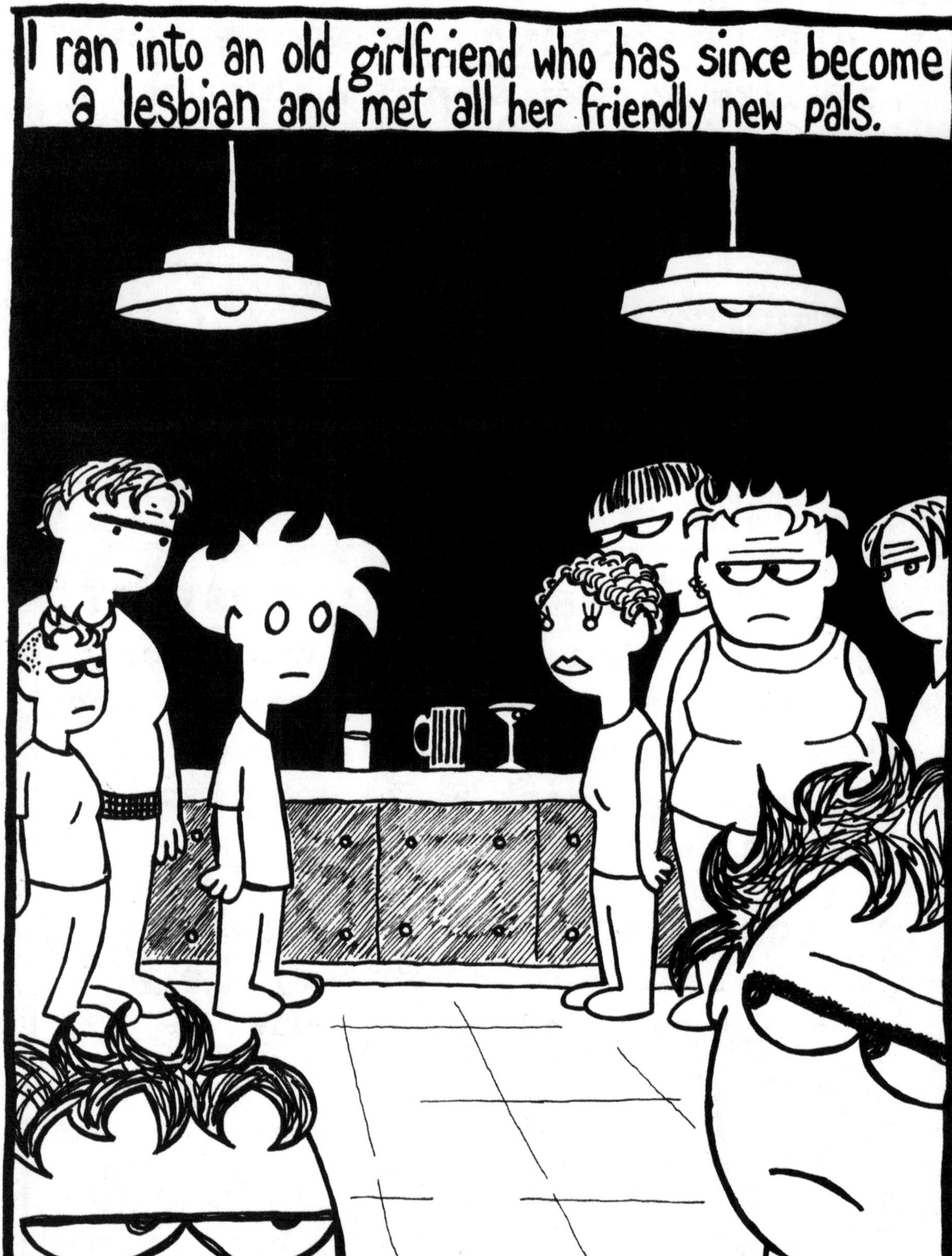
I ran into an old girlfriend who has since become a lesbian and met all her friendly new pals.

ASK DR. LEV

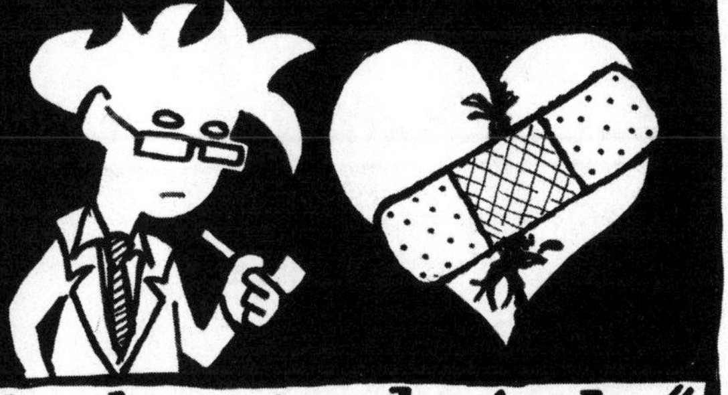

"Love advice for lovers who love too lovingly"

Dear Dr. Lev,

My girlfriend gets mad at me for almost everything I do. If I misplace the remote control, if I'm even five minutes late, if I wear shoes she doesn't like, she goes crazy. Even if I cook dinner for her she will complain that it's too hot or too cold. Nothing I do seems to be right. I love her very much and want it to work, but my self-esteem is getting badly damaged. What should I do?

Sincerely, Misery

Dear Misery,

Oh man, I HATE it when people lose the remote control. I hate it I hate it I hate it.

I think the problem here, is you're spending your time writing to me instead of getting a new pair of shoes, a new watch, and maybe learning how to use a thermometer. It is indeed an unhappy thing to feel like you're doing everything wrong, but this feeling will go away as soon as you stop doing everything wrong. Your self-esteem will repair itself in the process.

And for Christ's sake, leave the remote control on the coffee table.

Dr. Lev

Dr. Lev

U N T I

I am a horrible person of no virtue or worth.
1)
I could never get tired of talking to you.
2)
You're a lot smarter than you think you are.
3)
I feel safe with you.
4)
You have beautiful eyes.
5)
You mean the world to me.
6)

T L E D

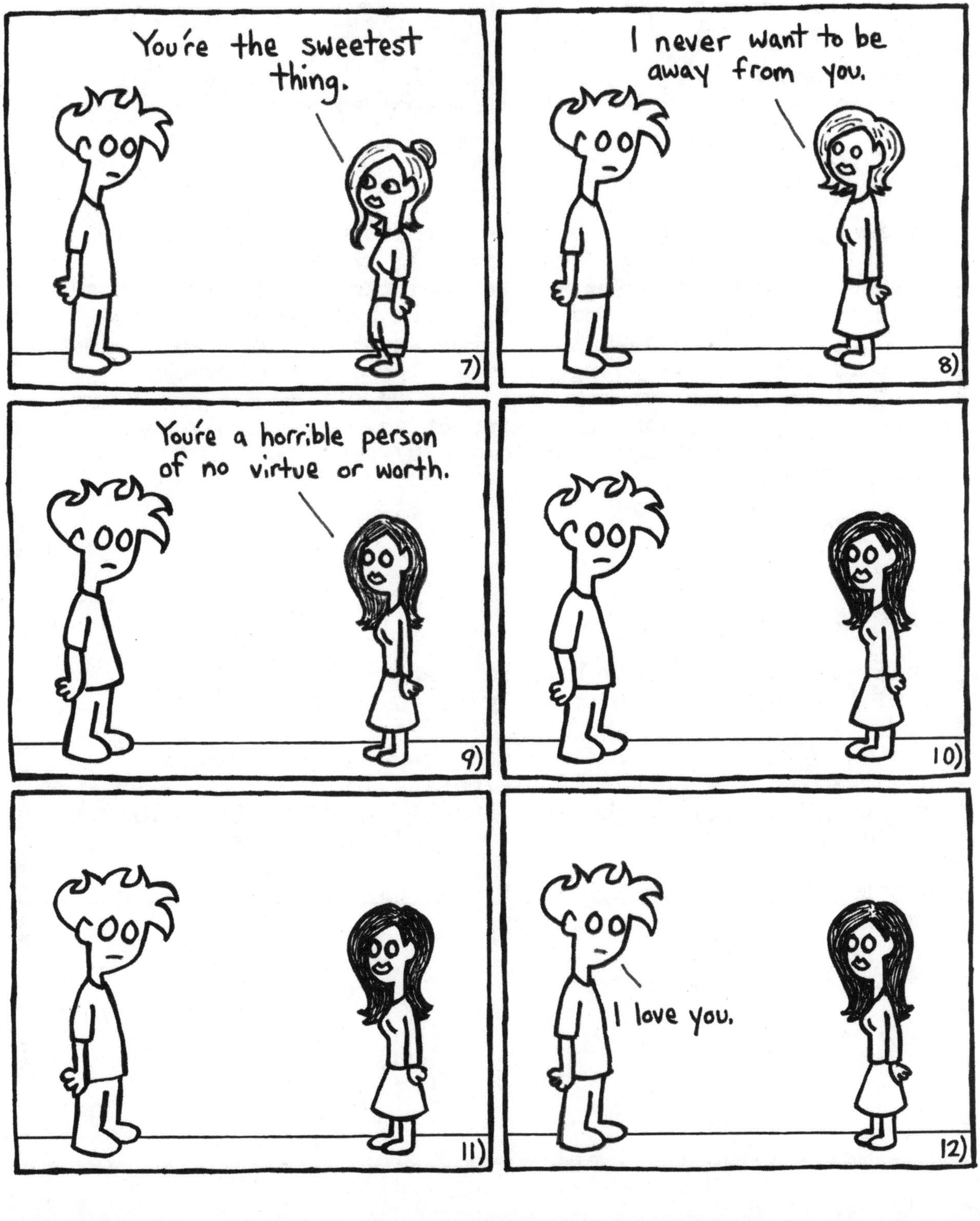

You're the sweetest thing.
7)
I never want to be away from you.
8)
You're a horrible person of no virtue or worth.
9)
10)
11)
I love you.
12)

ask DR. LEV

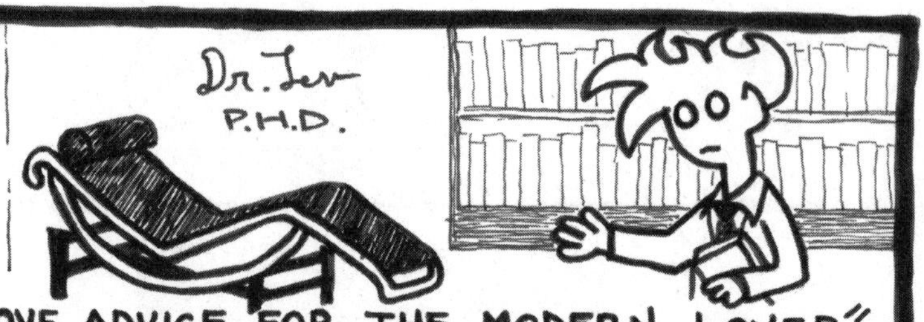
Dr. Lev
P.H.D.

"LOVE ADVICE FOR THE MODERN LOVER."

Dear Dr. Lev,

My dear, loving wife is on an extended business trip. I have always been true and faithful, but now I am being tested to my limits; The new receptionist in my office has been sending me notes and emails with her address & phone number, suggesting we "Discuss Business". It does not help matters that she is young, buxom, blonde and extremely attractive. I can see her desk from my office and she always turns in my direction and stares at me suggestively when applying her lipstick. I am losing my resolve. How do I resist?

Sincerely, TEMPTED

Dear TEMPTED,

Dude, she sounds pretty hot. How long is your old lady away for? I'll bet you could totally get away with it.

You're at little risk of anything happening long-term, because how long does a little potatocake like that ever stay in one place? Five bucks says she'll be off to LA to become an Actress-Model-Waitress before birdsong anyway.

Don't be a pussy. If you don't bone her while you can, you'll be kicking yourself for life.

Go get her Tiger,

-Dr. Lev

Dr. Lev

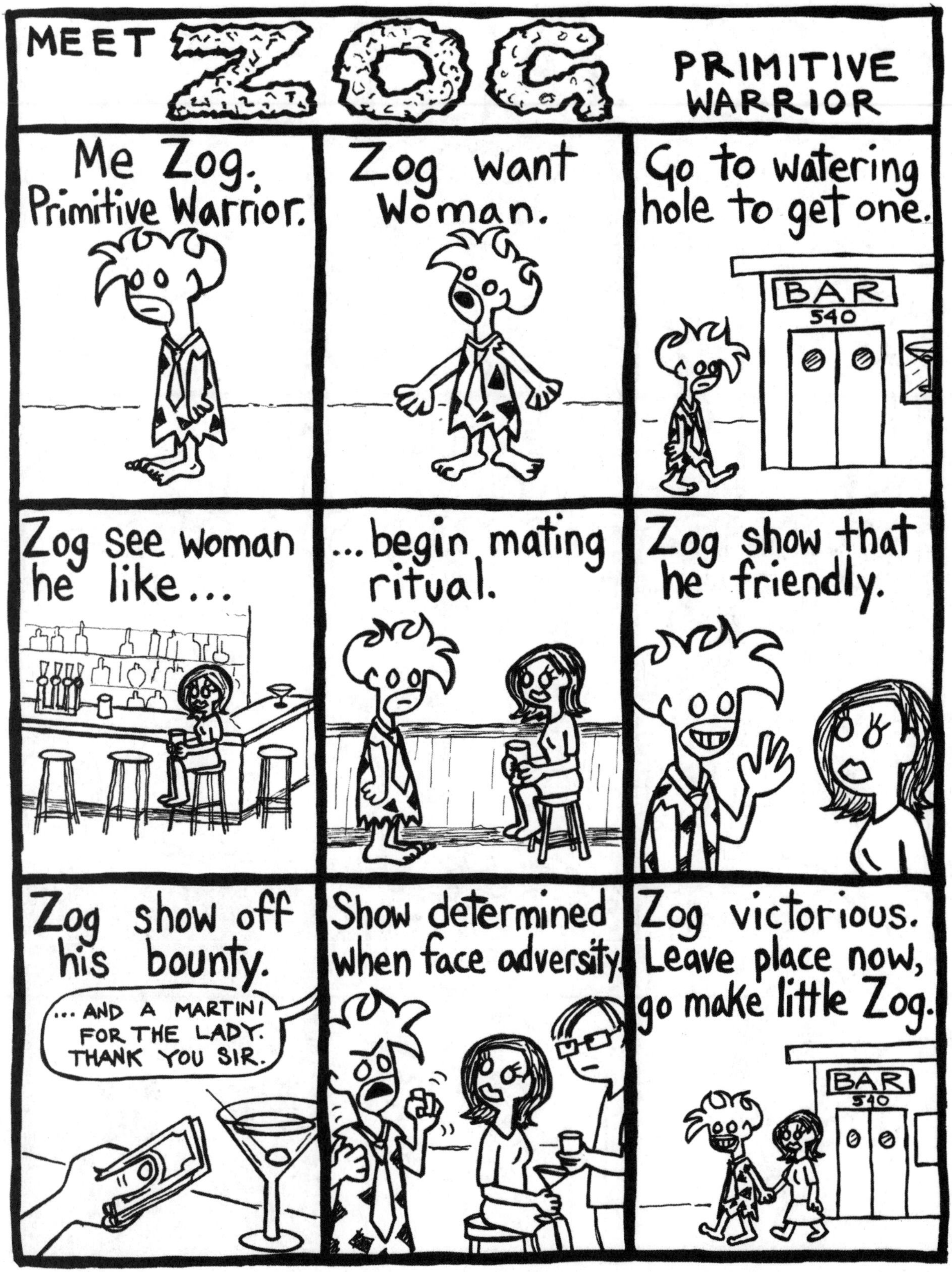
MEET ZOG PRIMITIVE WARRIOR
Me Zog. Primitive Warrior.
Zog want Woman.
Go to watering hole to get one.
BAR
540
Zog see woman he like...
...begin mating ritual.
Zog show that he friendly.
Zog show off his bounty.
... AND A MARTINI FOR THE LADY. THANK YOU SIR.
Show determined when face adversity.
Zog victorious. Leave place now, go make little Zog.
BAR
540

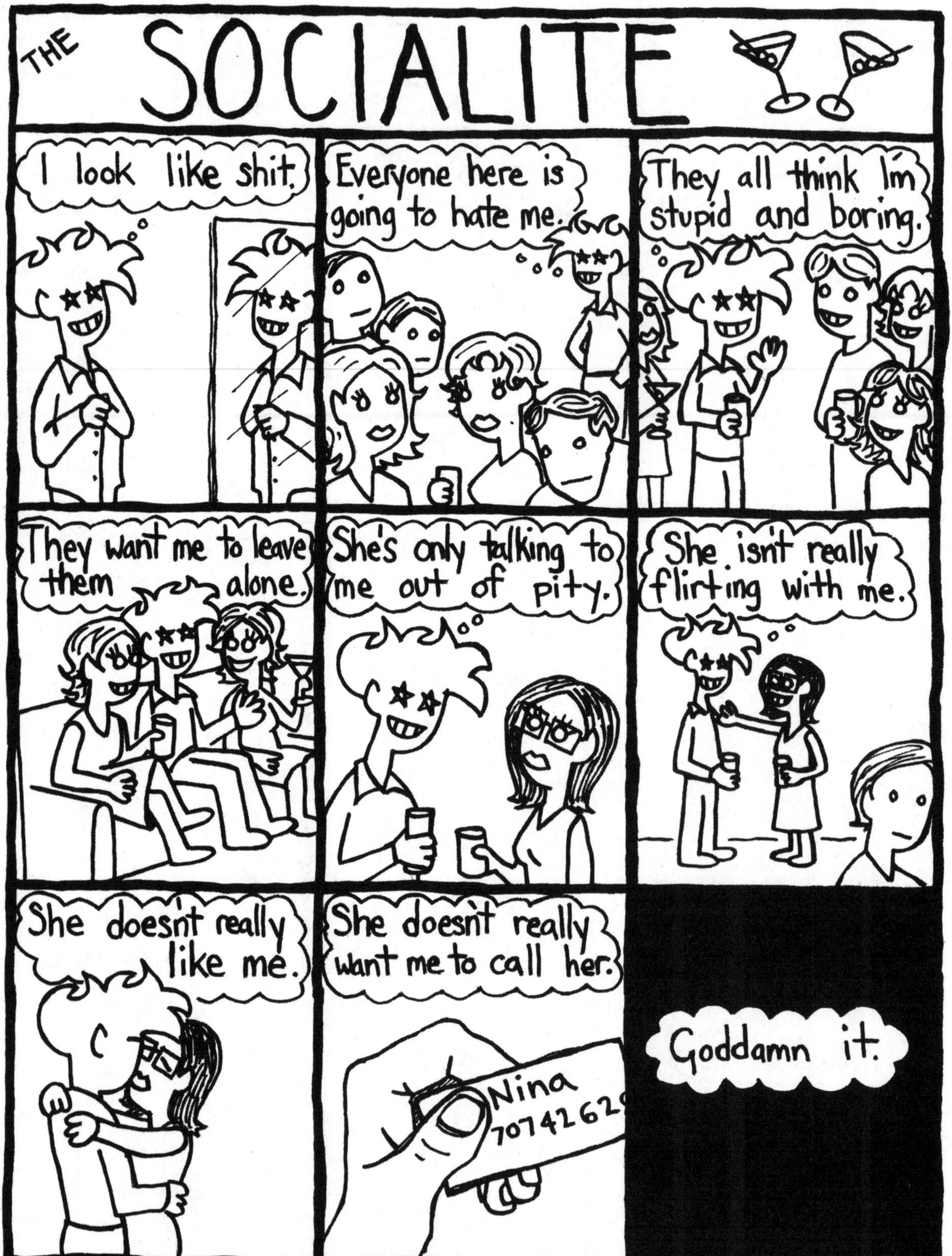
THE SOCIALITE
I look like shit.
Everyone here is going to hate me.
They all think I'm stupid and boring.
They want me to leave them alone.
She's only talking to me out of pity.
She isn't really flirting with me.
She doesn't really like me.
She doesn't really want me to call her.
Nina
Goddamn it.

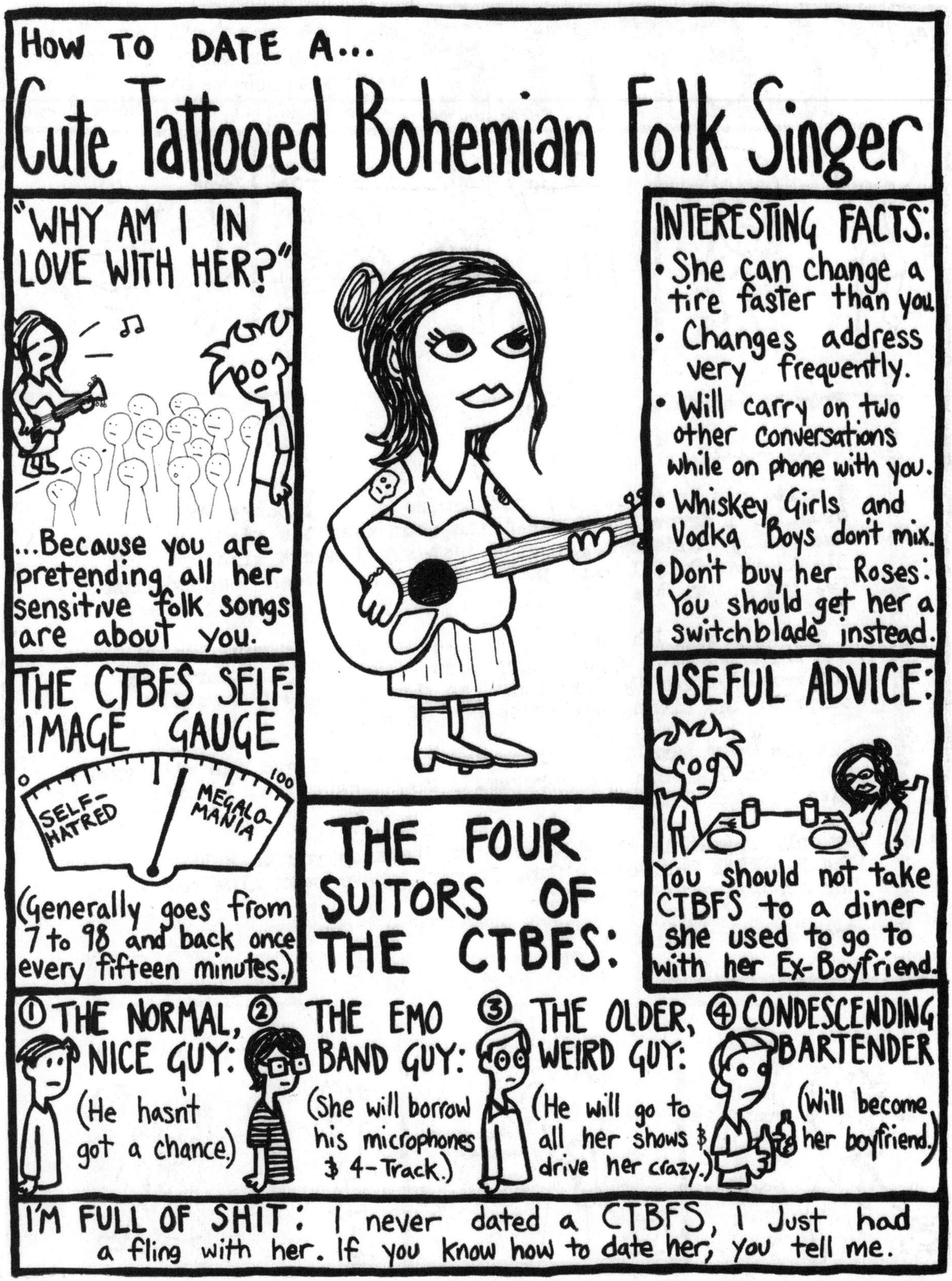
HOW TO DATE A...
Cute Tattooed Bohemian Folk Singer
"WHY AM I IN LOVE WITH HER?"
...Because you are pretending all her sensitive folk songs are about you.
THE CTBFS SELF-IMAGE GAUGE
0
100
SELF-HATRED
MEGALO-MANIA
(Generally goes from 7 to 98 and back once every fifteen minutes.)
INTERESTING FACTS:
• She can change a tire faster than you.
• Changes address very frequently.
• Will carry on two other conversations while on phone with you.
• Whiskey Girls and Vodka Boys don't mix.
• Don't buy her Roses: You should get her a switchblade instead.
USEFUL ADVICE:
You should not take CTBFS to a diner she used to go to with her Ex-Boyfriend.
THE FOUR SUITORS OF THE CTBFS:
① THE NORMAL, NICE GUY:
(He hasn't got a chance.)
② THE EMO BAND GUY:
(She will borrow his microphones $ 4-Track.)
③ THE OLDER, WEIRD GUY:
(He will go to all her shows $ drive her crazy.)
④ CONDESCENDING BARTENDER
(Will become her boyfriend.)
I'M FULL OF SHIT: I never dated a CTBFS, I Just had a fling with her. If you know how to date her, you tell me.

007 LETTER

Letter I wrote to a girl who I dated for a few weeks and watched James Bond movies with. She stopped calling me back, and then I saw her hanging out with her old boyfriend.

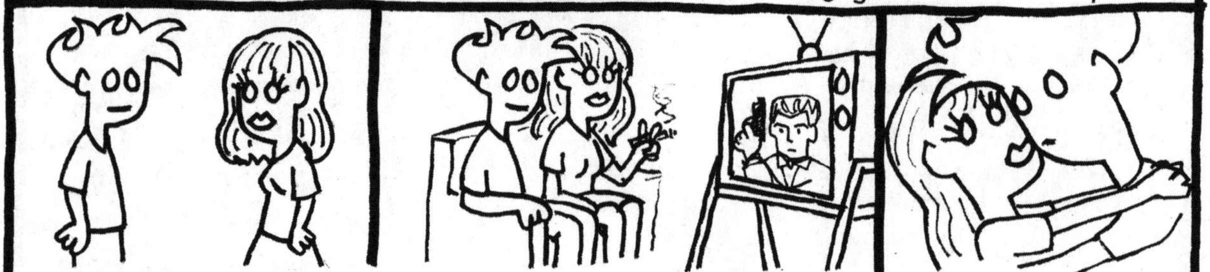

From he who is no longer On Her Majesty's Secret Service,

Hello Sally.

I write you in Peace, I'm not taking out a License To Kill. Usually, I Never Say Never Again, but when the sight of you two hit my Goldeneye... let's just say I don't wish to Die Another Day. I will just assume I have been demoted from Dr. Yes to Dr. No.

I actually saw John waiting at the bus stop by your house one morning about a week ago. That View To A Kill warned me you were not For My Eyes Only, so this all doesn't really surprise The Living Daylights out of me.

But You Only Live Twice, Live And Let Die. I had fun with you, and those Diamonds Are Forever. I don't hate you, I don't give you the Goldfinger .

My only regret is that I never got to show you that I'm The Man With The Golden Gun. It would have been nice to Thunderball your Octopussy.

From Russia With Love,

-Lev

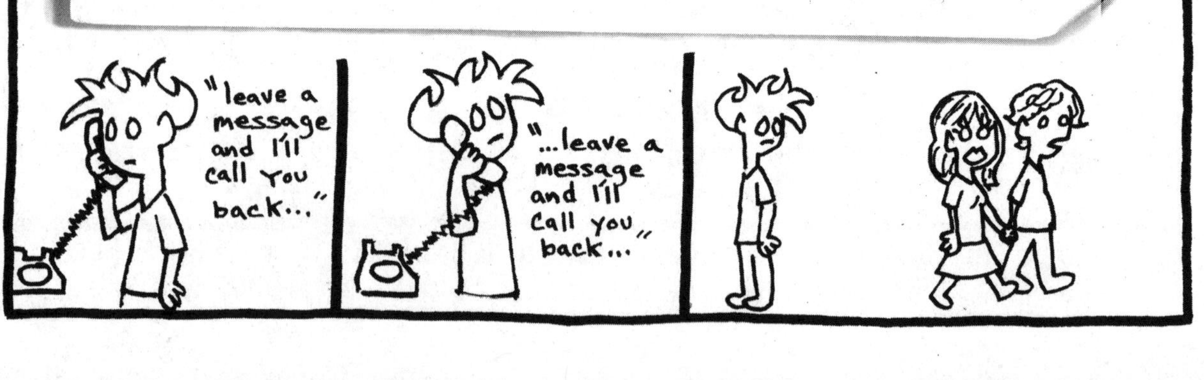
"leave a message and I'll call you back..."
"...leave a message and I'll call you back..."

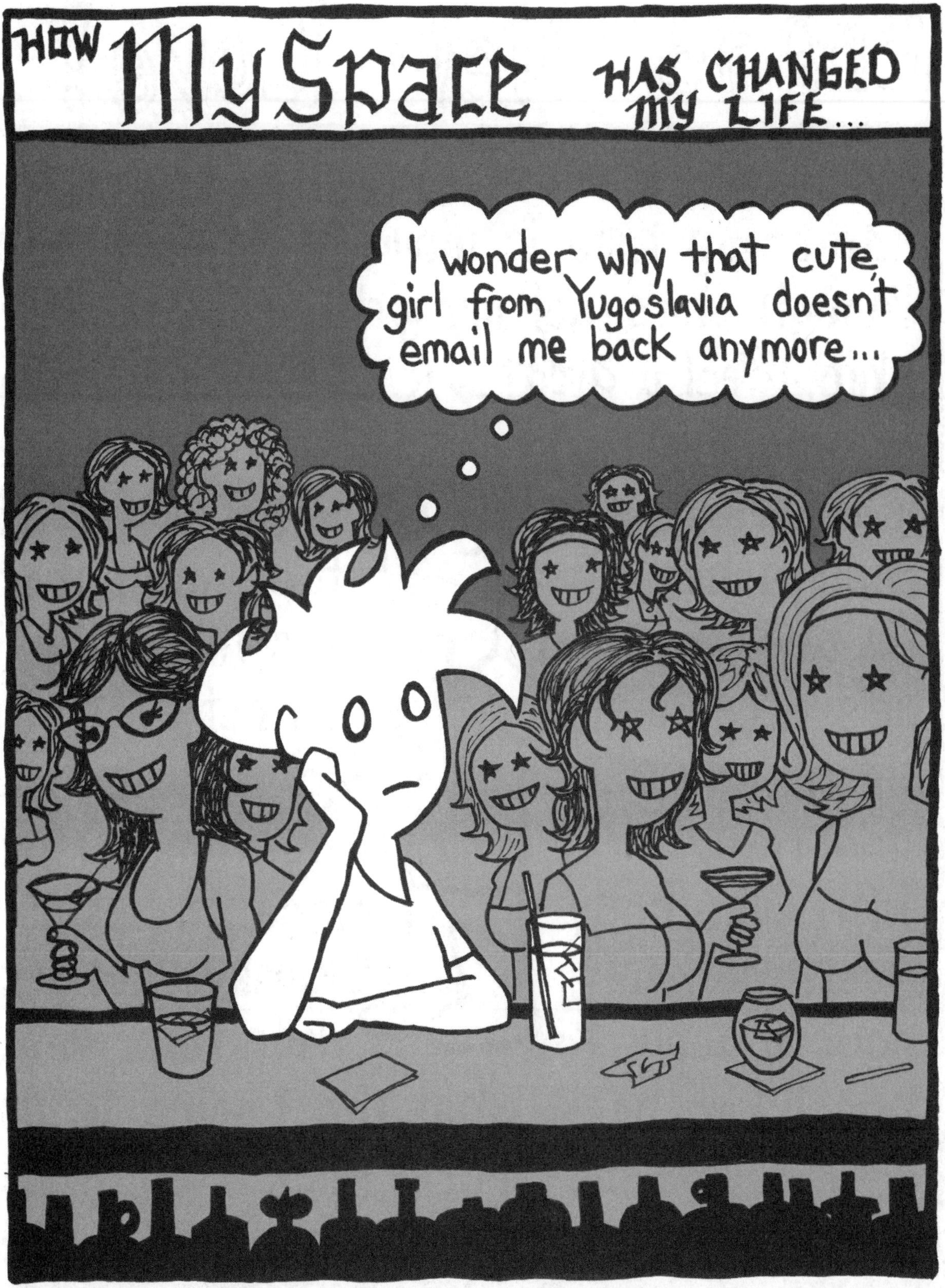
HOW MySpace HAS CHANGED MY LIFE...
I wonder why that cute girl from Yugoslavia doesn't email me back anymore...

Brand New Love!

Wow, she's neat! Wow, he's great! S amazing taste in movies. She's beautif though she's not my girlfriend. I want to ship. I feel a great emotional attac going like Q: "What are Is it a sign that our footste though he's a foot taller than I'm annoyed that I miss him. Wow. W he's eccentric. I'll bet I like her I think any minute now married. Hmmmm... Hmm with everybody since she slept w Just another Skanky McFuckp hour to reply to her text messa to call him back. What am I going to do if he dumps me? Fuck. Fuck. Well, if it e least now I got my red wings, so I suppos

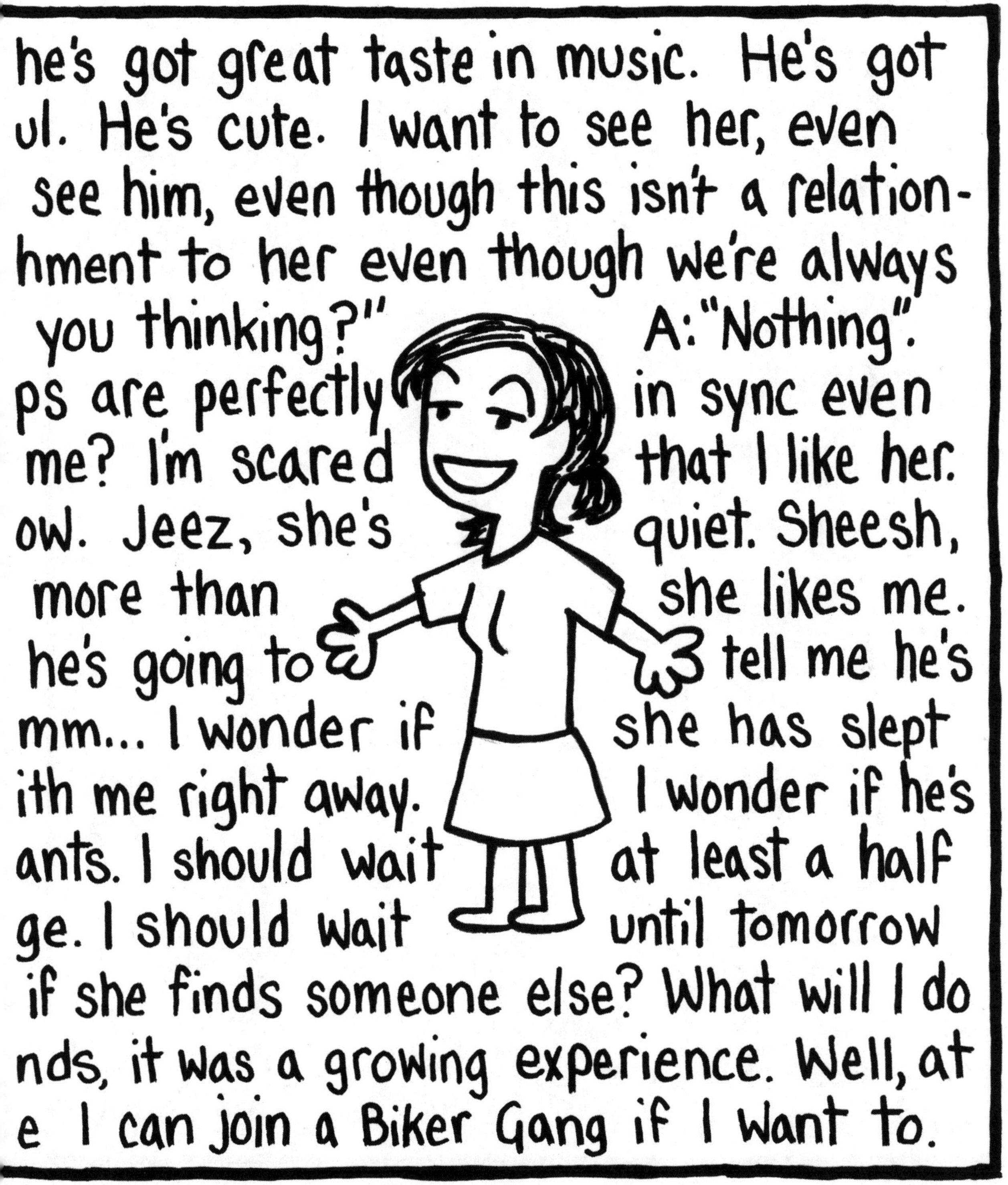
he's got great taste in music. He's got
ul. He's cute. I want to see her, even
see him, even though this isn't a relation-
hment to her even though we're always
you thinking?"
A: "Nothing".
ps are perfectly
in sync even
me? I'm scared
that I like her.
ow. Jeez, she's
quiet. Sheesh,
more than
she likes me.
he's going to
tell me he's
mm... I wonder if
she has slept
ith me right away.
I wonder if he's
ants. I should wait
at least a half
ge. I should wait
until tomorrow
if she finds someone else? What will I do
nds, it was a growing experience. Well, at
e I can join a Biker Gang if I want to.

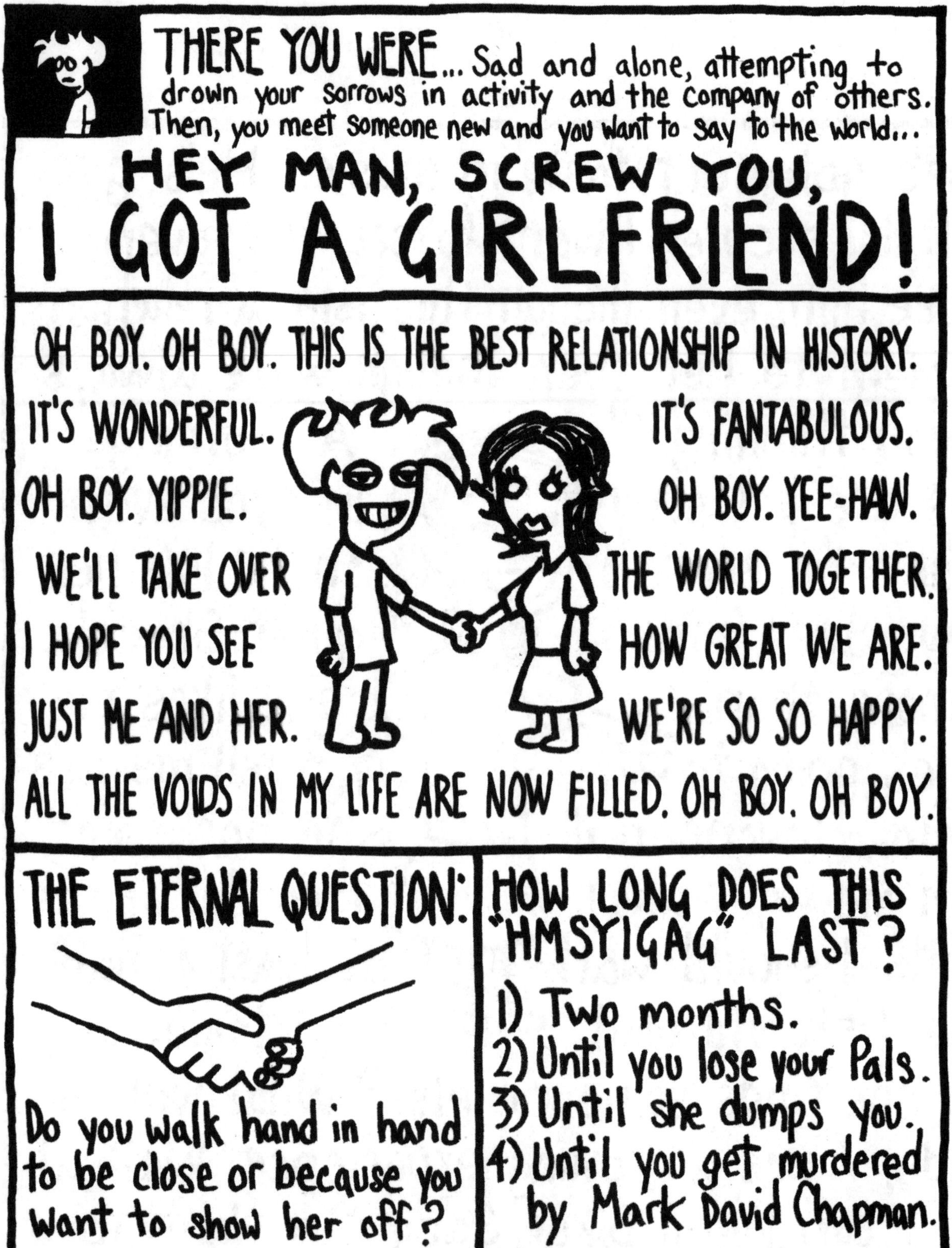
THERE YOU WERE... Sad and alone, attempting to drown your sorrows in activity and the company of others. Then, you meet someone new and you want to say to the world...
HEY MAN, SCREW YOU, I GOT A GIRLFRIEND!
OH BOY. OH BOY. THIS IS THE BEST RELATIONSHIP IN HISTORY.
IT'S WONDERFUL.
IT'S FANTABULOUS.
OH BOY. YIPPIE.
OH BOY. YEE-HAW.
WE'LL TAKE OVER
THE WORLD TOGETHER.
I HOPE YOU SEE
HOW GREAT WE ARE.
JUST ME AND HER.
WE'RE SO SO HAPPY.
ALL THE VOIDS IN MY LIFE ARE NOW FILLED. OH BOY. OH BOY.
THE ETERNAL QUESTION:
Do you walk hand in hand to be close or because you want to show her off?
HOW LONG DOES THIS "HMSYIGAG" LAST?
1) Two months.
2) Until you lose your Pals.
3) Until she dumps you.
4) Until you get murdered by Mark David Chapman.

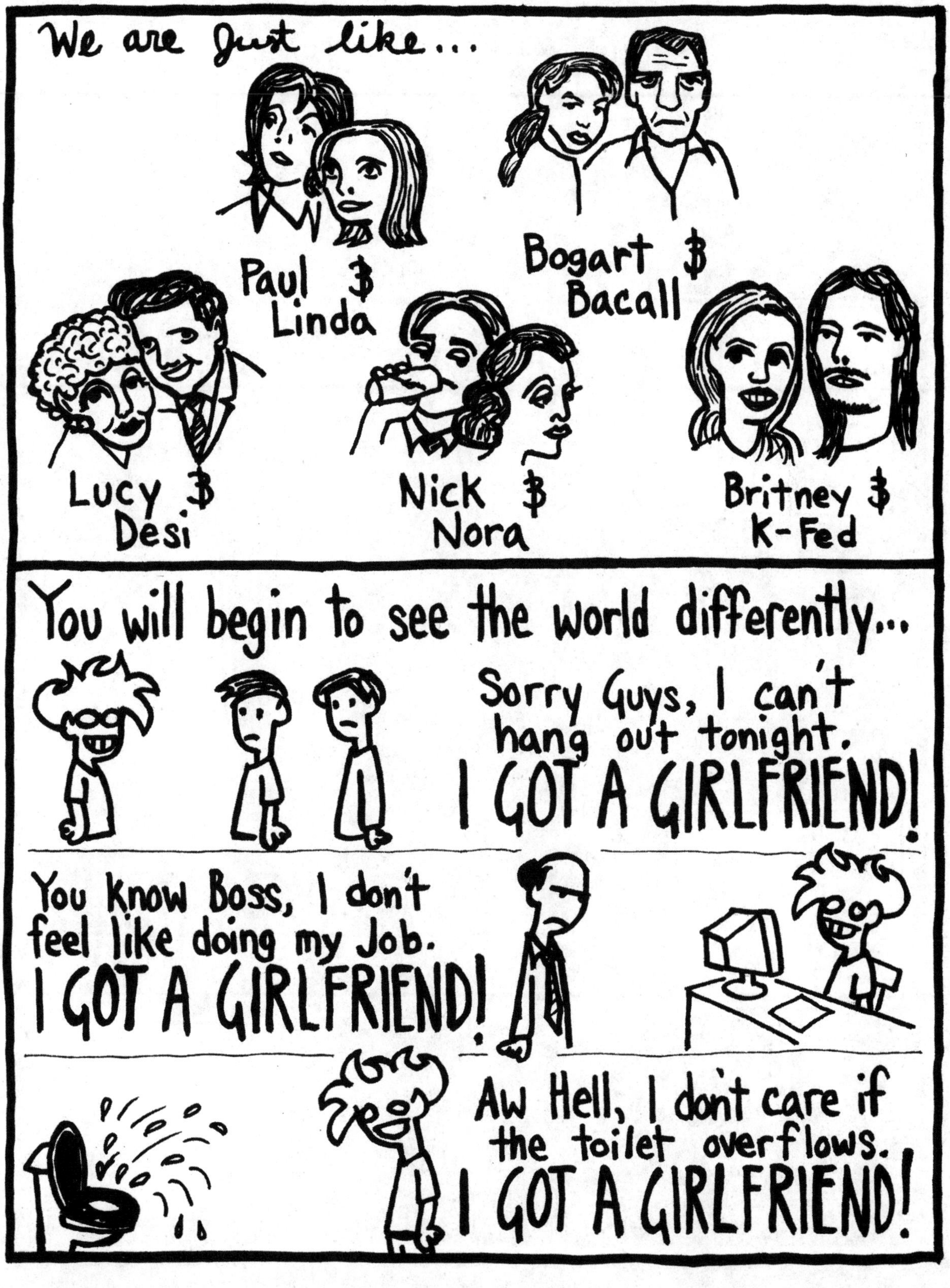
We are Just like...
Paul & Linda
Bogart & Bacall
Lucy & Desi
Nick & Nora
Britney & K-Fed
You will begin to see the world differently...
Sorry Guys, I can't hang out tonight.
I GOT A GIRLFRIEND!
You know Boss, I don't feel like doing my Job.
I GOT A GIRLFRIEND!
Aw Hell, I don't care if the toilet overflows.
I GOT A GIRLFRIEND!

"CONVERSATION"

An epic story of a couple in a video store

We got to the video store and she said, "So what do you want to watch?" and I said, "I don't know, what do you want to watch?" and she said, "I don't really care, anything will do." and I said, "Yeah, I'm not that picky either, whatever you want is fine".

So we were going thru the comedy aisle, and she picked up a Julia Roberts movie and said, "How about this?" I didn't say anything for a moment, and then I said, "Well maybe, but let's keep looking." and she asked, "Why, what's wrong with it?"

I said, "Nothing, nothing, but we just got here, let's look around a little more." And so she put it back and then about two seconds later she picked up "Sleepless In Seattle" and said, "Have you seen this?"

and I said "No, I don't think so..." and started to walk out of the comedy aisle. I heard her say, "I've seen it, it's good..." as I got over to the drama section.

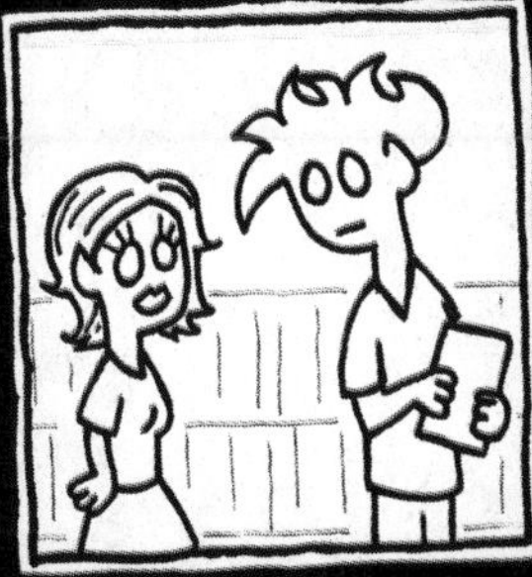

I started looking through a few titles and found a movie I liked. I was reading the back of the box when she joined me and said, "I guess you don't want to see a comedy tonight?"

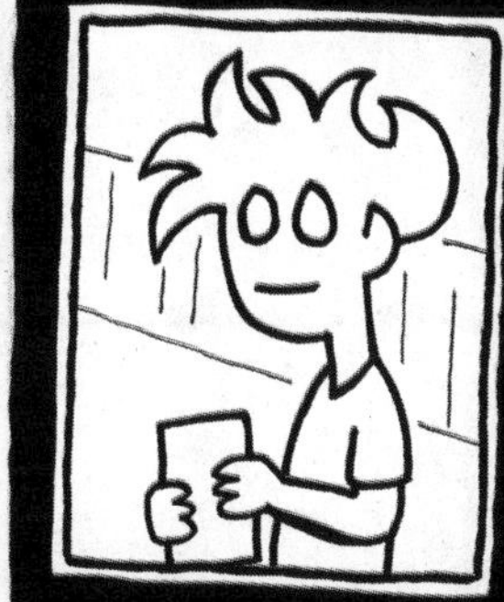

I said kind of jokingly, "Well, a comedy is fine, I guess I'm just not in the mood to see one where everybody gets married in the end."

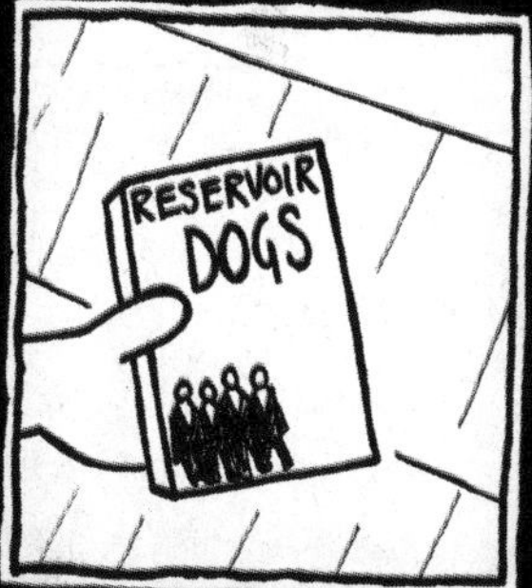
RESERVOIR DOGS

And then she said kind of seriously, "Well, okay, but I don't want to see one of those where everybody dies in the end either." And she went browsing around the aisle. I put the movie I was looking at back where I found it.

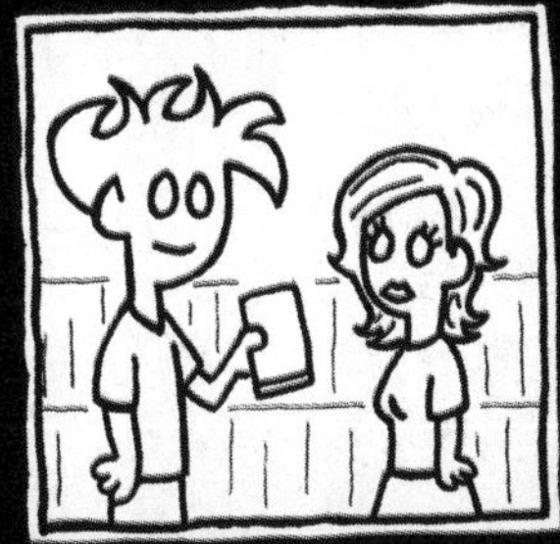

Then I got an idea: "Hey, I know a good one..." so I went down to find 'S', and pulled out "Shawshank Redemption." I said "This is a really good one, I think you'll like it."

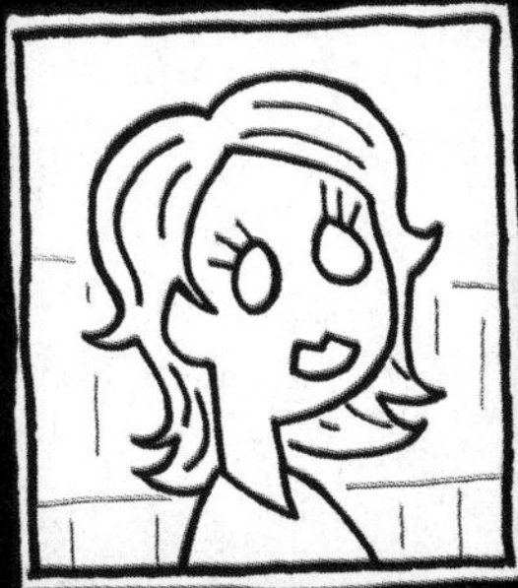

"Oh," she said. "Oh... uh, okay." I kept going: "Really, it's good. I saw it over Jim's house and it's great." and she said, "You want to watch one you've already seen?"

I said, "I'd totally be into seeing it again, and I think you'd like it." And she said, "Well... um, okay, if you really want to, we can get it."

I said, "Not in the mood for a serious one huh?" and she said, "No no, we can get it," and I said, "We can keep looking if you want," and she said, "No, we can get that," and I said, "Nah, let's keep looking."

I looked at my watch. I had to be up early the next morning. She pulled out "The Hunt For Red October" and said, "Have you seen this?" and I said "I don't know, I don't remember seeing it." and she said "Do you want to watch it?" and I said "Sure, that will be fine."

And she said, "What do you mean by 'Fine'?" and I said, "That will be fine, I wouldn't mind seeing that."

and she said "What do you mean by 'You wouldn't mind'?" and I said, "I mean I'd be all right with seeing it."

and she said a little louder: "Well 'Fine' means 'Fine', it doesn't mean you want to see it, so what you're saying is that you don't really want to see it..."

I interrupted and said as brightly as I could: "Hey wait a second, why don't we get one of those 60s musicals that you like?" and she said "Why? You don't like them."

I said, "Well, I'm usually not too into the stories, but you know, they're really colorful and the choreography is interesting..." and she said, "But you don't like the stories."

and I said, "Well not usually, but they're still kinda fun because they're so melodramatic..." and she said, "So you want to get a movie I like so you can laugh at it, so you can make fun of me, is that what you're saying?"

I stopped for a minute, and took a deep breath. Then I smiled at her and said as gently as I could: "Look, we may not be able to settle on something tonight, so why don't we just go back and watch something we've already got at home?"

She didn't say anything. I asked again: "Honey, why don't we just watch something we've already got at home?"

She still didn't say anything.

"Honey, Baby, what's the matter?"

And she said, "You don't love me any more." and I said, "Of course I do!" and she said, "No you don't." and I said "What has this got to do with it?" and she said, "I don't know."

And I said, "Of course I still love you!" and she said "No you don't." and I said, "I just don't want to argue tonight, and since we can't agree on a movie, I thought we could just watch something we've already got!"

And she said: "You're yelling at me! Why are you yelling at me? Don't yell at me..."

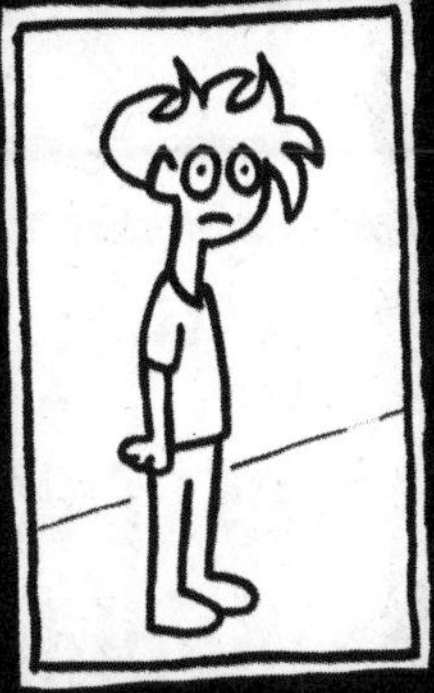

I stopped again. Then I said, "Look, please, I don't want to fight." and she said, "I don't want to fight either."

And I said, "Let's get out of here." and she said, "Okay." and I said, "Okay?" and she said, "Okay." and we left.

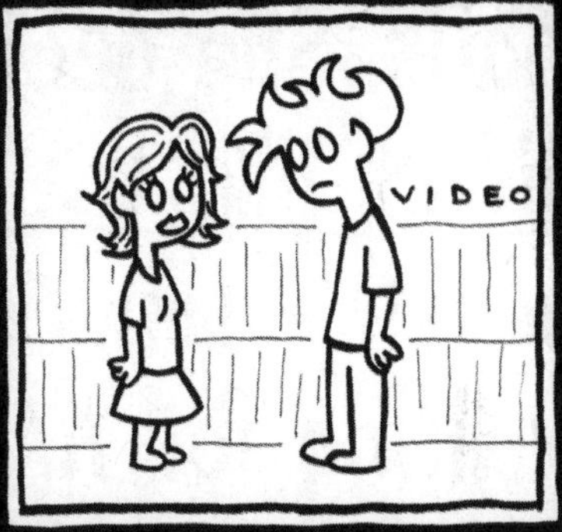
VIDEO

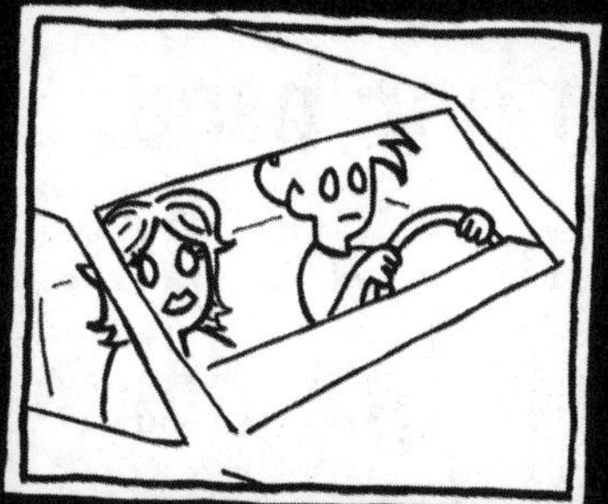

We didn't really say anything on the way home, and we didn't say much while cooking dinner.

We didn't really say much when we sat down with our plates on the couch.

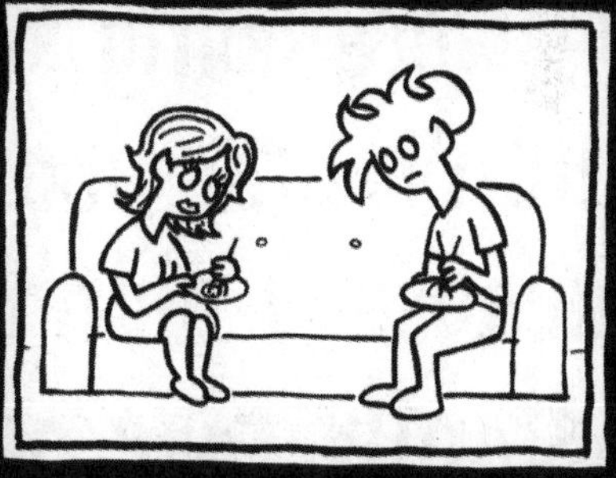

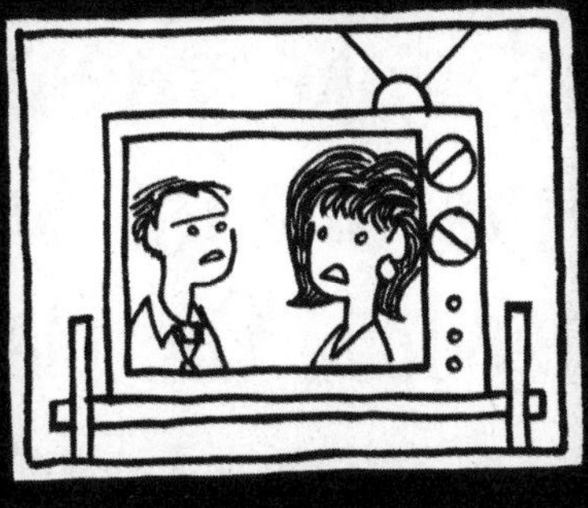

I was putting my feet up on the coffee table as she turned on the TV. An old rerun of "Married With Children" was on.

25 POSSIBLE

She's in the shower. She fell asleep. She's was She's on the phone with her mom. Her best fr nails. She decided I was boring. She decided I didn't like the sweater I wore. She left her pho ballet lesson. She's at the grocery store. She go waiting for AAA to show up. She is working o walking around with a book on her head. She i mixed up her name that one time. She decided ause I asked her what she felt like doing inst we were going to do. She decided I wasn't con I didn't brag too much about myself. She decid because I didn't act like enough of an assho instantly take all her problems away, but I did enough, and therefore could not take them aw telling them how in love with me she is. She's notebooks. She decided that her love for me wa piness. She smoked a joint and is now watchi

REASONS

WHY SHE ISN'T CALLING ME BACK

hing her hair. She had to stay late at work.
iend is very depressed. She's painting her toe-
was ugly. She decided I was too skinny. She
ne at home. She's at a
t a flat tire and is
n her posture
s mad because I
I was spineless bec-
ead of saying what
fident enough because
ed I wasn't an alpha-male type
le. She was looking for someone who would
n't figure out what her problems were quickly
ay. She's still on the phone with all her friends
writing "I Luv Lev 4-Eva" on her spiral-bound
s too great, and she didn't deserve such hap-
ng Huckleberry Hound cartoons on YouTube.

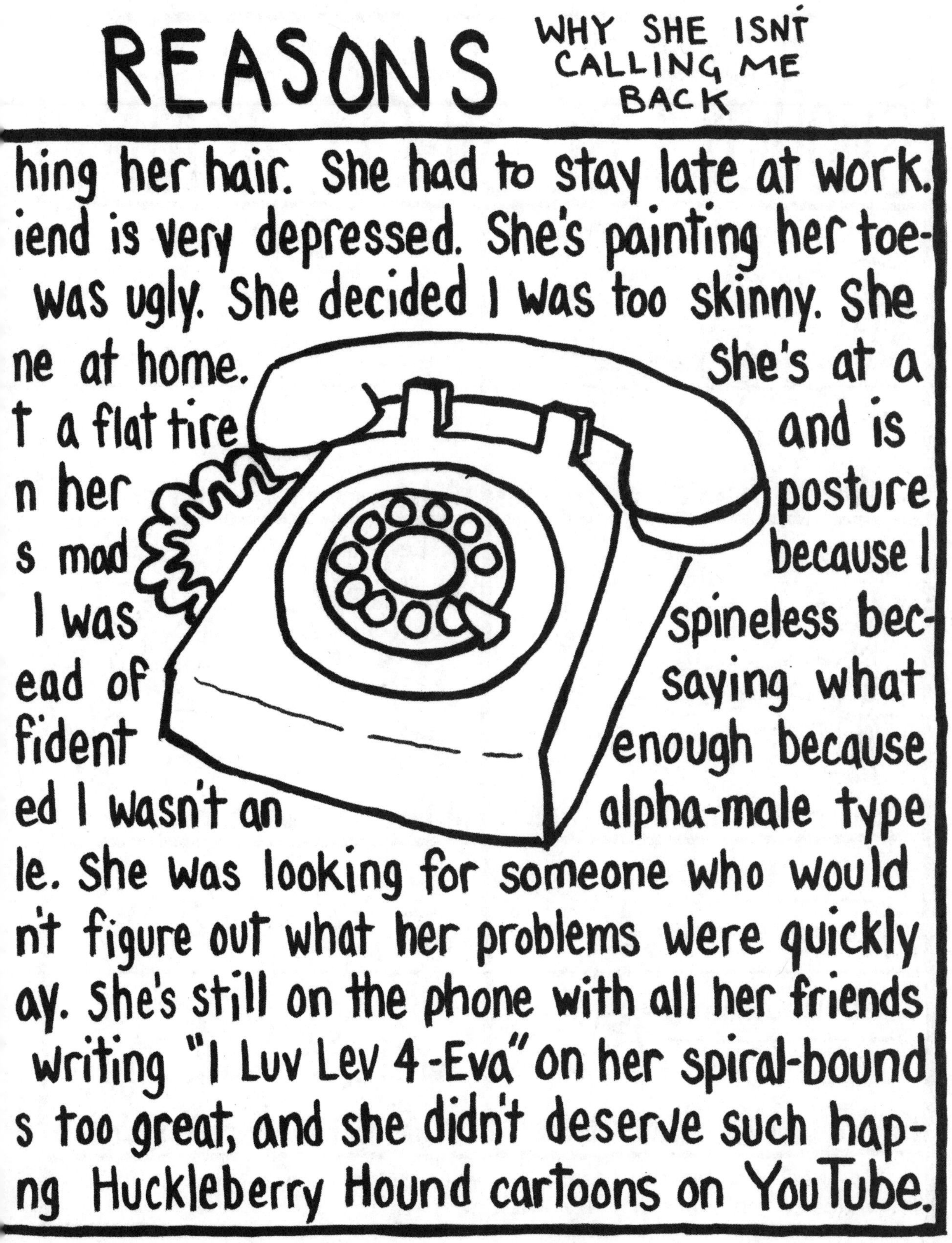

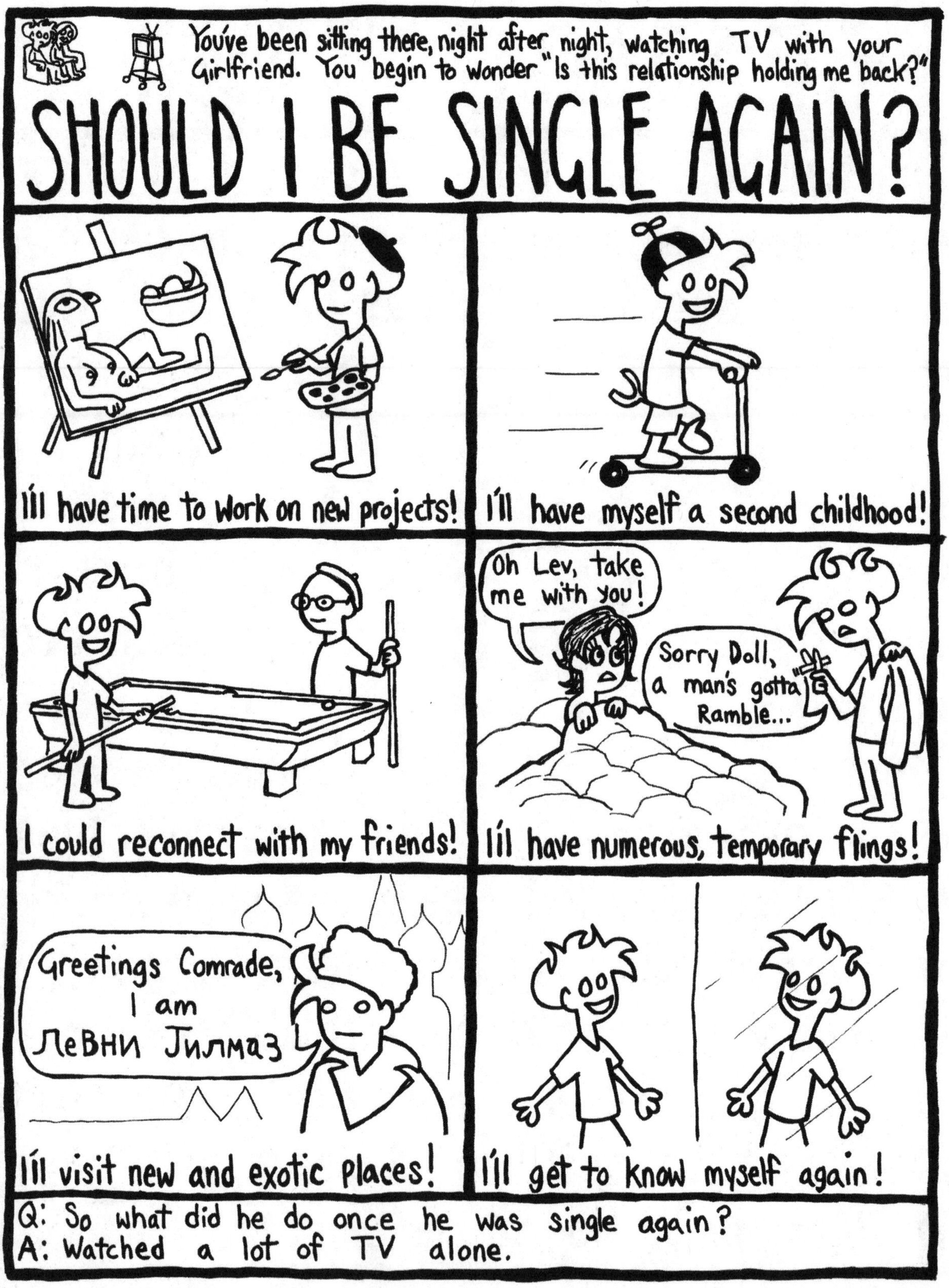
You've been sitting there, night after night, watching TV with your Girlfriend. You begin to wonder "Is this relationship holding me back?"
SHOULD I BE SINGLE AGAIN?
I'll have time to work on new projects!
I'll have myself a second childhood!
I could reconnect with my friends!
Oh Lev, take me with you!
Sorry Doll, a man's gotta Ramble...
I'll have numerous, temporary flings!
Greetings Comrade, I am ЛеВНИ JИЛМАЗ
I'll visit new and exotic Places!
I'll get to know myself again!
Q: So what did he do once he was single again?
A: Watched a lot of TV alone.

ASK DR. LEV

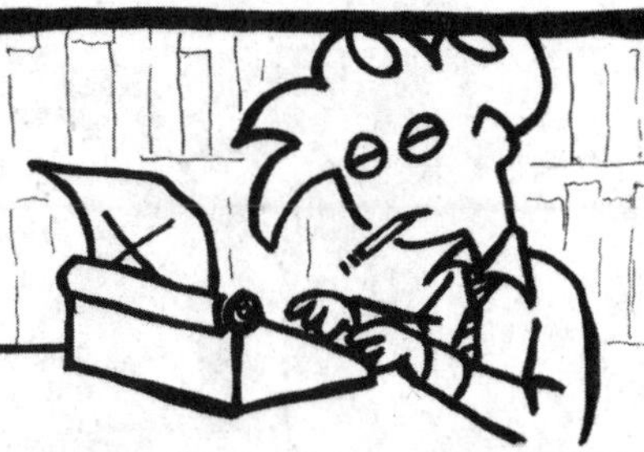

"Because who else are you gonna ask?"

—Dear Dr. Lev,

I very much love my Boyfriend of two years, but I feel the relationship isn't going anywhere. I think I need to end it, but I don't know how. Sincerely, DREADING IT.

—Dear DREADING IT,

Breaking up with people is always difficult, so the best way to deal with it is to not deal with it at all. Stop answering the phone, move out of your apartment if you can & don't tell him where you're going.

This may sound cruel, but it is nature's way. Look at the Ostrich: When he's nervous, he buries his head in the sand and waits for the problem to go away. You get it? Nobody ever messes with an Ostrich. I know an Ostrich can kick you to death, but this is beside the point.

—Dear Dr. Lev,

I am in my thirties, but the only kinds of girls I seem to attract are around 19 to 23. I have been thru so many young girls, but no matter how many I date or sleep with, I feel unfulfilled and empty. How do I change to find a relationship with substance? Sincerely, HOLLOW INSIDE.

—Dear HOLLOW INSIDE,

Fuck you.

Dr. Lev

HOW TO BREAK UP WITH YOUR GIRLFRIEND...

...in 64 easy steps

PHASE 1: The Buildup

Get a girlfriend.

Be together for a while.

Know you're going to be together forever.

Think you're going to be together forever.

Assume you're going to be together forever.

Start to wonder if you really are going to be together forever.

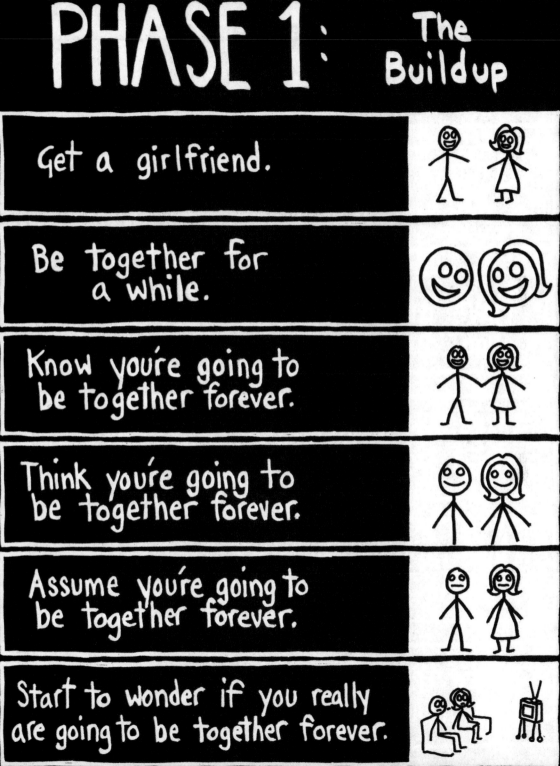

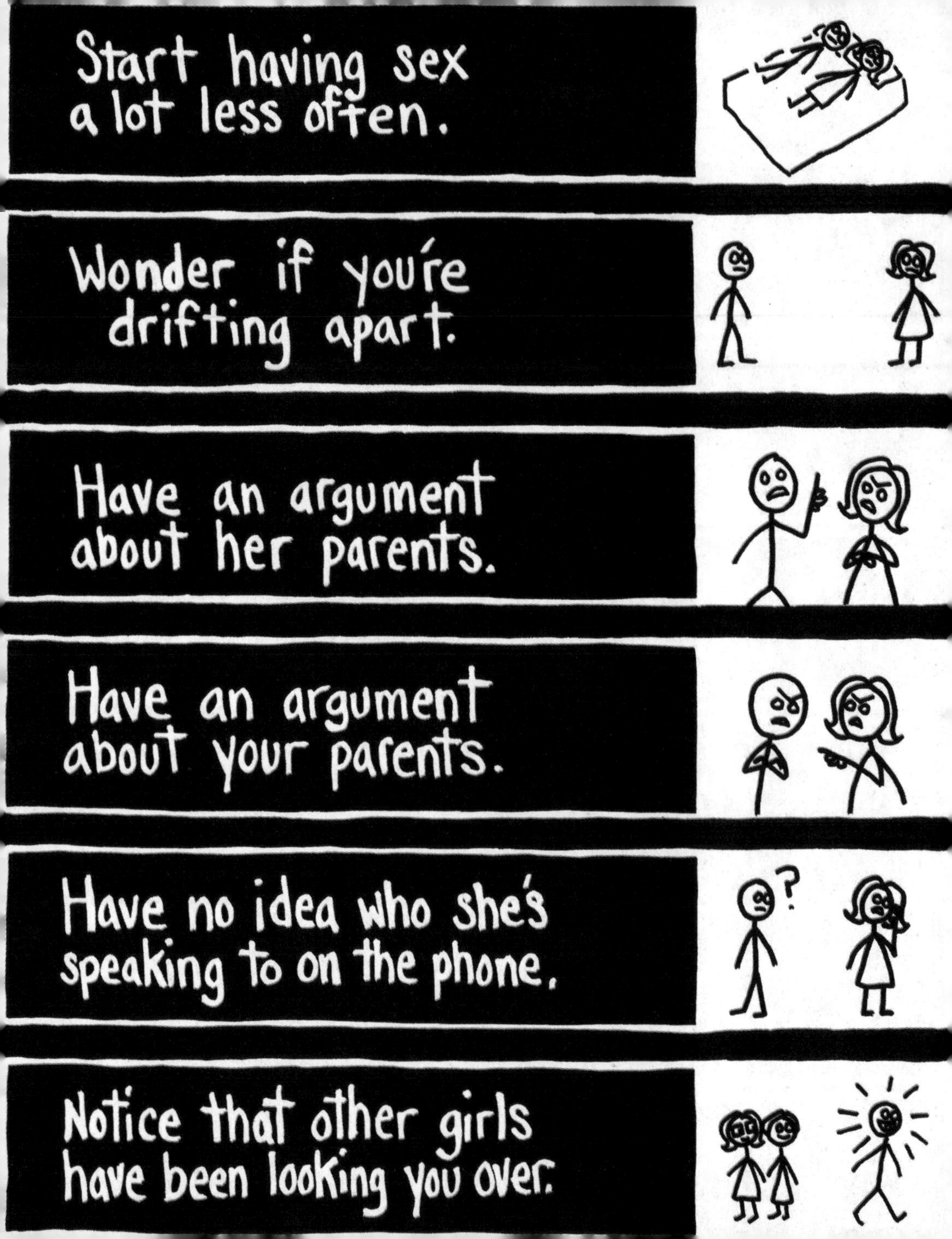

Start having sex a lot less often.
Wonder if you're drifting apart.
Have an argument about her parents.
Have an argument about your parents.
Have no idea who she's speaking to on the phone.
?
Notice that other girls have been looking you over.

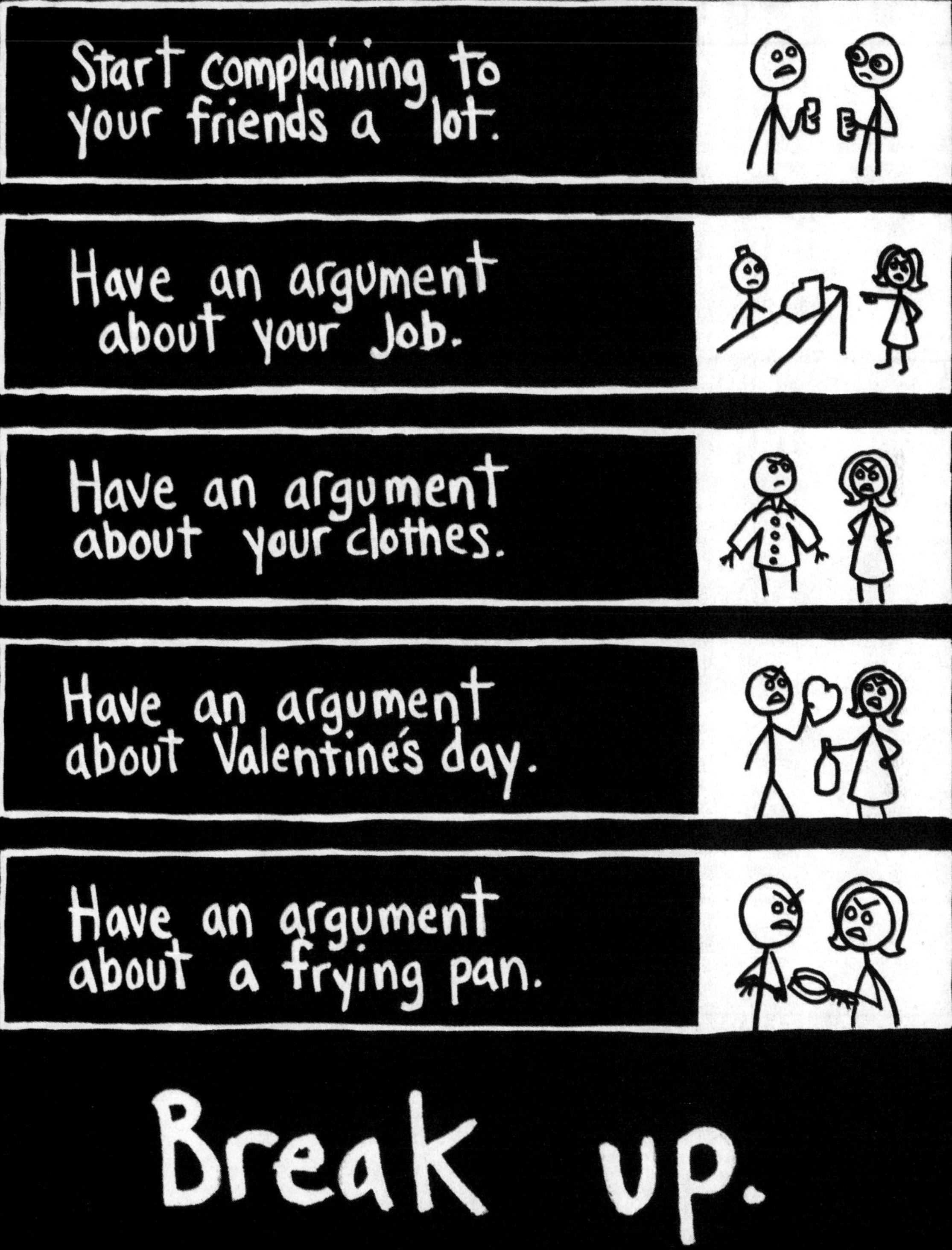
Start complaining to your friends a lot.
Have an argument about your job.
Have an argument about your clothes.
Have an argument about Valentine's day.
Have an argument about a frying pan.
Break up.

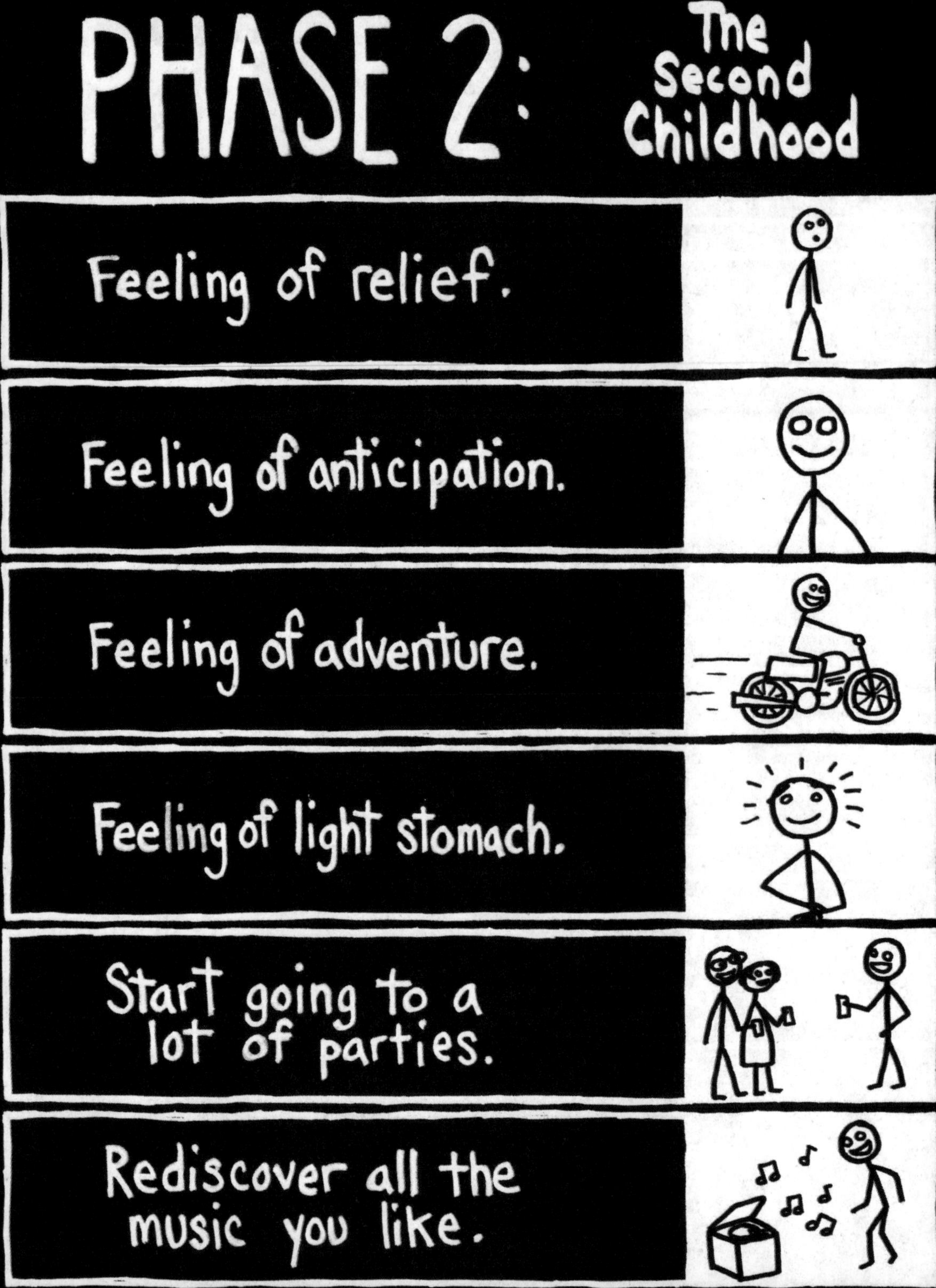
PHASE 2: The Second Childhood
Feeling of relief.
Feeling of anticipation.
Feeling of adventure.
Feeling of light stomach.
Start going to a lot of parties.
Rediscover all the music you like.

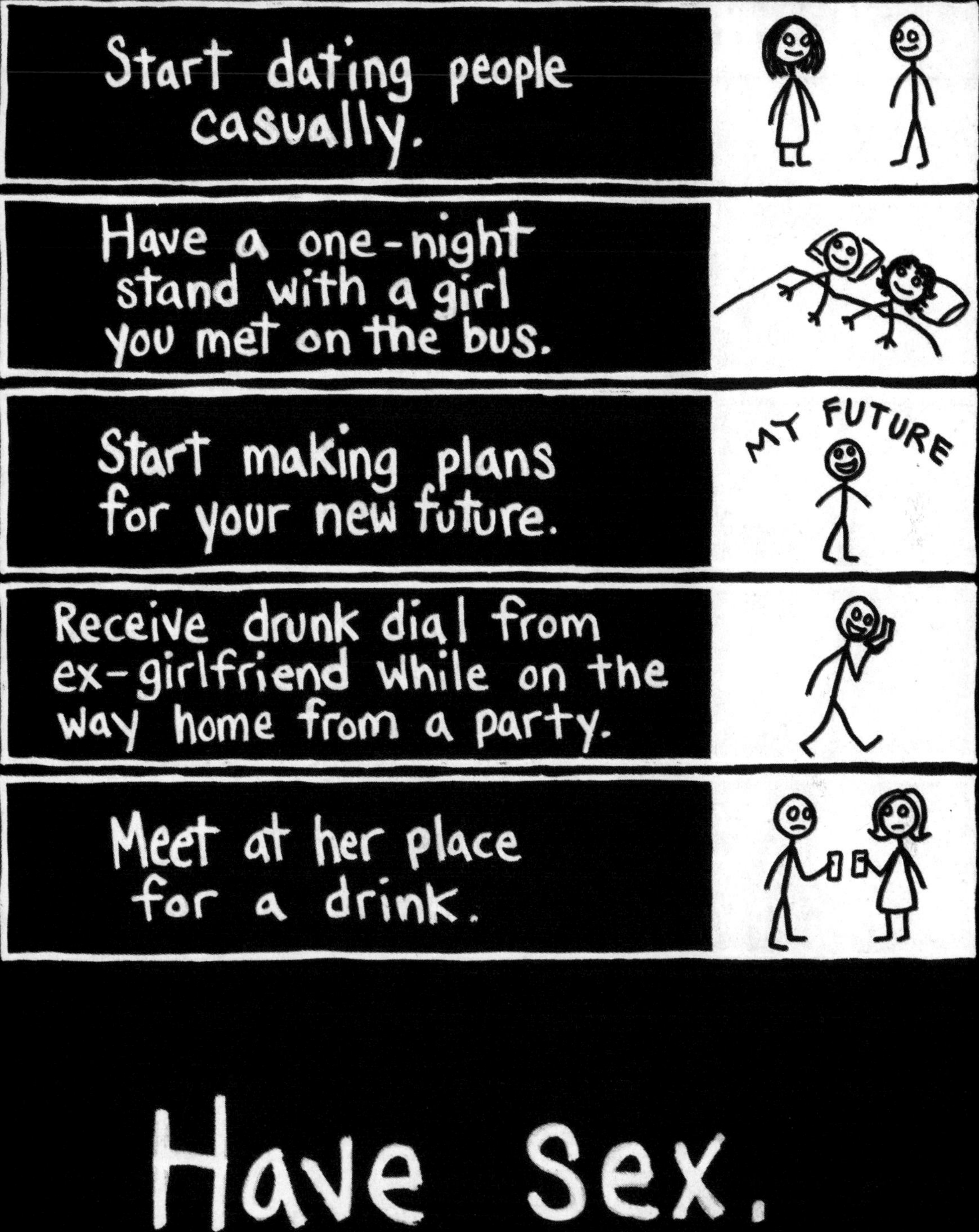
Start dating people casually.
Have a one-night stand with a girl you met on the bus.
Start making plans for your new future.
MY FUTURE
Receive drunk dial from ex-girlfriend while on the way home from a party.
Meet at her place for a drink.
Have sex.

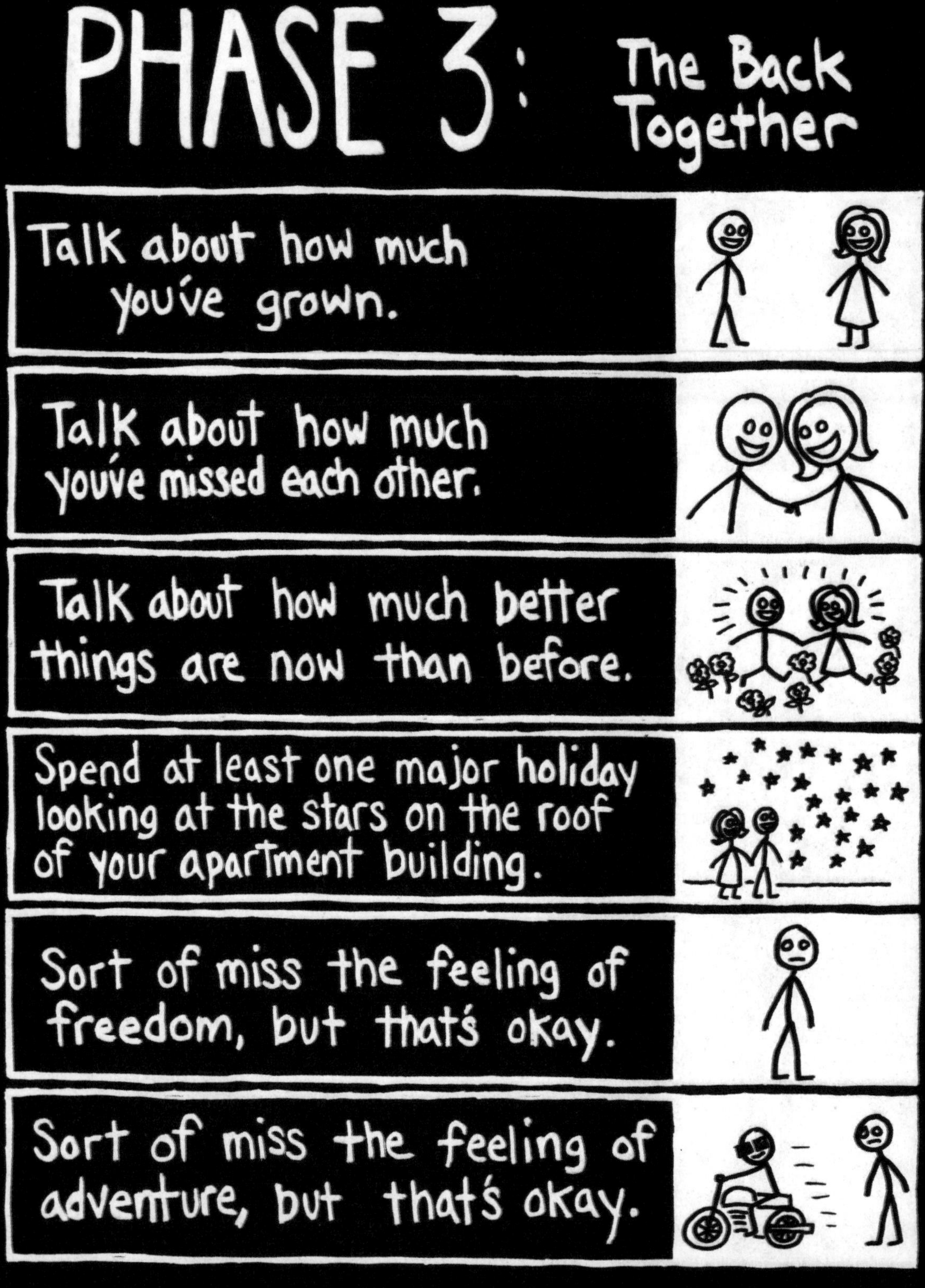
PHASE 3: The Back Together
Talk about how much you've grown.
Talk about how much you've missed each other.
Talk about how much better things are now than before.
Spend at least one major holiday looking at the stars on the roof of your apartment building.
Sort of miss the feeling of freedom, but that's okay.
Sort of miss the feeling of adventure, but that's okay.

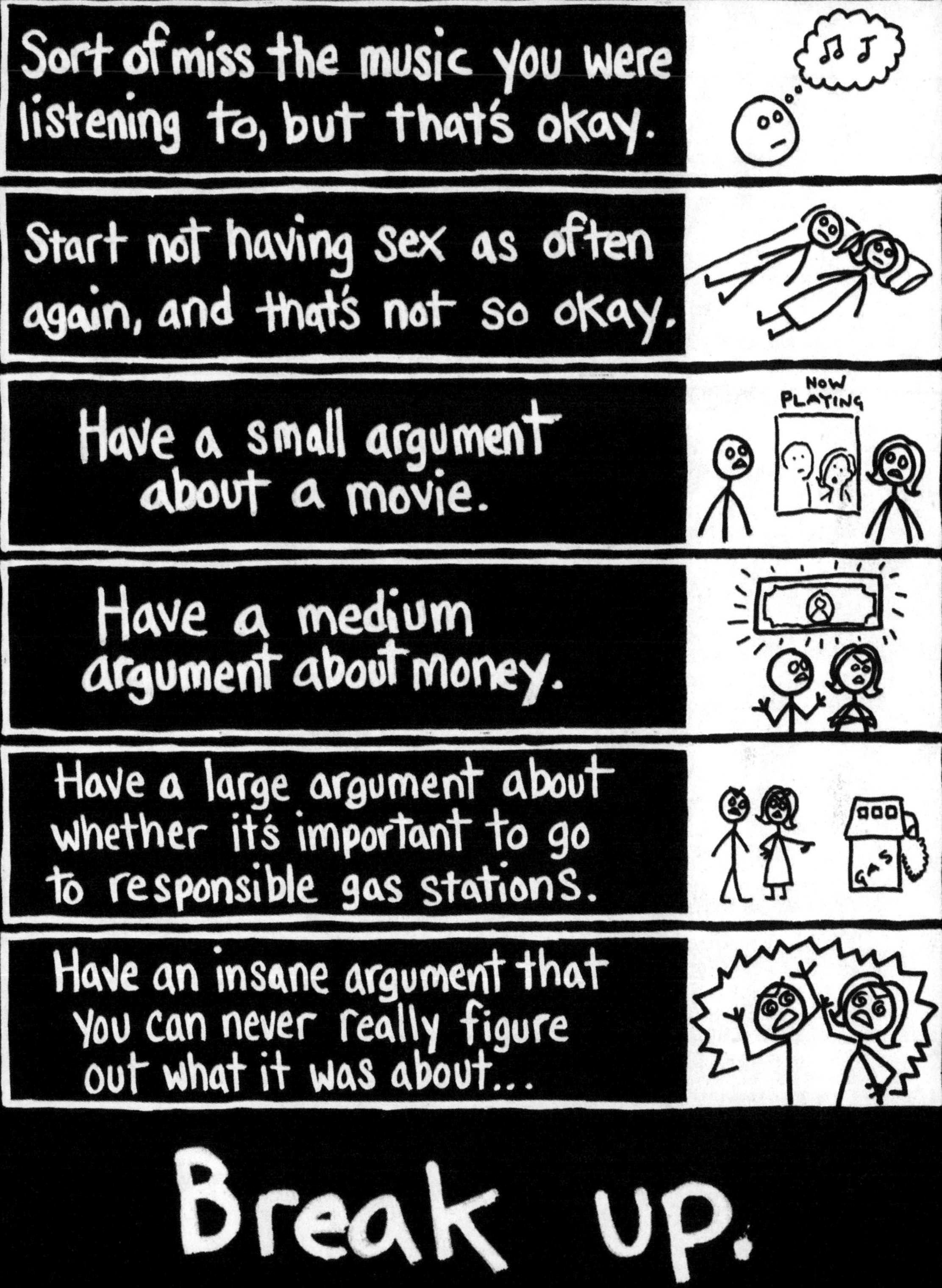

Sort of miss the music you were listening to, but that's okay.
Start not having sex as often again, and that's not so okay.
Have a small argument about a movie.
NOW PLAYING
Have a medium argument about money.
Have a large argument about whether it's important to go to responsible gas stations.
GAS
Have an insane argument that you can never really figure out what it was about...
Break up.

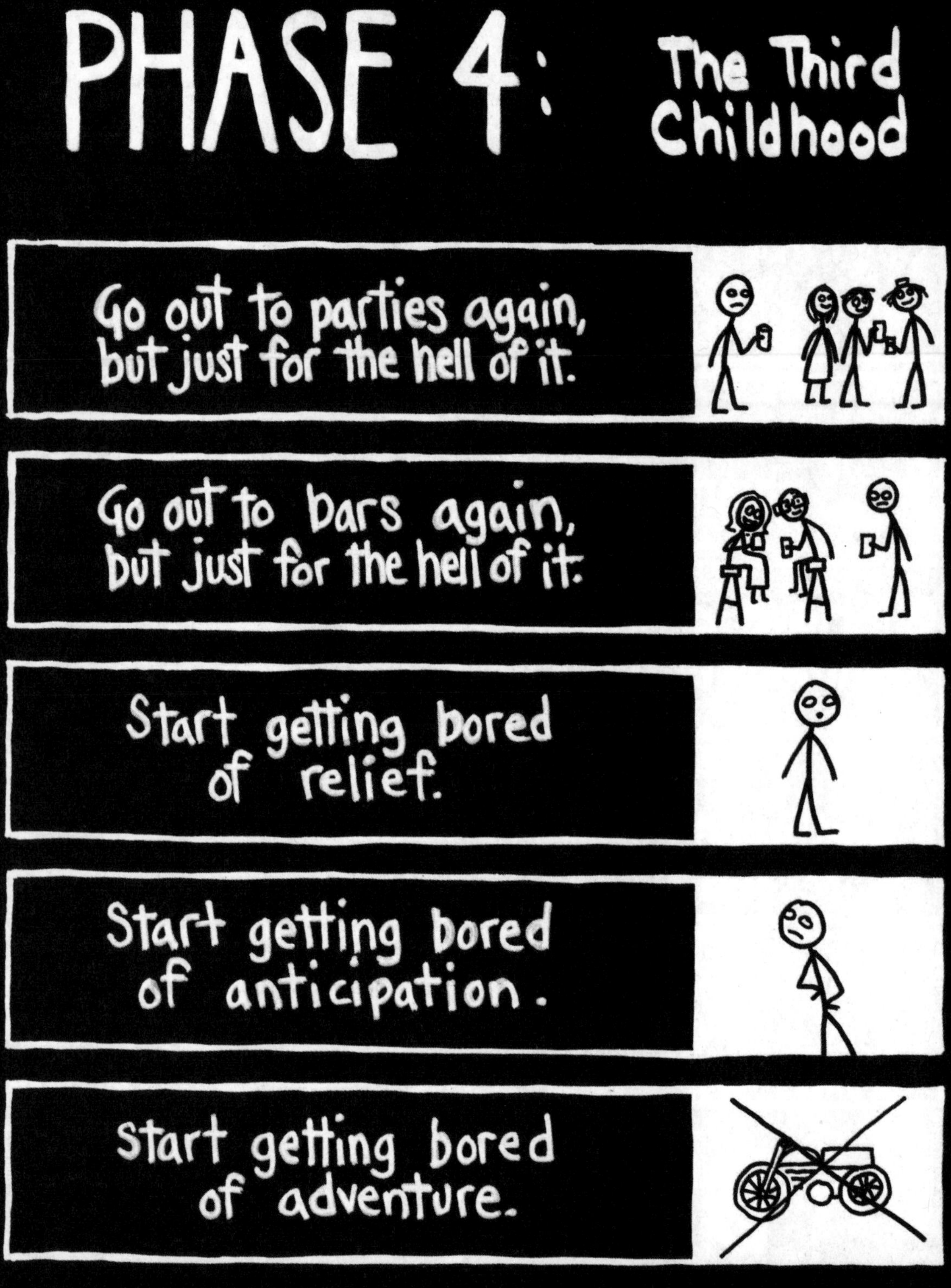
PHASE 4: The Third Childhood
Go out to parties again, but just for the hell of it.
Go out to bars again, but just for the hell of it.
Start getting bored of relief.
Start getting bored of anticipation.
Start getting bored of adventure.

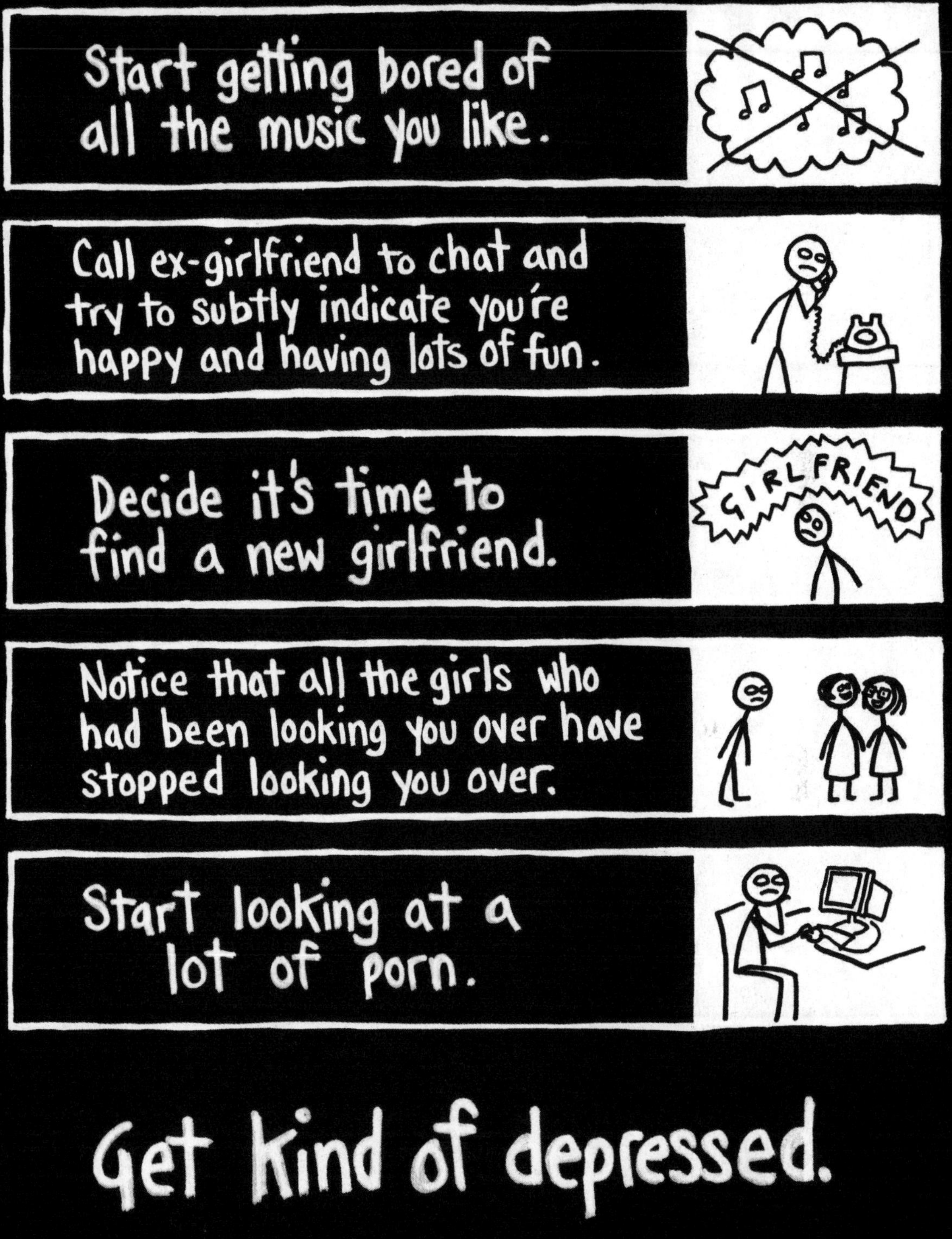
Start getting bored of all the music you like.
Call ex-girlfriend to chat and try to subtly indicate you're happy and having lots of fun.
Decide it's time to find a new girlfriend.
GIRLFRIEND
Notice that all the girls who had been looking you over have stopped looking you over.
Start looking at a lot of porn.
Get kind of depressed.

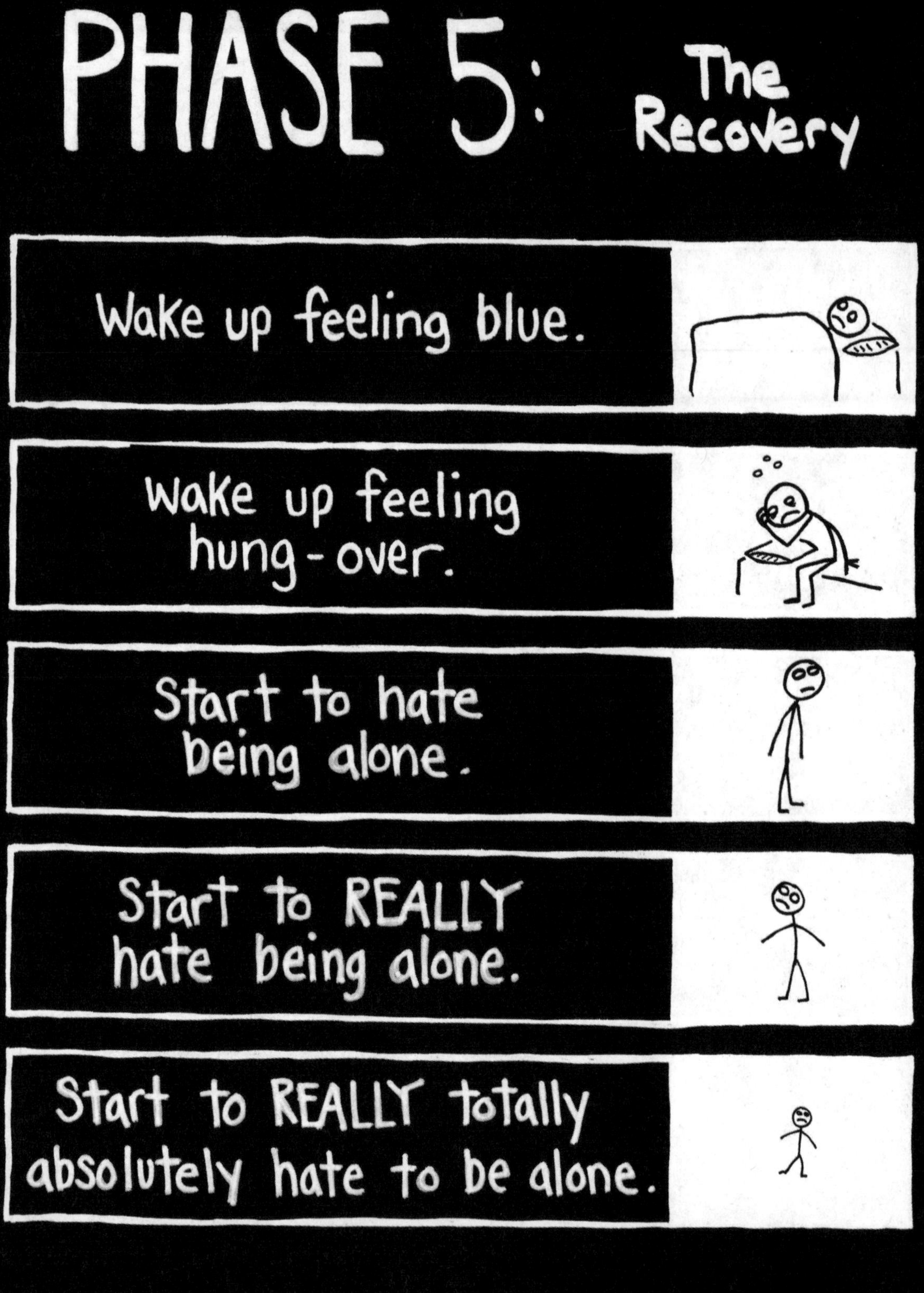
PHASE 5: The Recovery
Wake up feeling blue.
Wake up feeling hung-over.
Start to hate being alone.
Start to REALLY hate being alone.
Start to REALLY totally absolutely hate to be alone.

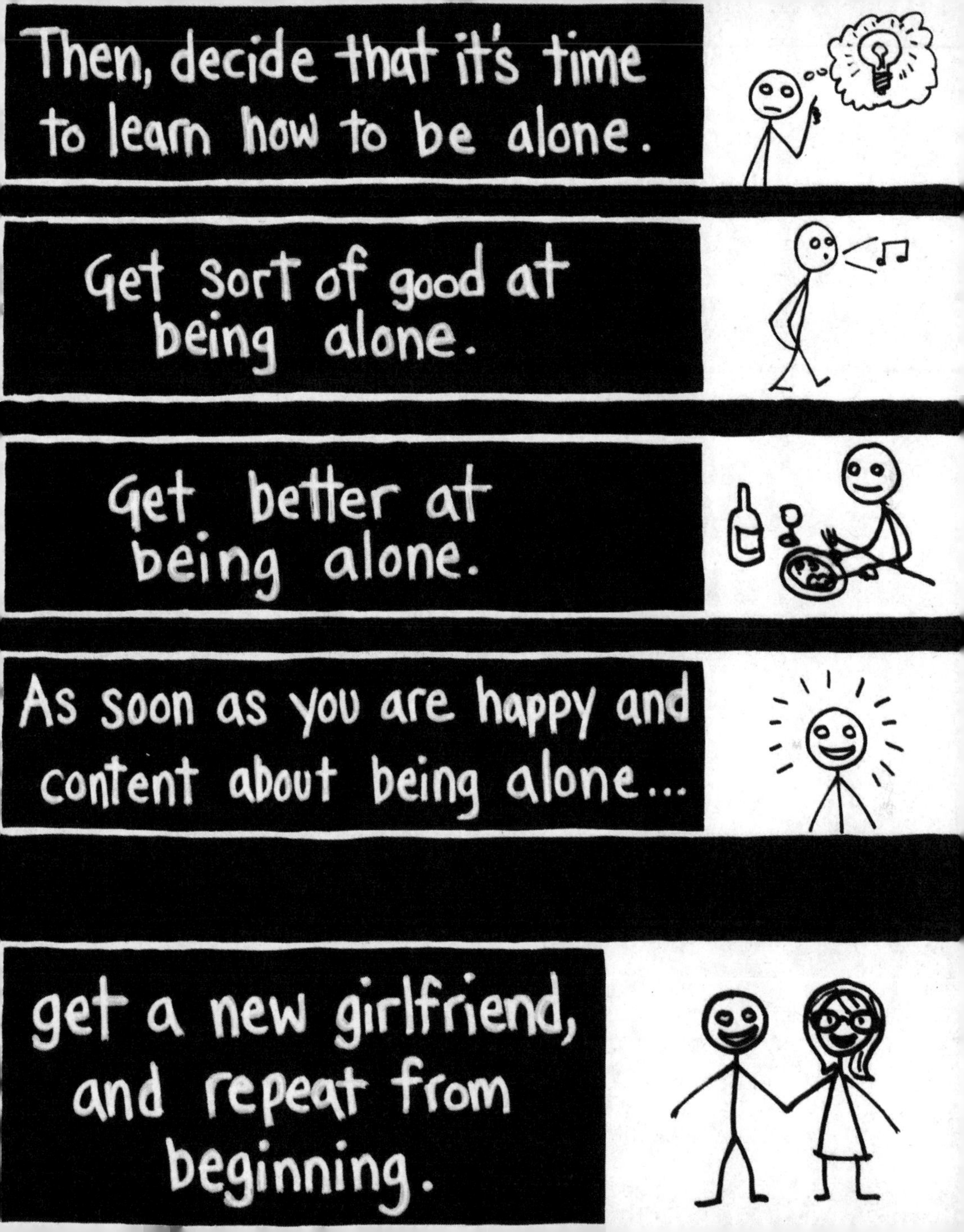
Then, decide that it's time to learn how to be alone.
Get sort of good at being alone.
Get better at being alone.
As soon as you are happy and content about being alone...
get a new girlfriend, and repeat from beginning.

Maybe I should check to see if I locked the door.
I sure wish I had never seen the photographs
in the RESEARCH "Modern Primitives" book.
If I'm going to feel this crappy every time I eat
Tofu, I may as well say screw it and eat Brisket.
There's a monster at the end of this book.
I wonder which will come first,
White hair or liver disease.
I wonder if that guy Pudgy Henry from High School
Who carved "Ozzy" into his arm is any happier
than I am today?
I could easily spend a full and happy day
thinking about nothing but how much I hate Sting.
"Breasts, Buttocks & Vulvas" is the way they
would say "Tits, Ass & Pussy" in a medical journal.

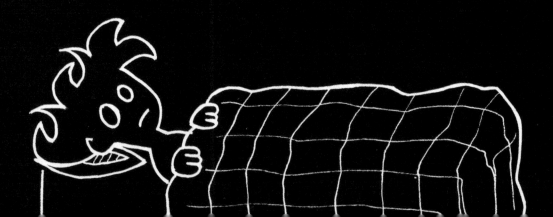

CHAPTER 5:
I have no idea what is supposed to happen next.

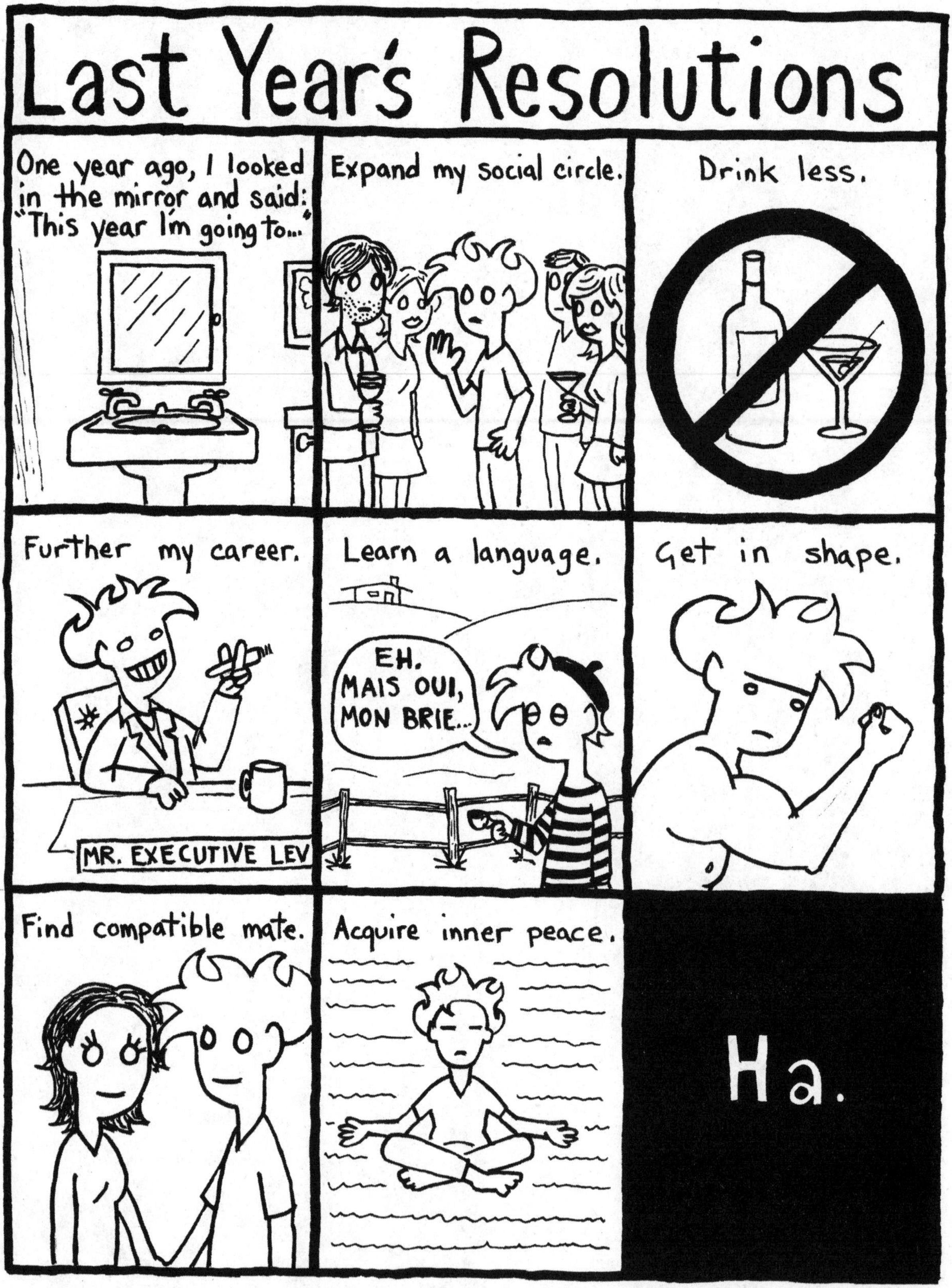
Last Year's Resolutions
One year ago, I looked in the mirror and said: "This year I'm going to..."
Expand my social circle.
Drink less.
Further my career.
MR. EXECUTIVE LEV
Learn a language.
EH. MAIS OUI, MON BRIE...
Get in shape.
Find compatible mate.
Acquire inner peace.
Ha.

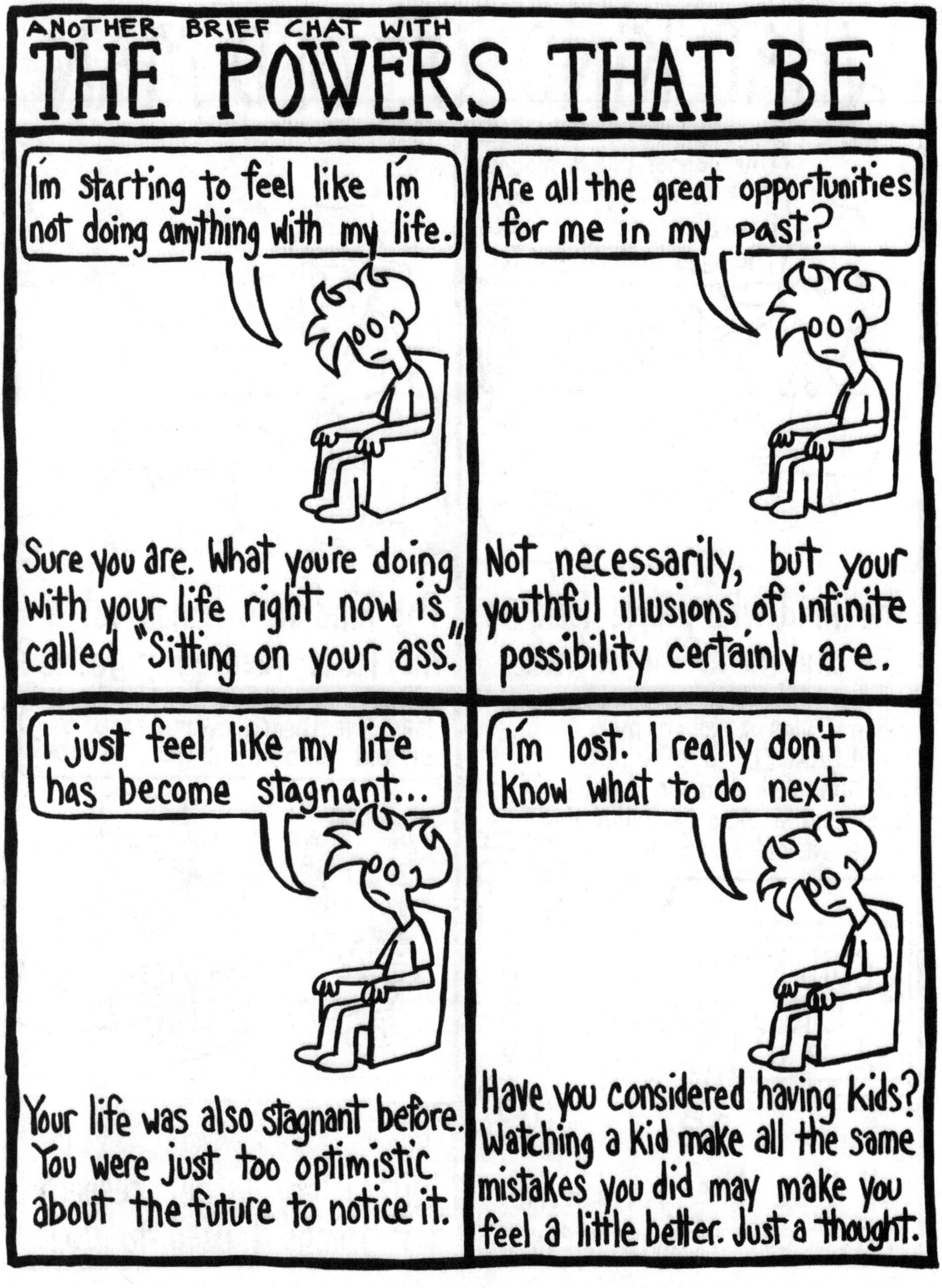
ANOTHER BRIEF CHAT WITH
THE POWERS THAT BE
I'm starting to feel like I'm not doing anything with my life.
Sure you are. What you're doing with your life right now is called "Sitting on your ass."
Are all the great opportunities for me in my past?
Not necessarily, but your youthful illusions of infinite possibility certainly are.
I just feel like my life has become stagnant...
Your life was also stagnant before. You were just too optimistic about the future to notice it.
I'm lost. I really don't know what to do next.
Have you considered having kids? Watching a kid make all the same mistakes you did may make you feel a little better. Just a thought.

WHAT KIND OF OLD MAN

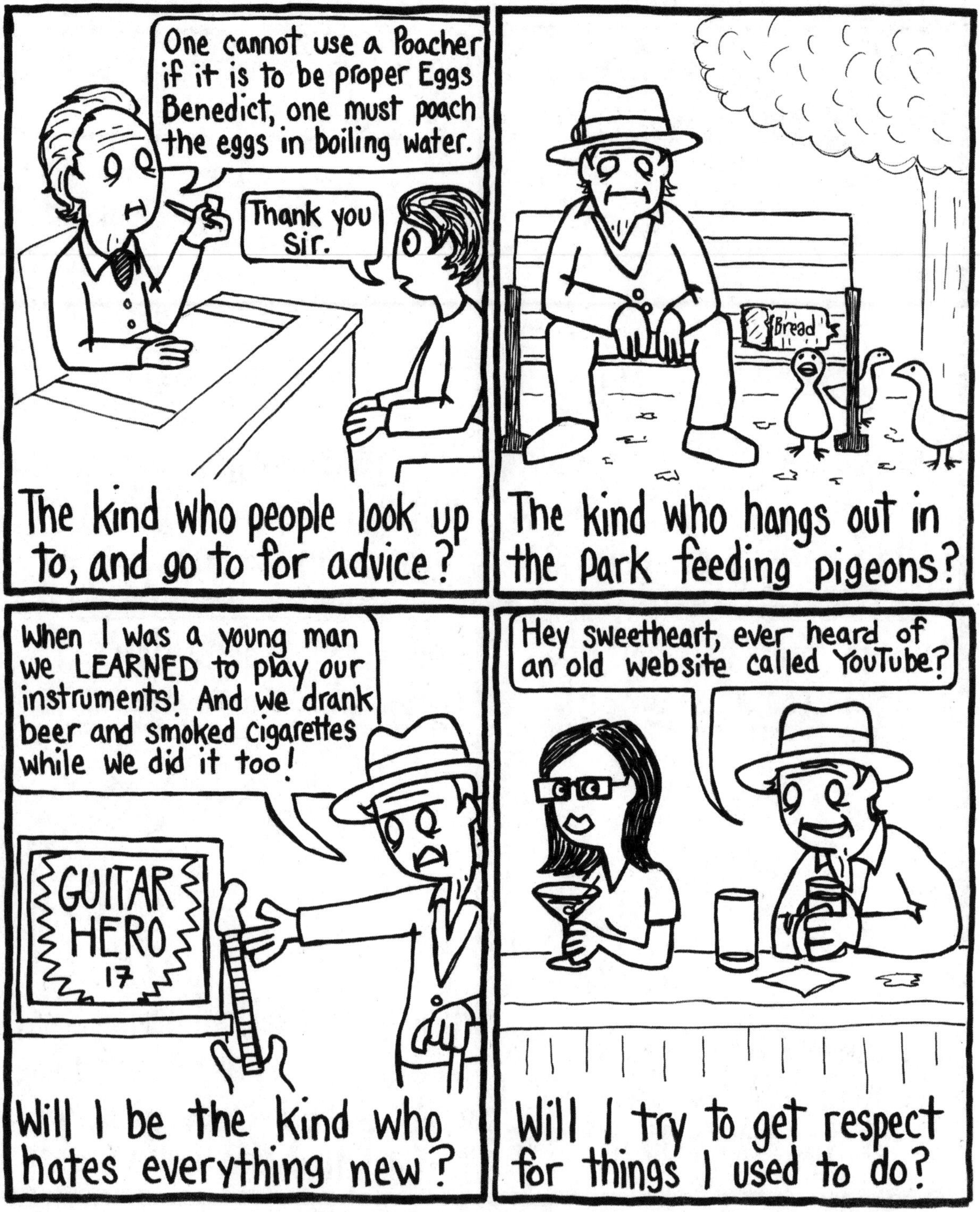
One cannot use a Poacher if it is to be proper Eggs Benedict, one must poach the eggs in boiling water.
Thank you sir.
The kind who people look up to, and go to for advice?
Bread
The kind who hangs out in the park feeding pigeons?
When I was a young man we LEARNED to play our instruments! And we drank beer and smoked cigarettes while we did it too!
GUITAR HERO 17
Will I be the kind who hates everything new?
Hey sweetheart, ever heard of an old website called YouTube?
Will I try to get respect for things I used to do?

WILL I BE?

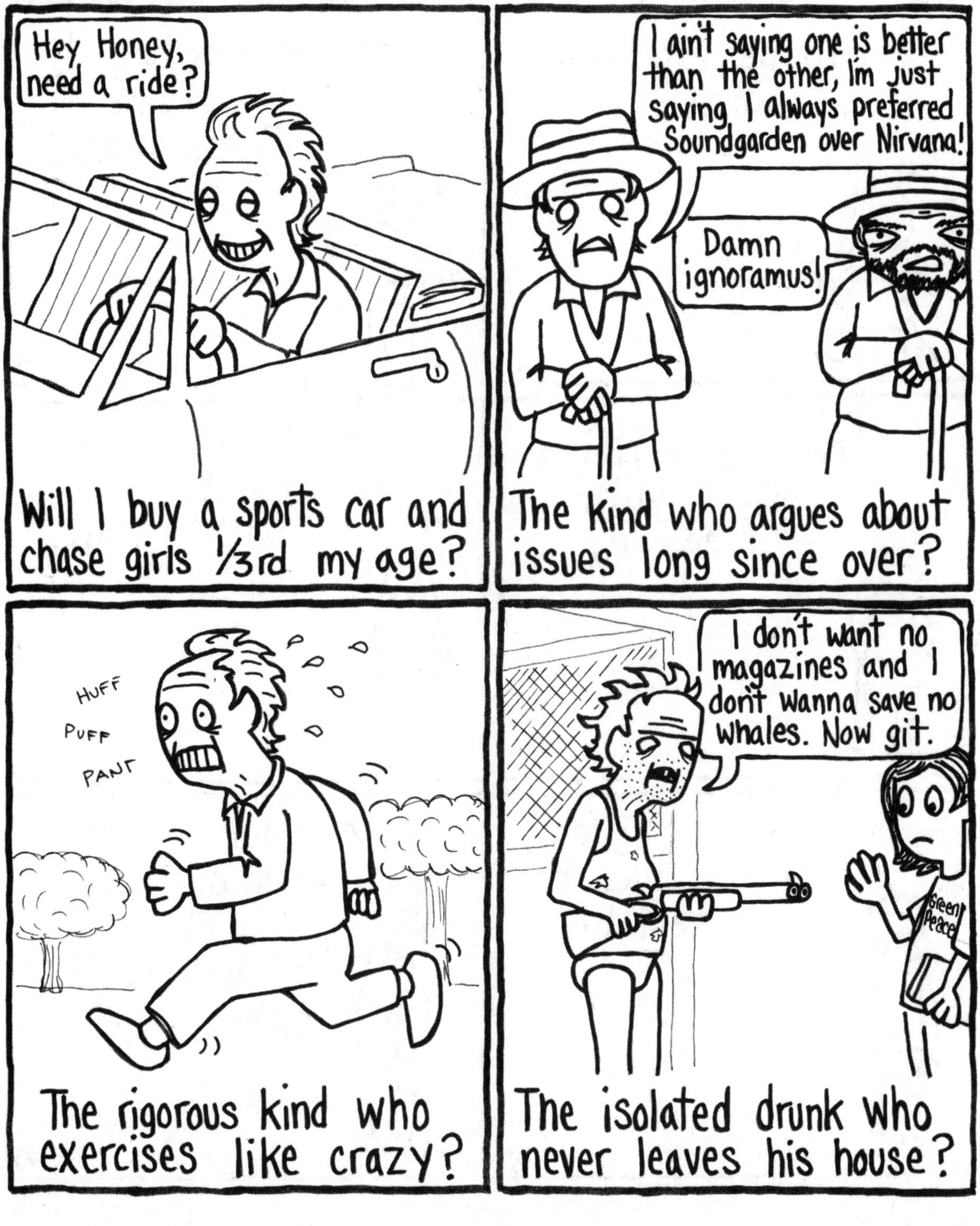
Hey Honey, need a ride?
Will I buy a sports car and chase girls 1/3rd my age?
I ain't saying one is better than the other, I'm just saying I always preferred Soundgarden over Nirvana!
Damn ignoramus!
The kind who argues about issues long since over?
HUFF
PUFF
PANT
The rigorous kind who exercises like crazy?
I don't want no magazines and I don't wanna save no whales. Now git.
Green Peace
The isolated drunk who never leaves his house?

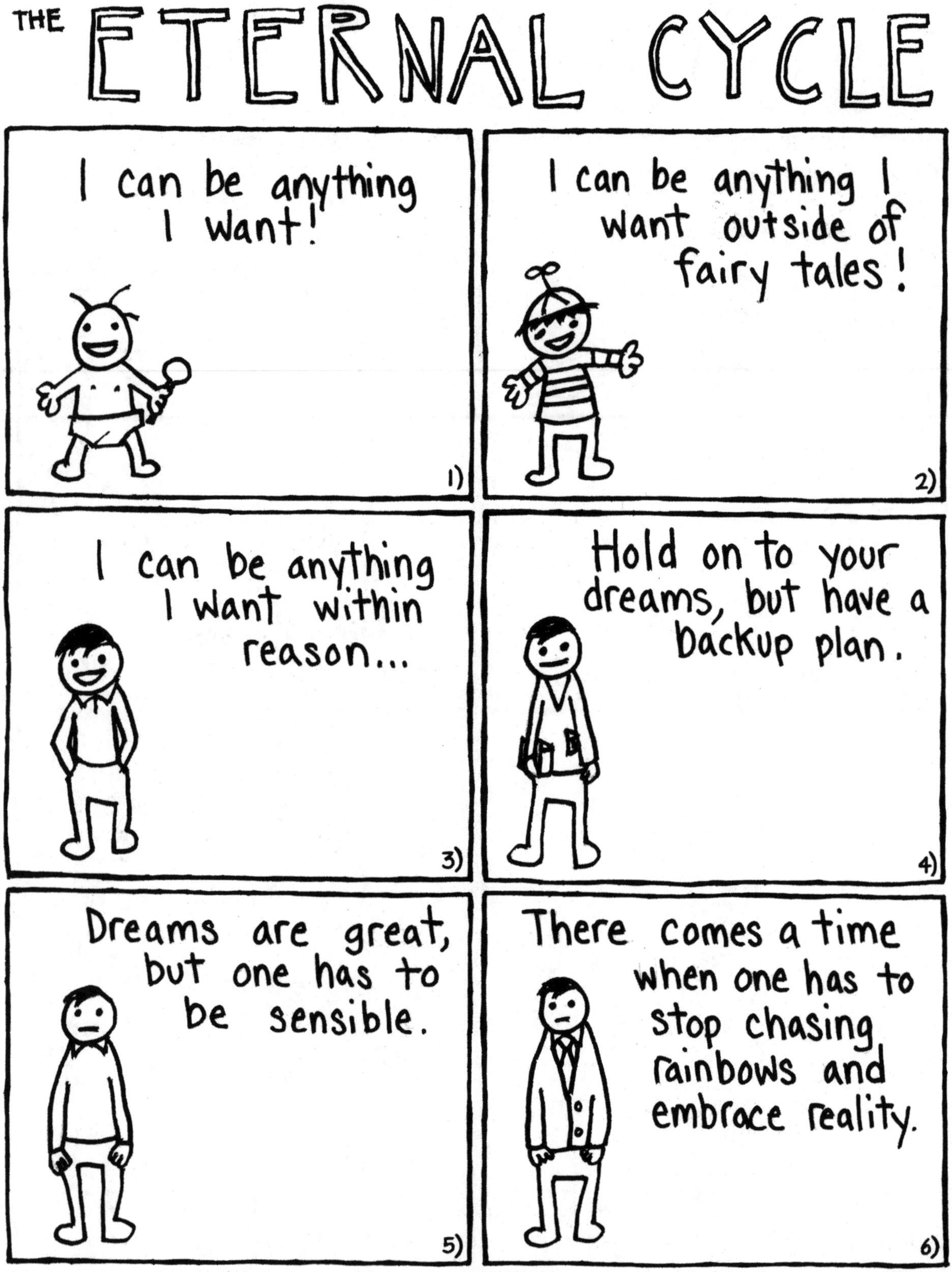
THE ETERNAL CYCLE
I can be anything I want!
1)
I can be anything I want outside of fairy tales!
2)
I can be anything I want within reason...
3)
Hold on to your dreams, but have a backup plan.
4)
Dreams are great, but one has to be sensible.
5)
There comes a time when one has to stop chasing rainbows and embrace reality.
6)

OF HUMAN DISPOSITION

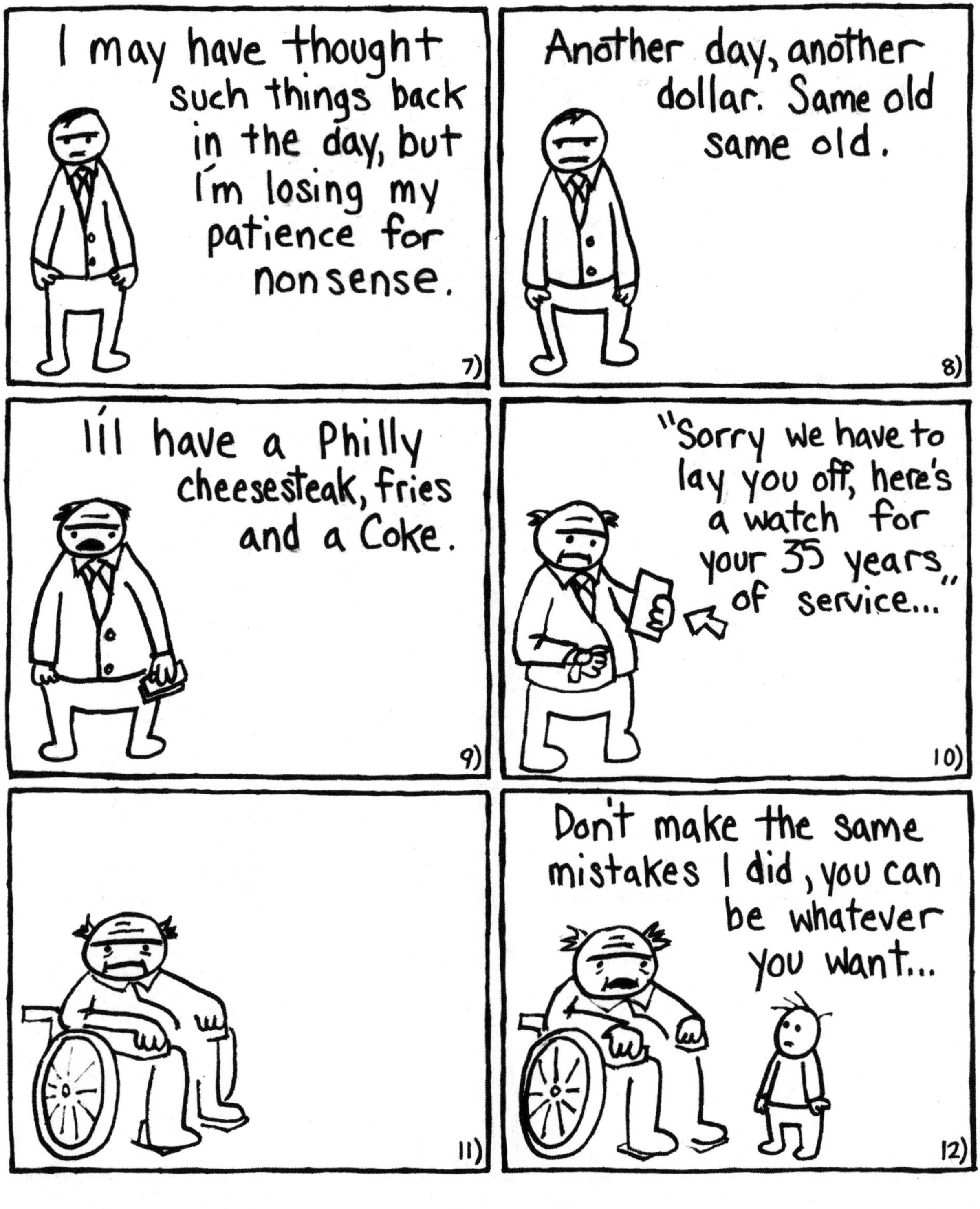

THE 7 HABITS OF HIGHLY NEGATIVE PEOPLE

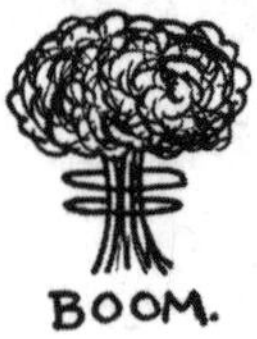
BOOM.

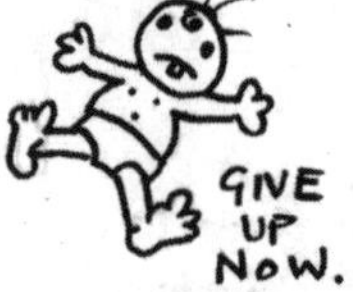
GIVE UP NOW.

1) BE MOODILY INACTIVE

Explore a lack of initiative taking, and a deep resentment toward well-adjusted people around you.

2) BEGIN WITH YOUR FAILURES IN MIND

When approaching long-term goals, remember that nothing you have tried has ever worked out before, so whatever idea you have now is unlikely to bring different results.

3) PUT FIRST THINGS WHEREVER

Fight the common misconception that anything in your life is less unimportant than anything else.

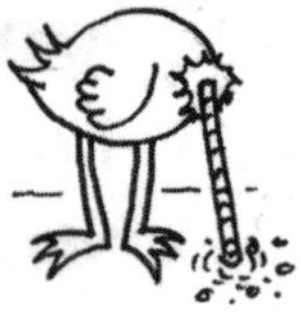

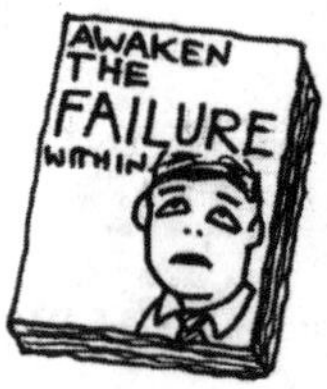
AWAKEN THE
FAILURE
WITHIN

4) THINK LOSE / LOSE

If you can bring others down far enough, they may wind up on the same level as you.

5) SEEK FIRST TO BE UNDERSTOOD...

Then to complain that nobody understands. If there is a way to do this kicking and screaming, do so.

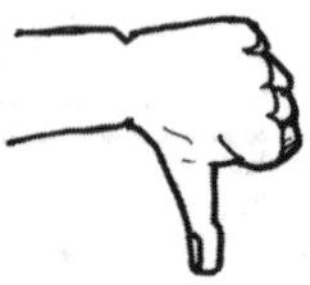

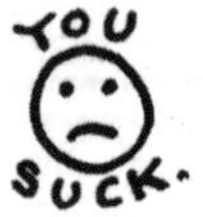
YOU
SUCK.

6) UNDERSTAND SYNERGY

Realize that the whole is greater than the sum of its parts, but also realize that your part sucks the most, so you may as well give up now.

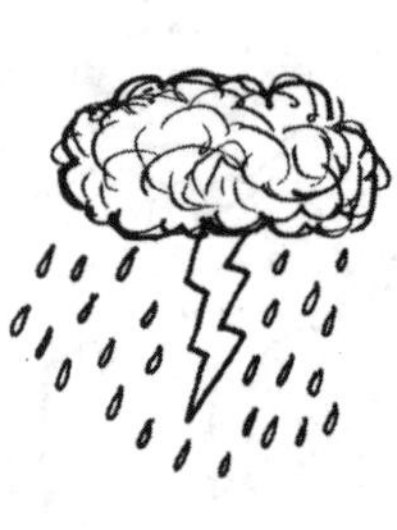

7) LET THE SAW GO DULL

Then, you can blame everything on the saw.

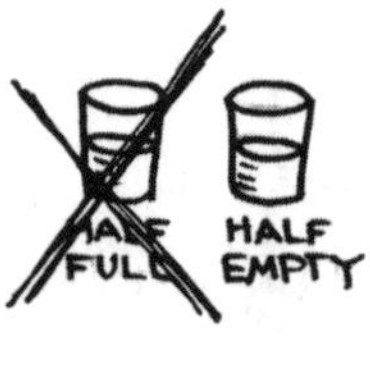
HALF FULL
HALF EMPTY

TOGETHER
EACH
ADMITS
MEDIOCRITY

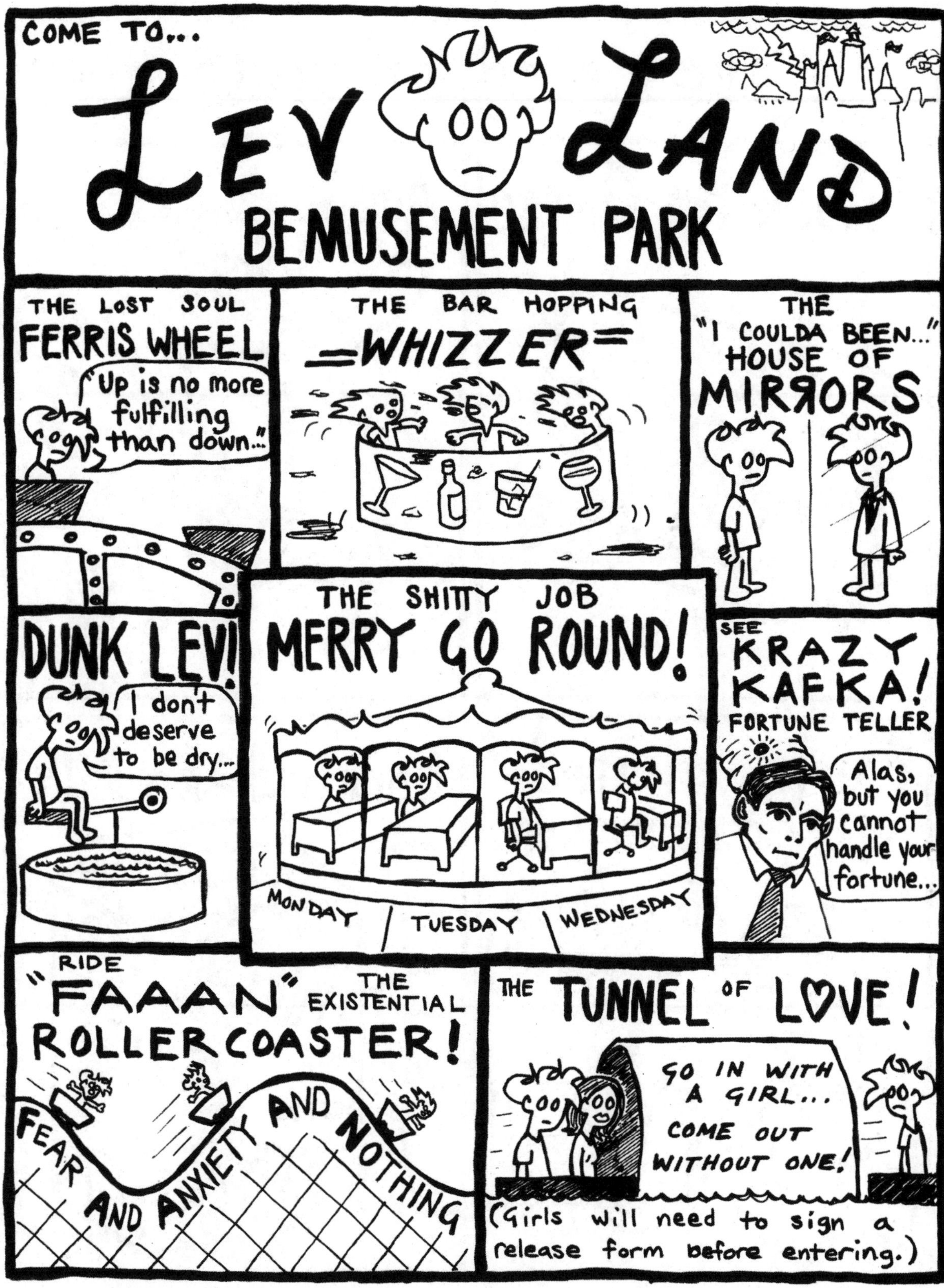
COME TO...
LEV LAND
BEMUSEMENT PARK
THE LOST SOUL FERRIS WHEEL
"Up is no more fulfilling than down..."
THE BAR HOPPING WHIZZER
THE "I COULDA BEEN..." HOUSE OF MIRRORS
DUNK LEV!
I don't deserve to be dry...
THE SHITTY JOB MERRY GO ROUND!
MONDAY
TUESDAY
WEDNESDAY
SEE KRAZY KAFKA! FORTUNE TELLER
Alas, but you cannot handle your fortune...
RIDE "FAAAN" THE EXISTENTIAL ROLLERCOASTER!
FEAR AND ANXIETY AND NOTHING
THE TUNNEL OF LOVE!
GO IN WITH A GIRL... COME OUT WITHOUT ONE!
(Girls will need to sign a release form before entering.)

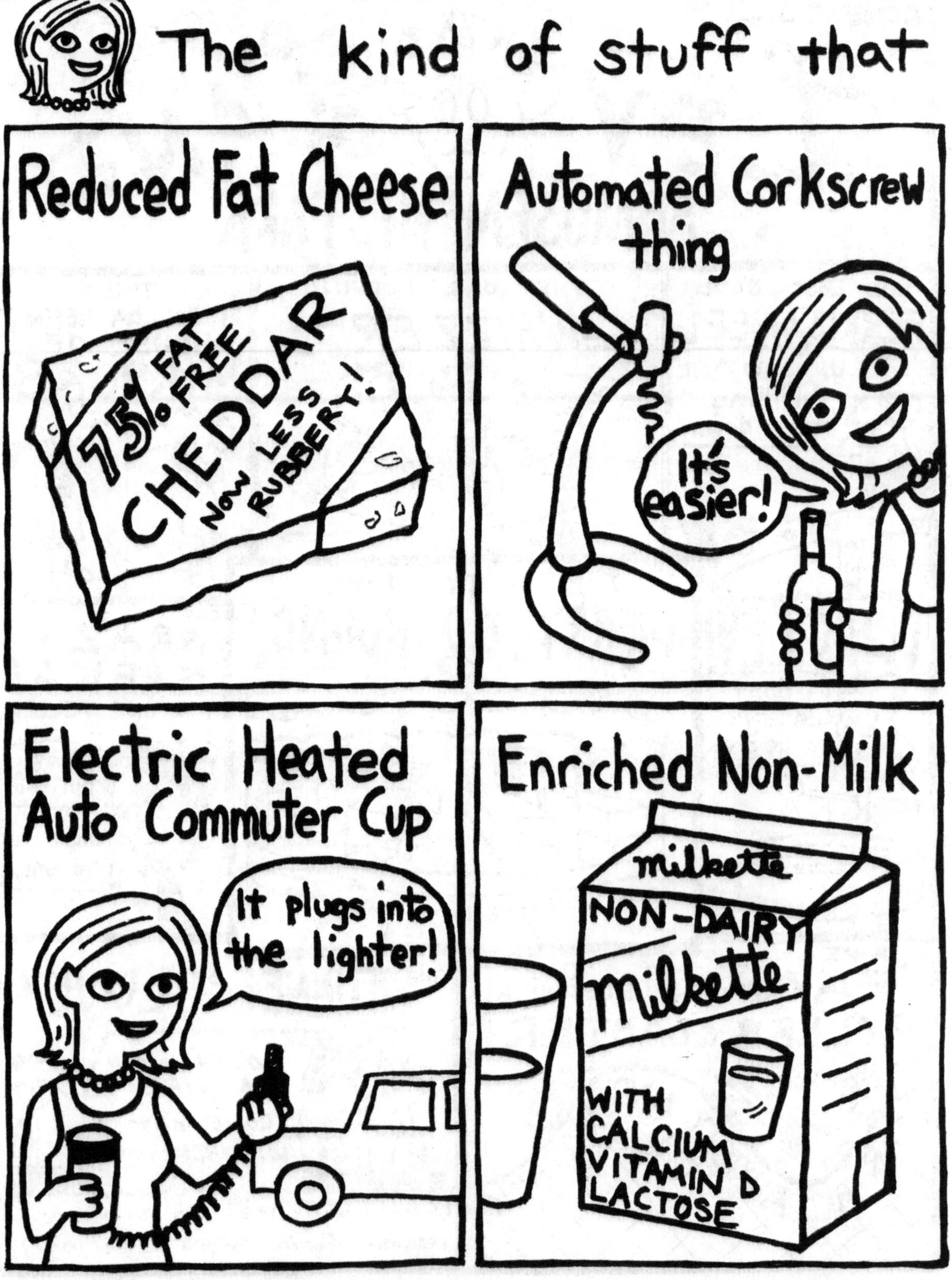
The kind of stuff that
Reduced Fat Cheese
75% FAT FREE
CHEDDAR
NOW LESS RUBBERY!
Automated Corkscrew thing
It's easier!
Electric Heated Auto Commuter Cup
It plugs into the lighter!
Enriched Non-Milk
milkette
NON-DAIRY
Milkette
WITH CALCIUM VITAMIN D LACTOSE

MY MOM BUYS

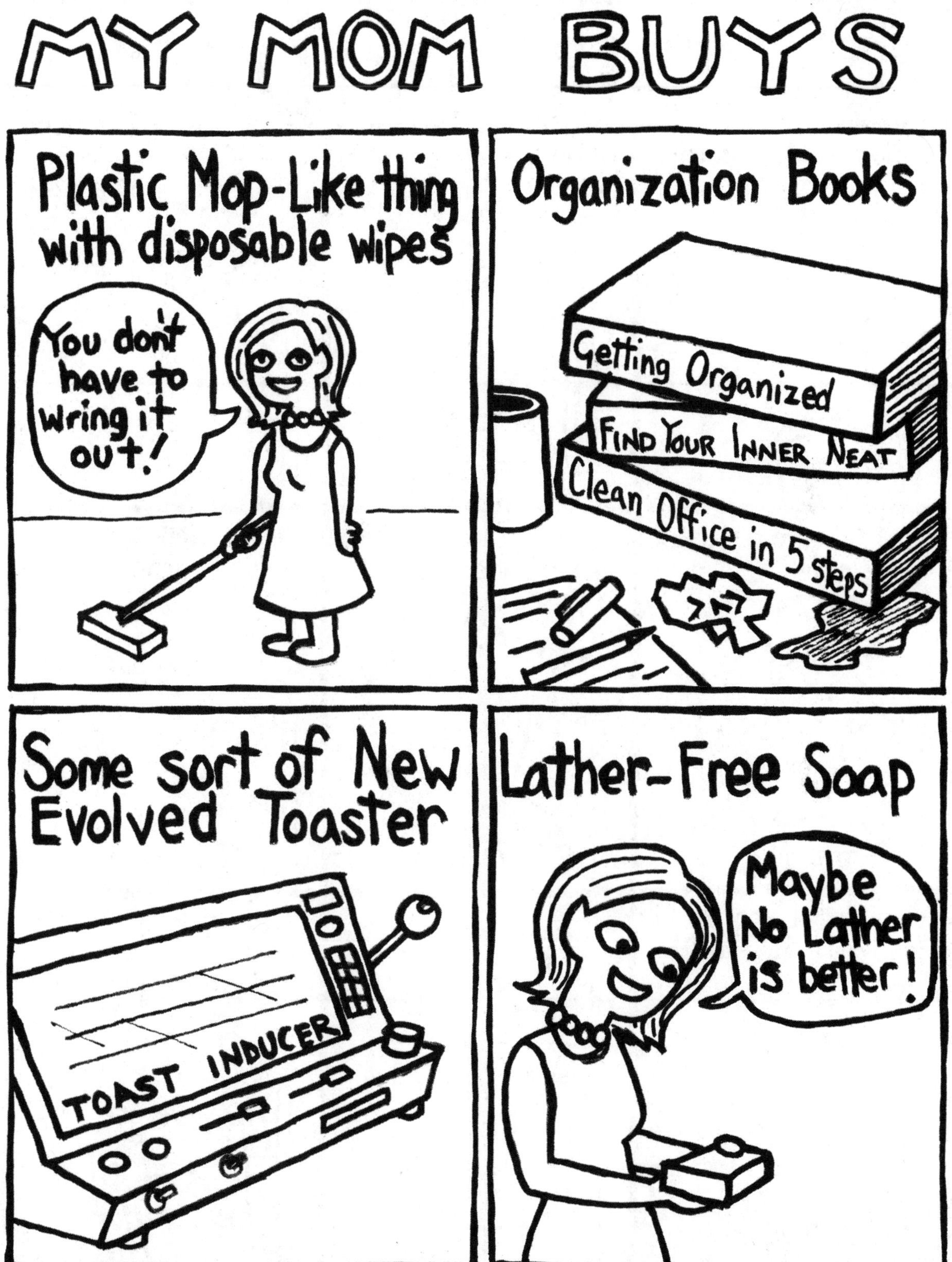
Plastic Mop-Like thing with disposable wipes
You don't have to wring it out!
Organization Books
Getting Organized
FIND YOUR INNER NEAT
Clean Office in 5 steps
Some sort of New Evolved Toaster
TOAST INDUCER
Lather-Free Soap
Maybe No Lather is better!

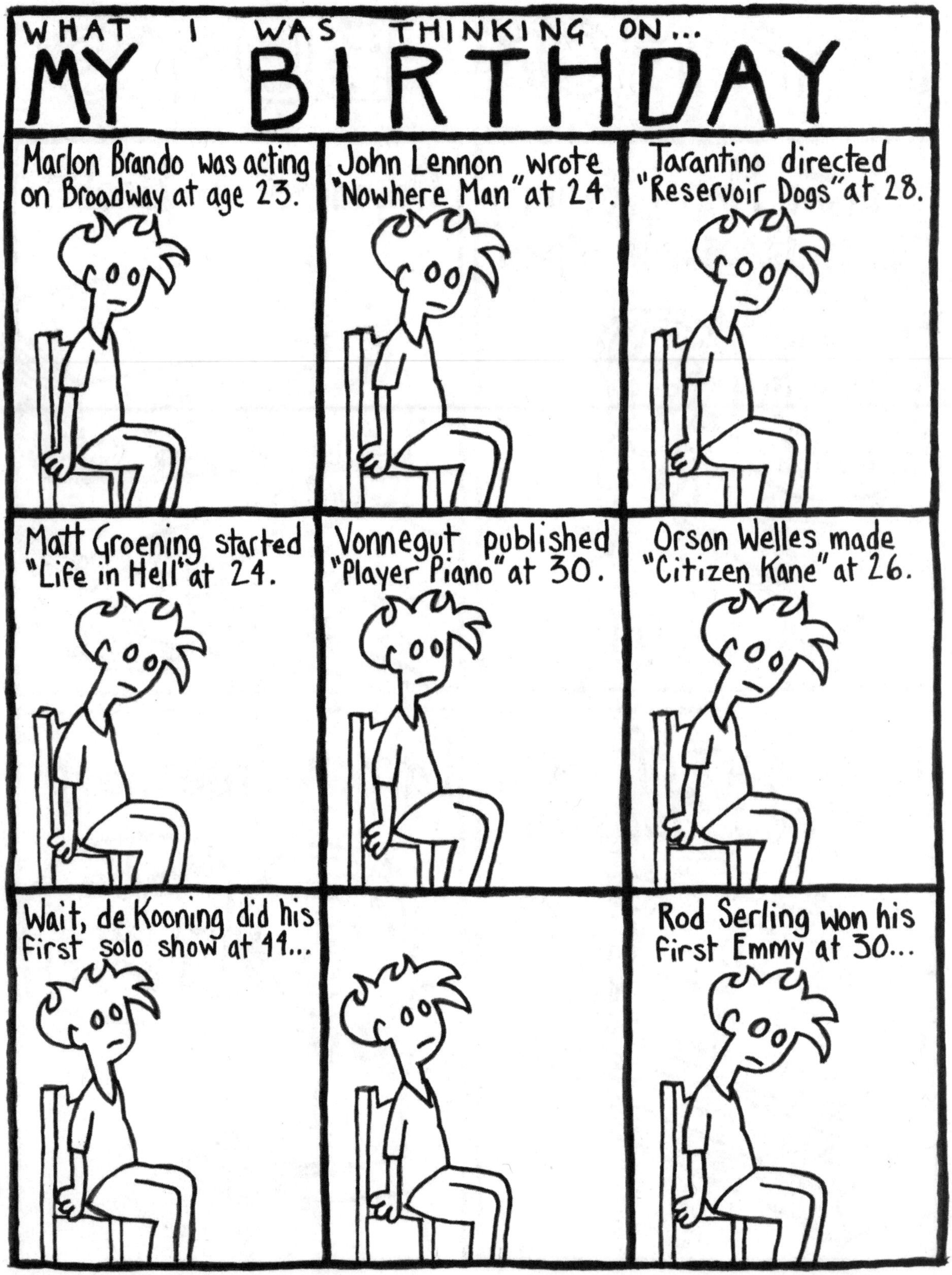
WHAT I WAS THINKING ON...
MY BIRTHDAY
Marlon Brando was acting on Broadway at age 23.
John Lennon wrote "Nowhere Man" at 24.
Tarantino directed "Reservoir Dogs" at 28.
Matt Groening started "Life in Hell" at 24.
Vonnegut published "Player Piano" at 30.
Orson Welles made "Citizen Kane" at 26.
Wait, de Kooning did his first solo show at 44...
Rod Serling won his first Emmy at 30...

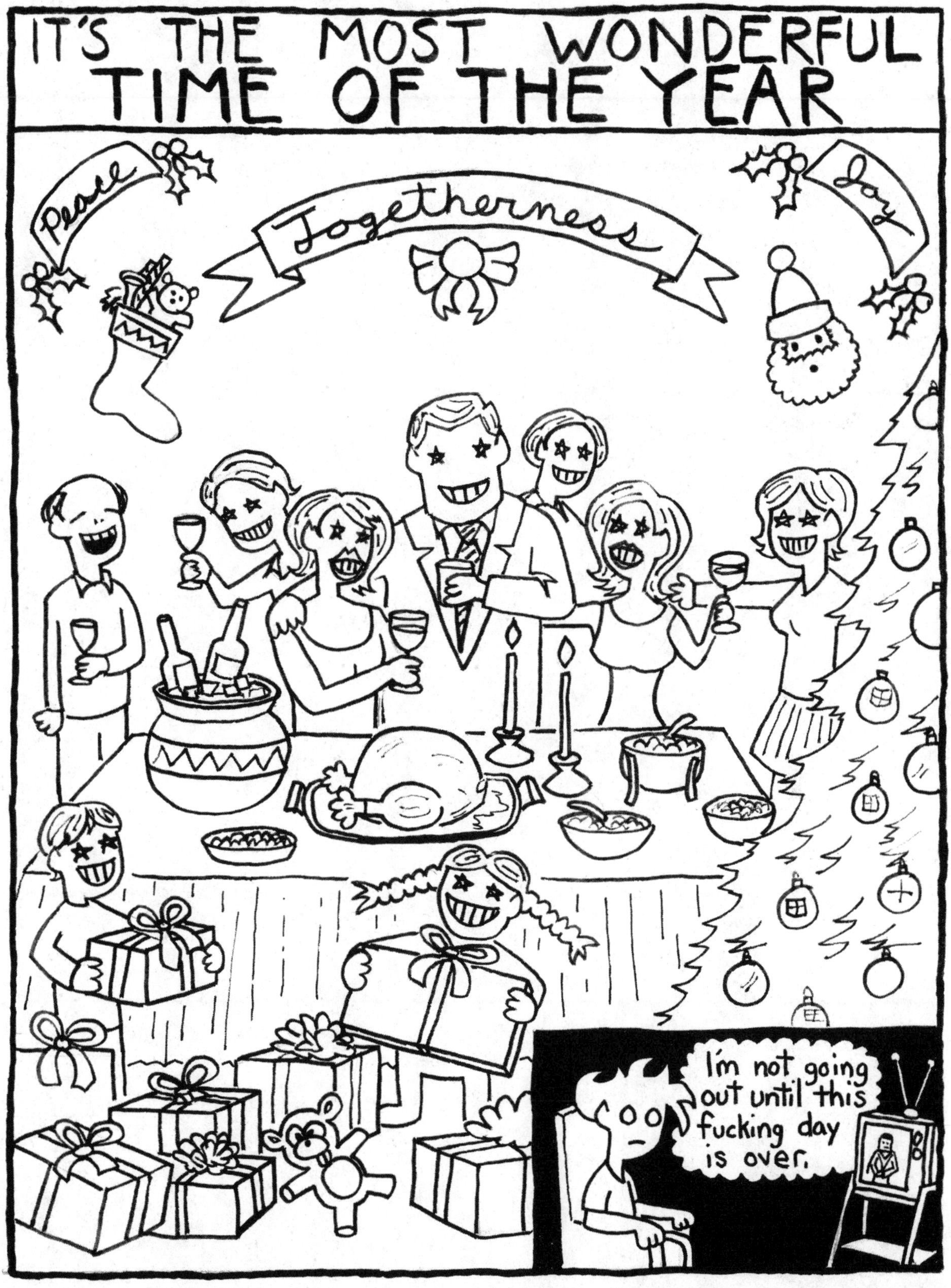
IT'S THE MOST WONDERFUL
TIME OF THE YEAR
Peace
Togetherness
Joy
I'm not going out until this fucking day is over.

I'm not going to think about her.

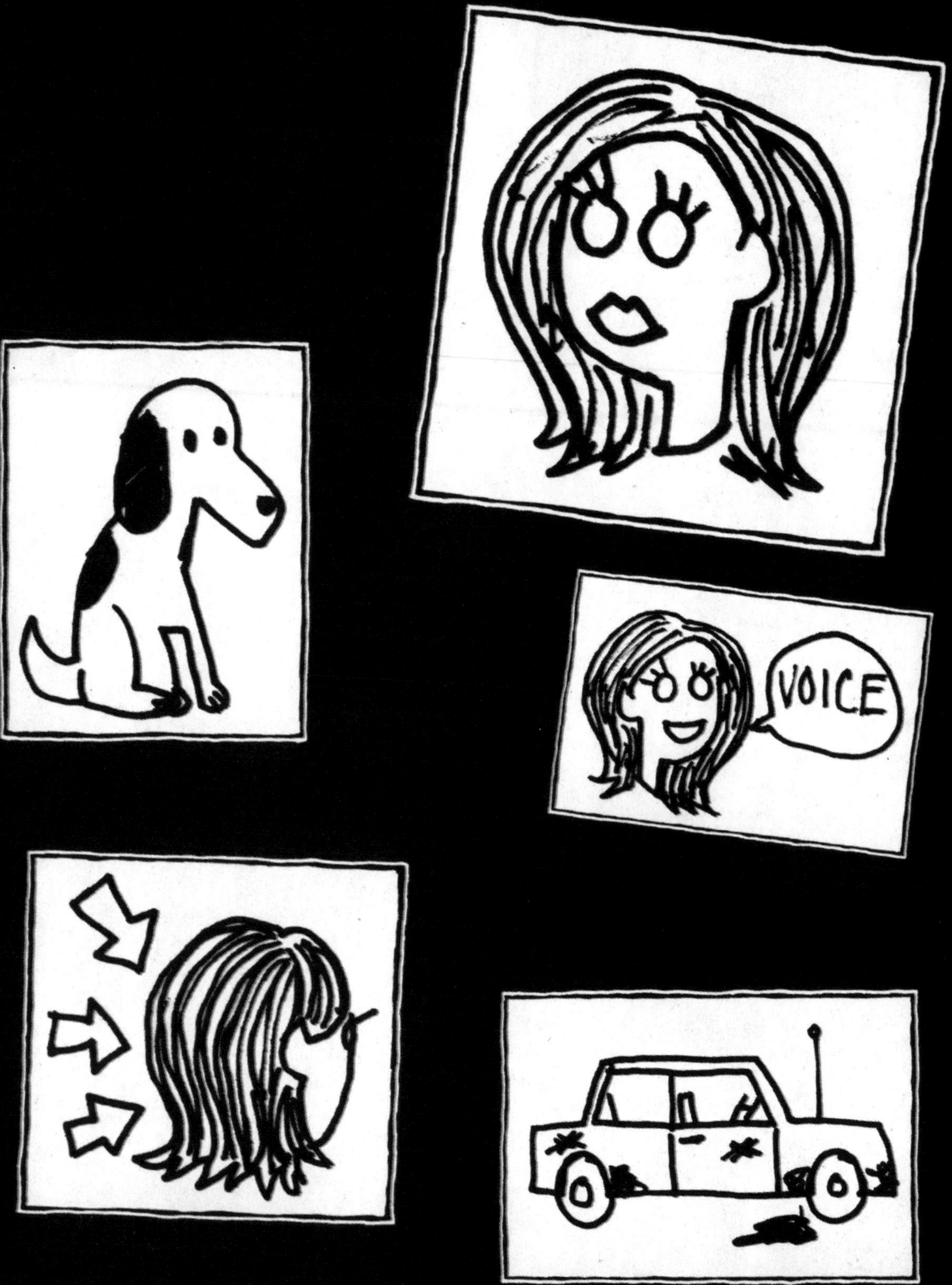
VOICE

I'm not going to think about her.
I'm not going to think about her.

I'm not going to think about her
anymore. I'm not going to think
about the way she looked. I'm not
going to think about the sound of
her voice. I'm not going to think
about the way her hair smelled.
I'm not going to think about how
she never cleaned her car. I'm
not going to think about how she
once had a dog named Romeo.

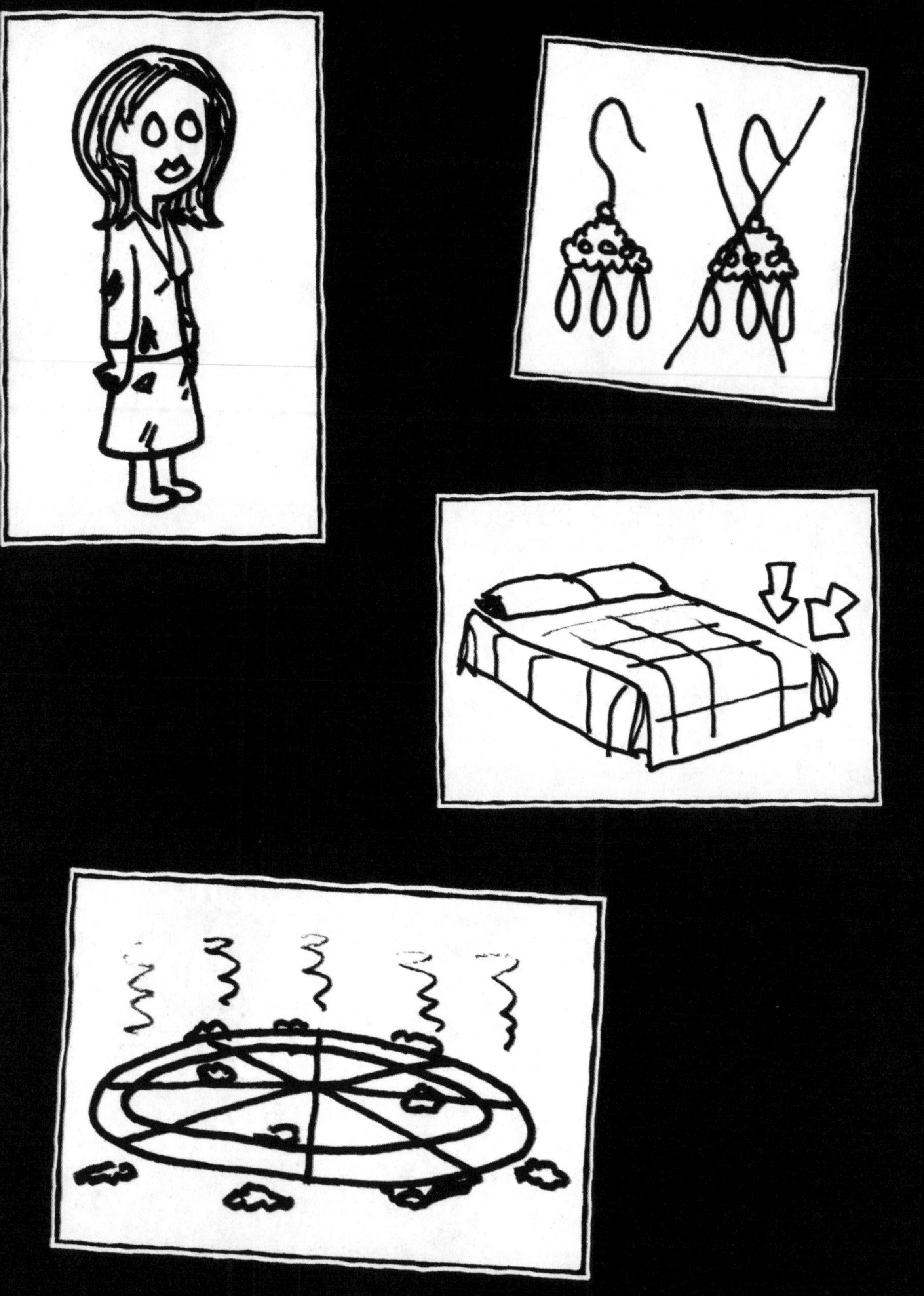

I'm not going to think about how she was never able to hang on to both earrings from a pair for more than a week. I'm not going to think about how she always untucked all the sheets after I made the bed so they wouldn't squash her feet. I'm not going to think about how she had these funny burn marks on all her good clothes because she always set the iron too hot. I'm not going to think about how she got drunk and cooked a frozen pizza with the cellophane still on it because the box didn't specifically say to remove it.

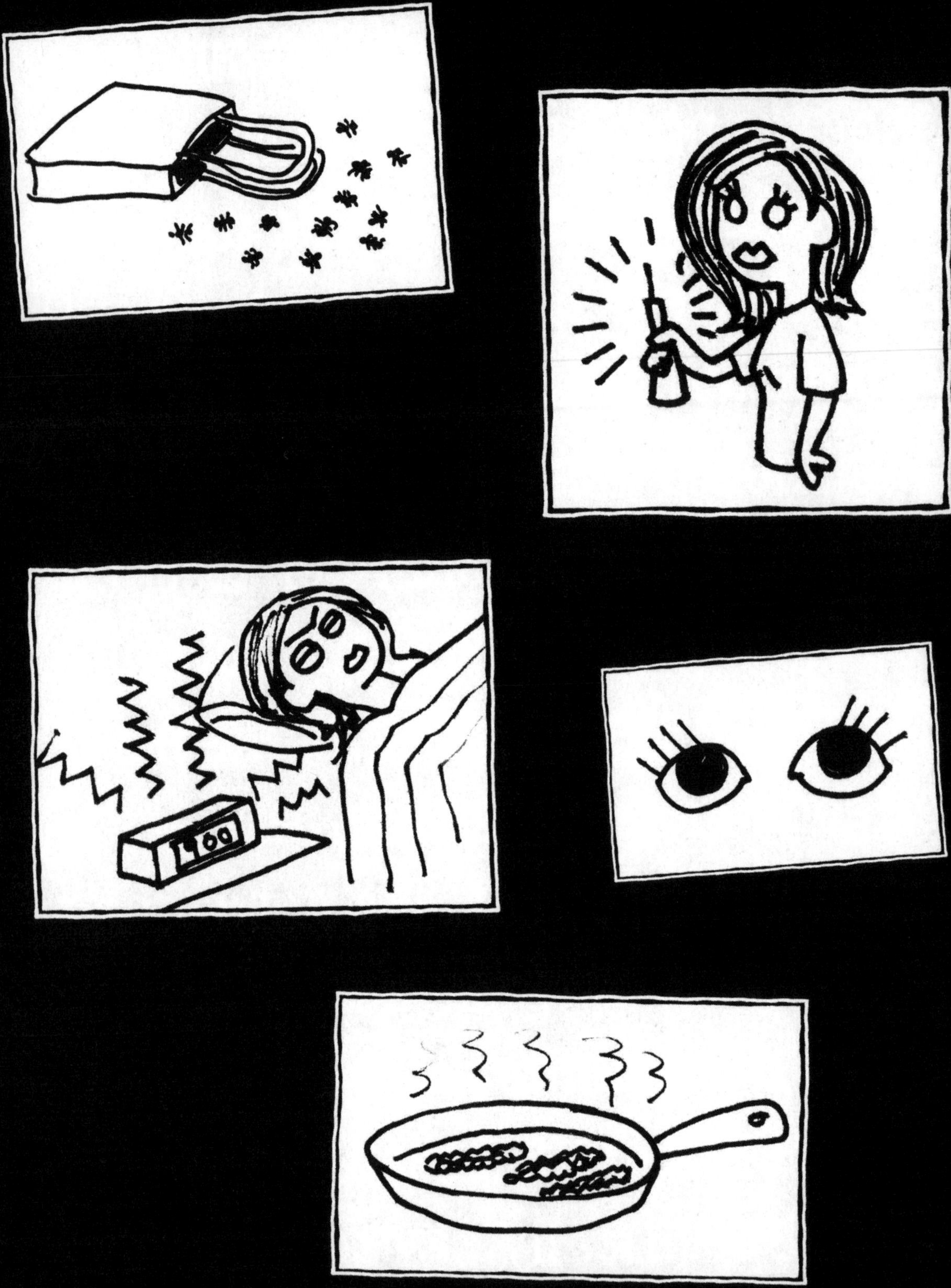

I'm not going to think about how she once left a bunch of open candies in her purse for a week and I spent an afternoon killing ants in her apartment. I'm not going to think about how she bought this cheap button-sewing thing off the TV. I'm not going to think about how she was really pretty good at cooking bacon. I'm not going to think about how she really hated the buzzer on my alarm clock. I'm not going to think about how one of her eyes was slightly bigger than the other.

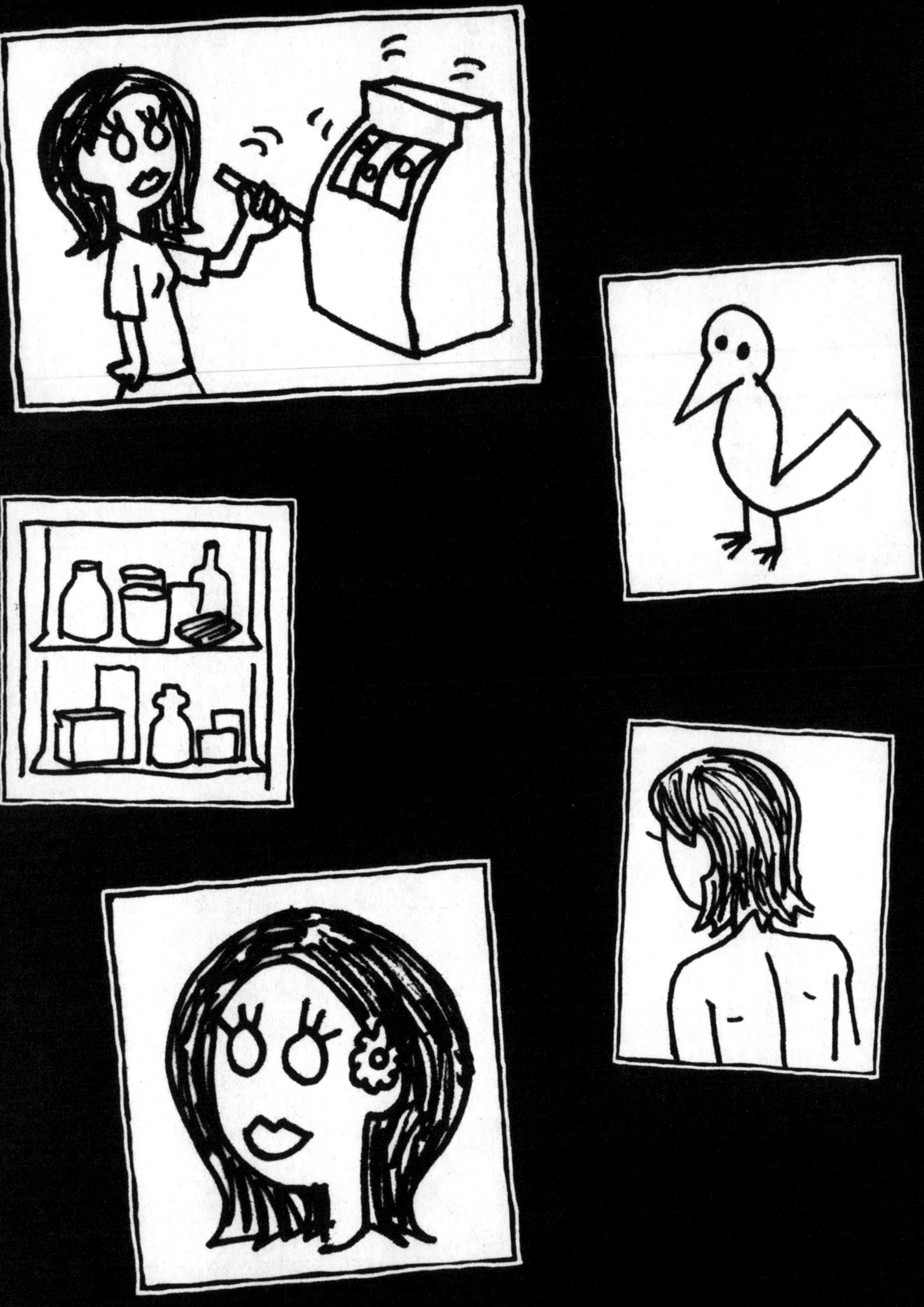

I'm not going to think about how we had a running joke in Reno that all the slot machines were broken because they weren't giving us any money. I'm not going to think about how she was so tiny & delicate that holding her was like holding a little bird. I'm not going to think about the time I came home one day and opened the fridge and realized she had bought me groceries. I'm not going to think about the dark, smooth skin of her back. I'm not going to think about what she looked like when I put this little white flower in her hair.

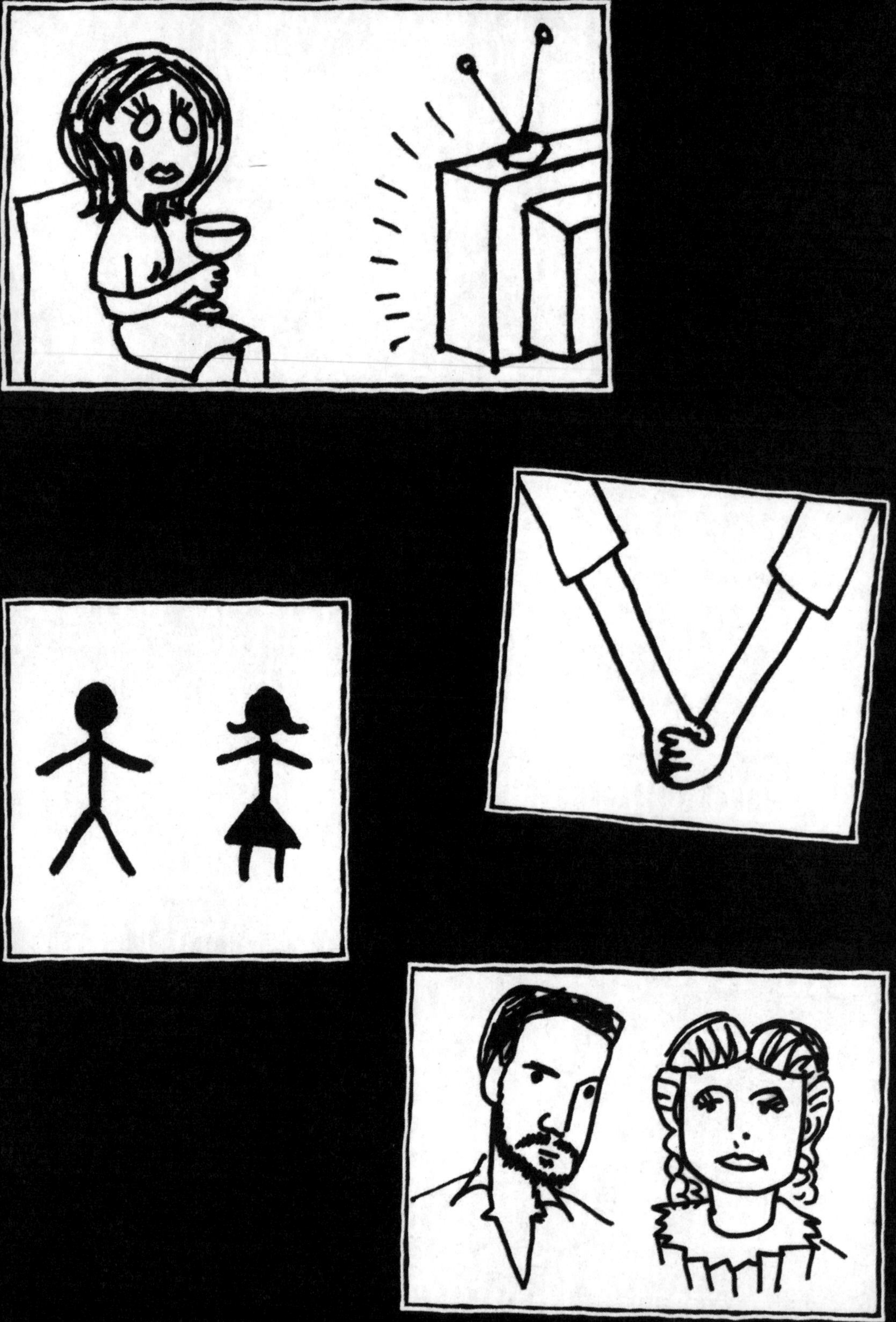

I'm not going to think about how she got drunk and cried during the scene where Chewbacca puts C-3PO back together in "The Empire Strikes Back." I'm not going to think about how she would always hold my hand in public. I'm not going to think about how we made a deal that I'd buy her "Shakespeare In Love" for her birthday only if she promised I'd never have to watch it, but she made me watch it a few times anyway. I'm not going to think about how it sometimes felt like we were the only two people on Earth.

I'm not going to think about how for a long time it really seemed like it was going to work out. I'm not going to think about how I found a box on my doorstep full of everything I had ever given her. I'm not going to think about whatever she may be doing right now. I'm not going to think about how she always used to call me to change light bulbs or fix door hinges in her apartment, but she doesn't call anymore and so she must have found somebody else to do it.

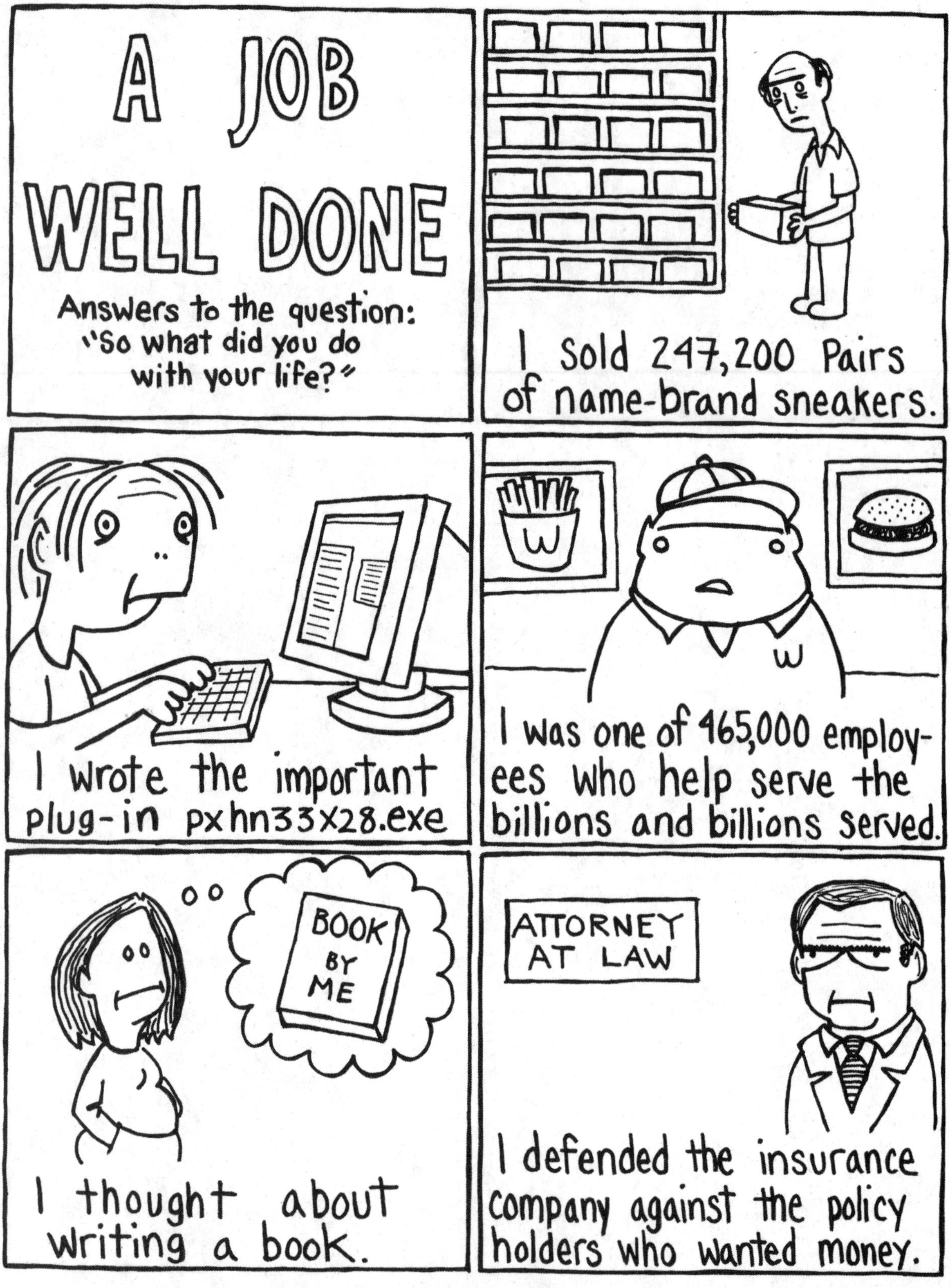
A JOB WELL DONE
Answers to the question: "So what did you do with your life?"
I sold 247,200 Pairs of name-brand sneakers.
I wrote the important plug-in pxhn33X28.exe
W
W
I was one of 465,000 employees who help serve the billions and billions served.
BOOK BY ME
I thought about writing a book.
ATTORNEY AT LAW
I defended the insurance company against the policy holders who wanted money.

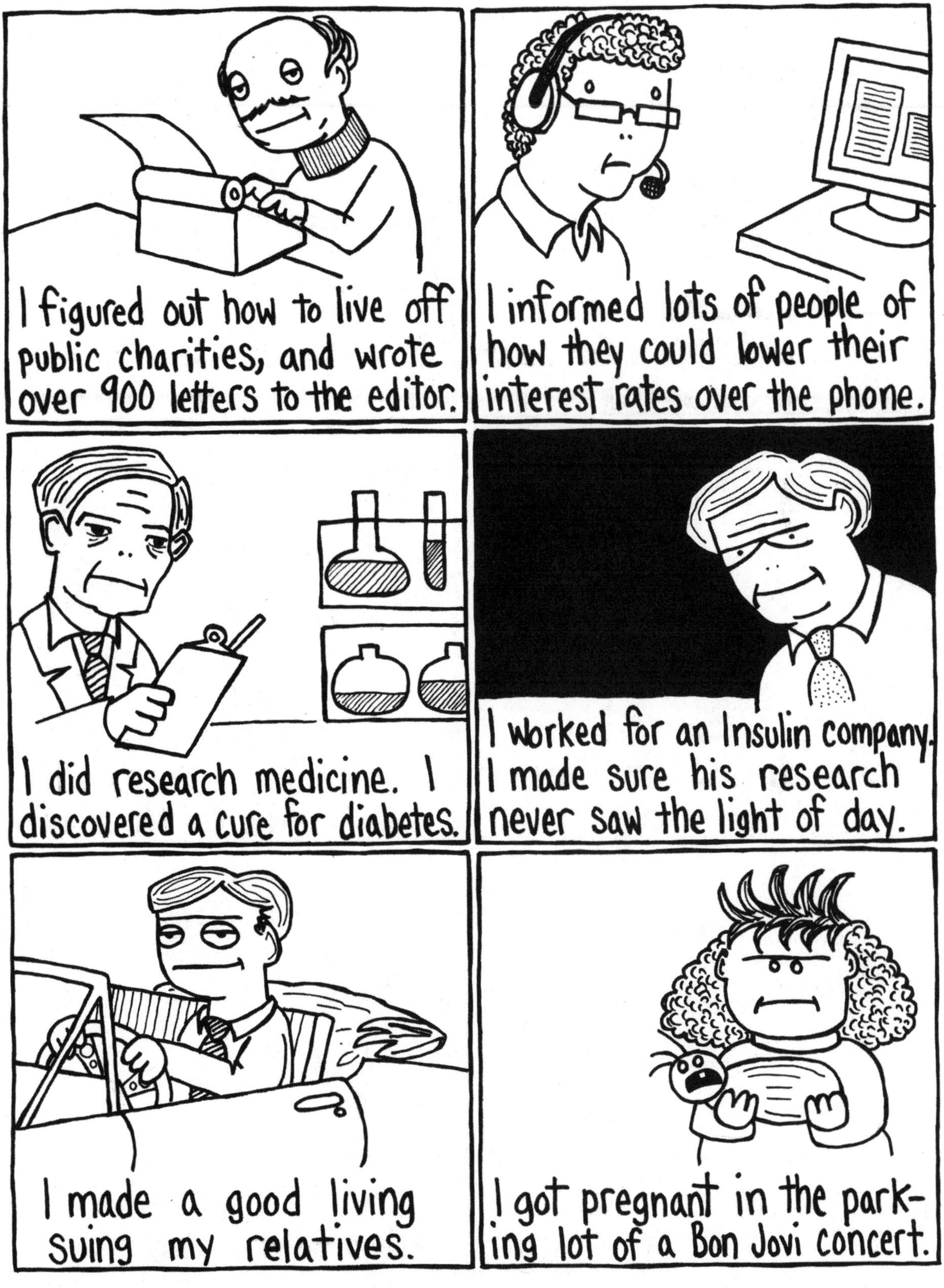
I figured out how to live off public charities, and wrote over 900 letters to the editor.
I informed lots of people of how they could lower their interest rates over the phone.
I did research medicine. I discovered a cure for diabetes.
I worked for an Insulin company. I made sure his research never saw the light of day.
I made a good living suing my relatives.
I got pregnant in the park-ing lot of a Bon Jovi concert.

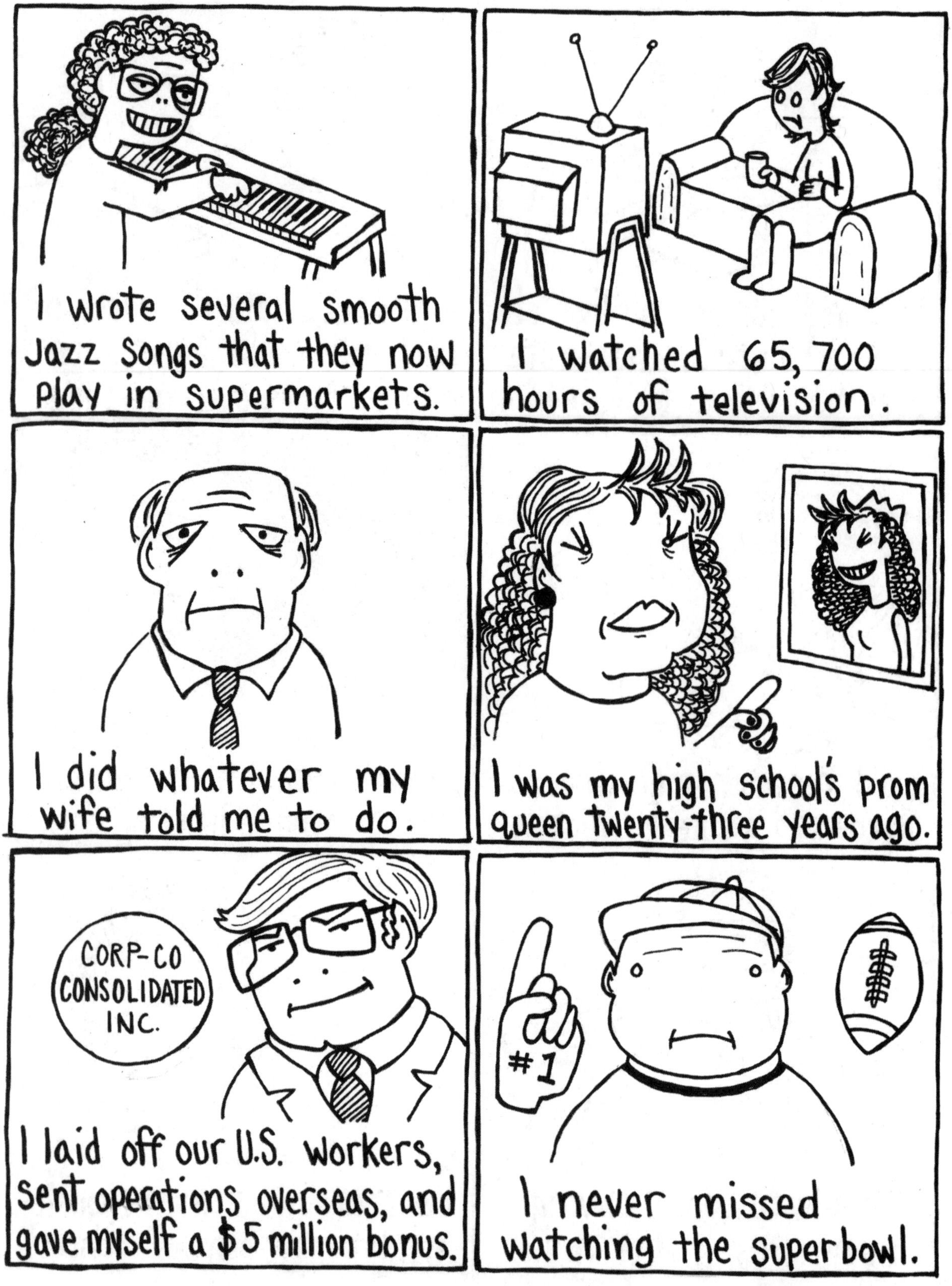
I wrote several smooth Jazz songs that they now play in supermarkets.
I watched 65,700 hours of television.
I did whatever my wife told me to do.
I was my high school's prom queen twenty-three years ago.
CORP-CO CONSOLIDATED INC.
I laid off our U.S. workers, sent operations overseas, and gave myself a $5 million bonus.
#1
I never missed watching the superbowl.

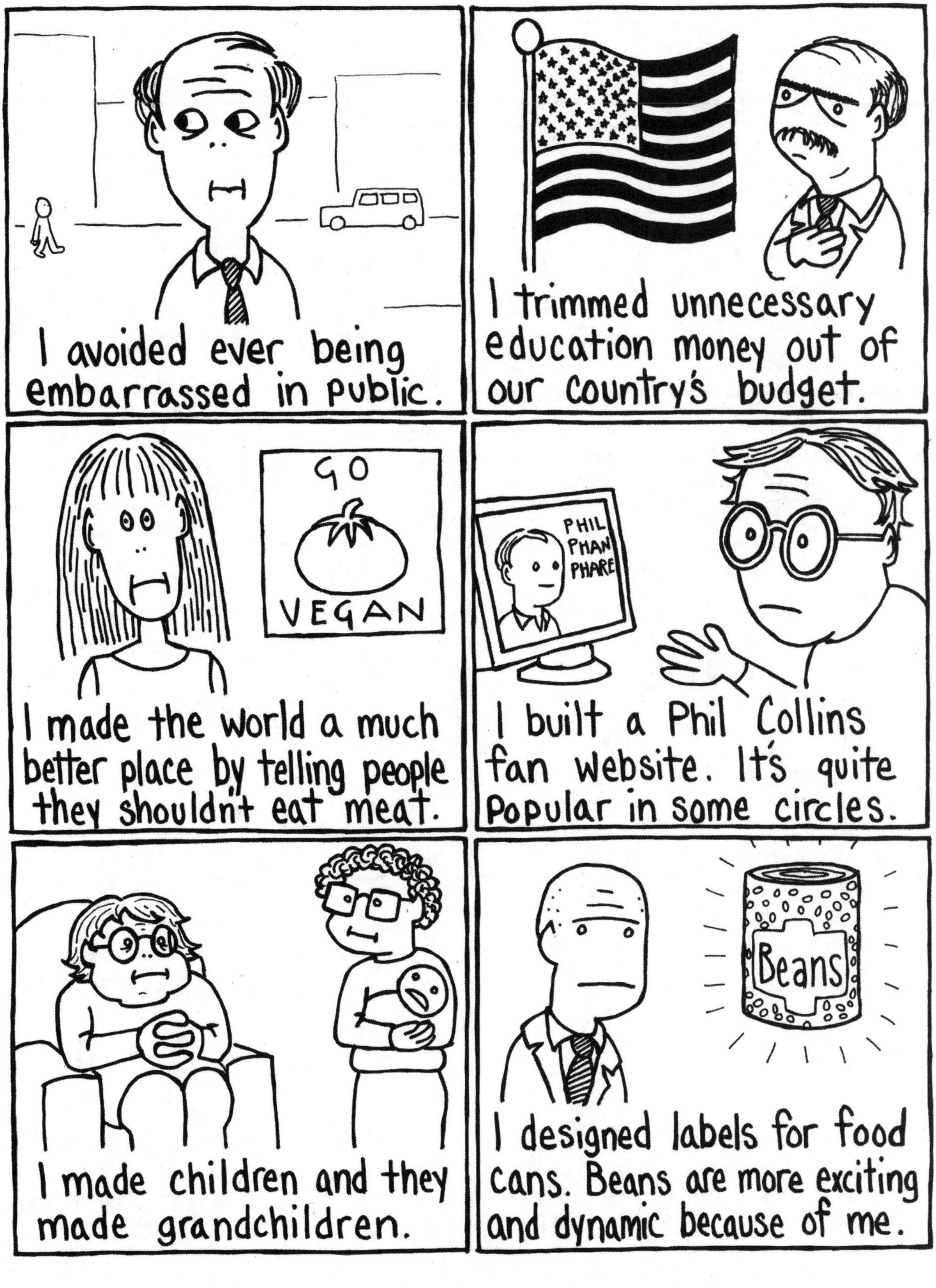
I avoided ever being embarrassed in public.
I trimmed unnecessary education money out of our country's budget.
GO
VEGAN
I made the world a much better place by telling people they shouldn't eat meat.
PHIL PHAN PHARE
I built a Phil Collins fan website. It's quite popular in some circles.
I made children and they made grandchildren.
Beans
I designed labels for food cans. Beans are more exciting and dynamic because of me.

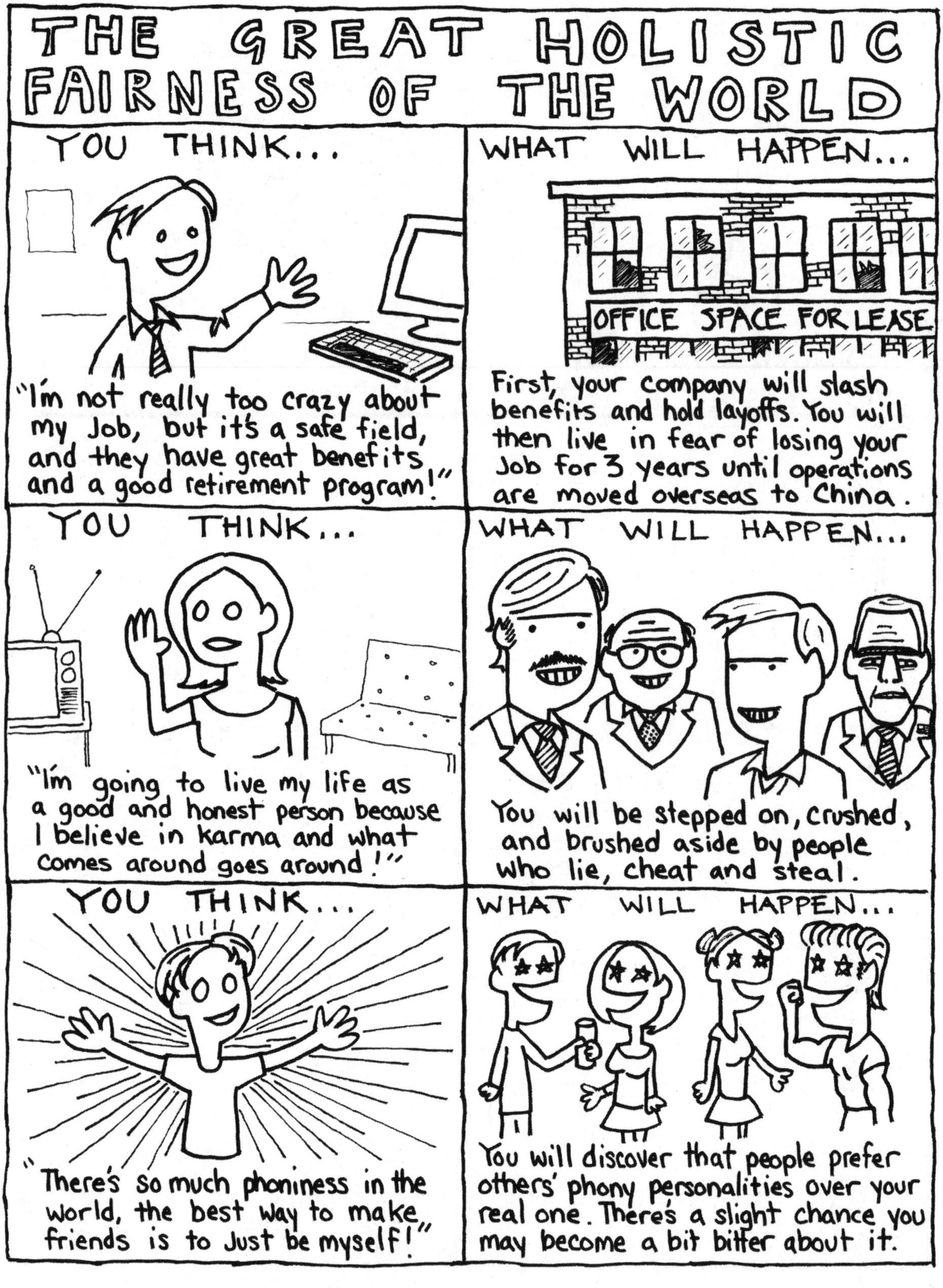
THE GREAT HOLISTIC FAIRNESS OF THE WORLD
YOU THINK...
"I'm not really too crazy about my job, but it's a safe field, and they have great benefits and a good retirement program!"
WHAT WILL HAPPEN...
OFFICE SPACE FOR LEASE
First, your company will slash benefits and hold layoffs. You will then live in fear of losing your job for 3 years until operations are moved overseas to China.
YOU THINK...
"I'm going to live my life as a good and honest person because I believe in karma and what comes around goes around!"
WHAT WILL HAPPEN...
You will be stepped on, crushed, and brushed aside by people who lie, cheat and steal.
YOU THINK...
"There's so much phoniness in the world, the best way to make friends is to just be myself!"
WHAT WILL HAPPEN...
You will discover that people prefer others' phony personalities over your real one. There's a slight chance you may become a bit bitter about it.

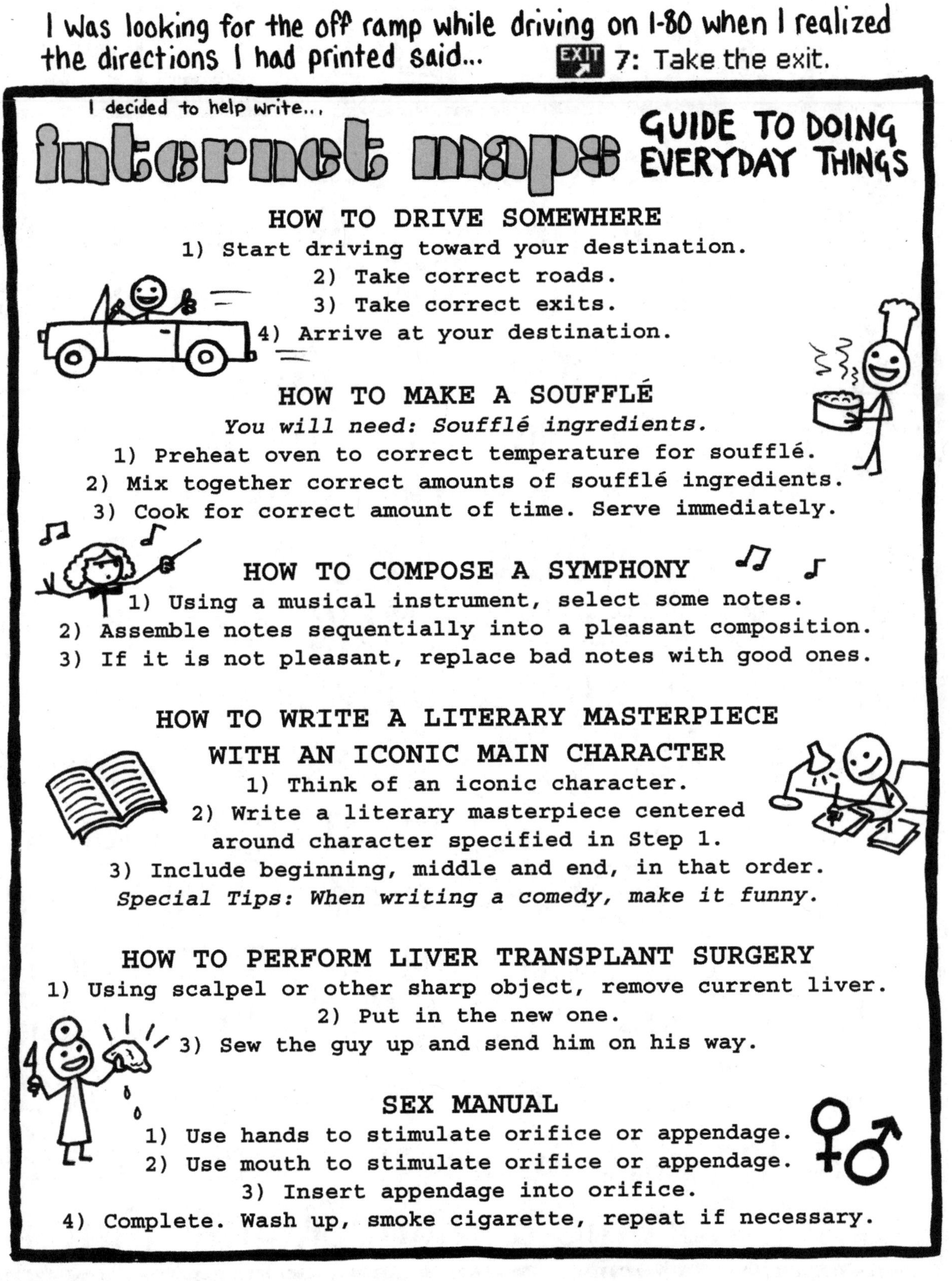
I was looking for the off ramp while driving on I-80 when I realized the directions I had printed said...
EXIT 7: Take the exit.
I decided to help write...
internet maps GUIDE TO DOING EVERYDAY THINGS
HOW TO DRIVE SOMEWHERE
1) Start driving toward your destination.
2) Take correct roads.
3) Take correct exits.
4) Arrive at your destination.
HOW TO MAKE A SOUFFLÉ
You will need: Soufflé ingredients.
1) Preheat oven to correct temperature for soufflé.
2) Mix together correct amounts of soufflé ingredients.
3) Cook for correct amount of time. Serve immediately.
HOW TO COMPOSE A SYMPHONY
1) Using a musical instrument, select some notes.
2) Assemble notes sequentially into a pleasant composition.
3) If it is not pleasant, replace bad notes with good ones.
HOW TO WRITE A LITERARY MASTERPIECE WITH AN ICONIC MAIN CHARACTER
1) Think of an iconic character.
2) Write a literary masterpiece centered around character specified in Step 1.
3) Include beginning, middle and end, in that order.
Special Tips: When writing a comedy, make it funny.
HOW TO PERFORM LIVER TRANSPLANT SURGERY
1) Using scalpel or other sharp object, remove current liver.
2) Put in the new one.
3) Sew the guy up and send him on his way.
SEX MANUAL
1) Use hands to stimulate orifice or appendage.
2) Use mouth to stimulate orifice or appendage.
3) Insert appendage into orifice.
4) Complete. Wash up, smoke cigarette, repeat if necessary.

Meaning Of Life

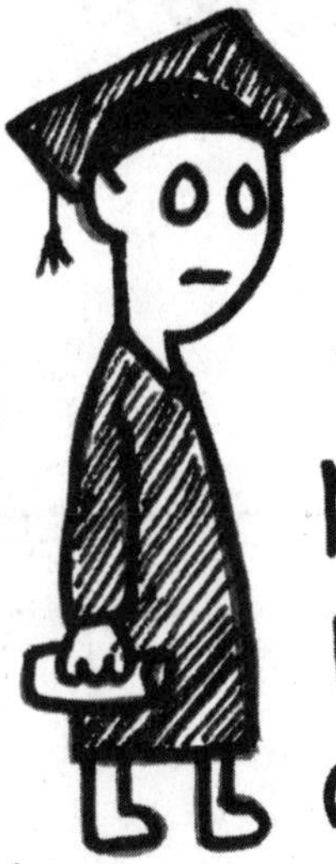

Be born. Go to school. Do well. G
some money. Make more money
somebody. Move in wit
Make money. Move up t

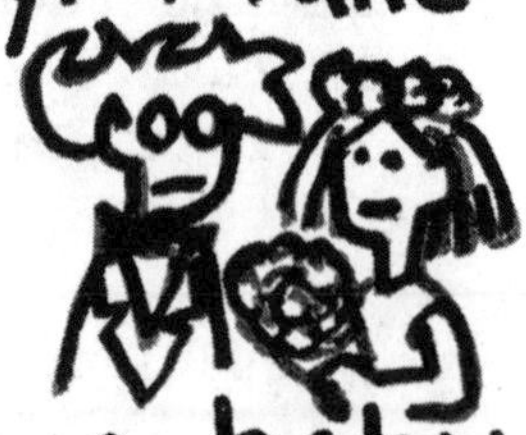

money. Have a baby. Buy a house
and go to work. Come home and
Have another baby. Make money. Buy thi
malls. Mow the lawn. Make more money.
car that can seat a family of six. Buy Elm
another baby. Go see the latest ro
Take a vacation to Florida.
Sink is broken. Make more

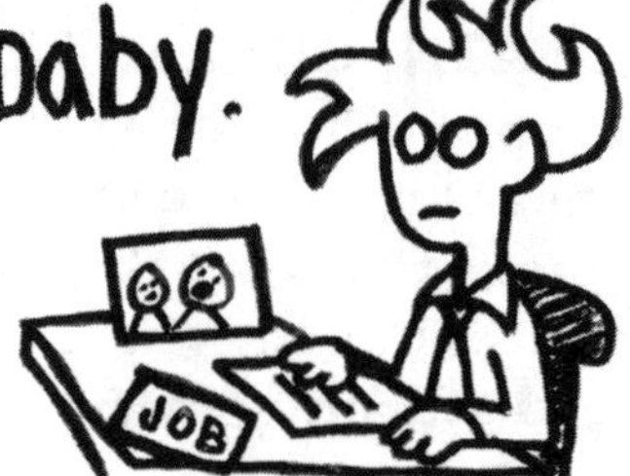

JOB

on occasion. Send the kids to school. Ma
vote for "American Idol." Go to your high
money. Take up golf and bowling. Give th
Send the kids to college. Take aspirin fo
of fat. Become a grandparent. Finish

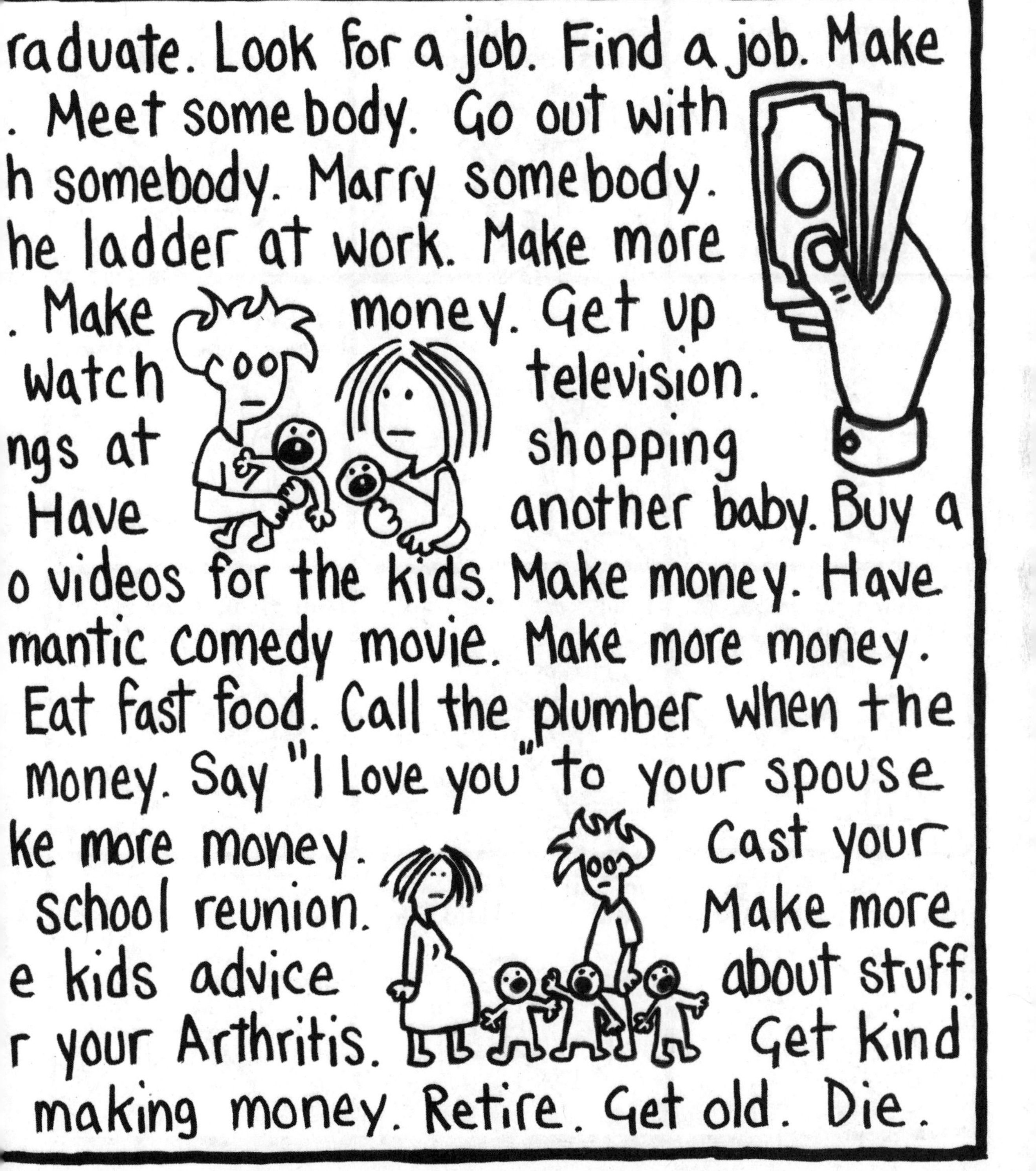
raduate. Look for a job. Find a job. Make
. Meet somebody. Go out with
h somebody. Marry somebody.
he ladder at work. Make more
. Make money. Get up
watch television.
ngs at shopping
Have another baby. Buy a
o videos for the kids. Make money. Have
mantic comedy movie. Make more money.
Eat fast food. Call the plumber when the
money. Say "I Love you" to your spouse
ke more money. Cast your
school reunion. Make more
e kids advice about stuff.
r your Arthritis. Get kind
making money. Retire. Get old. Die.

KING OF THE

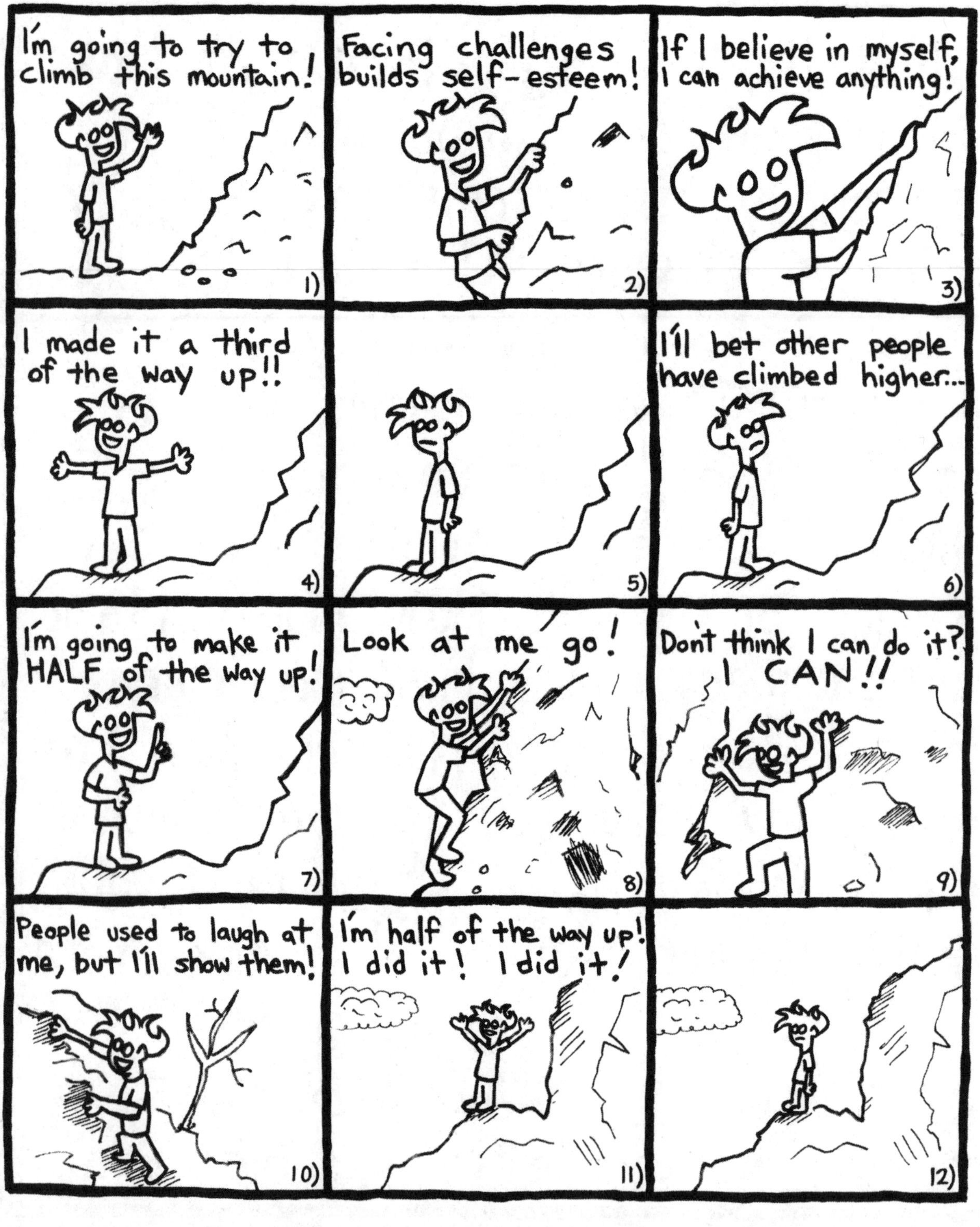

I'm going to try to climb this mountain!
1)
Facing challenges builds self-esteem!
2)
If I believe in myself, I can achieve anything!
3)
I made it a third of the way up!!
4)
5)
I'll bet other people have climbed higher...
6)
I'm going to make it HALF of the way up!
7)
Look at me go!
8)
Don't think I can do it? I CAN!!
9)
People used to laugh at me, but I'll show them!
10)
I'm half of the way up! I did it! I did it!
11)
12)

WORLD

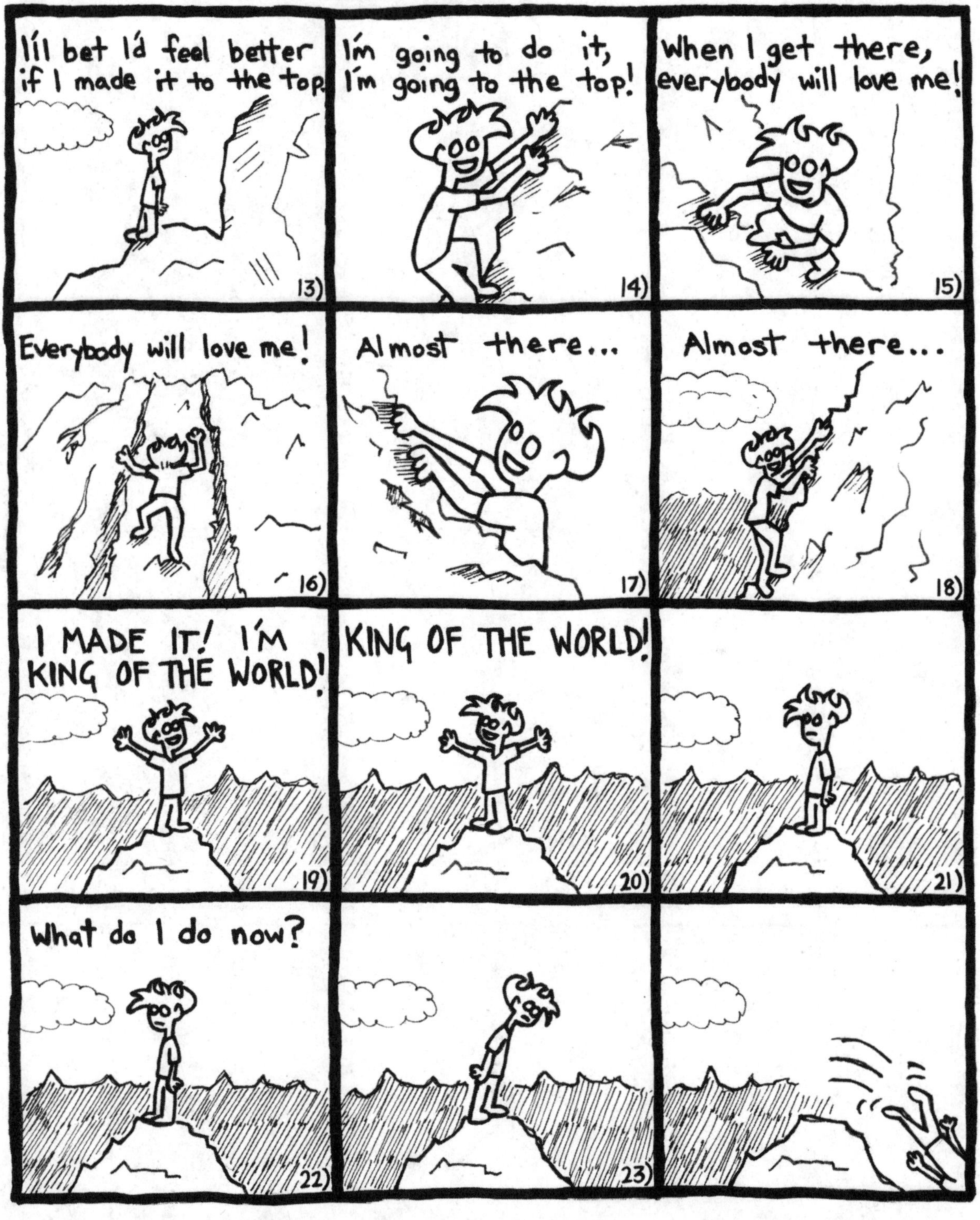

I'll bet I'd feel better if I made it to the top.
I'm going to do it, I'm going to the top!
When I get there, everybody will love me!
Everybody will love me!
Almost there...
Almost there...
I MADE IT! I'M KING OF THE WORLD!
KING OF THE WORLD!
What do I do now?
13)
14)
15)
16)
17)
18)
19)
20)
21)
22)
23)

Special thanks to:

Emre Yilmaz, Adrienne Davich, M $ P, Stacy Stranzl,
Yann Broly, Tami Marcaran, Tranh Pham, Keith Knight,
Colin Ferm, Jim Potter, Cara Bedick, Tricia Sherrer,
Joel Bachar, Futureshorts, Peaches Christ, Davy Rothbart,
Green Apple Books, Eric Calderon, Cory Wynne, George
Fifield, Megan Miller, New England Comics, O'Keefe's,
540 Club, Zam Zam, The Deluxe, Ed's Diner, Howard's Cafe,
In N'Out, HRD Coffee Shop, Hamburger Haven, Smirnoff,
Dr. Grabow, Comte De Galleyran, Captain Black.

And most of all, thank you Maryann Lim.

Levni Yilmaz grew up in Boston, Massachusetts.
He currently lives in San Francisco.

For more comics, movies $ info, go to
www.talesofmereexistence.com

LEV ON THE WEB:

www.talesofmereexistence.com
(Main website)

www.ingredientx.com
(Old website)

www.myspace.com/tales_of_mere_existence
(MySpace profile)

www.youtube.com/AgentXPQ
(My YouTube channel)

www.facebook.com
(Search for "Levni Yilmaz" and/or "lev yilmaz fan club")